About the Author

Tom Plate is an experienced American journalist whose international career has seen him working at brand-name media institutions from London to Asia. Born in New York, he completed his undergraduate studies at Amherst College (Phi Beta Kappa) and Princeton University's Woodrow Wilson School of Public and International Affairs. His twice-weekly syndicated column focusing on Asia and America runs regularly in a number of major newspapers, from Dubai, Singapore, Hong Kong, Seoul, Tokyo, Seattle and San Diego. He has received many awards, including from the American Society of Newspaper Editors, the California Newspaper Publishers Association and the Greater Los Angeles Press Club.

Professor Plate is now a full-time adjunct (contract) in the communication and policy studies departments at the University of California, Los Angeles. He teaches courses about American media and American governmental ethics, as well as courses on the media and politics of Asia. He now lives in Beverly Hills with his wife Andrea and their four cats.

Confessions
of an American
Media Man

28 Sept. '09

Dear Damon,

Never give up that searing commitment to quality — and to innovation. Jump the Midget!!! (see p.17)

With Appreciation,
Andrea & Tom Plate

Confessions
of an American
Media Man

Tom Plate

mc Marshall Cavendish
Editions

Front cover photo by UCLA magazine
© 2007 Marshall Cavendish International (Asia) Private Limited
Reprinted 2007

Published by Marshall Cavendish Editions
An imprint of Marshall Cavendish International
1 New Industrial Road, Singapore 536196

All rights reserved

No part of this publication may be reproduced, stored in a retrieval system or transmitted, in any form or by any means, electronic, mechanical, photocopying, recording or otherwise, without the prior permission of the copyright owner. Request for permission should be addressed to the Publisher, Marshall Cavendish International (Asia) Private Limited, 1 New Industrial Road, Singapore 536196. Tel: (65) 6213 9300, fax: (65) 6285 4871.
E-mail: genref@sg.marshallcavendish.com
Online bookstore: www.marshallcavendish.com/genref

The publisher makes no representation or warranties with respect to the contents of this book, and specifically disclaims any implied warranties or merchantability or fitness for any particular purpose, and shall in no events be liable for any loss of profit or any other commercial damage, including but not limited to special, incidental, consequential, or other damages.

Other Marshall Cavendish Offices:
Marshall Cavendish Ltd. 119 Wardour Street, London W1F 0UW, UK • Marshall Cavendish Corporation. 99 White Plains Road, Tarrytown NY 10591-9001, USA • Marshall Cavendish International (Thailand) Co Ltd. 253 Asoke, 12th Flr, Sukhumvit 21 Road, Klongtoey Nua, Wattana, Bangkok 10110, Thailand • Marshall Cavendish (Malaysia) Sdn Bhd, Times Subang, Lot 46, Subang Hi-Tech Industrial Park, Batu Tiga, 40000 Shah Alam, Selangor Darul Ehsan, Malaysia

Marshall Cavendish is a trademark of Times Publishing Limited

National Library Board Singapore Cataloguing in Publication Data

Plate, Tom.
Confessions of an American media man :- what they don't tell you at journalism school / Tom Plate. – Singapore :- Marshall Cavendish Editions,- c2007.   p. cm.
ISBN-13 : 978-981-261-315-8
ISBN-10 : 981-261-315-3

1. Plate, Tom. 2. Journalists – United States – Biography.
3. Journalism- – United States. I. Title.

PN4874
070.92 -- dc22   SLS2006041132

Printed in Singapore by Craft Print International Ltd

*... to my daughter, Ashley Alexandra Plate
who, at this time of writing, is twenty.
She now has a book she can read, when she gets the time,
that explains why her dad was away and
at the office so much of his time.*

Contents

	Preface	*11*
1	**Jump the Midget:** The Life of a Newspaper Columnist	*17*
2	**Long Island *Newsday*:** From Potato Fields to a Field of Dreams	*79*
3	***New York* Magazine:** Helping to Start Something Up is So Much Better than Winding Something Down	*113*
	Photo section: Famous People and Me!	*139–149*
4	**London Calling:** Good Newspapers Don't Have to be Dull	*150*
5	***Time* Pressures:** The Businesslike Bureaucracy of Quality Control	*190*
6	**With CBS:** Where I Wished Spanking Were Back in Fashion	*228*
7	***New York Newsday*:** Another Fabulous Start-up, Another Journalistic Lease on Life	*248*
8	**The *Los Angeles Times*:** The Responsibility of a Major-League American Newspaper	*272*
	Conclusion	*334*
	My Thanks	*340*
	Index	*343*

Preface

WHEN I WAS YOUNG, I was on the whole, an extremely serious person. I was the first guy in my junior high school to start reading *Time*, and one of the last, probably, to start perusing *Playboy*. I was an early bloomer intellectually and a late bloomer in almost every other way.

In junior high school, I bought a tiny printing press that consisted of rubber letters and basic illustrations, and published a weekly newspaper known as the *Hicksville Bugle*. Yes, I lived on Long Island—first in Levittown and then a place, not inappropriately named, called Hicksville.

Despite my nose for the news—or nosiness for others' business!—I never saw myself as a journalist. The craft was too vulgar, too ordinary, too unrefined an occupation. I imagined that someday I would wind up as secretary of state, or even president; or head of the United Nations. The fact that my origins were humble, that I was not especially telegenic, and that I had absolutely no significant connections perhaps spurred me to imagine all these things.

I certainly never imagined myself as a media man.

But, how well did I really know myself? I was always opinionated and had no shyness about expressing opinions to anyone who would listen. At this early age—as a pre-teen—I was rarely in doubt about much.

In high school I became an editor of the school paper, the weekly *Whitman Window*, a position that conferred little prestige. I was convinced back then, however, that when I grew up, I would be doing something actually important with my life.

That was also what I told myself at Amherst College, where I became managing editor of the *Amherst Student*, a title that impressed only myself.

But we coolies who ran the paper did have fun. The most useful project was undoubtedly the annual food survey. Polling the student body, we were able to report conclusively that the food in the campus was, in the opinion of the students, terrible. The finding was extremely unsurprising but delightfully exploitable. And, in the aftermath of the media exposé, there was a lot of scurrying about by the college administration—but no real change in the quality of the food. And so I learned my first media lesson: always remember, Tom, that the mere fact that a newspaper uncovers an incompetence or injustice or abuse does not automatically mean an end to that incompetence, injustice or abuse—it only automatically guarantees that the exposed incompetents will run around trying their best to cover their butts!

My best friend at college was Aaron Latham and he was a great friend to have. In our senior year—bored again—we co-wrote a best-selling guide to dating men in the Ivy League. It was called *Where the Boys Are*. The *New York Times* gave it major play and we were on the "Today" and "Tonight" shows the same day. With his ill-gotten gains from the book, Aaron put his money into a mutual fund; I bought my first sports car. Tells you something about the two of us—he's worth millions now; I am not!

Fortunately, I then went to a great graduate school, the Woodrow Wilson School of Public and International Affairs at Princeton. Somehow politics and political issues had always attracted my deep interest in ways that little else did. In high school, I "masterminded" the election of the student body president. In college, I was a political science major—and the Amherst political science faculty was superb (as was the English department, where I minored).

It was at Princeton that I began to realize that I had a better chance of interviewing a president than becoming one. Who the hell was I, after all? Answer: the son of a former Marine who never graduated from high school, and who got wedded to painkillers; and of a mom who was too often wedded to the bottle.

But there are advantages to struggle. You just push down your inferiority complex and never let it stand in the way! Never, never, never give up, Winston Churchill was to say, and that became my motto, too. But sometimes I was tempted to give up. Later in life, I was to turn too often and too readily to alcohol. But in my youth, what kept me going—and firing up those afterburners of ambition—were two things: great music and great women.

I loved classical music and I adored classically complicated women—at least those women who had the public look to compensate for my own meager looks. Glamour surely figures into it. From drab Levittown to glamorous Princeton, from undistinguished Long Island to (journalistic assignments at) the White House, 10 Downing Street, the Japanese prime minister's Tokyo residence ... these places were a long, long way from Hicksville.

Media work offered just enough of the touch of glamour—however superficial—to keep me hooked. Always in the wings were travels to faraway places to interview history makers. There were invitations to parties and receptions and briefings that would never have come my way had I chosen almost any other career.

I was thrilled when I was accepted as a graduate student at Princeton. I imagined delivering eloquent speeches at the UN Security Council or negotiating a tough security accord with the Russians or helping extricate hostages from some extremists' hell.

I never got to do any of those things. I did get to observe many of those things, sometimes at close hand, sometimes vicariously via in-depth interviews with the key participants shortly after the fact; but I was never on the field, or "the pitch," as the Brits put it (save for a summer stint as a state department speechwriter), or even in the dugout as a batting boy. But I did have a season's ticket to history—and sometimes I was lucky to have one of the best seats in the house.

I never set out to be a journalist. Even now, I do not believe it was an act of free will so much as some kind of predestination. But would-be careerists be warned: there is a significant downside to this field of endeavor. It is fundamentally an unspiritual and superficial life; there is often the sense of intruding on, if not sometimes even ruining, other people's lives; and the totalitarian bootstrap of the deadline is as suffocating as it is exhilarating.

There are thus two sides to the news media story—actually, about four or five. I will try to tell as many of them as I can, as well as I possibly can, but I must start with a disclaimer: there was never any ambition here to write a book about the news media because I rarely find books about the media very compelling. But then a funny thing happened in my life: I became a professor and I began to spend a lot of time with young people. And for them—besides the subject of sex—the most important matter in life is the question of career.

I cannot possibly explain how exciting I find teaching, how energizing this new life is, and how stimulating I find many students. I know I would not be anywhere as happy today if my life had not taken this turn. I now teach full time at UCLA, with offices on the beautiful main Westwood campus. I teach four or five courses an academic year, serve as a mentor to special honors students, and organize campus events about the news media. I take students over to the faculty club for coffee, supervise innovative term projects, and speak at special events.

It is at such times—and at many others—that UCLA students tend to ask: How did you get involved in the media? How does one get hired? What is it really like to be an editor at *Time* magazine or a writer at *New York Newsday* or a boss at the *Los Angeles Times*?

How does one answer such questions?! Well, actually, there are two ways. One is superficially—with a few stories or quick comments—and the other is with a full-length book on the American news media, designed for anyone who wants to know what it is really like to be a professional journalist in the United States. And so this book is for everyone and anyone, but the truth is, if it had not been for the persistent and sincere questions of my terrific students, not to mention sharp ones from my daughter, I would never have overcome my aversion to writing a book on the news media.

So this is not at all intended to be one of those relentlessly and boringly bitter and negative accounts about tyrannical bosses or flesh-eating corporate takeovers. Nor will it be a book that takes a view about the US and British press no less unkind than a Marxist's. Frankly, I do not much like, even detest, books that complain, that seek to even old scores or try to start new fights. This is not me, nor is it my way, nor my intention.

I have spent more than three decades in the news media and have had good jobs at some of the fanciest joints. I feel honored to have had those opportunities, believe that on the whole I was treated fairly and well, encountered unforgettable characters, and made good—and sometimes great—friends. In my experience, truly boring people do not tend to become journalists and the life you will be lucky to lead will probably be anything but boring. (But if it ever does become tedious, then start searching for another job—or another career.)

The many photographs on the wall of my office serve to remind me of the boring life I missed out on—the dull life I might have had if I had taken another route. (And the best part is that it is not over: I am still committing to journalism, writing an internationally syndicated column, traveling and meeting challenging political figures.) My students (somewhat) fondly term my office photo display of prime ministers, presidents, prominent diplomats, cultural gurus and other internationally known personalities—and me: "Prof. Tom's Ego Wall." Right.

Indeed. I have been lucky.

And I still am, with a twice-weekly column about Asia and America that theoretically reaches millions of readers a week.

My daily office life at UCLA, where I teach communication and policy studies courses, is a gift from the heavens. It not only provides me with a thinking environment but also eager, thinking students. At UCLA, I teach courses in Asian politics and the media, and American media ethics, and have lectured on business and governmental as well as media ethics at many venues. I also founded the Asia Pacific Media Network, a nonprofit organization, and the UCLA Media Center.

In my lectures at UCLA, a great research university with a daunting enrollment, I face a sea of faces less than half of whom are Caucasian, and/or in some instances more than half of whom are Asian-American. It is a wonderful environment for writing a weekly American perspective on the Asian half of the world. In my life at UCLA, I often refer to myself as the "token Caucasian."

With the guidance and inspiration of my dean and my former chair—Scott Waugh, the last of the true gentlemen, and Neil Malamuth, a "rocket-scientist" social scientist—UCLA has given me the time and the environment to develop a deeper perspective on American journalism and I have begun to recognize and understand as never before certain structural problems inherent in the media business that are extremely problematic for a healthy democracy. In my most pessimistic moments, I fear that regulating the media (in some non-governmental way) may not be a cure worse than the disease if the news media is becoming the disease of democracy itself.

And this is the great historic conundrum I put before my students and anyone who reads this book.

A WORD ABOUT the frequently employed term "Higher Authority" (with thanks and apologies to my colleague Robert Berger of the University of Southern California).

This is not a book of hate but of love (or at least of deep appreciation) for a mainly terrific life in the American news media, and therefore of special appreciation for the people, especially supervisors, who have had to put up with me over the years. Accordingly, I have absolutely no axes in my backpack to grind or to wield. I believe that my particular mercurial and neurotic personality often made me not easy to relate to, much less to supervise. So I have, on the whole, no serious criticism of any of my supervisors (or "betters"), only sincere thanks for their forbearance. Of course, honest disagreements about policy and taste and editorial judgment among adults sometimes do surface, as in any profession and organization, and I apologize in advance to anyone who feels I failed to present a balanced view of the issues of disagreement. Every supervisor in my career who has had to deal with me deserves indeed an employee-relations' Purple Heart. When this book does delve into honest—honest!—differences of opinion, norms and goals, I will employ the literary device of referring to the person with whom I disagree as "Higher Authority." You see, in every job, no matter how high your position in the hierarchy, there is always some Higher Authority to deal with. My advice to students is to deal with it more skillfully than I sometimes did.

Chapter One
Jump the Midget:
The Life of a Newspaper Columnist

Here is a dilemma for you. You decide what you would have done in this case. I have been reliably told that this story is utterly true. But I was not there when it happened. I believe it did happen. But even if it is at least partially apocryphal, it is so iconic of my profession that it is a story that just must be told. And it is a story that my students love to hear, no matter how many times I tell it.

It goes like this. The big American city, which shall remain nameless, had not seen a crime spree quite like this one in a long time. The very best penthouse apartments in the city's very best sections were being looted one after another by some kind of gifted burglar who had a way with tight places and fancy electronic anti-burglary equipment.

For the police, the serial burglaries were a nightmare; for the number-one paper, the metropolis' up-market broadsheet, they were at best minor fodder to be buried at the back with the used car ads. But for the editors of the perennially troubled number two paper, they were a gift from heaven.

For what hath a number two paper to peddle, if not sex, celebrities, sports and crime? And so with every new inexplicable burglary at yet another expensive address, the number two went out of its way to spotlight the story. Before long, the serial burglaries became a running spotlight feature as crime after crime went reported—and unsolved.

Until one night when the paper's second-in-command ran into the office of the paper's first-in-command and said, "Boss, you won't believe whom the police have arrested in connection with the serial burglary case!"

The boss listened intently, all ears.

"They think they've got the man, and the man is a midget."

First-in-command looked at his second as if to say, "There is a God, after all—and He/She/It favors troubled second-in-line newspapers." The two editors then discussed how to play the story. They both agreed it belonged on page one, but that was the easy part. The tough issue was how to spin it and, to this end, the boss editor, who himself was not especially tall (but especially intellectually and physically fit), had an unusual idea, as he often did in his multi-decade journalistic career.

"Why don't we jump the midget?" he said, as if reasonably suggesting expanding the weather page.

"What?" asked his sidekick.

"We'll run the usual tab-style headline, 'Nabbed' or 'Busted' or whatever, but then we will splash a life-sized picture of the suspect on page one."

"Boss, he's small ... but, gee, he's not *that* small!"

"Right, so we'll have to jump the midget. At around his belt buckle line, we'll put a dash across and say 'continued on page seven.' Then we'll run his bottom half. People can put the two parts together, hang it up on the fridge—a life-sized picture of the alleged perpetrator. It'll be the talk of the town!"

Second-in-command stared at his boss for a long time. Then the staff, getting word that the paper was seriously thinking of jumping the midget's life-sized picture, started to drift in, some to register very strong objections: small-sized people would have their feelings hurt; vertically impaired non-profit organizations would protest the utter insensitivity, perhaps even sue the paper under the civil rights act; worst of all, the paper would lose face, look silly, perhaps even be laughed out of town. "I'm not sure we can jump the midget, boss," the second-in-command said, slowly.

It went on like this for some time, but in the end, taste won out; the boss relented, the paper ran a smaller photo with the usual overheated tab-style coverage, the midget went un-jumped.

Many years later, I asked the Boss Man whether he thought the decision to take the high road had been the right call.

"Absolutely not," he said. "How many times in life do you get to jump the midget? Not many, for damn sure. I regret it to this day."

Very recently, as my friend the Boss Man's age climbed up in years, he casually mentioned to me that I might want to offer the eulogy at his funeral, when inevitably the time came, as it will eventually for us all; and would I also see to it that the epitaph on his tombstone read: "As I lie here now, unable to do much, I realize I should have jumped the midget."

And so this book is in large part about those jump-the-midget decision points in one man's journalistic career: why I jumped, or did not, my own midget opportunities when I had the chance; when, and when not, to take the big plunge. Some of my decisions raised ethical issues; some raised related questions of self-definition. But in life—whether you are in journalism, medicine, law, business, politics, whatever—you will be faced with those "jump-the-midget" moments. And so this is a book about life in the crazed American media. Everything in it is, as far as I know, true. I made nothing up—I did not have to.

I NEVER HAD much hope of rising to anywhere within ten thousand miles near the pinnacle of American journalism. But as a foreign affairs columnist with a major paper and then as a syndicated columnist, I got closer than I had ever thought possible. The road to this was rough and unpredictable, which in part is what this book is about. But the job was worth waiting for, and I am lucky indeed to still have it in today's morphed version.

My column now runs more or less regularly in a bunch of terrific papers from Singapore to Seattle. I wish I had started out in 1995 writing twice a week, but maybe I didn't know enough then about Asia, which is what I mainly write about, to maintain that disciplined pace from the start. That, in any event, was the advice of Higher Authority, which, being the authority that was higher, was the advice that had to be adopted.

The original *Los Angeles Times* version of the column was a weekly; it spanned five years, and led to a lot of great experiences. (Half of those columns were reprinted in 1999 in the *International Herald Tribune*, a prestigious spot.) It now appears twice a week in syndication. The *Los Angeles Times* column always appeared on the opinion editorial (op-ed) page and was intended to express a kind of US West Coast thinking about foreign affairs. Its publisher Dick Schlosberg and editor Shelby Coffey allowed me to travel widely. This latitude permitted extensive emphasis on reporting, an important aspect of the work of a journalist, as was proffered to me in a piece of fatherly advice from a special Higher Authority—the redoubtable William Safire, then a *New York Times* op-ed columnist. He told me, "Tom, people won't care what you think about an issue if you only know as much as they do. Find out more than they do: report, report, report. That's the secret if you want to be read and want to be influential."

I wanted to be read, and so I reported, reported, reported. I promise you, this particular Higher Authority was right, because this process led to the column being viewed in Asia, generally, though not universally, as low in stereotype and high in reportage.

Let me give you an example of what the great Safire had in mind, but you should keep in mind that Safire himself was not exactly giving away trade secrets. It is entirely obvious that reportage is essential to journalism, whether of the opinion kind or the so-called objective, factual kind. But good reporting often requires access and the hardest part is getting that access. Bob Woodward of *The Washington Post* is a great reporter, no doubt, but when you have his reputation and a legendary newspaper behind you, access to the top people is not exactly impossible to achieve. Access and reporting go hand in hand; it is very difficult to give a good interview if you cannot get the interview!

In 2000, I was invited to attend, as a so-called "media leader," the elite annual week-long retreat of "thinkers and leaders" in Davos, Switzerland, the intellectual and spiritual home of the World Economic Forum, a pro-business organization based for the other 51 weeks of the year in Geneva.

My column was focused, as it was then with the *Los Angeles Times*, and as it now is in syndication, mainly on political, economic and cultural issues of the Pacific Rim, especially Asia.

Several times I had asked the White House for a foreign policy interview with President Clinton—and had come close twice to nailing it. In the end, though, I would always get penciled out for some last-minute reason. About this recurrence, I was non-paranoid; on the other hand, would they have penciled out Tom Friedman?

And so it was in Davos that I was to finally get my man. As Winston Churchill said, "Never, never, never, never give up." I don't, I didn't, I won't.

The 2000 World Economic Forum (WEF) in Davos, Switzerland, was my second Davos. This annual retreat of the rich and ritzy (and then me!) was a mainly irresistible smorgasbord for self-important policy wonks. I would have accepted the invitation anyhow, but the fact that Clinton was going to be there put my enthusiasm over the top.

I knew enough people I liked who had been close to Clinton—true talents like Charlene Barshefsky, Mickey Kantor, Warren Christopher—to accept that Clinton was the real deal. He was often brilliant with issues, sometimes mean with his staff, but always on the job, 24/7. The country probably would have been better served had the oral sex period of his second term been covered up by the media rather than exploited. We all have our needs and that kind of issue is best left inside the marriage than out of it. In general, the Asians handle this kind of trivia with more delicacy.

Back to the 2000 WEF. You should know what a mini ordeal it was to get to Davos—a twelve-hour flight from Los Angeles, but then enduring a winding three-hour train ride up the Swiss Alps, then living in a near-constant snowstorm for a week. Even so, there was no way I would pass up the opportunity to be there.

As it turned out, neither could Clinton, and so in January of 2000, he became the first sitting American president to give a speech at Davos. It was befitting that he be the first, being the policy wonk of all policy wonks, for Davos is true Wonk Heaven—which is why I so enjoyed my annual Wonk Pilgrimages there.

Clinton chose to speak on the wonk topic au moment: globalization—which really was *most* appropriate considering that a mere six weeks earlier all hell had broken loose at the World Trade Organization's big shot meeting in Seattle. Anti-globalization protestors, gathering in considerable number, virtually closed down the northwestern US city and all but closed down the international meeting itself. It was an absolute and total debacle, and it had shaken the ideological foundations of the Clinton presidency, with its emphasis on the positive values of proliferating world trade, ever more market openings and intense globalization.

Are multinational corporations and institutions the primary beneficiaries of globalization at the expense of the poor people of the world? No one can say for sure right now. Only history will tell. Nonetheless, that this is today's specific and widely held perception is what makes globalization the convenient whipping boy for a variety of people with a myriad of bones—many disassociated—to pick in public.

Security was understandably tight at Davos. The only people invited to Clinton's speech were the WEF's delegate participants, of which I was one. General media reporters assigned to cover the WEF typically were handed a second-class pass that prohibited them from getting inside many of the

Davos main functions. They were allowed to mill about outside the main conference building in the freezing cold and interview participants as they exited, and were given standard press releases and occasional press conference opportunities. One such media person was a reporter from Hong Kong whom I shall call, to disguise her true identity, Fong Sze Yeung and whom I was lucky to befriend.

As an extremely industrious, clever—and noticeably comely—journalist, Fong Sze Yeung used sheer brain power to slip past WEF security in the conference hall. She had put herself smack in the middle of a tangle of Asian leaders—as if she were herself a delegate—and in the dab center of a demographic surge of Hong Kong delegates pushing to get in and secure seats up front. And so when I sauntered in some many minutes later, just a few ticks before Clinton went on, Fong Sze Yeung had already reserved seats way up front for her and me in a section she had no business being in (she wasn't even supposed to be in the hall!).

I was touched. I had made her acquaintance only once or twice before—but we had hit it off—and she waved dramatically to me as I walked into the hall. There were not many seats left by the time I got there. Actually, there may not have been any, certainly none up close (and potentially personal!).

Soon after we sat down, Clinton jumped up on stage from a side entrance and began his chat. It started rather slowly but in the end was superb. In the audience of several hundred were CEOs from all over the world, from Bill Gates to the head of Sony, famous artists, prominent statesmen, and an occasional (very occasional) nonprofit or humanitarian organization guru, not to mention a handful of weary-looking "media leaders."

At first, the president was lackluster. I later found out that he had flown directly from Washington to Geneva without sleep, and then had taken a bumpy helicopter ride, courtesy of the Swiss police, to make the Davos scene just in time. The man was plainly dead tired. But he somehow sucked tremendous energy from the people around him, and so by the midpoint of his speech, he seemed to have pretty much inhaled the energy of half the audience and exhaled his prepared text. You could almost see him flinging it off to the side as he went forward on his own.

Maybe we do not particularly like the man for his womanizing or whatever, but intellectually there was no question that he had got it. The audience gave him a rousing round of applause, and then, after a brief question-and-answer period, he started to leave the hall. I immediately saw my jump-the-midget opportunity.

I turned to the obviously gorgeous Fong Sze Yeung and said, "My young lady, how would you like to have a picture of yourself with the president? You could give it to your mom when you get home."

Her eyes opened wide. "Do you think you can do that? How?"

That innocent demurral prompted me to want it even more. I said, "Absolutely. I know my president. Just watch the people around you. This is, by and large, an international audience that doesn't know that Clinton will stay behind to chat and schmooze until the last janitor has left the lecture hall. Sit tight. You'll get your picture."

Indeed, Clinton exited the stage but stayed inconspicuously in the hall by walking off-stage, as if he had left the hall; and then around and down the stairs into the orchestra pit where half his cabinet were huddled. There, Sandy Berger, Charlene Barshefsky, Madeleine Albright and Bill Daley could see him, as could we; but the big shots in the hall could not. They figured he was back on *Air Force One*, jetting to the next crisis or opportunity. They thought he had left the hall, if not the little Swiss skiing village of Davos itself.

With half the cabinet milling about in the orchestra pit, the Secret Service had roped it off as a secure arena in which the president could meet and greet. Clinton was about 80 per cent through shaking hands with a gauntlet of people. I said to my Hong Kong knock-out: "Come with me, young lady. You are about to get your picture taken with the president of the United States."

Strolling up to the pit, I waved my WEF badge at Clinton. It read, "Media Leader, Tom Plate, *Los Angeles Times*."

Clinton looked at my credentials and grimaced in an I-really-don't-want-to-do-an-interview-right-now sort of way, but I quickly said before he could turn away, "No, no, Mr President. I don't want an interview. I just want you to meet Fong Sze Yeung. She's from Hong Kong. If it's possible, we'd like to take a picture of the two of you for her to take home to her mom."

Well, once he set eyes on Fong Sze Yeung (she was brainy eye candy indeed, and not unwilling to throw you a devastating Suzi Wong look as a way of getting your attention), he zoomed over with the speed of *Air Force One*, and was more than happy to stand next to her and put his arm around her for the camera. But as he stood there waiting to say "cheese" and beaming with his arm around her, and with Fong Sze Yeung all too happy to be there too (for, at bottom, Clinton offers women enormous charm and respect, despite what you may have read), I made believe that the camera was jammed—this was, after all, my jump-the-midget moment—and so while I was allegedly seeking to fix the camera, I said, "I'm so sorry, Mr President! This will take just a second to fix. By the way, regarding your speech on globalization, what do you really think is the best post-Seattle strategy?"

He had several quick thoughts on the issue and we began to chat and exchange views. At the end of it, I got some wonderful quotes that eventually formed the basis of a good column.

Bear in mind that this interview was taking place just weeks after the Seattle mess. The Clinton administration had been greatly shaken by the orgiastic anti-globalization protest that had all but closed down the high profile conference of international big shots, and so I asked the president about the durability and implacability of this burgeoning movement.

His response was that politics begot politics. By not engaging all parties to the protest, said Clinton, in a genuine discourse about the pros and cons of globalization, the net effect was to meld what in fact was a huge and diverse group into a seemingly seamless network of feral opposition to modernity. The president's prescription was to detoxify the overall fear level by dividing the opposition—separating those who had sincere concerns that could be addressed with reason from those who regarded the issue as nothing more than a convenient protest vehicle with which to burnish one's stature as a protest impresario. While holding onto Fong Sze Yeung with respect and affection, Clinton added that too many CEOs failed to appreciate that not all anti-globalization criticisms were ill-conceived and not all such spokesmen deserved little but CEO contempt.

In essence, then, I had an exclusive interview with the president of the United States. I was to later learn that it was caught on official WEF tape. Unbeknown to me at the time, the mezzanine cameras in the conference hall were still rolling as I spoke with him, even though, because of the camera angles, Clinton and I were visible to them but Fong Sze Yeung was not. The president of the Free World was, after all, still in the room, and the camera crew was high up on the mezzanine, shooting at the orchestra pit even as none of the gradually exiting delegates had any idea of what was going on.

At the big gala ball of the annual Davos Forum that night, a main wall decoration was the repeated replaying of the Clinton speech, the Q and A, and then, at the very end, his impromptu mini-interview with me. At least 30 people must have come up to me and said, "I see you speaking with the president, and he spent a lot more time with you than he did with anyone else. Why is that?"

You could just imagine how much I enjoyed that, especially when one of the taunters was a famous *New York Times* correspondent who was a better journalist than I ever was. Nonetheless, I had prepared a neat answer—I had had a few hours to polish it to shining. I said, brandishing a mysterious smile, "Well, the truth is, I just know my president!"

What I did not tell them was that I had a secret weapon with me that I knew would work. Clinton liked very attractive and very smart women (how weird, huh?). In truth, this was one of the things I liked about him—and, as a journalist, was able to use it to what I hoped was the reader's advantage.

> "Jumping the midget" means knowing whom you are dealing with and jumping it does not mean you have to go to unethical lengths.

To be successful in the journalism business, you have to know your politician and what he likes. New York City Mayor Ed Koch liked Chinese food. Bill Clinton had a different dish in mind.

How much would a life like this—interviewing powerful and pivotal figures on the very edge of contemporary history—be worth to you, I ask my students. A million dollars? Five million? Priceless?

I tell them of meeting the founder of a famous West Coast bank over dinner. He had invited me and my daughter Ashley to dine with him, his wife and their young granddaughter, a schoolmate of Ashley's. Her grandmother, it turned out, had been a regular reader of the column in its first five years when it appeared on the *Los Angeles Times'* op-ed page. I surveyed the vast expanse of backyard, adjacent to the late Frank Sinatra's Palm Springs home, the colossal pool, the beautiful furnishings ... and, catching my breath in awe, said: "I never made remotely your kind of money." And the tycoon, recovering from the recent partial stroke from which full recovery was still underway, responded this way: "At the end of the day, money is just accounting. What wouldn't I have given up to have had your life as a journalist."

IN ANY CAREER in journalism, or in any field, down moments happen; there's no way to avoid them. For me, the downest moments are not when I screw up (everyone does that), but when my integrity is questioned. This is when I get sad.

If there is one good thing about me (and maybe there is only one!), it is that I cannot be bought. I can be charmed, fooled, whatever—but never bought. When you read a column by Tom Plate—or by the worthy Tom Friedman or the wily Maureen Dowd or the brilliant Nick Kristof—you can be assured that the perspective, while it may be ill-conceived or misreported or just plain wrong, is an honest viewpoint.

Integrity and ethics are not often used in the context of American journalism, as my British friends are most delighted to point out. But a reputation for such can prove to be extremely useful to one's work, as an experience in Britain was to demonstrate.

While still the editorial pages editor at the *Los Angeles Times* one morning, I was working at my desk when the phone rang. Did I feel lucky? Was it the governor or the mayor calling? Or was it that little old lady in Pasadena who was angry with the morning's political cartoon?

It turned out that in the paper that morning, we had published a "Column Left" commentary by a well-known socialist polemicist, attacking the Labour Party of England, and when I gambled and picked the phone up, it was a Labour Party official named Gerald Kaufmann who was visiting Los Angeles. A well-regarded former Fleet Street journalist himself, he took vigorous exception to the opinion editorial.

I listened carefully and, Anglophile that I had become, responded in this way: "Well, Mr Former Shadow Foreign Secretary, you make a persuasive and, I must say, entertaining point. Why don't you write up your objections into a tidy 800-word-or-so opinion editorial and I'll do whatever I can to see that it is published in exactly the same space?"

It is my (almost uniquely held) belief that newspapers and magazines owe it to those who had been unjustly wounded, comparable editorial positioning when they or their position had been grievously wronged, as seemed the case in this instance.

"Are you serious?" His voice barely hid the astonishment.

I said I was.

"When do you want it?" he asked.

I said, "How about in an hour or two, so we can have the option of publishing it tomorrow?"

Kaufmann liked that option, and the challenge, quite a lot. One knew he would.

As expected, the piece came in over our fax before noon that day—in mint condition, of course, as befitting a former journalist-turned-political figure. And, yes, we published it the next day, in the same spot as the piece that had instigated the telephone call.

In time, Gerald Kauffman was to become one of my favorite people of all time. We would see one another as often as we could, whether I was visiting in London or he in Los Angeles.

One time, years later, we were leaving the House of Commons, and, with the sky pouring down rain like slabs of wet cement, we were forced to share a taxicab with someone else. Inside, Gerald introduced me to a colleague on the seat opposite. He was a snapshot of sheer ambition, his mind churning constantly, his eyes rotating a little nervously, utterly self absorbed and glowing with luminosity.

Gerald introduced us this way: "Tony, this is one of America's opinion editors. He's with the *Los Angeles Times*. He's in town to interview the prime minister (John Major) ... Tom, this is Tony Blair, a young man of whom I am especially fond, and who is to become the next prime minister of Great Britain. He will succeed Major before long, I promise."

Blair, shark-like teeth beaming under the fast smile, shook my hand.

The next day, I—together with Bill Tuohy, then the paper's London bureau chief, whose reporting from Southeast Asia had once won a Pulitzer—was to interview the then-current prime minister of Great Britain, John Major. The session was held at Number 10, as it is called, the prime minister's official residence.

It was a great afternoon and a terrific interview. I started by thanking the very busy prime minister for acceding to our request. "Well," he said, a plain-appearing man in a dark suit and forgettable tie but with eyes twinkling and a common man's manner, "It's not every day we get such a request from Los Angeles!" The interview flew by in an hour, amid the usual downpour of rain. Major seemed to me extraordinarily non-greasy, humane and even—is this the word?—decent.

In retrospect, the prime minister may have regretted dropping his guard for the out-of-towners.

The interview was well noticed. The *Times* of London bannered the interview this way: "Major Tells US that Tories Must Take Blame." Wrote correspondent Ian Brodie: "The prime minister has admitted that, after 14 years in office, the Tories have no one to blame for the problems that beset them. John Major made the comment in an interview published yesterday in the *Los Angeles Times*, in which he also claimed that the day after his election, he made an extraordinarily accurate forecast about a downward turn in his fortunes. He said he told a number of people: 'Within the next twelve months, the government will be the most unpopular we have seen in a long time.'"

Major had tendered what the Londoner Brodie dubbed a highly "graphic turn of phrase;" it concerned the Tory Party's internal finger-pointing and blood-letting: "At the moment, if you have a number of backbenchers in our Conservative Party forming a circular firing squad, there is going to be a bit of blood on the floor, and that, broadly, is what we have seen."

About a year later, in a London café outside an office of the BBC, Peter Mandelson—then Blair's image manager—came up to the table at which Bill Tuohy, Gerald Kaufmann and I were sitting. We were plotting our approach to the impending interview with Tony Blair, on the eve of his inauguration as leader of the Labour Party.

"I just hope," he said, with that British twinkle in the eye, "that you don't do to my man later today what you did to John Major last year!"

It was a compliment from Mandelson, now a European Union official. The comment came about an hour or so before Bill and I were to have an exclusive interview with Blair, arranged by my friend Gerald. But the interview almost did not take place at all, and it would not have—had I not been an American journalist. Let me explain why.

Gerald had put to Blair's office our request for an interview. Blair, though exceedingly ambitious to get Major's job, wasn't giving very many interviews—and none, I believe, to foreigners. But Blair thought of the elder

Gerald as a kind of political mentor, almost like his godfather, and always found it difficult to say "no" to his requests. Reminded that he had met me in the taxi that bloody awful night, and that I had done the damaging Major interview, Blair, perhaps reluctantly, consented.

I was in the airplane jetting toward London from Los Angeles when the deal fell through. In the snap of a heartbeat, Blair's boss—John Smith, then occupying the position of leader of the opposition—had keeled over from a stroke. By the time my plane landed, the Labour Party was in official party mourning, and the several candidates to succeed him had agreed, to a man and woman, that they would observe a strict press blackout until the official funeral had been held and a full week had passed to enable the family, friends and party members to observe a proper mourning. Then, the usual media games could—and would—resume.

When I checked into the Savoy Hotel, a note was waiting for me at the front desk. "Tom, with apologies, the death of Party Leader John Smith must be observed with a proper week of dignified silence. All press interviews have been canceled. I am afraid this includes yours. I know you have come a long way. But there is nothing I can do. Warmest regards, Gerald."

I was beside myself with disappointment. I left my bags to be taken up to the room, and went directly to the bar for a measure of self-medication. I needed a drink. I had come too close to a journalistic daily double—the only US journalist to exclusively Q/A the present prime minister, and then the next one. Oh why, said this craven journalist, couldn't have John Smith's stroke waited at least a few days longer?!

Then it hit me. There just might be a way ... just maybe.

I asked the bartender for a phone and dialed Gerald's number.

"Gerald, this is a bloody awful thing to do to me. I came 8,000 miles just for this interview."

"I know ... but we're up against unyielding British custom."

I paused a few ticks. "The issue, I take it, is a decent interval before the usual press posturing begins."

"Exactly, all the competitors agreed to it. Tony's going to win the leadership position, of course. It won't be remotely close. That's more the reason why Tony needs to look statesman-like and humane in the wake of this great tragedy."

I offered a Plan B. "Since everyone would agree that I am the only journalist who has come thousands of miles for this interview, and the only one who absolutely cannot stay in London for the week of mourning or however long the ritual is to last, I have an idea.

"We go to Blair's people, explain the unique circumstances, and request that the interview take place tomorrow as scheduled..."

"Tom, they won't do that..."

Ignoring the interruption, I continued, "On strict condition that the interview is withheld by the *Los Angeles Times* for publication until it receives official and explicit approval from Blair's office that it can run."

Pause on the other end, then: "Hmm ... interesting, very. But they will be sure to ask: what assurance do they have, can you give them, that the embargo that you propose will in fact be faithfully honored?"

Interesting and fair question, especially from a former Fleet Street journalist. I answered, "Just tell them they are used to dealing with amoral and cut-throat Fleet Street editors, who can't be trusted to honor their dying grandmother's death wish..."

"So?"

"Tell them that I'm an American journalist. We have ethics."

Believe it or not, it actually worked. Gerald bought it and, in the end, so did Blair.

Mandelson convinced Blair that I was on the up and up. The interview would take place as long as it was held back until the all-clear signal sounded, and if I committed to not telling any British journalist or anyone at all that it had taken place (because then they all would be furious to be scooped by an American journalist parachuting in). When I quickly signed off on the second condition (meaning, for one thing, that I was not permitted to brag about it to my London friends—darn), Bill Tuohy and I got to see Blair the next day.

The interview was memorable. It took about four minutes to come to the firm conclusion that Blair would, in fact, prove to be the second coming of Bill Clinton—brilliant, elusive, conniving, for all appearances sincere, the complete package.

I could not remember the last time I was so impressed by the fast-footed adroitness of a politician. Blair well understood that the future of his party as a plausible governing institution had no future at all if its craziest inmates were to be the ones proposing to run the show, even as Labour had to stand for something different from the Tories to retain the loyalty of its army of adherents. Whatever current public opinion of him, Blair, back then, stood for a steadiness of sensibility at a time when Labour was sinking fast from an overloaded loony bin of ideologues. Gerald was politically more liberal than Tony but, like many in Labour, was bone weary of being constantly out of power all through the Thatcher—and now through the Major—years.

(In the end, after his long tenure, Blair's fateful decision to link his prime ministership to the American intervention in Iraq was to turn the British people against him. But in truth, his years in power, on the whole, invigorated British politics and brightened Britain's future.)

That night, my phone rang at The Savoy. It was ... yes ... none other than Sir David English. (You will learn a lot about David and his band of merry men and women at *The Daily Mail* later on. For now, let me just say that David, regarded by his colleagues as the most skilled editor of his generation in London, had been my mentor, supporter and friend for years. When he died a half dozen or so years ago, it was as if I had lost a godfather.)

"Tom, you little scoundrel ... you sneaky and you amazing conniver ... And so you slip into my London on a secret mission, nail an exclusive interview with Blair who is granting no mere British newspaper even a private word, much less a kiss and a hug, and then you fail to inform your blood mentor, without whose celestial guidance your career would be in abject misery. I am truly chilled to the bones by all this manifest perfidy, truly saddened and betrayed..."

Hah! This was Sir David at his Edwardian, blow-hardian best—right out of some exaggerated West End comic production (he had married a famous actress, incidentally. He courted her outside the theater at night and when the curtain fell to the inevitable ovation, he would howl for Lady Irene from across the street.) His carriage and manner were that of a shining blend of the American actor Cary Grant and the British David Niven.

And so there was a hastily arranged lunch the next day at The Savoy Grill. I was as full of myself that day as perhaps I have ever been—and that's saying a lot! But I was prepared to fend off David's questions about the actual content of the interview. I was, after all (and for worse as well as better) an

American news media man. I have ethics—not nearly enough, perhaps, but at least some!

But David was too shrewd to intrude where he would have known to be unwanted; and his searing journalistic ambitions notwithstanding, was too considerate to force me to choose between English and Blair, because he knew that, aside from violating my pledge to Mandelson, I would have done almost anything for him.

"I just have one question," asked The Master, "only one. Will he beat John Major?" Understand that Blair's Labour Party, with its many leftwing kooks and unionist fascists, had been out of power for such a long time; understand that David was Tory (Conservative) to his bones, and so would have preferred Major in the upcoming showdown for who would be next to be prime minister; and understand that *The Daily Mail* institutionally and, David personally and professionally, had been as close to Major's predecessor, Margaret "Iron Lady" Thatcher, as almost anyone.

I took a deep breath. I wanted to give my mentor as clear and precise a picture as possible without betraying the agreement in any way so I plunged into summation: "David, Tony Blair will clean John Major's clock. He will eat his lunch. He will wipe the floor with him. It's over for Major. And, like you, I do like John."

My mentor's eyes bulged like those of a goldfish. The *Mail* was so politically Conservative—as, indeed, was most of Fleet Street—what would *The Mail* do? What could his newspaper do?

David paused for a few seconds, then asked, "What do you think we should do?"

I was flattered to be asked the question by one of the most amazing journalists I have ever met.

"If I were you," I responded, very carefully, "and of course I am not, I'd try to reach an understanding with Blair's people as soon as possible, certainly before Rupert (Murdoch, the owner of *The Sun*, a downmarket tabloid but also a Tory paper) does. Blair is a killer. I like John Major a lot but John Major is toast. It will be Jaws III."

The rest is history ... oh, yes, Sir David did make the deal: a honeymoon period (no extra effort by the Tory paper to embarrass the new Labour Party prime minister) in return for high-level access to the administration until the ceasefire was declared over and the knives came out on both sides.

The Blair people were happy to be approached. To be a Labour Party prime minister in a London of mainly Conservative papers is to be a distinct underdog. That Blair coped so well for so many years reveals much about his tremendous ability.

> All that a journalist can do is to do his or her best with total honesty. The job we journalists are given is, in its essence, a tremendous civic and cultural resource, and we must use it with wisdom and integrity.

FLEET STREET NEWSPAPERS, as a whole, do not waste a lot of staff energy worrying about ethical questions (though a distinguished high-end paper like *The Daily Telegraph* or *The Guardian* would), although all serious American newspapers are supposed to. But do they?

I had begun to worry about news media ethics, if at a mundane level, long before I was invited to teach news media ethics at the University of California, Los Angeles (UCLA). I was then nineteen, and with an internship at *Newsweek* had managed to finagle a trip to Houston to do a baseball story from the Houston Astrodome.

The Astrodome management could not have been happier to accommodate me, and this gave me my first taste of media royalty: I was only nineteen and was being treated like a true prince of Bel Air. There I was, sitting in the press box, which was right in front of an excellent array of food and drink, including beer. I do not recall if I got blasted but I know I did have a few free beers.

Leaving aside any implications about early-appearing alcoholism, the key word here is "free." What does a journalist do when accepting virtually anything that is free? The optimal answer is: he or she is doing wrong.

And so at an early age, then, the flat principle of accept-nothing-for-free seemed the right way to go. But the principle slammed into reality when I launched the column and was to travel so often to Asia. There, the custom of offering gifts to American visitors from so far away was commonplace. Today, my home cabinets contain I-don't-know-how-many trinkets and tea sets.

> To be effective, sometimes you actually have to rise above your ethical principles but when you do, never lose sight of their existence or their vital importance to your identity and self-worth.

How did I come to rise above my own ethical principles? By developing a new one of my own: the principle of reciprocity. When a source or a government official lays a gift on me, I reach into my travel bag and pull out a reciprocal trinket. In fact, on lengthier trips, I typically haul across the Pacific two suitcases—one for my traveling wardrobe; the second filled with UCLA tee-shirts, sweatshirts and sports caps. (I believe that, in 1999, I was the single largest non-corporate purchaser of UCLA sportswear. You might be able to look it up.)

There is no point in insulting the customs of another country by denying your host the opportunity to be gracious, especially when there's the opportunity to be gracious, rather than condescending, in return, although to be sure, there's not always that opportunity for graciousness.

MAKING SENSIBLE, non-ethnocentric, non-ideological and helpful observations about China is arguably the greatest journalistic challenge for an American news media man. For one thing, the stakes in the Sino-US relationship are enormous; second, the country's total population (more than 1.3 billion) is enormous; and, not least, the inner contradictions and complexities of a politically communist country turning into an economically entrepreneurial country are also enormous.

The enormity of the challenge is made no easier by the fact that there are surely several Chinas—the coastal (rich) and inland (poor), the modernizing (fast) and the traditional (reluctantly), and the pro-West (the emerging middle class) and the anti-American (various sectors, for various reasons); as well as the fact that strong generational differences in training, education and cosmopolitanism threaten to, before too long, bring China to the edge of a political crisis.

The challenge is further aggravated by serious methodological problems: China is not exactly Sweden. It is not only exceedingly bigger and more complicated but far less open and almost impossibly difficult to penetrate.

Government officials, especially in the foreign ministry, both those posted in Beijing as well as in the States, can be quite helpful and decent, but they still are more the exception than the rule.

US correspondents who are stationed in Beijing or Shanghai—though perhaps not in Hong Kong—face constant surveillance. The Chinese translator in the office is probably dating or married to an intelligence officer in the PLA (People's Liberation Army) or a party official or agent. Worse yet, they sometimes face surveillance not only from Western intelligence agents on the Chinese mainland but, in a sense, even from their own foreign desks back home.

That's because until relatively recently, the US news media lived by its own journalistic ideology regarding the world's most populous country. That is to say, the vast majority of the stories coming to America were confined to certain story categories, particularly human rights (abuses), government activity (screw-ups) and oddball communist behavior (cute or bizarre). If you were a foreign correspondent stationed in China, and you sought to convince your US-based editor to publish a story that did not fit neatly into one of these categories, good luck.

When I started my foreign affairs column which focused on Asia, I regarded China as my single most important issue. I then established a set of priorities that pointedly hoped to avoid my profession's conventional wisdoms. That is, I would try not to file any column on China that was like any other column or story on China that had appeared in the last few years in the mainstream US press.

This meant I would seek to avoid telling readers about the "olds"— the usual and continuing human rights violations, ongoing government inefficacies, communist ideological rigidity. Those stories may be old, but nonetheless, they were real, however dated, but they were certainly being amply covered, over and over and over again, in the mainstream US media. Instead of emphasizing the olds, therefore, I would point the spotlight on what was changing.

This approach would seem oddball only to deeply entrenched American rightwing anti-communists—and to many US newspaper editors who were of course anything but. Yet, they shared the same predilection for not wanting to confront what was new—the government's remarkably focused prioritization of economic development, the rise of an entrepreneurial and indeed a somewhat Western-like middle class perhaps 200-million strong, the decline in mass malnutrition and indeed starvation, the rather careful evolution of a slightly higher-profile foreign policy that was calculated to soothe neighbors' nerves rather than to raise alarms, and the utter moral, political and, of course, economic imperative for the US to engage China positively and in the manner of mutual benefit, rather than to foolishly seek to isolate China, which would inevitably be done ineffectually. China is far too big to be isolated, no matter what anyone might prefer.

This new approach caught the eye of at least three important sectors.

One was the leadership in Beijing. In late 1996, President Bill Clinton was urged to break the inherited policy of cooled bilateral relations with China (a result of the political fallout from the godawful 1989 Tiananmen Square bloodshed) and to travel to China on a state visit, which was what he did in 1998.

The column was also the first to urge China's admission into the World Trade Organization, which was to happen several years afterwards; and it was the first to argue that for the foreseeable future, the People's Republic of China would have but three main national goals, with every other goal in another, minor league category:

Priority One: economic development
Priority Two: economic development
Priority Three: economic development

That was not an attempt at humor, and when I would rattle this little joke off to truly knowledgeable adults, whether in China or America, they would nod in agreement.

The column was greatly assisted by important interviews. One, in 1997, was an exclusive with Tung Chee-hwa, the new master of Hong Kong, at a time when few Western journalists were permitted access; another, in 1998, was an exclusive with then Foreign Minister Qian Qichen, China's master diplomat who inherited the foreign affairs bishopric of the legendary Chou Enlai; and a third, in 1999, was an exclusive chat with Beijing's cross-strait relations rabbi, the aging but wise former mayor of Shanghai, Wang Duohan, in Shanghai.

These interviews were instrumental in helping work out a sensible and honest line about China in the column. While the country is not to be loved as long as there are communists in power who are worthy of the appellation "communist," neither is it to be feared. The world needs to work with this new giant if it is to get on with its history. What was the point of Western journalists grinding the same old ideological axes if what people needed to know was how China was really evolving and what this actually meant?

One particular interview in Hong Kong that took place two months before it became official Chinese property in 1997 illustrated the territory's feral hostility to Western journalists. I had secured an interview with a highly-placed woman on the pro-China transition team. This was not easy to get, but when word got around that I did, a US reporter based in Hong Kong asked to come along. I liked and respected her, so what could I say? Besides, as a reporter from a major US newspaper based in Hong Kong, she was masterful on Chinese issues. But whether through her own professional perspective or through the force majeure of her US editors' predilections, she was scorned by much of the Chinese elite in Hong Kong, as were most Western journalists.

Quite naturally then, she had not been invited to the interview, and in fact, her prior requests to meet with this top lady had been rebuffed. But out of professional courtesy and personal respect, when she telephoned me about the appointment, I suggested that she simply show up as if she were passing by and we would enter the official's office together and see what happened.

You should have seen what happened! As I walked in, the official turned to me and greeted me warmly, as if I was the only other person in her corner office. She then turned to my companion and spewed forth venom. Locking her eyes on the female journalist, she said scathingly, "We agreed to this interview with you, Tom, because we are well aware of your work, both here and in Beijing. While we do not always agree with it, it almost always seems fair-minded and well-reported, and never anti-Chinese. But you, [name deleted], you are anti-Chinese, you are working for the enemy, and once we are in power, your access to official sources will be completely cut off."

My American friend tried her best to defend herself but it was at first useless, with shrill shouts back and forth, and then it plunged into the shameless and near-hilarious, with the two of them going at it like prize-fighters at the rematch.

Sliding into my best Henry Kissinger-like pseudo-Teutonic mediator imitation, this peace-loving columnist implored the two warring sides to sit down at the peace table, negotiate their differences and, while they were at it, conspire to deliver me a sensational international scoop.

That intervention stopped them. Suddenly ratcheting down the bile, the pro-Beijing powerhouse turned to me and, ignoring my uninvited and unwanted companion, said sweetly, "Now, Mr Plate, how can we help you?"

What followed next was a fascinating 90-minute briefing (my US friend said very little; I said as little as possible, having concluded long ago that the more I talked, the less I learned).

Sessions like these make a big contribution to the column. In its first ten years, leading political figures from Junichiro Koizumi to Tony Blair to Lee Kuan Yew to Bill Clinton to Donald Tsang have helped by sharing some of their thoughts with me. I have especially courted sources who have had special knowledge of China, surely the single most significant economic and geopolitical story of our time.

My interview attitude toward sources was almost never confrontational. If I rode in like the galloping literary gourmet on my high American horse, sources would close up and hide from the Ugly American or the Quiet American or the Know-it-All American out of fear of media culture imperialism. It's our way or the highway, we American journalists tend to proclaim. But it is not that way in many parts of the world—and, besides, is cultural arrogance ever an efficient route to getting your source to relax and tell you more than he or she should, all for the benefit of readers?

That level of access in China and Hong Kong helped make the columns more informed; it also may have irritated other journalists, I don't know. My columns about China in the 1990s sought to highlight the changes inside the country rather than the continuities of repression and incivility, which were always well reported in the US media anyway. Did this make me "pro-China"? A good and fair colleague, well respected in the profession, suggested to me once, in a friendly way, "Tom, if I were you, I'd mix in an anti-Beijing column every third or fourth time or so, you know, just to maintain your credibility." In effect, this suggestion would make my columns more like everyone else's—to recycle, every so often, the "olds" at the expense of "news." This I would not do.

Another way to describe the arrogance of the American journalist is to reveal that sympathetic portraits are regarded professionally as evidence of a lack of manhood, that slash-and-burn journalism is viewed as inherently courageous (even when the "village had to be burned in order to save the village"), and that anything that remotely smacks of appreciation or understanding is generally quickly labeled as being a "court painter to the powerful," in the zesty phrase of famed American journalist Pete Hamill.

You see, it is real easy (isn't it?) to run a country, balance a national budget, provide for the national defense and solve serious social problems. It is especially a snap in China, which just forty years ago was economically less than even a Third World nation, with more people within its borders than any country on earth. To China, I am, and probably will always be, sympathetic but skeptical and cynical about its leaders. But only up to a point: I will not sneer until I hear. I do not fear to listen carefully to what they have to say, and I do not listen with an attitude of fear.

This stubbornness on the China issue led to attacks.

One was from US politicians, especially Congressman Christopher Cox, the Orange County Republican. He was to co-head the "Cox Commission Report on Chinese Spying" which triggered an avalanche of anti-Beijing stories about how commie spies were just about everywhere (under school desks, in industrial parks, inside your computer hard drive, etc.).

The truth was, yes indeed, there was a lot of spying done by China—as there was by France, Israel, Russia (still) and many others. Former Secretary of State Henry Kissinger, whose sophistication about China is widely respected, put it well when asked about the issue. He readily averred that there was a lot of spying "by everyone, not just the Chinese ... I don't see what all the fuss is about. Everybody spies on everybody else."

My column took the long view. If we were spying on the Chinese, why not they on us? The Cox report seemed juvenile and partisan, designed not so much to enhance national security as to undermine Bill Clinton's rock solid hold on the American people; and so, when the opposition couldn't get his presidency impeached over his dalliances with Monica Lewinsky, it tried to impeach his credibility and impugn his patriotism over his security lapses with China.

After a column appeared decrying the media hysteria over the Chinese spy report, co-chairman Cox (why in the world did this otherwise nice guy get involved in this slime?) wrote a letter to the *Los Angeles Times*, accusing me of "parroting the communist party line."

The former editorial pages editor in me was pleased to see the letter in print: the right of reply must be fully and unconditionally applied. And the heat-seeking columnist in me was enamored that Cox would make a fool of himself in public by establishing a red-baiting profile. (I was, though, surprised that the *Los Angeles Times* hadn't extended the courtesy of giving its columnist a heads-up about the imminent publication of a personal attack. Perhaps the editors simply didn't want to put me at risk of laughing myself to death?)

(Some years later, an extremely reliable source said that Cox, who is, by the way, a University of Southern California (USC) alumnus, Harvard law graduate and an otherwise smooth operator, had more or less come to rue the day he had been co-opted into fronting anti-Clinton forces by fanning the China hysteria. Cox, he said, is a serious man and not at all a demagogue. I asked him if he thought the congressman would be willing to go on the record with a disavowal. His response: "No, that would be too politically embarrassing.")

Another attack that was laughable came in the predictable cascade of hate email messages, especially from conservative parts of Orange County. One delightful zinger accused me of being a communist. Another from one idiotic professor at one of the California State University campuses charged that the nonprofit setup based at UCLA that I founded some years ago—the Asia Pacific Media Network (APMN)—took contributions from communists. When it was pointed out that such untruths are legally classifiable as slander, the attackers calmed down and returned to their caves. (APMN never took a dime from any government, communist or otherwise, or from any front.)

But here was my all-time favorite truly stupid attack: "How much does Beijing pay for those columns?" the emailer from a small interior city in Orange County, California, asked.

This one stopped me. "Well, you got me," came the effort at closure, "The truth is, about $10,000 a month. Pretty good pay, don't you think?"

How do you respond to arrant idiocy? If you ignore it, the malicious mosquito won't go away; if you tell the truth and deny it, the mosquito will spread the denial like malaria. Instead, try an email response designed for maximum confusion; it might just work.

It worked. I never heard from the emailer again.

UNDOUBTEDLY, YOUR HAPPIEST MOMENTS are when you are able to do some good with a column.

That does not happen often, but when it does, it is memorable and makes you feel better about continuing on down the questionable, if not roguish, path of the journalist.

One January evening early in the ten-year history of the column, I was dining with an official from the government of the Republic of Korea. Though the South Korean official was a pleasant fellow (someone I had spent some time with at various functions and later came to love dearly), the dinner went on seemingly for no purpose until the appearance of dessert—which is exactly when you would expect anything of any significance to come up.

It was over crème brulée that I popped the question: "Anything on your mind in particular? Anything bothering you?"

The Korean diplomat, as if suddenly comfortable with me, said carefully, "Well, one thing is, to tell you the truth. As you know, your president is planning a trip to Tokyo in April, after which he's flying directly to Moscow. We're upset by this because not only is Korea just a little 90-minute flight from Tokyo but it's also on the way to Moscow, so it wouldn't be a detour for the president to stop in Seoul."

"Why should he do that?" I countered. "There are a thousand places he could visit in Asia."

"That's true. But again, as you know, the North Koreans have been acting strangely lately. They have been trying to cut us out of their talks with Washington and isolate us. And they may be expanding their missile program. So, we're fearful that if President Clinton doesn't visit, they may come to believe that we're not so important to Washington anymore, and thus, they can get all they want in bilateral negotiations with Washington, leaving us out. Official American policy, as you know, is that fundamental differences between North and South Korea must be solved by direct bilateral negotiation between the two Koreas. But North Korean diplomacy seeks to improve its economic situation by dealing directly with Washington, to our exclusion. They want to split us. The Americans aren't stupid, of course, and won't bite. But if Clinton doesn't visit, those in the North would believe that they could actually work around us. They might even interpret his not stopping by in South Korea as a deliberate snub—and find hope in this."

"So you think it's a mistake for the president to not visit South Korea, leaving aside the obvious wishes of the South Koreans to have an American president in their midst?"

"Yes. We think it could open the door to serious misinterpretation by the North Koreans."

I flashed back to a historic mistake Dean Acheson made in January 1950 when he was secretary of state. In a wide-ranging speech, he had attempted to define "America's strategic interests," but inexplicably omitted any reference to Korea, an oversight thought later to have emboldened the North Koreans into invading the South and inciting the Korean War.

Mulling this possible precedent over, I thanked the Korean diplomat for his thoughts and went home scratching my head. Just another disgruntled and overly emotional Korean? Or grist for a pretty good column?

As it happened, I had scheduled for the very next day a discreet luncheon with a Japanese diplomat who was later to become a top foreign policy aide to a famous Japanese prime minister. I liked him a lot in part because he was delightfully blunt—there wasn't much diplomacy in his soul but he had tremendous intelligence and integrity and wit (he was stylistically almost un-Japanese, as it were, which might suggest that national stereotypes are probably of marginal usefulness at best, as well as ethically risky. But, we all use them all the time, alas...).

At this time, relations between South Korea and Japan were still careering along their historically frosty track. I thought if I raised the Korean complaint with him, he would dismissively say, "Oh, those emotional Koreans, they're always whining about something or other."

But he did not say anything like that. And that stopped me. He acknowledged that he was fully aware that President Clinton was not planning on stopping in Korea, but instead would go on directly to Moscow, and that naturally the Japanese were very pleased that he was going to Tokyo, even though this very limited itinerary hardly made the Koreans happy.

What I was missing was the quiet Japanese gloat (that is, too bad for those hapless Koreans, we never liked them anyhow…).

Instead, there was a very loud silence and then a prolonged quiet, and so (being a typically vulgar straightforward American), I looked at the diplomat straight in the eyes and said, "So, what do you think?"

Finally, he returned my stare and said, "I have to admit I think the South Koreans have a point. We have our own difficulties relating to the North Koreans. We find them unpredictable, impossible to decipher, and any possible or conceivable ambiguity that you add to a situation like that is a mistake."

"So you think the president really ought to go to South Korea?"

"He should. I don't want to be quoted in the column, of course."

I said, "No, no, I understand that. I just wanted your judgment. It seems to me that if you, as a member of the Japanese government, believe the Korean case has merit, then maybe the Korean complaint really does have merit."

"It has merit."

This was like, in baseball, a Boston Red Sox fan actually agreeing with a Yankee fan on something or other—besides their mutual hatred.

The next day I put through a telephone call to Washington. I had a top source in the State Department—let's just call him Deep Throat for fun—who always knew what was going on.

"Hey, Deep! It's Tom Plate."

Deep said, "Hey, Plato! What's up?"

Like many people, the famous diplomat liked to make fun of my patronymic name, not to mention my philosophical pretensions!

"What's all this nonsense about the president going to Tokyo and then to Moscow in April and not stopping off to give a kiss and a hug to our long-standing and oft-suffering friends in South Korea?"

"Oh, that's just those whiny, overly emotional Koreans complaining. They're always unhappy and they're very competitive with the Japanese. The president of the United States can't be everywhere, visit every country in East Asia. You know that."

"Yes, but Deep, these North Koreans have been in one war with us already, granted it was many years ago. So who's to say they wouldn't go instigate another if they thought—however foolishly—that our resolve and determination to defend South Korea was waning in any way? Or ignore peace overtures from the South because they figure they can cut Seoul out of the dialogue with us? This is risky business, Deep. It seems we're allowing an unnecessary ambiguity to arise, unless it is our intent to be ambiguous."

"No, it's not our intent. I just think the president has a lot to do and he's on a tight schedule."

"Oh, come on, Deep, tell me what the hell is going on here! Stop parroting the State Department line."

There was a sigh, there was a pause, then there was this: "Can we go off the record?"

I said, "Absolutely."

Another sigh, another pause, but longer now. Deep actually trusted me. The nature of my Asia column was not to slash and burn, and ruin people's lives (I really do *not* care how many blow jobs the prime minister of Japan gets from his girlfriend, and I'd rather not know, unless, of course, his girlfriend turns out to be a Chinese spy), but to illuminate important issues and understand key leaders (in a non-boring and honest way, and from the vantage point of the US West Coast).

"Tom, those egomaniacal jerks in the White House who are running Clinton's campaign,"—this was in early 1996 and the bid for re-election was well underway, so the president's time was even more parceled out than ever—"they only think of domestic politics, electoral votes, interest groups, 'Get him out of the country and back as quickly as possible.' They have no idea of the broader implications on the world landscape of who the president sees and does not see. The only way that anything like this can get to the president's eyes is if the media takes up the issue."

There was another pause. He said: "Do you think you might do a column on this?"

"Damn right!"

Deep said, in a low voice, "Good. Very, very good." And he hung up.

So I wrote the column—strong and to the point. It basically said a slight detour of *Air Force One* toward Seoul would reap big dividends, and I threw all I could into the argument, including the serious fact that there were roughly 200,000 Korean Americans in California—as well as the wholly improbable prediction that they all might en masse get peeved with the president and the Democrats if he were to snub South Korea on his Asia trip!

This doomsday electoral scenario was not likely to happen, of course, but for a White House concerned with securing California's 54 electoral votes later that year without having to shell out a fortune for statewide media advertising (California is the most expensive media buy in the US), this scary thought might get the issue attended to by the re-election wizards and pollster wonks in the White House—and thus get the column into the president's inbox.

Those of us in US media and foreign policy circles knew that, during the first term, the Clinton administration based many (though not all) foreign policy moves on its perception of the probable reactions of the American people to the media coverage of foreign events—rather than on any coherent conceptual scheme of its own. For it had none.

So, an appeal of the Korean over-flight plan based on sincere international relations concerns would fall on deaf ears. But, at the same time, Clinton could forward his position in domestic election polls by appearing in the media as a world leader with initiative, instead of just some guy smilingly manipulating re-election votes. In print, I argued: "A sitting president seems better cast for the job when acting presidential, especially when the other party's candidates are flinging primary election dirt in all directions." Impending election or no, Clinton was still the president of the free world and, as I pointed out in my column, "important foreign policy considerations must take precedence over political ones."

The *Los Angeles Times* published these perfervid thoughts the next day under the nifty headline (by the brilliant associate op-ed editor Judy Dugan): "Short Detour Could Pay Out Big Dividend."

I waited.

A few days later, I called Washington and got Deep on the phone.

No pause this time. "Well, you did it," he said.

"Did what?" I savored the moment.

"You put it on the radar screen. It's on the president's desk, thank God, those jerks."

"Really?"

"Yeah, it's being reviewed at the Oval Office level now. Someone put it in front of the president, and he looked at it hard. He's no idiot, you know. And you raised some good points in there. Plus, it's in the *Los Angeles Times*, which is the leading newspaper in California, hell, in the West. As you know, he has an election to think about so he doesn't want to get the *Los Angeles Times* pissed off at him."

"So, the president will change his travel plans?"

"Well, I wouldn't say that. They're still being very, very tight with his schedule. You know as well as I do that foreign affairs in general isn't that important in this administration but who knows? It's on the radar screen and it wasn't before."

I figured I did what I could. I thanked him for trusting me and we signed off by agreeing we would just have to wait and see but, I was not going to hold my breath for it.

> In journalism, as in anything else, you just do the very best you can and then let fate take its course. You can never do better than the best you can do. Don't even try.

Months before, I had planned a trip to Asia, and, as scheduled, I left the week after the column appeared.

The column was also re-published in *The Korea Herald*, then my regular outlet in South Korea (today, it is *The Korea Times*). My next to last stop on this Asia trip was Seoul, South Korea, where I was to meet with several government officials.

Invariably, as I walked into each of my eight meetings over the two days in South Korea's bustling capital, each official would have on their desk a copy of the column or had already committed it to memory. Their first question was always, "So, do you think, Professor Plate, that your column suggesting the president should make a visit to us in Korea before going on to Moscow will be acted upon?"

I laughed and chuckled, and always tried to make a joke of it. What was I supposed to say, that the president doesn't do anything without checking with me first? So I said, "Naturally, the president doesn't do anything without checking with me first."

They would always laugh, and it would be a nice warm moment, and then we would move on to the substance of the interview. But at every meeting, this first question (and my silly reply) went first.

My final appointment in South Korea was at the Blue House, which is the Korean version of the White House, except that it was not white, it was—surprise—mostly blue. I was received by Kim Young Sam, the first democratically elected president of the Republic of Korea.

What had been billed as a ten-minute courtesy call wound up lasting over a half an hour and yielded a solid interview.

Kim was a real ham politician—all back-slapping and jovial. In fact, the first issue President Kim wanted to raise was actually not political at all, but the fact that the previous night the Korean national soccer team had actually defeated the Japanese national soccer team in a dramatic win. That was a bigger deal in Asia than an American Superbowl—or the Red Sox winning a World Series.

So I said something diplomatic to the president, something like it was such a delight to be with a winner. That eased things a bit (no doubt he quickly concluded that I was as full of the b*llsh^t as he was). He then asked me about my column.

"Do you think it will have an effect, Prof Plate?" Although my column was pretty well-known in Asia, and so my profile was as a journalist, many Asians I would meet when traveling addressed me as "professor," precisely because, according to Asian values, being a respected educational figure was more prestigious and commendable by far than being a media person. Funny things, those Asian values!

"You mean the column I wrote in February?"

He said, "February 6th."

I had to laugh. He had actually taken the trouble to memorize the precise date of the column! And so, I used the line I had used everywhere else. "Well, who knows, but generally President Clinton doesn't do anything without checking with me first."

We had another nice chuckle and then went on to discuss other issues. After the interview, I went back to my hotel—the lovely Seoul Hilton, with its gorgeous lobby—made a few phone calls, took a much-needed shower, and started packing my bags in order to get to Kimpo Airport for my night flight to Taipei. And then the phone rang.

"Professor Plate? I'm Jin Park, press secretary to the president of the Republic of Korea."

I liked Jin a lot (Park was his last name. In Korea, as it is throughout much of Asia, the actual order of the name would be Park Jin). A whip-smart graduate of the John F Kennedy School of Government at Harvard, he would kid me about being an alumnus of the competing policy institution at Princeton, the Woodrow Wilson School (the better one, of course).

"Oh yes, Mr Park! How are you? What can I do for you?"

"You've done everything you could possibly do for us. That's why I'm calling. I've been authorized by the president of South Korea to thank you for your help in arranging for the president of the United States to revise his April schedule."

"Oh? Wow!"

"Yes, we have just heard—as you know, our foreign minister has been in Washington for meetings with Secretary of State Warren Christopher, and he has just told us that the president will stop off here before going on to Moscow in April."

"That's excellent, Mr Park. One win for the good guys!"

"In fact, we at the Blue House think your column was a substantial factor in helping change the decision not to visit Korea."

I decided to have a little fun. "Substantial factor? Are you crazy? It was the *main* reason for the switcheroo!"

Jin Park chuckled giddily. "You know, life offers so precious few delightful moments like this, moments of pure triumph, that you might as well take full credit for it. You deserve it. Hey, if there's anything we can ever do for you here, you just let us know. We'll do our best to do it."

"Thank you, Mr Park. Your legendary Korean hospitality has been more than enough."

It was true—Korean hospitality at its fullest is perhaps second to none. But right then, I felt like a gambler in Vegas who had been piling up hundred-dollar chips at the roulette table. The only way I was going to leave the table as a winner, with that pile of chips in my pocket, was to stop gambling, pay a friendly and real quick visit to the cashier and get the heck out of the casino.

"Jin, I've got to go. I'm ahead and I want to leave here a winner. I have to finish packing, head for the airport and catch my flight to Taipei. So, off I go! Good luck. And enjoy Clinton's visit."

WITHOUT THE COLUMN, would the president's schedule have changed? Who knows? But knowing as we do the susceptibility of that administration (hardly unique) to what the news media was doing and covering and saying—heck, the mere fact that a column in the *Los Angeles Times* bothered to raise the issue was enough to beam it onto the radar screen of the White House. The US media barely covered international events, unless the US was at war, and it covered Asia poorly. How many foreign affairs columns in America focus on Asia?

So when Clinton looked at it—being the reasonable man that he is—he undoubtedly said something like, "How much time does stopping in Korea really add to our trip? If it really is not that much, then maybe we ought to do it, especially given what is potentially at stake here."

There are several lessons here. The impact of a heavyweight institution such as the *Los Angeles Times* committing itself to something as relatively obvious as an Asia-oriented foreign affairs column cannot be underestimated. I was so happy that it made the commitment, but five years later, after *The Chicago Tribune* bought all of Times-Mirror Corporation, closed it down, took over at the *Los Angeles Times* (and *Newsday* and elsewhere), and killed my column, I was really sad. Happily, the column was to live on in syndication, appearing in roughly a dozen different newspapers in America and Asia over the last six years. The combined circulation of these papers is at least three or four times that of the *Los Angeles Times*, which recently has sunk below the iconic one-million mark.

Second, whether a column is a piece of sand on a very lengthy beachfront, or a huge sand barrier, it is in its essence something—and, especially, in this age of the internet, a material member of the news media food chain. In the case of the Korean visit column, it generated questions elsewhere in the news media and raised doubts in the White House about whether dissing Korea on the trip to Asia was worth the geopolitical risk, not to mention the news media criticism. Some months later, visiting with my former *Time* magazine colleague Steve Smith, then editor-in-chief of "US News and World Report," I was relating a few of my very rare column successes, and happened to mention the Korean visit issue. "Oh," said Steve, "so you're the one who stirred that one up!"

Yes, I was—and proud of it.

Solid international journalism is crucial not only for the American public but for the American government. It is the one thing large media corporations are likely to chintz on, but this is a terrible cultural error and, over the long term, a formula for national disaster.

PRESS SECRETARIES ARE probably the most unheralded and under-appreciated slaves in the labor of politics. They do an important job as go-betweens for their powerful bosses—president, prime minister, defense boss, whatever—and the news media. Some of them, I have come to greatly admire.

Years after that interview with Kim Young Sam, the first non-military head of the Republic of Korea, Park Jin was to become a major political figure in his own right. At this writing, he is a prominent figure in the Grand National Party, an established political party in the nation. Some day, Jin may just wind up as president or prime minister or foreign minister of South Korea.

But when I met him for the first time, he was "nothing but a flak" for the president of South Korea. The morning before the presidential interview, he came into a small antechamber at the Blue House with a small pot of tea. As part of this ritual for every official interview I have ever had in Korea, the presentation of the tea was all too often accompanied, if a man were proffering the brew, with the whispered advisory that the tea was *ginseng* tea and—drum roll—"good for the manhood."

This had happened so often during the trip that I joked afterwards that I was starting to wonder whether my wife had been secretly telephoning officials from Los Angeles with marital complaints! So to Park Jin, who was obviously as sharp as blades come, I complained: "Hey, all I want is to have an interview with your president, not have sex with him!"

Jin roared and said: "In two years in this job, that's one I absolutely have not heard!"

"Nothing but a flak" is such a demeaning phrase but this is exactly how many journalists in the news media view press secretaries. This assessment probably says more about us than about them. There are different kinds of press secretaries, just as there are different kinds of journalists. The ones I tend to meet are dedicated professionals who work just as hard as we do.

I will never forget years ago checking into the ANA Hotel in Tokyo one night—four hours late. A typhoon had forced my flight from Los Angeles to divert north to Sapporo until the turbulence calmed down long enough to head back to Tokyo for a landing, and, by then, I figured the press aide to the Japanese Foreign Ministry had long ago gone home.

I dragged my bags to the check-in line, half-asleep around midnight, when a tap on my shoulder brought me back to the land of the living. "Professor Plate," said the voice coming from a quietly dressed middle-aged man with a black portfolio in one hand and an umbrella in the other, "my name is Kazuo Kodama." The press aide to the Foreign Ministry had been right there waiting. How many of us would have sat there in the lobby that long for what could have been done the next day? I was impressed by the exhausting evidence of sheer, dogged dedication.

Kodama-san, a career diplomat in Japan's famed Ministry of Foreign Affairs, was very special but not, as he would be the first to argue, unique. Press spokesmen like Akira Chiba and Koji Tsuruoka add luster to the idea of public service. So do ace diplomatic players like China's Han Tao, for a few years the witty press spokesman for the Chinese government in Los Angeles.

The funniest press secretary I had ever met, though, was undoubtedly the American Mike McCurry. He labored for Warren Christopher in the State Department and then wound up as White House press secretary. Eventually, the job of deflecting all the hand grenades lobbed at his boss Bill Clinton wore him down, but during his stoic run, I cannot think of a single serious enemy he made.

He certainly won my daughter Ashley over when she and I made a visit to Washington one July 4th weekend. Almost no VIP of any consequence was in town, but there Mike was, in his comically cramped office, when I called to ask if I could pay a personal call and whether I could bring my daughter along. Of course, he said, come on over. And yes, Ashley was probably the only ten-year-old kid in America that year to be personally escorted to the Oval Office by the president's press secretary to tour the historic room.

The list of press secretaries of distinction is frankly as long as any list of distinguished journalists. Ken Bacon, an Amherst College colleague, was Pentagon press secretary for six years (somehow) and set a standard of performance for that job that will be hard to beat. David Bergen served more than one president, and wound up, nicely on his feet, at Harvard. Bill Moyers, a former Texas preacher, struggled with his soul as White House press secretary under President Lyndon Johnson, pushing forward the war in Vietnam, but before too long, left for *Newsday* to become its publisher and helped lead the moral crusade against the war.

I never served as a press secretary and I don't know how I would have reacted had I been offered such a position by a political figure I admired. The revered journalist and historian Richard Reeves once warned me that I'd probably face that very job dilemma at least once in my career but, up to now, that hasn't happened. I am glad it hasn't but I greatly admire those who have done this job and left with their reputation and integrity intact. That isn't easy to do but it is something to behold when it is done very well.

I HAD BEEN WRITING my Asia column for hardly more than a year when a bright student of mine named Gwendoline Yeo (now an accomplished actress in Los Angeles and occasional guest star on "Desperate Housewives") suggested that I visit Singapore, where she had been born and raised until early adolescence. Initially, I scoffed at the idea. I'd only been to China once at that point and the young column was progressing just fine; why should I waste a trip on tiny little Singapore? Who would care? But, being a bright young woman, and a trilingual one at that, Gwendoline justified her assertion in the language a political writer could comprehend, "You should go to Singapore because you will meet a political genius named Lee Kuan Yew."

I was intrigued by her characterization of the founder of modern Singapore. It was certainly true that the country had become a city-state of extraordinary influence and success, especially considering its minute size and population. But it had a political system that ran things, shall we say, not exactly in the American way. It was a one-party goliath that squeezed out—or absorbed into the ruling party—all of the significant political opposition. That was the bad news (from the US political values perspective).

The good news was this: Lee had built a top government team that single-handedly transformed impoverished Singapore, which was abandoned a half century ago as a lost cause by the ever-pragmatic British, into one of the most impressive little places in the world. But again, he did not do it the American way.

The seeming duality of the place—the contrast between enviable achievements and questionable process—fascinated me; so did the political enigma of Lee Kuan Yew, who, to say the least, had not received a very good press in the United States, at least in the nineties.

I decided to call on the government of Singapore and phoned to ask for a journalist's visa so as to travel there for a column or two.

Initially—and to my surprise—they were not enthusiastic. "Oh sure, we know what you're going to do," said the government official who handled the foreign press. "You're going to come to Singapore, you're going to spend 2.1 days here, you're going to write 3.1 articles and you're going to mention that caning incident 17.6 times."

They had a point.

The Singapore government had been keeping track of foreign journalists who parachuted in (and stayed for some time, then write the one dominant story on caning) for quite a long time. Indeed, before I left for Southeast Asia, I had reviewed the *Los Angeles Times*' database of previous columns and stories, and found that the vast majority of those done in recent years (or ever!) had focused on Singapore's use of caning as criminal punishment and social deterrence, and about its first known American recipient thereof, the notorious Michael Fay. He was more or less a typical young irresponsible American goofball who decided to publicly display his spray painting skills on walls and cars in a political culture whose entire goal was absolute public respect for authority—and control of deviance of almost all kinds. In such a small and well-policed city-state, the young American was quickly arrested and promptly sentenced to a handful of whacks from the strict Singaporean caning rod.

The US media outcry was instantly condemnatory. How primitive! How animalistic! But it never occurred to the American media so loudly lynching Singapore—and telling it how to run its affairs—that American public opinion was far more in favor of than against this practice, probably because we wish we could be at least a little sterner with our own errant children, perhaps even without getting slapped with an ACLU (American Civilian Liberties Union) lawsuit.

But let's go back to my conversation with the Singapore government.

"Okay, I'll make you a deal," I said. "I'll stay 5.0 days, a whole work week. I won't go to Malaysia, I won't go to Indonesia, I won't go anywhere else in Asia during that time. I'll look, I'll learn and I'll write one column in which I'll likely only bring up caning once because as an American journalist, I'm going to have to mention your caning law at least once or I'll lose my journalistic license!"

I was joking, of course, or was I? Of course, American journalists don't have to be licensed, but should they be? Now, that's an interesting question; you might be surprised by my answer!

The Singapore official threw my pitch right back at me: "Okay, here is what you are proposing: you'll stay one week, you'll write one column, you'll keep an open mind, you'll observe, you'll listen, you'll look and you'll only probably mention caning once?"

"Correct. But I will have to mention it once or I won't be able to get the column into the *Los Angeles Times*."

"There must be a catch."

"There is a catch."

"Uh-oh, right. What's that?"

"Before I leave Singapore, I must have an interview with Lee Kuan Yew."

The media relations official said he would get back to me and hung up.

I never thought I would hear from him again.

Word came back from Singapore two days later. "Okay, here's the deal as we understand it. You come, you stay a week, you see what you want. No one will follow you around. You write whatever you want, of course. We'll be helpful to you in any way we can, and at five o'clock on Friday, since we know you are leaving on Saturday on a Singapore Airlines flight 868 (Singapore's government officials, to generalize, are extremely precise and always do their homework better than you had done yours) to Hong Kong, you can have 45 minutes with Lee Kuan Yew in his office at the Istana."

The Istana was an old but lovely British colonial residence. It had its own nine-hole golf course. It was gorgeous. Lee Kuan Yew, as a proud ethnic Chinese Singaporean, may have been happy to have the British vacate the premises but no one had ever said he was dumb. Istana soon became his government's equivalent of the White House.

So off I went to Singapore, and, as I laughingly tell my students, as soon as I touched down at the airport, had gone immediately to the information booth and asked, "Where does the caning take place? Where are the caning centers?" They looked at me like I was crazy. I was joking, of course.

What I found in Singapore was a modern state with a high standard of living where roughly 90 per cent of all families own their homes. There is almost full employment; the place is as clean as a whistle; and many, if not all, government offices have air-conditioners—thank God—because the temperature in the country gives lit ovens a bad name!

Sure, Singapore had its problems—ethnic tension, excessive political uptightness, constant worries about employment. But they've done one heck of a job in many respects and any fair-minded parachute journalist had to be duly impressed. The city-state has one of the highest per capita incomes in the world. The environment is so clean that it is a Western environmentalist's paradise. There is no littering. On the ride from the airport, you look out from the car and search in vain for trash on the roadside. The public education system consistently rates as one of the best in the world. The Singapore cabinet invariably fields a team whose collective IQ is at least equal to that of its neighbors' cabinets combined; its civil servants are paid well and its appointment process is, by and large, merit-driven; and its much-maligned, if always pro-government, news media—while not a "rock-'em-sock-'em" negativistic pile driver like its counterparts in America—serves all its ethnicities pretty well by not sensationalizing frictions and counts one world-class daily newspaper, *The Straits Times*, among its holdings.

This was not the Singapore I had read about in the Western press—a lifeless, uninteresting, robotic, hell-hole equatorial humidor of a place. On the contrary, it was something else and I rather liked it.

Such was my general impression as the much-anticipated Friday appointment with the senior minister approached. Lee Kuan Yew took that invented title after stepping down as the founding prime minister a half dozen years before. (Lee later assumed the post of minister mentor in 2004.)

Who was this man—so glibly portrayed in the US media as some kind of political control freak, as nothing more than a "soft authoritarian"—who managed to engineer one of the most remarkable national development success stories in the postwar history of nation building? The answer turned out to be anything but a disappointment.

The interview was long and deep. Instead of the 45 minutes I was scheduled for, Singapore's founding prime minister laid out his views for nearly two pleasant but intense hours, replying to every one of my questions with astonishing precision, careful thoughtfulness and a charming British lilt acquired in his years as a Cambridge student in England.

What was the biggest problem he faced when he and his People's Action Party began to piece Singapore back together in the 1960s? Surprisingly, Lee said it wasn't the economy, national security nor public schools, but rather the omnipresent, oppressive, lawless, marauding drug gangs who roamed the streets, terrorized the citizenry and kept the decent people of Singapore indoors at night. The British had largely ignored the gangsters during their reign. As a result of this debilitating carte blanche, the problem mushroomed into a living nightmare. Roaming gangs controlled the streets not only by night but also during the day, and the threat of being an innocent but dead bystander in a drug gang gun battle or drive-by was real. It was impossible to build a peaceful society with that kind of arrant misconduct, insisted Lee.

I asked him what he did to combat the gangs.

"We had the army arrest them and put them in jail."

"So, how did the trials go?" I said, reasonably.

"We didn't have trials," the senior statesman replied directly.

"What?!" I tried to seem unruffled but I think I failed. My Americanness was shining through too obviously.

"You see, Tom, we inherited the British system of justice which requires the first-person testimony of one gang member to convict another one. But the gangs would kill off anybody who talked, so what developed was a revolving door system in which an arrest would be made and there'd be a trial which hinged on the testimony of a witness who then would be killed by agents of the indicted gangsters, and out the door would go the criminals, back onto the streets."

"Why couldn't the police protect the witnesses?"

"They weren't strong enough."

"So what did you do?"

"We let the army round them up and put the gang members in jail," Lee said.

"So, where are they today?"

"By and large, they are still in jail."

"But that's preposterous!"

He looked me in the eye clearly and evenly, and said directly, without a trace of apology, "Mr Plate, haven't you noticed? The streets of Singapore are safe."

He had me there. Years later, my spunky wife Andrea put this to me: I want to go away for a week, by myself, without obnoxious you or pain-in-the-neck child around me. I need a week all to myself. What, in your view, is the most interesting and safe place for a woman alone? Easy, I answered, Singapore. She went and mainly loved it. She went several times again, and again mainly loved the place, though she has been developing the very strong view that the former prime minister ought to lighten up a little and let his people enjoy themselves more. Then the place might be near-perfect.

We switched to other topics. I asked him about dealing with China. He was of the emphatic view that the key to stability in Asia was the stability of China, and believed that to no little extent the stability of China was directly related to the state of its relationship with the United States. If that relationship was "gotten right," in the senior minister's phrase, or in other words, if it could be a civil one that minimized antagonism and maximized cooperation, China—and Asia—had a good future ahead of it. But if something akin to the Cold War erupted, Asia would become unstable since much of Asian prosperity depends on its political stability and lack of confrontation.

I left the interview session convinced that Lee Kuan Yew—love him or hate him—had an exceptional mind and a very steely will.

I banged out my Singapore column from the gorgeous Shangri-La Hotel near Orchard Road, faxed and emailed it to the *Los Angeles Times*, and then I went to the airport for the long flight back to California. I slept like a puppy.

When I arrived back in Los Angeles, an urgent phone call was waiting for me. It was from an editor at the *Los Angeles Times*: "Tom, this column on Singapore, are you sure you want it to run?"

I said, "Sure, what's wrong with it?"

"Well, it's, um, how do I put it ... it's kind of soft on Singapore."

"What do you mean?"

"Singapore is a terrible place, Tom! You're too easy on them."

"Have you ever been there?"

It was allowed that the editor had not ever been.

"I just returned after a week of reporting and I do not think it is a terrible place at all. I think the column is quite fair. No one followed me around; I didn't see any caning; and Lee Kuan Yew is a helluva lot smarter than Dan Quayle."

"I don't know. There are some mumblings about this column from Higher Authority."

"Look, Singapore's press, whatever its strengths, is obviously not as free as a free press in the West. But isn't it one of our press' most revered calling cards that we're *totally* open and free, and thus any well-substantiated point of view can get into print?"

I was inadvertently asking if we wanted the *Los Angeles Times* to be as repressive as he was accusing the Singapore news media of being.

The ploy worked. The *Los Angeles Times* shrank back and the column ran, and there really was nothing in the piece that could be construed as blatantly anti-American. If anything, it revealed the many ways in which Lee looked favorably upon the United States. It said, in part: "Lee, like many Asian leaders, never permits his anti-Americanism to go more than a tenth of an inch deep. In fact ... [he] views the United States as the world's only credible guarantor of the nation-preserving principle of non-aggression—an important and much appreciated trait in the eyes of a tiny country wedged amidst a bevy of larger and more powerful ones. Lee even inadvertently forwarded the multi-ethnic values of the United States by warning Japan 'to moderate its emphasis on its uniqueness if it [wants] to be fully accepted by the international community.' "

Lee was equally pragmatic in his criticism of the US. He calmly pointed out that the US itself should be careful not to ignore festering domestic issues, especially inner-city poverty and under-education, while experimenting too much with "new lifestyles," because a domestically stable America "is the keystone of the all-important triangular relationship with China and Japan." That sounds more like the musings of a thoughtful statesman than some crackpot despot. (A few years later, I was to interview South Korean President Kim Dae Jung, who was awarded the 2000 Nobel Peace Prize. He enthusiastically characterized Lee as "a political leader of insight" who single-handedly "led a tiny country to a prosperous modern society amid the tidal waves of modern politics.")

Lee understands world politics to be an interrelated net of ideologies and practises, some of which correspond to the American way while others do not. Lee's own political leanings obviously fall into the latter category but I saw no reason to slam him for that, especially since he used his un-American beliefs to create a safe, prosperous and peaceful new country.

A week or so after the column ran (which the *Los Angeles Times* aptly titled "More Homeowners than Hard-Liners"), I got a phone call from the inimitable Dimitri Simes, director of the Nixon Center in Washington which was planning to honor Lee Kuan Yew as "Statesman of the Year" at a dinner in November that year.

He said, hilariously, that he had just gotten a telephone call from Henry Kissinger in New York, who had just read William Safire's column in the *New York Times* that excoriated Singapore and referred to Lee as a "little Hitler." An irate Kissinger had called Dimitri and said, "[Insert heavy German accent here] Dimitri! I am so angry with Bill. His piece was garbage. How could he write such junk? He's never been to Singapore. Lee Kuan Yew is one of the great statesmen of Asia and the world. In fact, that columnist "Platt-ay"—he was mispronouncing my last name, which is really pronounced like dinner *plate*—"in *Los Angeles Times*, he had a much more nuanced view."

Obviously, there was enjoyment in hearing this. My "Higher Authority" of yesteryear, Bill Safire, had not only gotten the Singapore story wrong, but he had gotten it wrong because he violated his own essential First Principle: Report, report, report. Safire was later to revise his view about Lee Kuan Yew, but only after spending some time with him, for the first time. Before that, the brilliant columnist had never visited Singapore. I had, many times. This was the difference.

> Always report. A journalist's First Principle should always be: report, report, report.

In fact, Kissinger was so upset by Safire's uninformed column that he proposed to the Nixon Center that he would delay his long-planned business trip to Turkey if the Center still wanted him to introduce Lee. The Center officials had proposed this several months before but Kissinger had politely declined due to the prior commitment.

The Nixon Center, of course, was not stupid. On hearing the offer, they were elated. "Absolutely! We'd love to have you, Henry." This was tough for Turkey but sweet for the Nixon people.

Well, the Nixon Center felt I had started the ball rolling by writing a column that not only unsettled the editors of the *Los Angeles Times* but outright infuriated Bill Safire, who in turn wrote a column that outraged Kissinger. It then came to pass that I, too, was invited to the dinner and to the private reception before the main event. I was the delighted beneficiary of the ultimate political bank shot—how could I not go?

On the day of the dinner, in a private downstairs reception room at the Four Seasons Hotel in Georgetown, I sat meekly in the corner and watched the East Coast "A" list enter the room, preening. This was the who's who in political Washington. There was also the "B" list. This was the who's who from the Singapore diaspora (and who not coincidentally are also rich) from the Great Washington Area. Then, finally, there was the "C" list—"Platt-ay" from Los Angeles, with his guest, a former Singaporean who was visiting relatives in Washington DC and whom Dimitri had said I could bring.

Kissinger, of course, made his grand entrance—as did Newt Gingrich and Bill Bradley and many other big shots. I watched with fascination.

The charismatic Lee and his wife (a "Double First," signifying top academic honors at Cambridge) arrived to claim the spotlight. There was a sense of ceremony. Everyone bowed and scraped and congratulated. It was a largely Republican audience but as I looked at my guest for the evening—a Singapore-born student—I could easily understand that, even though she represented the younger generation of Singaporeans that viewed Senior Minister Lee with a combination of admiration and loathing (wishing for the day that a less rigid generation of leaders would come to power), there was also pride in her eyes that her own country's founding father was receiving such a high accolade in the capital of the world's only superpower.

Lee saw me and dramatically pointed in my direction. "*Los Angeles Times!*" he said in a strong voice. The reception room, packed to its edges, quieted a little.

I thought to myself, laughing: "Oh God, he can't remember my name but he's going to cane me anyhow!"

Instead, he said, "That column of yours ... I well know and appreciate the ideology of the American media. That column was brave of you."

This was an amazing moment. Sure, Lee would not be the first person to seek favor with a columnist by flattering him but I do not think that was his motive. He does not care that much what the Western press thought about him, unless Singapore's overall image was hurt. His point was that the American news media had an overarching ideology that is all but invisible to us, but extremely obvious to those outside our borders; he also implicitly understood that if the American journalist deviated from that ideology by too wide a margin, the journalist runs certain risks, especially professionally.

I had deviated by not slamming Singapore; I had run some risks; and I don't think the *Los Angeles Times* was ever happy with that column, nor with a lot of my columns about China which emphasized the tides of change sweeping that country rather than human rights abuses or outdated Chinese ways, nor even my columns about Japan which preached understanding instead of condemnation.

You see, in the American media, if you're not bashing, you're not a real macho journalist.

I did say in the column that Lee is indeed "another Asian authoritarian without remorse ... whose flinty intolerance of such things as a vigorous free press seems buffered by [his] donnish accents of Cambridge." That was balanced with the assertion that America "doesn't have to agree with everything [Lee] says. But why not listen? We could learn something about Singapore [from him]—and about ourselves, too."

Well, a balanced perspective doesn't fly for very long in the American political press. As a journalist, you're considered bland, a milquetoast, a pushover. You're written off as a dork by those who long for the sharp teeth of the ever-hungry self-appointed watchdog. Lee Kuan Yew had his faults, as do we all, and one must freely acknowledge that. But even his worst critics acknowledge that he is a man of superior intellect and extraordinary experience, and possessed an iron will put to the good use of his country. Yes, he did things the Singaporean way, and not the American way, but that's precisely what America needs to understand. It works.

> The American way is not everyone's way and never will be. There are many modes of successful operations outside of our own. And maybe

we ought to start respecting others more. The all-pervasive US news media could use more nuanced and less ethnocentric reporting.

ANOTHER FASCINATING PLACE to visit that also proved a special challenge to cover as a columnist was Hong Kong. Like Singapore, it was small in population but punched above its weight on the world stage. Under the British, it had flourished as an economy but had been kept down, purposefully, as an infantile polity. But history keeps on happening, in Hong Kong as everywhere else; the sole constant is change.

A little background first: In 1982, the British agreed that in 15 years' time, they would hand over sovereignty of the Hong Kong territories to Beijing. When 1997 finally rolled around, much of the Western media was predicting the worst. I took a different view, which was that whatever the flaws of the communist regime in Beijing (and there were of course many indeed), it would put in place, in its own self interests, a government that, whatever its ideological leanings, would prove at least as competent as its predecessor. And perhaps in some ways, even more so—because, after all, the government would be truly Chinese.

Either way, I was determined to find out firsthand by somehow landing an *exclusive* interview with the incoming leader of Hong Kong, Tung Chee-hwa.

Exclusive interviews are rarely obtained in a conventional way. They take immense preparation and a lot of scheming. It is the scheme-lover who becomes the interview-lander.

Of course, so was everyone else. There had been at least a hundred requests for interviews and the list was filled with true giants from around the world—*Newsweek* and *Time*, the *Washington Post*, the *London Times*, *Corriera della Serra*, *Le Monde*, etc.

The problem was that Tung Chee-hwa, the former shipping businessman selected by Beijing to be the new governor come July 1, 1997, was extraordinarily press-averse. He distrusted it immensely and I did not totally blame him. The Western media, with its inherent negativistic ideology, doomsday prophesizing and endless anti-China anti-communizing, were out to sink their teeth into him. So my Western press credentials would be absolutely no help in securing that exclusive—in fact, they would be a hindrance.

On the eve of my 1997 trip to Hong Kong, it finally hit me. Several months before, I had the very good fortune to have met Ronnie Chan, an intellectually astute, wealthy Hong Kong tycoon and prominent political figure. I liked him immediately because he was not afraid to take a chance and had once said to me, "You know, Tom, I liked your last column, but the one before that really sucked."

I can live with that, even respect it. As a USC graduate and member of the university's board of trustees, Ronnie was familiar with and liked the Los Angeles lifestyle. The fact that I was a professor at rival UCLA posited a theoretical rivalry between us, but our time together was always absorbing.

On the night before I planned to go to Hong Kong, I realized (finally) that Ronnie and only someone like him (though he was like no one else) might be able to help me land an interview with the new chief executive. So I quickly banged out a short fax to Ronnie in Hong Kong. It said simply: "Dear Ronnie, I'm to arrive in Hong Kong in a few days and will stay for a week to see what's going on. Is there any chance you could get me in to see Tung Chee-hwa? Love and kisses, Prof Tom, UCLA."

It was a long shot but it might possibly work. Actually, it was my only shot. If Ronnie Chan was the well-connected multi-billionaire that I thought he was; and if he was as active in politics and the issues of his country and the world as I had known him to be (he was on the board of directors of the World Economic Forum in Davos, after all); then he might have some influence that would exceed what I had as one of a thousand begging-on-the-knees journalists pining for an interview with the elusive and reclusive and dismissive Tung Chee-hwa.

Sure enough, when I checked in at the hotel in Hong Kong, there was a message waiting for me from Ronnie: "Dear Tom, the new chief executive will see both of us Friday night at six o'clock for a social call. I think it will last long enough for your purposes. Call me if you can't make it. Otherwise, I'll pick you up at your hotel at 5pm." Not quite like winning a Pulitzer, but the feeling was exhilarating as it was very hard to get China's new man for Hong Kong to talk.

At five o'clock on Friday, Ronnie came by in his car and I hopped in. I could see he was in a good mood. Suzi (not her real first name) hopped in too. She was a former student now in Hong Kong who had grown to greatly admire Anson Chan, the head of the territory's famed civil service, and (unlike most Western journalists) wished Tung Chee-hwa the best. I knew Ronnie would like her serious manner and had cleared it with him that this outstanding future leader would be joining us.

But before I could even say "hi," even before the full impact of my friend's intellect and charm could be properly appreciated, Ronnie's car phone rang jarringly.

After speaking for a few minutes in Mandarin, he turned to me and said in English, "Tom, I have some good news and also some bad news. The good news is that the meeting is still on; the bad news is that it's off the record. You cannot quote anything that Tung Chee-hwa says to us tonight."

This was a devastating blow. I would be getting an interview that I could not use. My first instinct was to be furious and I suppose as a younger man, I would have loudly protested, knifed Ronnie in the back and jumped out of the car. But what could I realistically do? Should I say, "You tell the chief executive that there's no way I will see him unless he does things my way!"

I did not think so. That was not the way things worked in the world, certainly not in Asia.

So I just nodded and swallowed my disappointment, for which Ronnie no doubt had sympathy. And so the whole way up to Tung Chee-hwa's office, I was thinking: "Here I am, about to enter the new chief executive's office three weeks before the historic handover of Hong Kong to China, and I can't write a column that quotes him."

It was all I could do to not lose it.

Tung was a man of mystery to the West that I wanted to decode. The only thing I actually knew about him was that he was portrayed by the Western media as an aloof, calculating son-of-a-bitch businessman now making a living as a puppet of Beijing. As I soon found out, he was anything but.

For starters, Tung Chee-hwa turned out to be a portly, grandfatherly figure—warm, friendly, smiles often. Of course, as the three of us entered his office, he first said "hello" to Ronnie who then introduced me and my assistant to the chief executive.

We immediately sat down with his chief of staff and press aide, and began the session. As I asked my first question, my former student took out her Steno notepad. She was wearing a very conservative white linen dress and had her hair tied up in a bun. Her demeanor was that of the studious graduate student sitting in the penumbra of the master instructor.

Even so, the worried press aide immediately sprung into action. The chief executive's appointment book had only said, "Ronnie Chan and friend, 6pm," but the aide had earlier telephoned Chan's office and found out who that friend was. Having turned down a gazillion requests for interviews, he was not happy that Chan's friend was a *Los Angeles Times* columnist. He had talked Tung into keeping the session off the record. The press aide proceeded to interrupt and said, "Oh no, Miss. You may not take notes."

I looked at Suzi. She looked positively distressed, hurt, distraught; she was playing the part perfectly. I wasn't sure whether one should hug her or give her an Oscar.

The chief executive intervened. "No, it's okay," said Tung, in a courtly way, "Tom can use it as background." Smiling in a grandfatherly way at my friend, he said, "Don't worry. You may take notes."

The press secretary turned white in the face and I could only imagine what he was thinking, having turned down the world's leading press institutions and media egos. We had sat and talked for well over an hour. And when it was finally over, I thanked both the chief executive and Ronnie for arranging the interview. I also thanked the press secretary for his understanding.

"You are welcome, Mr Plate," he said. "But I must remind you and Mr Chan that although your assistant was allowed to take notes, they may be used only for background. This interview was off the record."

Well, some primal force suddenly took hold of me and I figured I had nothing to lose as I already had the interview in hand. So I actually stood up and gave an absurd, emotional and over-the-top peroration:

"With all due respect, Mr Chief Executive-in-waiting, I think it's absurd that this interview is off the record.

"The Western media is largely portraying the chief executive as a cold, robotic, calculating puppet of Beijing who has no interest in Hong Kong or the real people who live here. They say he's just serving the interests of the imperial power in Beijing. But what tonight's helpful conversation has made clear to me is that he cares deeply about Hong Kong and wants to do the right thing, and, at the same time, he respects the fact that the sovereign power is now in Beijing. This is a man who is well aware of the tightrope he will have to walk."

As I was giving this semi-calculated blowhard jury plea, I looked Ronnie in the eye and I could tell he knew exactly what I was doing. I looked at my assistant in the eye and I could see that she did, too. I kept going for another minute or two like this.

When I finished, the press secretary would not look at me in the eye but Tung Chee-hwa did. He stood up, shook my hand, and, staring at my friend, said, "Okay. Go ahead and put the interview on the record," he said. "Thank you for coming by."

In the elevator, I didn't know whom to kiss first: my alert assistant for taking such wonderful notes and then looking so forlorn, or Ronnie himself for his connections and wisdom. He knew I wouldn't act like a jerk in the interview. He also knew I could be the conduit to convey the other side of the Hong Kong story to the Western world. I was happy to do just that, for that was the under-reported story.

I later found out two interesting things. The first was that two days after my interview, Tung's press secretary hurriedly announced there would be a press conference open to all journalists for whom he previously had refused interviews. It was the first press conference Tung Chee-hwa had ever given to the Western press. I think the embarrassed press secretary pushed the panic button and thus the idea at the last minute, because of the unexpected grant of an exclusive interview to a *Los Angeles Times* columnist.

I may actually—my ego notwithstanding—have underestimated the magnitude of the scoop. The day after the session, I attended a luncheon hosted by the Freedom Forum in Hong Kong that had CNN China correspondent Mike Chinoy as its keynote speaker. His speech was a basic gloss on the book he had recently published, *China Live*. Mike believed China was undergoing enormous internal changes that could take the country in directions no one can predict. Unlike most Western journalists, Mike was different in that he would emphasize the *news* of China—that is, what it is about the place that is changing—instead of the *olds*, the usual human rights repression and so on.

After the speech, I bought two copies, one for my family and one for my helpful assistant. As Mike was signing the books, he asked me why I didn't want one for myself. Playing off the longstanding rivalry between print and video, I said, "I'm a print guy, you're a TV guy. What can I possibly learn from a TV guy?"

He laughed. "Well, I read your stuff and it's pretty good! So what are you doing in Hong Kong?"

"Oh, nothing much. Writing some columns and getting to understand the handover firsthand."

"What have you been doing and whom have you been seeing?"

"Oh, this and that, and well, I saw Tung Chee-hwa last night."

"With a tourist group or something?"

"No, I had an interview with him."

He immediately stopped writing and said, "You *what*?"

"Yeah, I spent an hour and twenty minutes with him. It was great."

"You son of a gun! How did you get that?"

"I just lucked out."

"You son of a gun! That's a world exclusive!"

"Really? I was wondering. Thanks for confirming that for me, Mike!"

"Jumping the midget" sometimes makes people mad or (delightfully) jealous—and sometimes that means you are just doing your job.

The moral of the story is this: to get an unconventional story that no one else has, you sometimes have to use unconventional means. In this case, I had three things going for me. One was an inside contact with influence, someone who knew and trusted me. The second was a gifted and enterprising student who helped by taking wonderful notes and appealing in her youth to the new Hong Kong chief's sense of being the ultimate gentleman. The third factor is that I approached the situation with an open mind: I wasn't out to get Tung Chee-hwa like some journalists in the Western press do and I think he saw that. To be a serious journalist who commands respect, one has to keep an open mind.

That open mind led to two other columns that same month. The second one, following the Tung interview column, focused on the outgoing British governor, Christopher Patten. Hated by the Chinese for arguable hypocrisy in raising last-minute democracy issues conspicuously dormant during Britain's long colonial rule, he was much admired by the Western press. He said all the right things, fitted into all the ideological preconceptions and was great quotable copy. No wonder many Chinese, in both Hong Kong and Beijing, found him infuriating. So did I, in the sense that I found Patten too clever by half—and that's what my column said. It caught the eye of every Western journalist googling articles about Hong Kong. Was it influential? Who knows? Generally, the Western press marches to the beat of its own ideological ticker.

The third of those 1997 columns from Hong Kong was equally infuriating. Its bottom line was that many people in Hong Kong feared the "paratrooper journalists" of the West, perpetuating as they do their ideological preconceptions that could harm tourism and investment, more than they feared the People's Liberation Army, which the Western media suggested would be ever-present at every street-corner (it wasn't, and isn't).

These were three columns of a tenor and perspective unknown to the Western establishment media. I applaud my editor at the time—Judy Dugan and her boss Janet Clayton, my successor as *Los Angeles Times* editor of the editorial pages—for their forbearance and tolerance of what was then such an iconoclastic view. But these columns, on the whole, pretty much hold up almost ten years later.

> We journalists must make it an unbreakable practise to honor our word as a solemn bond. If a comment was proffered and accepted as "off the record," it needs to stay off the record. Period. If a quotation is offered you on a "not for attribution" basis and you accept it on that basis, don't go back on your word. In the long run, such dishonor will be the death of the news media profession.

WHEN THE COLUMN started in 1995, it seemed as if a standing title like "Listening to Asia" would be a perfect title. That was too much for the American editorial ego, of course, and for that of the US political elite. Lawrence O Summers, then Undersecretary of the Treasury in the Clinton administration, when Robert Rubin was still his boss, once told me frankly (in Davos, Switzerland, at a World Economic Forum retreat) that, while he liked the column, he found it on the whole "too pro-Asia."

I respect Summers, the former controversial president of Harvard University, for his passion for ideas and for his utter incapacity to offer sunny intellectual shelter to a cliché in either thought or language. There is almost none of the mediocre in him, nothing of the mundane. He can also be corruscatingly blunt, which people did not always appreciate. Once at an international conference, on a panel on the future of the Internet with a pompous French minister, he almost had to be restrained when the Frenchman declaimed (wildly erroneously) that France had one of the highest Internet usages in the world. (Actually, the French did not; the South Koreans did.)

Summers had an honest temper. A July 1997 column on the incipient Asian financial crisis anonymously quoted a US official as admitting that Washington was unlikely to intervene in the Thai currency meltdown, as it had famously in the 1995 Mexican financial plunge, because "Thailand isn't on our border." That seemed such an absurd statement in this age of intimate economic and financial globalization that I had to use it in the column (which sought to sound a very loud alarm about what was to mushroom into two years of region-wide financial misery), but I also did not have the heart to name the official who said it. I figured in a few months' time, the rampant currency contagion in Asia would prompt Washington to get more involved, whether out of a sense of naked self interest (that is, the dollar gets the disease too) or a more general geopolitical sense of obligation to the region.

When that did not happen—on the contrary, Washington remained mainly aloof until the undercurrent almost sucked a US hedge fund out to sea—I reprised the quote for a column on the first anniversary of the Asian financial crisis. A year had passed and I said the hell with it. The amazing quote appeared again but this time it was attributed to the high administration official who actually had said it the year before.

"But I never said it!" thundered Summers from Washington, telephoning the morning the column appeared in the *Los Angeles Times*. When he called, as I thought he might, I had my notes in front of me. Yes, he had said it and I had it all down in my notes (I always keep my notes).

We argued for five minutes. I held my ground; he was livid. I didn't say it, he yelled; but you did, I said.

Summers said, "Well, if I did say it, which I don't think I did, I said it off the record."

But he was mistaken; I had the notes right in front of me (I still have ten years of column notes in the basement of Haines Hall on the UCLA campus). "Mr Secretary, when something is said to me off the record or not for attribution, I circle it boldly and clearly. I have my notes in front of me. It was not off the record. I didn't quote you a year ago because I felt the comment was not you at your very finest and I have respect for you.

"On the other hand, I am a journalist and it is not my job to suggest to an official that he or she should retract something he or she says that is of considerable public interest, especially since you did say it, and it was not off the record. Hey, I gave you a whole year to solve the Asian financial crisis. How much more time did you need?"

At that sally, I could feel him chuckle a little and ease up a bit.

A few more endless seconds of silence went by, then Summers said something like: "Well, obviously, we have a misunderstanding, an impasse... What do you propose we do about it?"

For once, I was quick on the uptake. "Why don't we just do another interview? How about, er, right now?" I could feel his incredulity. "But this time, I will type up the notes," I said, "and fax them to your office, and you can check them out carefully, make any editing changes if I misunderstood you, and we will have another column, on an important subject, with you quoted, once again, accurately."

The future Ivy League president laughed. Sold.

I got another column; later, Harvard was to get a new university president in Summers. Who got the better deal? I do not know, but I liked Summers' irreverence—especially his willingness to confront us journalists when in his view we had violated the deal. Which I had not—never had and never will.

IF THE JAPANESE had a general gripe about us American journalists, it is that our reportage all too faithfully mirrors our culture of self-centeredness. Precisely because some of us think we know it all, there is no reason why we would bother to listen to them, to much of what they say. This observation is scarcely true of all US and Western correspondents, to be sure, but it is a valid critique of too many of us.

> One of the worst ethical offenses is the sin of ethnocentricity. In a world that is ever closer, if not flat, as Tom Friedman has put it, failing to nuance and balance your reporting against internationalist norms is about as un-cosmopolitan as you can get. It doesn't get much worse than that.

Even though Summers had scolded me for being too "pro-Asian" (whatever the hell that might mean!), he came to appreciate a pair of columns written in the heat of the open and public US critique of the Japanese government's management of its economy. For if in the eighties, Japan all but set the standard for economic efficiency, in the nineties it became the dismal poster boy for fiscal flatulence and virtually negative economic growth.

In the mid- and late-nineties, at the urging—and feeding—of the Treasury Department, the elite US news media went into its attack mode. Article after article and commentary after commentary excoriated Tokyo for failing to kick the bear of its somnolent domestic economy in the rear and recharge it into a bull.

The media assault was constant and withering, to which Treasury Secretary Robert Rubin (a very smart man, but not especially an internationalist) was happy to add fuel to the fire in a series of speeches urging Japan to open up (that is, let more US goods into the Japanese market), to trim down to realize labor-cost efficiencies (that is, fire people as presumptively and as uncaringly as in the United States) and to stop trying to micro-manage business development by supporting presumptive corporate winners and isolating predicted losers (which was the basic winning formula for the huge Japanese economic surge of the seventies and eighties that was to transform the nation into the world's number two economy).

The basic content of the Rubin/*New York Times* prescription for Japan was actually arguably solid—times have changed much faster than the Japanese economy—but the prescription was unarguably American medicine.

For the Japanese, the economy and society are inextricably connected. Individualism is less valued than teamwork. Government intervention in the economy is considered proper public policy if it helps maintain social stability. Above all, change must be gradual—certainly nowhere as fast as the *New York Times* and its high-level Treasury Department sources would prefer it.

I had been to Japan often enough to know that the constant bashing by Washington was getting under its skin. The Japanese were anything but stupid; they knew their economy was in the doldrums. But how bad was it? It was still the number two economy in the world. The editor of a famous Japanese newspaper once motored me around Tokyo in his Lexus, showing off this skyscraper and that, this gorgeous shopping area and that, concluding thus: people just don't see the dimensions of the disaster as outlined in Washington. Bear in mind that just a few decades ago, trying to rise up from the ashes of the war, Japan was a Third World economy. Now, it is number two in the world! If the economy screwed up dramatically for a couple more years, Japan would be number three—not exactly a catastrophe. So the country was not that eager to lay off hundreds of thousands of Japanese workers and sow the seeds of possible social instability.

One day, at an international conference in Europe, Summers' press aide came up to me and said, "You know, Larry will never admit it but those columns you wrote urging us to stop bashing Japan, a close ally, had an effect. In fact, Larry took the first one to Bob Rubin, who read it and asked him if he agreed with it. Larry said he sort of did. Bob, who respected Summers' views even when he did not agree with them, which was rarely anyway, then said, 'Let's make an appointment with the president and get his input.' And they did. From the Oval Office, Clinton read the column (in seconds, one suspects), and said to Rubin and Summers: This is basically right, we have interests with Japan that transcend the mere economic, strategic ones especially. We do need to tone down the rhetoric."

I laughed to myself as the press aide told me the story. I was being (shall we say) massaged. In crude New York-eze, one would have said: I know what you are doing to me, but it still feels good!

Then, from over my shoulder came a well-respected *New York Times* reporter—a nice guy, but all the same, a real hard charger. Surprisingly, he confirmed the story and added the delicious detail that Summers had personally asked him to read it, as he had Rubin, so as to understand that the administration would begin to tone down the anti-Japanese rhetoric.

And then—magically!—so did the US news media, especially the *New York Times*. Wonder how that came about...

> But don't ever try to jump the midget unless you can be yourself in the process. You have to be true to yourself; where you get into trouble tends to be when you try to imagine you are someone else.

YOU DO GET TO MEET very interesting people in this line of work. Two of the most interesting you could ever meet are Koji Tsuroka and Kazuo Kodama. Both were career diplomats at the Ministry of Foreign Affairs (MOFA) in Japan and both were dedicated patriots of their country; but both considered themselves little more than hardworking functionaries. In fact, they were extremely gifted diplomats.

Understand that, in dealing with such top-flight talent, you should never try to outsmart them; always play fair and respect that their loyalties and affinities are entirely Japanese ... or Chinese or Korean or Indian or whatever, not American. Also understand that professionals at this degree of accomplishment tend to deal at a level of subtlety and indirection that, as a general rule, is not the hallmark of the American way. More than of any other country or nationality, this trait is characteristic of the Japanese. I say this entirely as a compliment; we Americans could use a few skin grafts of this type to broaden our response mechanism. So when a Japanese diplomat speaks to an American journalist rather directly, this is—in the Japanese style—like having a two-by-four fall on your head.

"Tom," said top MOFA official Kazuo Kodama over a drink in a Tokyo hotel, "when you meet the prime minister tomorrow, just be yourself."

You cannot be serious, I thought. My true self, I admit, is a bit of the goofball incorporated. I tend to wear loud ties, a sports jacket, if not a suit, everywhere except in the swimming pool, and effect an excessively casual manner. Surely this is not what is wanted.

"What do you mean?"

Flamboyant Prime Minister Koizumi Junichiro, explained Kazuo, does not like excessive formality, especially in conversation. Whatever you do, do not read from your list of prepared questions. His aides have prepared written answers to the queries we required you to submit a month ago but he could not care less about the prepared material. So you just bounce questions off him right from the start. That's the best approach with him.

"But," he added, "... there is one other thing ... Koizumi likes to look deep into people. He will stare you directly in the eye. Try not to avert his gaze or lower your eyes to read from your notes. It'll be a little unnerving but stay with his eyes as long as you possibly can. He thinks if you look away, you're not up to the occasion."

"And," I added, finally, "be myself. Are you absolutely sure this is what is wanted? It's just an interview for me but it's your job that may be on the line, right?"

Kazuo laughed. "He will like you. He likes the random and unpredictable. Like you, he gets bored easily. And he is very self-assured so he is not leery of spontaneity."

This was going to be one interview I absolutely looked forward to.

Super-K—Koizumi—was the lion tamer of Japanese party politics. His trick was to go over the head of the party hacks through the use of appeals to the public, often via the medium of television. Relatively tall, with a flurry of lustrous hair, and a bachelor, the prime minister had gambled at key stages of his five-year run, at one point throwing a thousand token Japanese troops into Iraq to keep his US ally happy, and at another, dissolving parliament when the Upper House rejected a domestic reform plan. (Both these events occurred after my interview with him.)

The next day, I was seated in the guest chair at the Kentai, the new prime minister's office building. The old one had been something of a relic, if not a dump. The new building, however, was magnificent—elegant but spare, in the classic contemplative Japanese style, with a little UN modernism thrown in.

There were three aides with me waiting and when the prime minister walked in—Koizumi appeared more youthful-looking than the average Japanese politician—I looked directly at him and executed a cute little upshot with my hands on my own hair, which in its straight-up, white-wheat style could be likened to a "white man's Don King."

Without hesitating, Koizumi did the same. We laughed a little.

My first question was about my questions: "Do I need to ask you the prepared questions in the order I presented them to you?"

Koizumi said flatly, through a very adept translator, "No, ask anything you want. Forget about the prepared questions."

The interview had been booked for about twenty minutes but lasted 40 minutes or so. I was able to stretch it out to twice the scheduled length, despite the antsy protestations of his anxiety-ridden press secretary, because the questions got more provocative and interesting as the interview went on. This was by design. I always start with a sleepy question and progress as the session becomes more comfortable. The final pushy question came just as I feared the press secretary was about to hurl me out of the building. At this point, Koizumi had reaffirmed his promise to send troops to Iraq and bet his prime ministership on reform. On the Iraq troop issue, he was firm, though vague on the timing; on the issue of domestic economic change, especially postal reform, he was emphatic—he gave me the sense he would bet the House on it, which later he did (and won)!

Time for my last question. "Mr Prime Minister, your first cabinet appointment was as the minister of health, and in your first public press conference, someone asked you whether it was more important for the government in terms of the nation's health to accelerate its anti dioxin emissions campaign or to accelerate government approval of the sale of Viagra." Everyone in the room roared. Koizumi, of course, was Japan's best-known bachelor. "Well, Mr Prime Minister, you answered that, hilariously I thought, by saying 'Yes, Viagra ...' As prime minister now but still a bachelor ... do you answer that question with the same priority?"

Koizumi's aides practically fell off the couch but the prime minister, with a twinkle in his eye, was ready for me, explaining that it wasn't for his own needs that Viagra approval was important but for the general mental and biological health of Japan, with its falling birthrate and aging population.

"You mean," I said, really jumping the midget now, "that Viagra is needed not for the prime minister, but for, say, your tired staff!" The prime minister nodded, looked at his tired staff and chuckled.

That night, Kazuo called me. "I heard about the Viagra question; half of Tokyo is talking about it."

"He didn't seem very upset by it," I said, defensively.

"On the contrary, he loved it. In fact, he said it was the best one-on-one interview he has done as prime minister."

"You mean, with a foreign journalist?"

"No, not just with a foreign journalist. The best one. Period."

As you can tell by now, I thoroughly enjoy meeting and interviewing people who help make history. Part of the reason? As a Long Island-born, I am probably in a bit of suburban awe. But there is another, more compelling reason. Having been educated at a public policy school—and being a political science major in college—rather than at journalism school, either as a graduate or undergraduate student, I have good reason to be at least somewhat respectful of these historymakers at times, though not because of their positions, but because of the immense difficulty of their positions.

At Princeton, you come to appreciate how complex good government is (bad government is much easier to realize)—how excruciatingly difficult, for instance, it is to lower the rate of inflation without shooting unemployment through the roof.

Journalism schools—and journalism in general—had a different perspective and ethic. Rather than appreciating the prime minister's reform efforts, however modest they may be, the journalist comes at the political figure cynically—instinctively (and by training) believing almost everything is for show, nothing is sincere, politics is only about money (bribes, etc.), the Japanese (or the Chinese or the Koreans or the Indians, etc.) can't be trusted, nobody really cares about a little pocket-lining and so on.

Sure, I wasn't born yesterday, but I do not have an axe to grind everyday that says every single political leader is corrupt or incompetent, and no one is truly serious (or even sincerely patriotic). In American journalism, generally, to report sighting even a silver lining in the political and policy cloud is to risk being categorized as hopelessly naïve. Wouldn't you just love to see some of our editors and reporters on the receiving end of the prejudice they project!

THE TENTH ANNIVERSARY of my foreign affairs column occurred on 1 January, 2005. Over those ten years, it had become America's only regularly appearing syndicated column on Asia. The joke is that it is both the worst column about Asia and the best. Of course, both statements are true—because it is the only one. And I hope it stays that way!

Or maybe I don't.

Maybe I am slightly embarrassed that after 10 years I am still the sole regularly-syndicated Asia columnist. And maybe we should all be more than a little annoyed that Asia does not get more respect from the US media.

I guess it is a sore point with me, but I just have the feeling that as history is unfolding before our eyes in Asia like a giant wave, what with the rise of China and India and so on, the US media's eyes are peering off in all sorts of trivial directions. Even today, my column, which originated from Los Angeles, appears in far more Asian papers than US ones.

Where is the column at today? I don't know. I have a handful of world newspapers with a few million copies in combined circulation. After 10 years, maybe it is time to hand the torch over to someone from a younger generation.

After all, it has been too good a life, and from Davos to Singapore, an unusually fascinating and fulfilling one.

In fact, my wife Andrea reminded me just the other day that my very first column appeared in the *Los Angeles Times* the very day of the OJ Simpson verdict. So it is doubtful that many people read it. Maybe fate was trying to tell me something then. Maybe I wasn't listening. Maybe it is time to do that now.

As the great playwright Anita Loos penned, "fate keeps on happening."

We'll just have to see where fate takes us next.

But whatever happens—to me in life, to the column in the future, to you in life—don't forget to jump the midget.

The oft-asked question: Is journalism actually a profession, sort of like medicine? The answer to that, I believe, depends on the stated norms and actual behaviors of us journalists. What we do for all the world to see tells the world precisely who we are. If we strut around the world in ignorance, in prejudice, in deception, and/or with airs of superiority, few will take us seriously, except ourselves. So the more we listen carefully to others, the more we will learn ourselves—and learn about ourselves; but the more we preen, the sillier and more irrelevant we'll seem.

Chapter Two
Long Island *Newsday*:
From Potato Fields to a Field of Dreams

I FELL INTO MY FIRST GIG in the news media profession through a series of accidents. By accident, my junior high school newspaper needed an editor—and I was the only silly fool who wanted the job. In high school, it seemed like working for the student newspaper would be a fun place to hang out, and during my awkward teen years, it provided a network of social contacts. The truth is, if you have worked on your student newspaper in high school or college (or both), be very careful: you may be tragically fated to go the distance as a career journalist.

> The propensity to take chances all started in college. Many of today's journalists were journalists before they even knew it.

The *Amherst Student* was anything but a prestigious extra-curricular activity, but my best friend and I shared the position of managing editor and put out the bi-weekly by taking the helm each once a week and, boy, did we have a blast!

The *Amherst Student*, as it turned out, was the bridge that led over the moat into the castle of American establishment journalism. After the summer of my junior year, I interviewed for a summer internship at *The Washington Post*. As luck (fate?) would have it, the interview was conducted not by the personnel chief (delightfully, he/she was on vacation) but by the distinguished executive editor himself, who, as it turned out, was an Amherst alumnus. Bingo! (Better to be lucky than good, eh?)

Amherst is a very small New England college. It does not churn out tens of thousands of alumni like Harvard or Cornell or Stanford. And, for whatever reason, few graduates from those schools, or Amherst, go into the news media business. So what are the odds of the top news executive of the capital's powerful newspaper coming from Amherst?

Well, this is how it happens, boys and girls. Somehow you are standing there in the doorway and they figure you may be what they need—in fact, what they need right now! This is then one of those jump-the-midget moments. Will you choke and come off like a dork, or will you flash your true genius and razzle-dazzle them with your commitment, energy and determination?

By the time I arrived at *The Washington Post* for my summer internship, Amherst alumnus and trustee Al Friendly, after many years at the helm, was about to be replaced by *Newsweek's* Washington bureau chief and former roommate of John F Kennedy's at Harvard, Benjamin Bradlee. I was afraid that I had lost my alumnus mentor and would suffer accordingly. I could not have been more mistaken.

Bradlee, in his broad-striped dress shirt and tie with collar ajar, was a shot of triple expresso in the newsroom. Where Mr Friendly would confine himself within the four walls of his solidly walled and nicely decorated office, Bradlee spent most of his day prowling the newsroom like a cat looking for a good fight or for something to chase, and was certainly not one to rest on his laurels. Eventually, he even had his office re-done with glass walls, as if to say I-can-see-you-and-you-can-see-me and so, let's-work-and-not-play-games, boys and girls.

Bradlee's aim was to re-energize the newsroom. He did this with his presence and charisma. He not only inherited a soggy staff but a minimalist summer intern program—in my year, there were but a handful of interns. But we were very lucky kids.

For as the smog and fog of August rolled into Washington, the newspaper's big guns characteristically fled (except during the quadrennial presidential nominating conventions) to the comforting shores or cool mountains of Virginia or the beaches of Maryland or to their summer cottages, or, for the more affluent, to Cape Cod or Nantucket.

By mid-August, we hardy band of interns comprised about a fifth of the available reporting staff. In the ordinary summer of Washington, there were not many choice stories so a dozen or so reporters would often be enough. But when a few unexpected stories did pop up, the interns got a disproportionate share of them as they were among the few bodies around—and among the few that actually wanted to work.

This is why you should never accept a summer internship wherein your chief challenge is to master the intricacies of the copying machine or the reception desk. Find a real place for yourself in a real job, anywhere. It need not be at a brand name like CNN or *The Washington Post*, but a place where they will grow shorthanded and be desperate enough to actually use you. That kind of desperation does not happen a lot at places like *The Washington Post* anymore; luckily for me, it once did.

One day, the White House announced a raft of mid- to semi- upper-level federal appointments. That the announcement contained so many names and was delivered in the middle of August with little else going on in Washington (which is a city about jobs if nothing else) rendered it a page one story.

When word came of the numerous appointments, Bradlee surveyed the newsroom for someone to handle it. I smiled charmingly, innocently and with 101 per cent availability when he looked over in my direction.

"Hey, kid, come here." (In the wonderful film, "All the President's Men," about *The Washington Post's* Watergate triumph that forced President Nixon to resign, Bradlee was played by the late Jason Robarts, an extroverted actor known never to have a scene stolen from him. People who knew Bradlee well, however, thought the flamboyant Robarts underplayed the role!)

I hurried over. Bradlee set up the entire deal in very few words. (Other than Sir David English and perhaps Don Forst, both of whom you will meet later, I was never to work again for an editor who was so concise and clear about what he wanted.)

Bradlee said something like: A bunch of middle to upper-middle political appointments are happening this morning, not one of them big enough for its own story, but taken altogether, it will make a good story for this government town, especially in August. Why don't you figure out how to handle it? Maybe some kind of special packaging?

It was about one in the afternoon, leaving only a few hours before the deadline. How should one handle this unexpected assignment? I reflected on Bradlee's own background at *Newsweek*, which, like *Time* magazine, emphasized clever and concise packaging of related stories, and chose to jump the midget: let's try a *Newsweek*-ly approach.

You did not have to be a rocket scientist to figure out that if this dynamic new editor had wanted a conventional story, he would have given the assignment to one of the few experienced, conventional reporters not on vacation. But by pulling an intern rabbit out of the summer hat, he wanted something completely different.

About an hour or so later, a national desk editor sauntered over to my desk to check on my work. He seemed to be politely suggesting I was going off course, that the approach I was taking was "not the *Post*." I had no idea what to say—as in any new job, you want to please everyone and offend no one. (I was exceptionally guilty of this. The adult child of alcoholics, I spurned shouting matches like a draft dodger avoided war.) Fortunately, Bradlee periscoped his eyes from across the sprawling city room, saw what was going on and came to my rescue.

"Leave the kid alone!" the new editor fairly bellowed.

The national desk editor looked startled.

"Just leave the kid alone," repeated Bradlee. "Let him try it his way. Let's try something new for once around here! Jesus!"

The middle-level editor fled back to his desk for fear of his life.

Bradlee looked back at me to ask if I had it under control.

"I think so. Short 50–75 word portraits under the picture of each. With a short story introducing the entire photo-bio package that explains what the hell this is all about."

Bradlee smiled. God, he was a ruggedly handsome man—wish I were in his league! "Sounds great to me. Just be sure to give the photo editor a list of the appointees so he has enough time to round them up. Without a pix for each and every one, your approach won't be worth crap."

> Success on a job is not just showing up on time and being dressed right. Woody Allen said this but it is silly. It is running into the right people and having the youthful gumption to "try something different" when the Right Powerful Person is around to say: Hey, give the kid a chance!

The story package (eight appointments with eight pictures) was, by everyone's estimate the next day, a happy success. A (very very) minor star was born.

What were the essential elements of this success story? You needed an editor who wanted to innovate, and a worker young enough, ambitious enough, inexperienced enough, and maybe slightly dumb enough, to not realize the very steep risks inherent in innovation, especially at a well-established institution like *The Washington Post*.

You see, at many big-league institutions, management will proclaim, often grandiosely, the desire for innovation, but when it comes, will resist it like established antibodies fighting off foreign virus. As many years later we in management used to say, only half-jokingly at the *Los Angeles Times*, "Sure, we encourage staff innovation—just don't bring us anything new!"

Bradlee was a true, almost fearless innovator, at least in that period, and of course at least through the spectacular Watergate years. As a lucky intern, I was one of the first to benefit from that instinct for the daring and the new. I was not anywhere remotely as talented as Bob Woodward and Carl Bernstein, the legendary odd couple that cracked the Watergate mystery, but it could be that Bradlee's affinity for "reckless young people" helped him stay with those two young reporters longer than almost any other major editor might have. I mean, this was the guy who handed me a page one story on my third week as a summer intern.

Lower-level editors were not always so smitten with the intern from Amherst. One day, an old couple came into the *Post's* newsroom and was passed on to me as a penniless veteran and his wife from the historic "Lincoln Brigade." Like an idealistic humanitarian aid worker reviewing his first woebegotten case, I started earnestly calling up city agencies in search of housing and a temporary grant. Finally, a few editors cracked up with laughter and called me over. They explained that the couple's claim was preposterous and the whole pitch a hoax. They had wanted to see how gullible I would be. I passed the lack of cynicism test with flying colors—alas. Potential hotshot or not, I had a lot to learn. That was the point and it was a very valid one.

A week later, the national desk called on me, then 20, to cover a major political speech at the Mayflower Hotel. I was the hero intern of the previous week's Lyndon B Johnson-appointment package. Even the deputy managing editor, a crusty veteran *Post*-er of many decades, had come up to me the next day with a compliment: "That was one of the best deadline writing jobs we have seen around here."

That was a real newspaper person speaking! Writing on deadline is at the heart of what you do at a newspaper: some longer articles may take weeks or in very rare cases, even months of preparation; soft feature articles can be written quickly, but publication may be held over for a day or two or three—

with much opportunity to rewrite. But deadline writing must take place within the confines of a very limited amount of time. When your story is due, it must be done—no excuses! This is perhaps a very minor skill in the grand scheme of life but it is an essential one at a newspaper or a newsweekly. It took ten years to write *Madam Bovary*, an enduring classic; it was to take me an hour or so, years later, to write my columns. The latter are not classics, were not classics at the time, and will never be considered classics. But, they met the deadline. Writing on deadline is at the heart of the journalistic beast.

At the Mayflower Hotel political dinner—a boring and, ultimately, a minor story for the paper—I sat in the area roped off for the press. At many of these kinds of events, I was to sense that the news media would be treated as if it were a communicable disease and its journalists contained in an off-to-the-side petri dish under the supervision of a political management center for disease control.

One of the reporters in the petri dish was then the highly regarded education editor of *Newsweek*. I think he looked at me with some curiosity, as if I was not only very young then for a *Post* assignment like this but perhaps also looked very young for any serious journalistic job.

We chatted amiably and by the time we parted, he had asked me to accept the part-time position of campus correspondent back at Amherst for *Newsweek*. "What?" I said. "I'm only 20." He said, "If you're good enough for *The Washington Post*, you might just be good enough for *Newsweek*."

I accepted on the spot. Why hesitate?

AT ANY INTERNSHIP OR NEW JOB, your key move is probably to work longer hours than anyone. I suppose this is as true in law and medicine as it is in journalism, but it is an unvarying rule. When I am in doubt about what to do, I say: just be there, stay there, do something, make yourself useful! Forget the ease of the nine-to-five job. A young person who puts in but the minimalist seven or eight hours a day will go nowhere in an organization unless he or she is the scion of the owner, a mole for the CIA, a member of organized crime or incredibly lucky or gifted. So, sleep under the desk. Come in on weekends. Compensate for your inexperience by committing your time. Let them know that when the earthquake comes, when the roads are impassable and when the city's mass transit system is down, you will somehow get to the office—even if on all fours. (Seriously, I mean this.)

That summer, there being only a few interns—and many August vacationers—we were given many chances to prove ourselves. And, on the whole, we did. Not because we were so terribly talented but because we were unblocked enough to be courageous and hungry enough to not feel exploited. We were too young to fully comprehend our limitations so we did not feel we had any (or perhaps, we were in a blissful state of youthful denial). Besides, journalism at the level we interns were permitted to practice was not exactly rocket science.

What was required to succeed at this level of reporting is indefatigable energy, and the ability to shut up, deep-freeze your ego, listen carefully and rely on good old common sense. What is also needed is probably a kind of functional attention deficit disorder (ADD) and a talent to translate your own ability to become very quickly bored, into a compressed account of what happened, for the consumption of readers who have many other things on their minds.

I sure did fit the bill. I have had functional ADD (may I term it functional?) for as long as I can sit still long enough to remember.

By summer's end, I had compiled three dozen bylined stories. It is believed that this still constitutes the "Intern Record for a Single Summer" at *The Washington Post*. When I say "it is believed," I mean this: "I believe it and I challenge subsequent summer interns to show they had more bylines." The reason I believe it is this: since I was an intern, decades ago, editorial standards have risen so high that no one intern could possibly be published that often!

Bradlee was fantastically supportive all summer. He obviously loved being around young people (as I am today and always have been) and was not overly concerned about their lack of experience. In fact, he probably viewed too much experience as an impediment to innovation. To him, it was far easier to program a green man or woman than to re-wire a far more established careerist. It was surely this philosophy that induced this great and bold editor to stick with Bob Woodward and Carl Bernstein when the Watergate Hotel break-in mushroomed into a major political mystery. He stuck with "the kids."

At the suggestion of Stephen D Isaacs, then the energetic city editor (now an equally energetic and admired Columbia University of Journalism professor), I paid a final call on Bradlee before jumping into my erratic Triumph sports car and tooling back to Amherst for my senior year.

"So what are you going to do next?" he asked, feet propped up on the desk, a pencil in his ear, his jacket on the back of the chair.

"Back to school to finish up."

"Yeah, I know, but after that?"

"Graduate school."

"Why don't you come here and work for us?"

"Need that degree."

"Ah, fuck it. Graduate school ain't worth shit!"

That is actually what he said. He repeated it: "Graduate school ain't worth shit."

So—don't ask me why—I went to graduate school!

And so thus was the "leave the kid alone" field left wide open for Bob Woodward and Carl Bernstein—do they realize that they owe their fame mainly to me?!

Right, another road not taken, like the one in high school, where, as a committed classical clarinetist, a Julliard scholarship was suggested, and I looked the other way.

And so fate keeps on happening.

AN IVY LEAGUE EDUCATION is scarcely necessary for success in journalism. Indeed, very few graduates of the Woodrow Wilson School of Public and International Affairs—where I received my master's degree in public and international affairs—lowered themselves thusly into the gutter world of journalism. They did important things such as working in government or public service, or engaging in some nonprofit activity or humanitarian cause.

My best friend at Princeton as well as at Amherst—the brilliant Aaron Latham, who was to write the screenplay for the hugely successful movie "Urban Cowboy"—used to say only half-jokingly that the best reason for going to schools like Princeton was not that they were necessarily categorically better than other schools but rather that by having them tucked away in your background and résumé, you did not have to go through life saying, "Oh my, if only I had gone to a place like Princeton or Amherst..."

And no doubt a very good school does leave you with the intellectual self-confidence to tackle almost any intellectual or policy challenge. But this is important only for a certain brand of upmarket journalism because at the upper tiers of the profession, you are interviewing and evaluating enormously intelligent people. You need all the education you can get just to understand what they are saying—or, more likely, trying to avoid saying.

Certainly, all of the important forms of serious journalism (that is, not Madonna or Brad journalism) would be better off if their practitioners at least had quality master's degrees. The world is too complex to wing it anymore, which is what American journalism has been doing for too long. A graduate degree in public health or economics or public policy (my favorite) or in a foreign language or culture or even journalism (this would be my last choice though) can help equip you to cope with the many challenges you will face. Indeed, were I king of the US world, I would require a credentialed journalist to have, as a minimum, a master's degree, in at least something.

What might surprise you is my strong sense that a master's degree in a substantive subject would be better for America—and its young people—than one in journalism. I do not have an ideological prejudice against journalism schools—especially the very best ones, from the Columbia University School of Journalism in New York which is practically iconic, to the USC Annenberg School in Los Angeles where Dean Geoff Cowan and his team have been so effective in reform and upgrading—but the student's expenditure in time and money might more fruitfully be directed towards an advanced degree in a substantive area. Benjamin Bradlee and his successors can teach you all the "journalistic techniques" you need, but they cannot teach you the techniques of economic-marginal analysis, how to speak Mandarin, how to comprehend complex public health and public policy issues, international relations trade-offs and even the tender issues of social work, an under-appreciated subject.

BEFORE I HAD my first significant full-time job in journalism—after *The Washington Post* internship and after graduate school—I took a few months off to write a serious book that I figured few people would ever read. Commercial success was never my most important goal and I still have the bank account figures to prove it. The book was about the nuclear arms race, then raging like a firestorm in the vortex of the West's Cold War with the Soviet Union. Books of this nature are not destined to ring in the cash.

What was astonishing was that Simon & Schuster, one of America's most commercial-minded publishers, agreed that this book needed to be published. My editors there were Richard Kluger, a brilliant thinker and former book review editor of the *New York Herald Tribune*, and Bill Simon, a very young man then, who later went on to law school but before that owned one of the first BMWs ever imported into America (which tells you something—one of my best friends in my early twenties was one of America's first yuppie beemers).

Writing a book for a large audience is easily one of the most intellectually exhausting, ferociously complicated and at the same time, most deliciously breathtaking adventures imaginable. The late Sir David English, the legendary editor of the London *The Daily Mail*, told me it was the one thing in journalism he felt he could not do well and envied me the ability (slight as it was). He also said nothing was more difficult in print mass communication than a book and that to do it, one had to be prepared to make extraordinary personal and professional sacrifices. That picture of a road paved with cut glass only inflamed my ambition. I suggest to you that writing a serious book about a vital subject is a great thing into which to invest your time, psychic energy and talent; it is noble even, if you tell no lies.

I did the research for the project at the super-neat Woodrow Wilson School library and wrote it back at my super-messy apartment on Manhattan's West Side. I would take the train from Penn Station to Princeton two or three times a week and sit in the library like a young Karl Marx trying to figure out the world. I had enormous encouragement from my faculty advisors, especially the visionary Richard Falk, who was writing about global innovations like international war tribunals when most people were scoffing at the idea as utopian, if not Martian; and Richard Ullman, the most sensitive of professors and an enormously engaging commentator on world issues who once worked as a *New York Times* editorial writer.

Well, I am no Karl Marx in the manufacturing of classical books. His book *Das Kapital* inspired a political revolution, and is still sold and read today. My own book, *Understanding Doomsday: A Guide to the Arms Race for Hawks, Doves and People*, turned out to be not quite as influential or commercial. But writing it was one of the greatest privileges of my life. I was then twenty-three. I had the enthusiasm of my best teachers, a great publisher and a supportive and singularly caring literary agent, Theron Raines. I was a very lucky young man.

The book received no bad reviews and several excellent ones. *Scientific American* liked it a lot. It was published in both hardcover and paperback. It sold somewhat several billion fewer copies than Hillary Clinton's memoirs of life with Bill. But Simon & Schuster—under the legendary editorship of Michael Korda—published it even though they were under no illusions about its commercial potential. I always keep this experience in mind when students sermonize on the essential sordid commerciality of American publishing. This is usually a correct observation but not always, because the famous Korda was a special character.

The book finished, I had another job to do—to land a real paying job. Still only twenty-three, I somehow feared trying for a spot at the *New York Times* for the same reason I had feared trying to get into Harvard. These places were too damn big and cold and impersonal for me. I was offered admission to Harvard College but when much-smaller Amherst College accepted my transfer credits from the University of Pittsburgh where I finished my freshman year and proffered a full scholarship, I was theirs.

Amherst and Princeton were central to my future because they helped shape my sense of self. As the shaky product of a proud but uneducated father whose horizons were so limited that he opposed my going to college at all, and of a loving but timid mother who cowered in the shadow of my towering (six-foot-five US Marine) dad, I was an early bloomer academically but a late bloomer in terms of self-definition.

That self-observation may be true of many journalists. As the very process of journalism is more of a receptor position (of received ideas, of stories out there, of what *others* do), the journalist can hide for years behind the mask of receptivity and objectivity without having to flash more of an identity than a media press card.

I, too, would have probably been no more than some tabula rasa boy if not for the coddling of Amherst and Princeton which surely deserve all the credit and more for their worldwide academic acclaim. Indeed, whether at school or in the workplace, I am at my best when I am coddled and loved as if I were an only child.

It is important for young people to get a sense of who they are and in what environment they will work best. Some of my friends loved huge universities like Harvard and Cornell but for me, the smaller and more family-like, the better. To be sure, at both Amherst and Princeton, I was far from being the best student. But I was okay; I earned the added cachet of being the campus correspondent for *The Washington Post* (at Amherst) and then *Newsweek* (at Princeton).

These were unbelievably great gigs. For one thing, they paid a little bit of money, but more to the point, they taught you how to relate to a big headquarters institution from afar. I was never to become a foreign correspondent (which, if you are brave, is probably the best job in journalism; next is being a foreign affairs columnist), but the campus correspondent stringer jobs offered parallels.

I have to add one last odd note before going on to my first real staff job. The only time I ever had a job that was not in the news media was one summer after Amherst when I served as a summer intern at the US State Department in Washington. There, I wrote speeches for top US diplomats, and I loved it. People dump on the State Department in terms such as "foggy bottom" and a bunch of "cosmopolitan girlie-boys," but that was not my experience at all. I met dedicated foreign-service officers—men and women—who worked long hours for modest pay, were seriously intelligent and well-educated, and gave it everything they had. It was perhaps this singular summer experience, as well as my two years of graduate work at Princeton's public policy school, that tempered the American journalistic knee jerk conceit to wit—that probably most public officials are either incompetent or corrupt. This cynical, negativistic attitude pervasive in the American media is a fact of contemporary US journalism that I absolutely hate, in part because sometimes my own work perpetuated it.

NEWSDAY, UNDER THE TENDER LOVING CARE of publisher Bill Moyers and editor David Laventhol, was to become my Amherst; and after that, *New*

York magazine, under brilliant/zany Clay Felker and graphic geniuses Milton Glazer and Walter Bernard, was to become my Princeton.

Newsday, though already a pretty good paper in the 1970s, was destined for bigger things. It had a near-monopoly on Long Island, which was an increasingly wealthy suburb of the greatest city in the world. Under Dave's editorship, it was to become one of the ten best papers (on almost every such chart) in the country. I was to be allowed to play a small—very small—role in the success story.

Or perhaps, I proactively carved out a tiny role for myself. Destiny can be the product of circumstance, and in Moyers and Dave (who not only believed in young people but believed they were essential to success), I had another Benjamin Bradlee—they were the "let the kid alone!" kind of guys. They were reasonable adventurer types who leaned toward innovation rather than status quo institutionalization.

It is obvious that my academic degrees from fancy places opened the door for job interviews that perhaps I might not have gotten otherwise. That was probably the case with *Newsday*, when Moyers, Lyndon Johnson's former press secretary, came aboard as publisher. One of his first moves was to hire Dave as editor. And that was a real good move.

> Probably the single most important factor when you are young and breaking into the business is the person for whom you will be working. You could rise to your level of ability or realize your limitations. Mentors and the opportunities they offer are, over the long run, far more decisive at this stage than money or position.

The young Dave was no screaming movie star like Bradlee. He was shy and half-inarticulate, but armed with a spacious intellectual interior of deep thoughtfulness, constant reflection and caring for the individual. Shelby Coffey, who was to inherit the horrifying job of becoming my direct supervisor later at the *Los Angeles Times* in 1989, once characterized him precisely and appropriately, as a "sage." It was my good fortune that Dave was to become my first professional mentor.

As a former Yale graduate student, Dave was far more respectful of the value of higher education even in newspapering than Bradlee. Whereas

Bradlee thought that graduate school was not "worth shit," Dave was intrigued (or puzzled) that a young man coming out of the Woodrow Wilson School would choose journalism as his career route.

Interviewing for a job is of course the first hurdle to getting one, and, though this facet of working in journalism would prove the easiest of the tests for me, it was an inherently enervating task. One slip-up and one could lose the job; on the other hand, many interviews are not granted unless the employers are pretty sure one was what was needed.

Dave, often short of words (though never ideas), did not make it any easier with his barren economy of expression. In this atmosphere, you have two options: talk a lot and fill up the silence, or talk very little and let the would-be employer show his or her hand.

My own strategy would always be to assume that the person interviewing me was smarter than I because he/she had a job, a good one, and I did not—I needed the job. How could I impress the interviewer of the inherent wisdom of hiring me without my having to put on a performance? Therefore, I always chose the route of garrulousness: the no-guts-no-glory tactic.

As it turned out, that worked with Dave. He was a man who appreciated words from others even if he sometimes seemed to use them as self-consciously and sparingly as if they personally cost him $1 per syllable. By contrast, if anything, I was a good talker. Stories and jokes were my specialty. So I talked about Princeton—which I loved—and I told him the Bradlee story. He sat behind the desk like Humpty-Dumpty, if Humpty-Dumpty were an Oxford don, and took it all in. When I finally slowed down to a mere sprint, he said, "I could hire you as a reporter tomorrow. Would you like that?"

I might have said yes, and indeed, perhaps I should have. In newspapers, the route to top management—where I wanted to be—was through the city desk and then the national and/or foreign desk. But I was always more interested in ideas and policy issues than train wrecks and car chases or even cute little stories about the weird practises of foreigners. I could better imagine myself chasing welfare reform ideas than ambulances. So I pushed my luck and asked if a position as an editorial writer might be available.

AT JOB INTERVIEWS, *always* push your luck—but just a little. Don't be obnoxious or ungrateful, but whatever is offered or suggested can always be improved upon. Once you are employed, your leverage is greatly reduced for improving your situation over the near term, for what the employer wants then is outstanding performance—payback for his or her investment in you. But in the negotiation for the original position, before you agree to terms, your leverage is at the maximum. Once having agreed, you are where you are for at least a year.

> In job interviews, always push your luck—but just a little. Once you are employed, your leverage is greatly reduced for improving your situation over the near term.

I realize that this advise is "easier said than done"—we are always timid about pushing for ourselves. But as long as you tender your "can you do better or different" replies in a polite way, you will be even more valued as an employee, and your potential employers are even more likely to hire you and value you. For—they figure—if this is the way you handle yourself in front of your boss, then this is the way you will handle yourself in front of a source or the mayor or Deep Throat. Journalism (even the classiest kind) is nothing if not a little bit pushy.

Note that I did not ask for more money or more vacation or a large expense account. What I asked for was a job that I thought I could do better at than the one offered. But whatever you want, ask for it *then*—during the interview. Don't be a jerk but don't be a wimp either.

DAVE TURNED OUT to have a huge influence on my life. Because of his steely intelligence and ability to put up with weirdos as long as they put in the quality as well as quantity time, he "got me" better than almost anyone. I was a little (*little?*) weird, an inescapable truth over which not even Ivy League degrees could paper. But he was okay with that—in fact, he was a little weird himself, and he believed that driven talent and true weirdness were not only compatible but were often inseparable. This is the sort of supervisor you want, if you were a "little" weird (that is, like almost everybody else).

At the time of his hiring by Moyers, he was already widely thought of as one of America's most innovative journalists. Bradlee had made him the first

STYLE editor of *The Washington Post*.

STYLE was a new section of the paper that emphasized feature stories about health, profiles of prominent persons, movies, theater, music and whatever. Before there was this stand-alone section, such "soft" stories would crop up almost anywhere inside most American newspapers, though not on page one—but probably on the FOR WOMEN page. By consolidating and prioritizing such stories, *The Washington Post* led the country by adding what was, in effect, a daily magazine dimension to its daily newspaper. In the forefront of that change was the young Dave.

Dave was, let us stipulate for the record, not a sartorially stunning man. He was obviously exceptionally unconcerned about his appearance and we all used to joke about this with him. He could not have cared less, for brains were his daily wardrobe.

Outside his fishbowl office at Long Island *Newsday* was a frantic swarm of a newsroom—reporters on telephones, banging out stories, answering editors' fierce questions. But his eyes, if you stared at them long enough, gave him away. He was taking everything in. And he was a hard man to fool. Destiny was to have me work for him two more times after *Newsday*. Later, we used to joke that this frequency of employment recidivism violated the federal statute of how many times one person could be hired by the same employer. The truth was, anyone who has had the honor of working for Dave's *Newsday*, had been smiled upon by good fortune.

LONG ISLAND *NEWSDAY*, in the seventies, was more of an excellent adventure than the huge success story that it is today. That is why I wanted to work there—better to be involved in a dynamic work-in-progress, especially when you are young, than in a wholly finished work. This is what all young people should want—forget IBM, hook up with your generation's Bill Gates!

So, when, a few days after the interview, Bill Moyers (the publisher who, in the setup of most newspapers, is The Power That Be over the editorial pages—the publisher's play spot or sandbox, as it were) telephoned and asked me to drop by for a second interview, I felt this would work. The first quality I wanted in a job (I was then still in my twenties) is adventure, challenge and a great man/woman to work with. In Moyers and Dave, I had two great men to work with and thus I had all three.

Moyers had a Southern ocean-porch personality and a light sparkle in his eyes that was luminous and fun to observe. He was more than a superficial smiling man though; he was a true intellect. He made sure that I was relaxed during the interview in his office at *Newsday*, then at Garden City. It seemed to me that his only concern about hiring me was the possibility that I was "too Princeton"—too Ivy League or too *New York Times* (a great but back then stuffy old gentlemen's club of a newspaper that for some odd reason, I never yearned to work for as much as I should have) and not common folk enough. But his concern vaporized the minute I told him I was Long Island born and bred.

A few weeks later, I was on the editorial board of *Newsday*, penning editorials on national and foreign policy. What was wanted from me was a compatibility with others, a sophisticated but not affected approach to major issues and a lot of productivity. I liked meeting and talking to people, I read widely and I worked hard.

Newsday was anything but a struggling paper then though it was not the colossus that it was to become when it was later sold to Times-Mirror Corporation which owned the *Los Angeles Times*. So people really had to work extra hard. This was fine by me. I was a genetic workaholic, and, truth be told, the more time I spent working, the less time I spent drinking. I did not want to grow up and become yet another newspaper alcoholic.

The newspaper itself was brilliant. It covered suburban Long Island as if it were its own private backyard. Hardly a parent-teacher meeting could be held without encountering a *Newsday* reporter. The coverage was, on the whole, adult and helpful. To my way of thinking, *Newsday* was a newspaper that took the yokel out of local.

But local reporting was not my cup of tea; ideas and issues were. And so I especially liked working in opinion sections: I regarded editorial page work as the "thinking person's" section of the paper, concerned with the serious issues and difficult controversies of the day.

The one issue I was not allowed to write on was that of the Vietnam war. That was Bill Moyers' baby, almost 100 per cent. Having worked in the White House and having personally observed the grave error of America's ways in Southeast Asia, he was eager at almost every opportunity to explain to Long Island and the world the magnitude of this strategic blunder and moral calamity.

What was absolutely extraordinary about Moyers was the paradox of profile and conviction. Had this former Baptist preacher not wound up as press secretary to the president of the United States who expanded the Vietnam war so dramatically, he might have just been yet another anti-war voice; but because of that very job—arguably unacceptably evil in its essence (that is, PR flak for a tragedy that killed more than 50,000 Americans, and God-knows-how-many Vietnamese)—he wound up gaining a prominent pulpit to denounce the very war effort that the administration in which he shone advanced. This paradox aside, his editorials flew off the newsprint pages with powerful passion, arousing in the reader a deep if latent sense of profound decency and moral outrage. In my view, of all the many Pulitzer Prizes that over the decades have been unjustly un-awarded, Moyers' editorial Sherman-esque march against the American establishment ranks very high on the list of great journalism unrecognized.

REFLECTING ON THOSE DAYS, it is hard to recall if anyone in the editorial division of *Newsday* supported the war. I certainly did not. In fact, back in the days when I was managing editor of the *Amherst Student*, I had written the first editorial against the war to appear in an East Coast establishment school. We beat the *Harvard Crimson* with that editorial statement by a few weeks. I had gone to Cambridge to visit with Donald Graham, then the editor of the Harvard College daily, and quickly learned that the *Crimson* (often dubbed "The Crime") was planning a major anti-war issue. I sped back to Amherst in my British TR-3 to inform my college newspaper colleagues of Harvard's plan and convinced them, including *Amherst Student* chairman Marshall Bloom (who was very easy to convince—he was about as anti-Vietnam war as Mao Tse-tung) that we needed to rush into print with our break-the-glass anti-establishment editorial. The *Amherst Student* boded to become the first East Coast establishment college paper to declare itself against the war unequivocally, and I had had the honor of writing it.

It was not an absolutely terrible piece of work and it attracted a lot of attention. On campus, it was denounced by the late Professor Earl Latham, the chairman of the department of political science, my major field of studies. No matter—the wonderfully witty Professor Latham was perhaps my greatest fan and even as he read the intellectual riot act to me, he did it with caring and love; and I listened intently, almost reverently. But in my heart, I knew the war was a mistake and history was to prove this view not wrong at all. With an enthusiastic green light from all, we had set down the first marker.

I sent my editorial to Bryce Nelson, then an aide to Senator Frank Church, the eloquent Idaho anti-war Democrat. Bryce was a former chairman of the *Crimson*, a Rhodes scholar, Church's foreign policy aide, and someone I greatly admired and considered a true soulmate. (Bryce is now a distinguished professor at University of California's Annenberg School.) He had helped grace my way into Amherst, as had the late Dr Roy Heath, and was a personal inspiration who had urged me to go there even after I had also been informally offered admission to Harvard as a freshman. Amherst, with top-notch professors like George Kateb, Benjamin DeMott, Earl Latham, William Pritchard and the late Dean Scott Porter, was the single best decision made in my first 19 years of life.

Church wound up entering the editorial in the *Congressional Record* as evidence that Berkeley—whacked out, drugged up and even then over-sexed—was not the only major campus against the war. This was in 1965, and of course the uprising at Berkeley prefigured the huge anti-war student demonstrations that were to follow, the tragedy at Kent State and the utter self-destructive spiritual division of the nation into two warring halves.

> The notion of "being first" is one key to understanding the media, whether at a college paper or otherwise. I had not known this instinct to be so powerfully embedded in me until I realized Harvard might beat us to the anti-war punch. In reality, what would be the big deal, right? The point is, simply, this: You either have the competitive instinct inside of you to be the first, and the best, or the most imaginative, or you do not. If you do not, don't even consider the media as a career.

ON THE ISSUE of Vietnam itself, of course, Bill Moyers was on the right side of history, as the subsequent tragedy proved, but he was on the wrong side of *Newsday* politics. The family that then owned the newspaper—the Guggenheims—found the Moyers anti-war movement too strident and relentless for their taste, and before too long, Moyers was history.

One lesson here is that while at any institution, whether it is a student newspaper or *Time* magazine, you have to calculate carefully who the power is or where the power is. You cannot expect to win by fighting the power all the time, or even most of the time. You may land a cluster of tactical victories, even an occasional important one, but over the long run, if you push too hard against The Power That Be, you would eventually be crushed by it, rapidly or over time, whether you are the secretary of state serving the president of the United States, or an editorial writer serving a publisher, or in the case of Moyers, a publisher employed to serve the interests of the proprietor.

Years later, I was to learn this lesson repeatedly in London when I was to work with Sir David English, the editor-in-chief of Associated Newspapers, the Europe-based media giant, and, for decades, the unforgettably brilliant editor of *The Daily Mail*. He had a view that American editors lost more than they gained by pretending to have clean hands and excusing themselves from the business side of the decision-making.

In the end, the loss of the *Newsday* job actually worked to Moyers' advantage. An amazing personality with boundless energy, he then became a fixture at America's Public Broadcasting Service, and rightfully so. He was a superior human being and a deep thinker, and I learned much from him as a young man. He wrote as he spoke, with the passion and conviction of the young Texas preacher he once was. He taught me to care about individuals as well as causes. When he went on to greater things in journalism, he became one of the few major media success stories of which I was not jealous. Moyers had real talent, and, he was a good person—this is not true of everyone who has made it big in the news media. I do not know how much money he has made, but whatever it has been, he has deserved it.

As DID DAVE. Dave could be more fun than he would let on. At one point, he invited me (I was still only 23 or so then) to a night at the Trotters in Yonkers. *Newsday* had recently run a story about irregularities in the race results. One day, he casually asked me, "Want to go see some rigged horse races with me tomorrow night?" I guess it was then that I knew he liked me. I certainly liked him.

ALTHOUGH I WAS NOT on the news side and thus it was not my job to rake in hot news stories, I was able to bring in an exclusive for Dave and it made me happy. You always want to please the boss if he/she has gone out of his/her way for you. And the boss was indeed pleased. He was still flying after our story on Lyndon B Johnson's memoirs. The exclusive came courtesy of my college and graduate school best friend, Aaron Latham. After leaving Princeton with his PhD in English, Aaron was snapped up by *Esquire* magazine where the famous magazine editor Harold Hayes then reigned. When I was doing my book on the nuclear arms race, *Understanding Doomsday*, Aaron used to invite me to the weekly story-ideas sessions in Manhattan that Harold would organize at a nearby hotel bar. He and a dozen of his top people would sit around over drinks and come up with cover concepts or story angles. I was not a staffer but I think Aaron thought highly of my knack for stories and ideas, and liked to show me off, as I liked to show him off.

> When choosing close friends, choose carefully. If you have a choice between choosing a very intelligent friend and a low wattage one, choose the former.

In those early days, Aaron seemed to always be able to save me from disaster in a pinch. The classic Aaron-saved-me story happened at Princeton when I needed to pass a foreign language exam. My language skills in general were just terrible. I had fumbled with Russian in high school so I chose French. It had seemed less daunting than most options and besides, my roommate Aaron spoke it with some fluency.

Princeton gave me a $500 loan for a tutor while I interned for *Newsweek* over the summer in San Francisco. I spent very little money on the tutor. San Francisco was then and still is an exciting place for a young man.

A week before the exam, Aaron called me from France where he had been vacationing with his sweetheart, a super-sexy Avianca stewardess who basically taught Aaron a real usable kind of French. He was concerned about my exam. He was expecting to share an apartment with me at Princeton, but I would be expelled from the university if I failed the exam.

On the phone, he started to chat me up in French and quickly concluded I was one cooked non-French goose. He said, "You are going to fail." That meant I would be expelled from Princeton. What could I do?

He sat silently for many minutes, then he said, "I got it. Maybe the examiner will be a modern language professor who resents having to do the chore of examination. He will sit in a darkened room, pretentiously dressed, with the air of someone who'd rather be anywhere else doing anything but this." Aaron paused some more. "If so, he would probably open the examination with some condescending question like, 'What did you do on your summer vacation?' "

But what if he/she asks a different opening question? His answer: "Then you will fail and be expelled. So this is the only hope. In fact, no matter what he asks you, tell him what you did on your summer vacation."

Over the next three days, I rehearsed a grammatically and linguistically complex answer to the all-important and hoped-for question about my summer vacation. It was a very lengthy and pretentious answer.

At the end of repeated rehearsals, Aaron said, "Listen to me. Only say that; say nothing else. The answer is so good that the professor will agree with you that the whole ordeal is beneath the two of you, and he will end the exam as an absurdity."

That was the hope, but would that question be asked?

I knocked on the examiner's door. Come in, the French voice said. Guess what? Behind the desk, dimly illuminated by one tiny desk lamp, was an impeccably dressed, fulsomely bored professor. There was a long pause. I said nothing. I waited for the first question. Finally, he asked (in French): "So, what did you do on your summer vacation?" I gave him my one excellent (and long) answer. And so this is how I passed my French exam at Princeton. I had a very smart friend who bailed me out.

I WAS NEVER OFFERED A JOB by Hayes at *Esquire* but I stayed close to Aaron and did well at Long Island *Newsday*. Pretty well.

For some reason, I had a hard time at first writing editorials and slid over to the opinion-editorial (op-ed) page, where at the age of 24, I became its editor. They liked my op-ed page work at *Newsday* in part because it was innovative—but perhaps also because I put in so many hours. I worked like a dog because I never felt like I had an entitlement to job security once I had been hired. Constant insecurity bred constant productivity.

On the whole, to me, this bred better journalism. By that I mean journalism that is more entrepreneurial and more committed to offering the reader the best possible effort, day in and day out. For me, if I had done my job honestly and fully, when I left at the end of the day, I could say: I am exhausted; I did everything I could possibly do; I will go home, collapse and wait for tomorrow. (Both Bill Moyers and Dave Laventhol were similar worker bees. Notwithstanding their fame and accomplishments, they were often the first in the door and the last to leave at the end of the day.)

Good journalistic practise is as much energy and enthusiasm as it is anything else, especially daily journalism. By good journalistic practise (GJP), one means the equivalent of what lawyers mean when they use the term "due diligence" or "best practises." This goal, when consistently pursued, adds value to our civic culture because it leads to greater understanding and helps to prioritize problems and issues. Good journalism does not have to be dull but it is not good unless it seeks to enhance the public good. People who call the news media the "fourth estate" or the "fourth branch of government" draw attention to the central role of the news media in the US system.

Editorial and op-ed pages especially deserve to be ignored when they fail to excite, engage and inform. Listless editorial pages are like worthless abandoned boats in the low rent area of the harbor. They just sit there and bob, and take on water, leak and eventually sink without a trace, with no one caring except for the occasional bored water rat.

Editorial pages are the purest example in journalism of why the First Amendment can be justified. When the news media performs a serious public service, our fourth estate truly deserves constitutional protection. But when it simply exploits that constitutional privilege with an effort that does little to help people make sense of their lives, their government or their world—their lives, their health, their children—then the news media under-performs as a public trust and deserves the disgust from the public.

At *Newsday*, empowered by the enthusiasm of leaders Moyers and Dave, the young John Walsh and I were able to recast the editorial pages so that they leapt out at you, capturing your interest and attention, perhaps even before you headed directly for the sports or fashion pages. My trick was to use a lot of editorial art, especially poison-penned editorial cartoons that spiked up the energy level and cast issues in powerful imagery. I do think to this day that if there is very little true genius in most journalism, it may occasionally creep in around the edges in a lampooning political cartoon.

One day, I recall, I could not find much of value to put on the op-ed page. Just about everything seemed like yesterday's oatmeal. So I decided to jump the midget—to do something that I did not think had been done before. Instead of running one or two editorial cartoons, I ran a whole bunch. So when you opened the op-ed page, a riot of graphic opinion hit you and stopped you. The reaction in the newsroom was warm and upper management registered no objection so I instituted the practise on Saturdays, as a regular feature. You may see something like it in other papers around the country these days. The device also caught the attention of a cartoonists association which asked me to speak at its annual dinner. I did. I told them I really liked their work. They applauded lustily.

During this era, the trend for America's editorial pages was otherwise: listless, aimless political columns that more or less upset no one, enlightened few and deserved an unceremonious cremation.

So I tried a lot of different tricks, why the heck not, I was only 24.

One morning, as I was recovering from a night of drinking, Dave Laventhol walked into my humble office. Dave could be ominous even as he pined to be Santa Claus. In many ways, he is the sweetest man in the world but he is also a shy man who tended to mumble a bit. At first, as I did not clearly understand what in the world he might be saying, I thought I might be in trouble. I had tried something new again—a very splashy photo package surrounding a strong column on airline safety. But I had forgotten to clear the innovation with my supervisor who was the editor of the editorial pages.

The omission was not prompted by wilful defiance of authority, rather, my instinct when trying something new is to think it through inside my head (one minor talent I have is interior visualization), and then, once I am convinced it would work, I would go ahead and just do it. (My unoriginal if subconscious fear is that a committee could and would kill off anything of substantial originality. That is the whole point of most committees—to lean in the direction of the view of the least risk-taking member—no?)

There is an additional bias. I tended to work better as a lone ranger than as part of a group effort. This was due as much to my insecurity as to my ego. I hated quarrels, even well-intentioned and professional ones. If I were a shrink, I would probably psychoanalyze myself along the lines of: children who hail from fiercely argumentative and alcoholic parents generally shy away from confrontation that might lead to hard feelings, not to mention genuine hard knocks.

As it turned out, Dave was anything but critical. He loved the package—the complete deal: wrapping a piece on airline safety inside of several crash pictures. He hovered in my office for all of five minutes, at most. But that support meant everything. It taught me a lesson and gave me a measure of self-confidence that probably turned my career around and ratcheted my head on straight, because here was upper management rewarding the calculated risk.

The only mistake he ever made with me was hiring me twice more in different jobs after this one. Or that is how we would come to joke about it.

> At an early professional age, the most important factor in a job is who wants you to work there and why. Salary, benefits and whatever are secondary. If your goal is to excel, surround yourself with excellence. You cannot soar like an eagle if your boss is a turkey. And if a turkey is your boss, what kind of funny farm is the place that hired you?

NEWSPAPERS ARE A LOT MORE THAN simply editorial and opinion pages, to be sure. In fact, they are driven by the news, not by ideas—or, if you will, driven also by ideas about what constitutes the news. This is inherently the case with the newspaper that must come out everyday. Have we ever seen a paper published with a headline such as: "Sorry! No News Today!"

Of course we have not. Accordingly, newspapers need to have a voracious, shark-like, even bulimic appetite for news, though for sports and celebrity news more than anything else these days. So if you are in the news media, and you want to impress the Higher Authorities (and I did want to impress Dave Laventhol, especially, and Bill Moyers, whom almost everyone loved), then what you want to do is to come up with a big-time news story.

Here is another example of why it helps to have smart friends. Remember Aaron Latham—the close college pal who guided me through Linguistic Mission Impossible: passing my French exam at Princeton? Well, he had a humdinger of a story for me—and it made me look great at *Newsday*.

I got a phone call one day from Aaron when he was still a staff editor at *Esquire*. This was 1971. It seemed that former President Lyndon Johnson's memoir, *The Vantage Point,* was being shopped around to a few high-level magazines for second serialization of the soon-to-be published book, which no one until now had seen, except for Aaron.

Lyndon B Johnson, the principal perpetrator of both the Vietnam war (bad) and vital civil rights legislation advancing minority rights (good), was then a hot property. His views on the war would be especially marketable—and newsworthy—if he were to express them candidly in the book.

The publisher had sought to whip up commercial interest by permitting a very select group of editors to sit in a room for an hour or so and flip through the manuscript. The rules included no photographing of the pages and no note-taking. *Esquire* had Aaron represent the magazine. So my college and graduate school buddy entered a Manhattan hotel room and stayed there for an hour to inspect the manuscript so as to determine the magazine's interest in buying serial rights, as they are called (that is, to buy the right to run excerpts in the magazine at about the time the full book is available in the bookstores).

To Aaron, who (I hope you do not mind my saying once again) was brilliant, the key revelation of the book was its remarkable confession that Lyndon B Johnson, while prosecuting the war to the fullest, actually shared some of the doubts of its critics and dissenters. The publisher permitted no copies to be taken from the room, but Aaron, the ever-clever one, secretly scribbled (when the publisher's hall monitor was looking elsewhere) some direct quotes from the book to report to editor-in-chief Harold Hayes.

After he did that, Aaron telephoned me from his Manhattan office at *Esquire* with the scoop. I was all ears. Here was a terrific, exclusive story about what the former presidential protagonist of the Vietnam war had really been thinking and worrying about at the time these awesome (and awful) decisions were being made to send some 50,000 Americans to their deaths in what was once called Indochina.

I went into Dave's office in a flurried hurry. I thought I had a hot one. I relayed the basics, the quotes and the source. At first, Dave said nothing. Was I overselling the whole deal? Maybe it wasn't such a big story after all? Then

I remember him saying, almost inaudibly, two things: "Do you trust your friend to take very accurate notes?" (I said of course, hell, this was the same guy who got me through my French exam at Princeton); and then, "Good story!" (That is to say: Go Tom!)

Newsday ran with it the next day. And it was big national news.

The book publisher, predictably, was furious, because *Newsday* had creamed off the best stuff; lawyers were threatening to sue for theft of copyright. This stupid threat only prolonged the story, which went on for days. By the way, real newspaper and magazine editors—and I mean the real-deal ones, not the corporate fakers and climbers—almost love it when someone threatens to sue. Generally—rightly or wrongly—they view it as a sign that they are probably doing their job, which is to get something out into the public light that some people would prefer to keep hidden.

I worried that Dave might not wish to be so far out on a limb and would begin to distance himself from me because of the controversy.

The next day, he shuffled into my dinky office and said, before leaving, only this, and in a voice so low I thought he might be asking me to execute a mafia hit: "Tom, thanks for getting that story, and give my thanks to Aaron, too. I haven't had such fun here in a long time!" Wouldn't you have wanted to work for someone like that?

> Perhaps in many if not all fields of endeavor, if you are not having a degree of "fun" in your media job, what's the point? Unless you are being paid a lot of money, get another media job or go back to school and retrain yourself for a different, more meaningful career.

AARON WAS HIRED away from *Esquire*. And that was not easy to do. Harold Hayes at *Esquire*, then America's leading men's magazine, was an elegant Southerner with a charm as broad as the Savannah River and he had an intellectually flirty way with young talent that was wonderful to observe.

But then came along a real rake of a figure—Clay Felker. This incredible guy was one part a riverboat gambler, one part college cheerleader, one part Willy Loman and one part pure magazine genius. He was then the founding editor of a chic new weekly magazine, *New York*, and it was soon clear that he would be a notoriously successful Pied Piper for young and (in the early stages of the magazine's history) relatively cheap talent.

Until the great success of *New York* magazine in the seventies, the *New Yorker* was king of the weekly cosmopolitan magazine roost. Sustained by very fine literary journalism and fiction, and powered by an endless parade of often hilarious if not devastating editorial cartoons, the latter was such a giant that it was hard to believe that there was any oxygen left in the market to sustain the life of another magazine.

But Felker and a handful of others who launched the magazine after the death of the New York *Herald Tribune*, where the Sunday section had been titled "New York," found that niche, filled it with the oxygen of talent (as well as a lot of editorial hot air and hype) and flew with it.

The magazine then was in its early days. This is often the best time to seek out the kind of job in which you can find your real self. The publication's culture is not yet rigidly solidified; the staff is young, bright and experimental; and the contribution you can make creatively can dwarf the true reality of your talent, that is, the opportunities and challenges are so great that someone has to fill in the many vacuums and voids. The demand for immediate solutions is often far greater than the supply of available talent. In this chaotic circumstance, it is the case that even slightly better-than-average talent can rise to occasions of arguable excellence and even spot-on brilliance.

Aaron was the handsome yet shy type; I was the unhandsome but not-so-shy type. He bordered on social awkwardness; I bordered on social obnoxiousness. He was smarter than I was—certainly then, if not also now. At *Esquire,* he was a young legend, and when Clay Felker tussled him away, it was a serious loss for Harold Hayes. Magazines, especially, can be driven to great heights by the energies and talents of a small corps of over-achievers; on a magazine like *Esquire* under Hayes or *New York* under Felker, young people can have a huge impact.

When Aaron defected, Harold was furious with Clay. Soon, Dave Laventhol was also to be a bit irritated with Clay. Guess what happened? I received a call from Clay's office that was to change everything in my life.

It was a momentous moment for me, as this kind of experience is for many young people, because it was my first upward job movement lunge. I remember it with vivacity. Here is the background.

As Long Island grew and expanded—as potato fields became plowed under and tract homes built over—*Newsday* started to sprout on the East Coast newspaper scene as well. But it had no Sunday edition—leaving the growing Long Island market to the Manhattan-based *New York Daily News* and to a lesser extent, the very upscale *New York Times*.

Dave and Moyers were perhaps geniuses in their own ways but it did not take a genius to see that there was a rather large market opening here. So, in 1971, the *Sunday Newsday* project was launched.

It is important to understand that in the US market, a Sunday paper offers a special commercial opportunity. Advertisers love Sunday newspapers because surveys show readers spend more time with the paper on Sunday than on any other day. Mom and daughter (stereotypically) go for the style, home or fashion section(s); dad and the boy(s) dive for sports; and the younger kids rampage the color comics section (an innovation that originated in the US and was then exported to England and elsewhere).

What was more, newspapers that operated in markets that have upper-income families would also tend to include an "intellectual" section—either to help their readers feel intellectual, or to actually keep them informed about trends, controversies and issues. The goal of *Sunday Newsday* was not only to all but wipe out the *New York Daily News*' stranglehold on Long Island but also to chip away at the *New York Times*, which on Sunday sold pretty well in the most upscale Long Island neighborhoods, especially in the affluent North Shore.

So Dave asked me to start up a Sunday section to be called IDEAS and to find an assistant with whom I could work. Hiring talent turned out to be something I was pretty good at. I could spot talent and I was not usually threatened by it, even when it was superior to mine. So I asked John Walsh to join me in the section start-up. He was brilliant. Later, he was to become editor-in-chief of *Rolling Stone*, Inside Sports and then ESPN. We lured writers like David Halberstam and Isaac Asimov (whose delightful brother Stan was a *Newsday* executive) into penning major pieces for Long Island *Newsday*, of all places. We sometimes looked as good as the *New York Times*' Sunday opinion section. Dave was thrilled. John was incredible to work with.

In large part because I had him as my deputy, the Sunday opinion pages of *Newsday* were sometimes awesome.

As an elder mentor once put it about the true mentality of the prototypical quick-thinking editor: "I may be wrong but I'm never in doubt." In newspaper work, the one sure wrong decision is the late decision. Missing a deadline is a journalistic cardinal sin. One reason John and I worked well together is we liked to make decisions—and we rarely looked back. John was an extremely talented co-worker and great fun to be around.

> When hiring, look out for the potential employee who is described (whether by himself or someone else) as a genius. The probability is that in six months, you would be suicidal about having hired this so-called genius. This is because in real life there are very few geniuses. The gods don't make Goyas or Einsteins or Puccinis every day. What you probably would be stuck with is someone who is not a genius and someone who makes you miserable to be around. Talented and great to hang out/work with, the John Walshes of the world were extremely rare.

IDEAS, the Sunday opinion section, was so successful it attracted attention beyond Long Island. The concept was a bit oddball but therefore attractive. The section was deliberately designed to be visually conservative as if to suggest that a truly intelligent reader would not need the bells and whistles of an extravagantly loud design to be attracted to real "content." (Besides, my Monday to Saturday op-ed pages tended to have more bells and whistles on them than a cruising suburban ice-cream truck!)

Well, the stylistically conservative Sunday IDEAS section worked. It remained *Newsday's* Sunday opinion section until 1988 when I was asked to redesign it again as editorial page editor of *Newsday's* New York City edition.

BUT BEFORE I WAS to land that job, a whole bunch of jobs would come first. The next one came in a phone call from Clay Felker. (Aaron, now working at *New York*, had tipped me that a call would be coming.) Would I meet with Clay in his Manhattan office at 11am Thursday? I said sure.

My view is that no matter how happy you were in a job, if someone thought they had a better idea for you, why not listen carefully and hear them out? This is not about being disloyal; it is about looking after yourself.

Sunday IDEAS was always put to bed Wednesday nights. Clay had asked me to meet with him the next morning. But rather than hem and haw and ask for a different time, so that I would be better rested and more self-assured, I readily agreed.

I was—well—panting. *New York* had started to become hot. And the brilliant Aaron who had just given me that Lyndon B Johnson scoop was working there. I had to check it out, if only to make Aaron look good, because, to tell the truth, whether or not I was a good editor, I did give good, impressive interviews. And that in turn would make Aaron look good, whether or not I took or got the job.

John and I closed that particular edition of IDEAS in the *Newsday* composing room at around 2am. I dragged myself back to my tiny house on Long Island but had trouble getting to sleep, knowing that I had a pre-noon interview with an editor on the apron of stardom. In the end, I may have had 90 minutes of actual deep sleep before I got back in the car and headed for Manhattan.

I was still in my twenties then, so I was much younger than the aging, ancient, ramshackle Manhattan brownstone in the East 30s in which *New York* was then housed. Charming as it was to become to me, it had a leaky roof, oft-failing plumbing, unworthy heating system and no elevator. Love at first sight, of course.

Clay interviewed me in his office. The first thing I noticed was that it was very messy. Manuscripts and photographs lay everywhere, including on the rickety, coffee-stained couch. Clay cleared out a little space for me to sit.

I usually give a good interview but I could not possibly have been on my best game that day, and I must have looked like hell—tired as I was from the late close of IDEAS, from the lack of sleep due to nerves (was I smart enough for *New York*, the magazine on its way to becoming the smartest magazine in America? And, more to the point, was I feeling guilty about possibly leaving *Newsday* and my supportive mentor Dave?), and from the tedious trip into the center of the city in my run-down green Triumph sports car.

In fact, I returned to Long Island not knowing if I would be hired. About all I could remember of the interview was that the job opening was titled "senior editor" (whatever that meant—there were no *junior* editors on the masthead, so far as I could tell), and that at one point, Clay expressed what I thought was surprise at the salary *Newsday* was paying.

Of course, *Newsday* was well into the black and *New York*, still essentially a start-up, was still well in the red. Salaries were being funded by investors' monies, and Clay had to nurse what he had been given to work with.

Aaron telephoned me that afternoon when I was back at *Newsday*.

"Tom, it's Aaron."

"Hi, how'd I do?" I asked.

"Not bad," he said. But there was a problem.

"Salary?" I asked. The truth was, I was prepared to take the same amount or even a little less if I felt the opportunity was exceptional. Besides, I was growing tired of suburban-slow Long Island, even as I totally respected *Newsday* and its top editors. As a single man, I was drooling to live in Manhattan and, for a sometimes-sleepless young man, the city that never sleeps seemed like just the right crib for me.

The problem, Aaron said, was that Clay was worried that I was a drinker, and, having personally witnessed so many newspapermen drowning their careers in a bottle, was worried and apprehensive.

I told Aaron, who knew that I did like to drink, that I had endured a late close, and a night of little rest, and much tossing and turning.

"Ah, that explained why you looked like hell!"

I laughed.

"Well, Clay'll probably call and invite you to brunch on Sunday. Whatever you do, don't start downing Bloody Marys before the appetizer arrives!"

Sunday brunch took place at a fancy Manhattan restaurant around noon. When the waitress came, Clay ordered a bourbon and soda. I ordered an iced tea. Then Clay ordered another bourbon and soda. I stayed with the iced tea.

Later that day, Aaron called to ask how it had gone.

"Pretty well," I said, "but, tell me, is Clay a drinker?"

"No."

"Then why did he order two bourbons for lunch?"
"Hah! He did that?!"
"Yes."
"He almost never drinks," said Aaron. "He must have been testing you." Ahh..
"What did you order?"
"Iced tea," I replied. "Three of them."
"Good move," he said. "You'll probably get an offer."

Two weeks later, in Dave's office, I gave notice.

Dave was shocked and probably a little hurt, though he was, as usual, hard to read. But he believed me when I said I was sick of Long Island, where I was born and raised, and that I was looking forward to the Manhattan bachelor night life. Because this was all true.

He asked me what I had been offered monetarily.

I lied. I had to. I had not the heart to tell him that *New York* would be paying me less. I liked Dave Laventhol too much, and I liked *Newsday*, and always have. Sometimes, it is not about their limitations; sometimes, it is about your needs. So I said ten thousand more.

(It was actually two thousand less and that was actually three thousand more than what Aaron had accepted—how did I tell Aaron? Did I tell Aaron? I don't think so.)

But when he asked about the magazine's medical plan, he interrupted me before I could answer. "You probably don't even know if they have one."

He was right. I did not.

My exit line was: "I told Clay I couldn't start right away, however. I told him I really respected you guys and wanted to give you six weeks' notice."

Dave looked at me with disbelief. Almost no one gives that much notice when they have decided to take a new job. In fact, most employers want you out the door as soon as feasible once you have decided to leave. And most employees spit in the employer's face while exiting, laughing. Not me. I wanted to send *Newsday* a message. The defect was not in the newspaper nor the staff; it was in the locale. All my horrid family memories were but a few miles away from *Newsday* headquarters. I wanted to get further away from those memories, even as I refused to blame my parents for anything other than giving up too soon on hope.

(One day, my mother, who died years ago, took a taxi from the mental facility in which she was living, came to *Newsday* and proclaimed in the hallway that she was my mother. Like a coward, I hid for over an hour until the security guards had taken her away. Later, a secretary informed me that someone was just here claiming to be my mother. Unflustered, I said that was odd. I had thought for sure she had died years ago. Was this cold of me? Yes, but necessary for psychological self-preservation. Many years later, my sister yanked her family out of Long Island and started life anew in Florida. She took a whole lot longer than I did to make the escape, but when she did it, I was very happy for her. And she is very happy for herself and her family.)

I was serious about the six weeks' notice. That was what I offered to do. Clay was furious. He had wanted me on board the very next day, as it were, but I held my ground.

I believe Dave and the *Newsday* organization never forgot the gesture.

> How you exit a place is as important as how you entered it. In fact, unless an organization has been absolutely brutal to you, avoid spitting in their eye when you leave. Exit classily, offer to help find a replacement if you had not groomed one, and offer as much lead time before leaving as possible. There are two reasons for doing so. The first is that it is the right thing to do, and the second is that you would never know—you might wind up working for that organization again ... and they would not ever forget the way you left.

Chapter Three
New York Magazine: Helping to Start Something Up is So Much Better than Winding Something Down

UNDOUBTEDLY, magazines are to the print news media generically what a makeover is to a Los Angeles star: a flashier, shinier, and more visually oriented version of the genre. Their design is more carefully executed; they smell better; your hands do not get dirty when you touch them; and you tend to develop a kind of personal relationship with them.

I was fortunate to be hired at a magazine that was a little masterpiece in progress rather than a refined and done deal. I was fortunate to be a young man living in one of the liveliest cities in the world. I was fortunate to have as a boss someone who obsessed about magazine profits only half the time.

In America, the magazine industry has been tragically and completely overhauled to cater mainly to people who were itching to spend money, as if that was all there was to life. When I was to work later as an editor at the magazine division of CBS, we used to joke that CBS would start up a magazine based solely on some perceived marketing niche, no matter how obscure and boring. If Ted the hot shot in R&D discovered that 11 million high chairs were sold last year, you can bet that someone would propose launching *High Chair Monthly*.

Which, of course, would be the most boring magazine in the history of the world, but that was the way some (not all ... but *many*) marketing people think. This religious devotion to market analysis is exactly why so many magazines are born each year and why so many die soon after delivery. Not every market niche can sustain its own publication, or indeed, should.

On the whole, magazines are very popular in America but on the whole too, they are not that important. One would think that all the excitement and reader loyalty surrounding the magazine world would be symptomatic of the greater and enduringly important content that the magazines carry but the opposite is actually true. On a media spectrum measuring social contribution and impact, the serious broadcast media get top ranking, primarily due to the profound impact of images on the minds of the masses. Newspapers come in second, largely because they are out there 365-plus days a year, and they create constant hum and sometimes virtue amid the vices of sensationalism and commercialism which Alexis de Toqueville understood to be essential to democracy. Bringing up the rear are flashy magazines, which with the exception of the few publications, tend to spend their pages bouncing back and forth between pure entertainment and semi-journalism.

Under the bumptious but bravura editorship of Clay Felker, one magazine in the seventies seemed to define perhaps the most glamorous marketing segments in America: New York's real and wannabe upper middle class. It was there that the magazine portion of my print journalism career truly began.

New York magazine rose from the ashes of the *New York Herald Tribune*, a very decent newspaper that died in the late 1960s. Despite a cast of really brilliant editors—including James G Bellows, Sheldon Zalaznick, Dick Schaap and of course Felker, too, as well as many others—it was not able to overcome the superior, well-entrenched newspaper, the *New York Times*.

Clay and some other former editors at the *Herald Tribune* decided to repackage the paper's Sunday magazine and sell it as a weekly publication on news-stands and via subscription. I came on board in the early days, and was chronologically and emotionally tied with my friend Aaron Latham, a wonderful writer, for the dubious distinction of being the most juvenile (with me, though, in more ways than one) senior editor in the place.

Clay was, in all respects, the real leader and mercurial inspiration. He was funkily charismatic, tremendously charming, imaginative, and had titanic waves of energy that would begin as a devilish gleam in his eye. Clay occasionally would indulge in a pricey glass of wine over a superb lunch or dinner at Lutece, then the most famous French restaurant in Manhattan. But unlike most journalists I knew, he was anything but a drinker.

He was an educated Southerner in every sense of the word—raised in the region, groomed at Duke University, and briefly married to a lovely blueblood named Pamela Tiffen, who perhaps became more famous, both rightly and wrongly, for her heartstopping external architecture than the range of her well-schooled theatricality (right, I am trying to say she was hot.). He later married Gail Sheehy, one of *New York's* finest women journalists.

I once met Pamela, a few years after their divorce, at a Manhattan party. She did not know I was working for her husband until I told her. Until then, I think she thought I was some sort of second-rate intellectual (she was as perceptive as she was hot). The man with whom she had arrived at the party was a famous architect. He told me, after she excused herself, that Pamela did not usually bother to talk to strangers so therefore I must be worth something, because she had been chatting with me happily.

It was easy to see why Clay had fallen for Pamela. She was a knockout in every sense—warm in personality and glamorous in appearance.

There may be something in the yearning of the journalist for glamour that draws some of us to the theatrical world for our female companionship. At the time, I was seeing a young actress named Gwen, though I think I was probably almost as much of a disaster to relate to for her as Clay was for Pamela. Indeed, Pamela asked me several probing questions about Clay and when at one point, our eyes locked as if to agree that we had both been through the same hurricane, I almost asked her out.

And so it was a dashing ex-husband of a talented actress who crafted the up-and-coming magazine of Manhattan, a glittering little self-important planet all its own, a magazine which specialized in pointing out all the ins and outs, and do's and don'ts of America's largest city.

The famous architect came back for a chat and began to fire off all the usual questions asked by the intellectual crowd. "So tell me, Mr Plate, where did you get your education?"

"Amherst for undergrad," I said, "and then I got my masters at Princeton."

"Very impressive," he said. "And what is it that you do now?"

"I work at *New York* magazine."

"For Clay Felker?"

"Right."

He looked at me like I had lost my mind. "Whyever would you do something like that?" It was obvious that he felt the Ivies had wasted their quality on me.

"I'm not sure exactly what you're getting at," I said slowly.

The architect stared at me for a long moment and said, "Why don't you do something important with your life?"

Stunningly, this searing question, from a snooty New Yorker architect who gained fame from designing famous and enduring New York skyscrapers, stuck with me for weeks afterwards. Prior to that upsetting question, my primary thought processes at the time went something like this: "I'm the cat's meow. I not only work at the hottest magazine in America with Clay Felker and my friend Aaron Latham, but I've been made a senior editor at age 26. I'm single, never been divorced, don't owe any alimony, don't have any major diseases, and am having a glass of sherry with a knockout named Pamela."

But now my interior dialogue had a new line tacked on. "Then this apparently very smart guy asks me why I've descended to so low a state of professional employment."

The hubris of youth—and a few more wines—eventually papered over the fissure that the architect's comment had made in my cocky sense of professional direction. But as the years wore on, I more than occasionally found myself thinking about what he had said. It was not a malicious comment. In fact, it was sincere. I thank him today for making it, even if there is no chance in the world he would remember the moment.

I ALSO BEGAN to see that the architect had a point—and that Clay, in an inadvertent sense, agreed with him! In cover-story planning sessions, Clay would patiently sit and listen as Milton Glazer, the great design innovator of the time (the guru of Push Pin Studios), would almost visibly cringe at some out-of-left-field story idea by Clay and say, "But, Clay, if we do this, it will just be terrible! People will be..."

And then Clay would bark back at the cosmopolitan Glazer: "But Milton, it's only a magazine." That is to say: It is not nuclear science, not oncology, not a cure for some major disease, and not even remotely *Madame Bovary*. It is just a magazine.

Clay was not denigrating our work here but he was pointing out that we were not exactly covering national security issues and thus, if he bent the rules a little bit and pushed the envelope, nuclear war with Russia would not be thus triggered.

So in essence what that famous architect meant at that long-ago cocktail party was that most commercial magazines are fundamentally trivial. They are not of eternal value or importance; in fact, they are quite the opposite. Indeed, it was Clay's own view that a successful magazine even at the top of its genre provides at best merely a cultural snapshot—a fixed picture of the moment, and only one framed perspective of that moment.

Once, I was perusing an old 1938 issue of *Life* with the great Byron Dobell, yet another talented (but truly senior, in the sense of well-experienced) editor at *New York*, and I said something incredibly stupid, which, alas, was not wholly unprecedented of me: "Gosh, this magazine looks so dated!"

Byron, obviously the wiser of us two by a rather wide margin, said, "Tom, but that's the sign of a good magazine."

In other words, when you look at a magazine 20, 30, or 40 years later, it should look dated. All the good ones do. It means that at the time of its existence, the publication captured the contemporary zeitgeist, or a slice of the cultural essence of the moment. It is precisely because magazines are mirrors of their times that they offer little of value outside of the era that spawned them (except, of course, to cultural historians trolling for publication grist and scholarly footnotes). And so, let us all agree on this: if you are working on a magazine and you are not enjoying it, please, quickly, get another job, because you are not doing anything that is likely to make a lasting contribution for the ages.

THAT SAID, KEEP IN MIND that *New York* magazine was a happy community of intellect and creativity. Clay and his staff had gathered together a near-monopoly of the top young talent of the age. Tom Wolfe, one of our staff writers, was a towering legend even then. Another staffer, Gail Sheehy, was just beginning her triumphant trot through the bestseller list. Aaron Latham went on to pen a terrific screenplay for the hit film "Urban Cowboy." Andy Tobias wrote bestseller after bestseller on complex financial topics. Dan Dorfman, his later legal troubles notwithstanding, was surely the premier financial analyst of that day—indeed, he practically originated the genre. Ken Auletta became a leading journalist on the media, writing several bestsellers and in later years enlivening the pages of *The New Yorker*. Michael Kramer—also a classmate from Amherst—went on to become a *Time* magazine columnist and editorial page editor of the *New York Daily News*. If there was a better food writer/critic in the world than Gail Greene, she/he was not writing in English. Walter Bernard, the art director, was to go on to redesign *Time*, after working under Milton Glazer's wing (and Walter was really something!). The list is virtually endless.

It was an all-star team (with a few journeymen like me thrown in).

Clay was not only the trunk connecting all the branches of this talent tree but he really made the experience of creating the magazine fun. This, in turn, produced a magazine that the reader found consistently fun and relevant, week after week. It was this sense of fun surrounding *New York* that liberated us to do a lot of legitimately important work. We could and did run pieces on international and political affairs that were not remotely in the mental landscape of the then less-than-imaginative *New York Times*—where the editors would think of them as being too controversial or sharply angled.

Consequently, some of the tenets taught in journalism school were notably in rare supply at *New York*. For example, what is known as the separation of church and state in the business—the separation between advertising and editorial—did not exist at *New York*, at least not in the mechanistic way envisioned at many journalism schools. If we had advertising pages coming in relating to the virtues of a certain brand of mascara, we would gin up editorial copy about how to put makeup on, or "The 50 Ways to Entice Him with Your Mascara Brush." No problem. People had to eat and pay mortgages, especially editors and writers. Besides, I liked smart women with mascara enticingly arrayed—forgive me if you can.

Keep in mind that many publications—among them *Vogue, Cosmopolitan* and others—also engaged in similar practises. This is why you would never see a major publication in New York doing an investigative piece on Bloomingdale's mail order operations or Tiffany's diamond business. When it came down to it, magazines required a commercial base to survive and if they insulted the advertisers that provided it, they would die. Maybe it is sad and maybe it is wrong, but in commercial America, it is pretty simple and totally unavoidable.

Oddly enough, they do not emphasize this at many journalism schools. But if you go into journalism thinking it is going to be the way they say it is going to be in some journalism schools, then you probably ought to go into something else.

There was a second reason that our inherently lighthearted philosophy at *New York* enabled us to do important work. This philosophy freed us up from the shackles of objectivity. This statement obviously needs to be put into context.

One could argue—I personally would not—that the reporting of the *New York Times* is objective. Whatever your opinion happens to be, the fact of the matter is that we did not want (or claim to have had) that kind of objectivity at *New York* magazine in the seventies.

We wanted stories that were sharply angled. In this sense, I think Clay's journalism was at times more honest than mainstream journalism thought it was. True objectivity is very difficult to achieve, and in the effort to objectify fluid reality, you run the risk of freeze-drying the topic and manufacturing boring journalism. Sure, the facts need to be right: no one is going to be interested in what you produce if you could not get the facts straight. But Clay did not believe in journalism—objective or otherwise—if it was not compelling. "What's the point of this thing?" he would bellow, flinging an un-compelling manuscript across the room. "Let's get to the point!"

Banality would be his most frequent roaring complaint when, at the last minute, he would yank some piece from the magazine because he felt that if it was boring, no one would read it and thus, it would not make any difference one way or the other, even if it was important. If a physicist proposed a solution or proof regarding the famed but elusive Riemann Hypothesis, the *New York Times* would argue that no one would believe it if the physicist had no credibility, but for Clay Felker, that was not even relevant if no one could understand the proof and if it could not be presented in a compellingly enough way for people to comprehend it.

To simplify: Clay subscribed more to the general British press ideology of "story first" than to the more doctrinaire upmarket American ideology of "objectivity first." This is to say that both he and the British, by and large, preferred their publications to be sharply angled (that is, Conservative or Liberal) and to contain strong perspectives than to be credible, boring and bland. Londoners do not expect *The Guardian* to be complimentary to Conservatives, nor do they expect *The Telegraph* to fawn over Labour Party politicians.

Clay, in turn, was not looking for writers who would go into an assignment thinking: "I must collect twelve opposing facts on one side and twelve on the other, to represent all points of view in this story." He would instead look for writers who, with a "novelist's eye," would pick out, assemble, and pass along the most telling details to the reader: the lint around the collar that hints of carelessness, mismatched socks that speak of scatteredness or even substance abuse, magazines on the mahogany table revealing a fetish, either by their content or by their overly neat arrangement. He wanted his writers to be Emile Zola, not the Encyclopedia Britannica.

Of course, Clay had staff fact-checkers (well, not until after the magazine started to make money—only *then* did we have fact-checkers) to make sure that the things stated as facts were in fact (no pun intended) true. The magazine needed to show due diligence in its editorial process, though I do not really think Clay, with absolutely the greatest of respect, overly cared much about that. While he definitely did not want to be sued for libel, if he had to choose between a story that would not be read, and one that was entertaining and yet danced on the borders of whatever, he would choose the latter. There was no question about it—and I don't care what the former magazine guru says today now that he is a distinguished professor at the Graduate School of Journalism at the University of California, Berkeley!

Thus it was that *New York* magazine sometimes raised great controversies, but it also induced New Yorkers to become deeply interested in real urban issues that would affect their lives but may not have otherwise received widespread coverage.

An instructive example is the classic piece Gail Sheehy wrote about prostitution in New York, the point of which was that the sex trade had burgeoned into a full-fledged commercial business. While risqué in topic, the controversy surrounding the story arose from the fact that Gail's main alleged informant, a particularly outspoken streetwalker by the name of Red Pants who was the centerpiece of the astonishing article, did not really exist as one person in one body at the same place and time.

True, Gail had gone out and hung out with hookers, but rather than portraying any single one of them, the talented journalist stitched the details, color and atmosphere of her experience together and created a composite that conveyed the totality of her reportage better than a narrowly delineated version would have. No problem here, in my view. There is nothing wrong with that if we had simply included a disclaimer in the published piece that said: "Red Pants is not one real person, but a composite," but Clay did not feel it necessary to do this. He made a mistake. He knew it.

The establishment press was infuriated to discover that the intriguing, streetwalking protagonist of Sheehy's exposé was in actuality a whole bunch of streetwalkers blended together in the Cuisinart of a writer's mind. There was a big hullabaloo. And rightly so, to be sure. But again, Gail's style of journalism had the value of proffering a unique way of bringing things to life and making them extremely arresting, and thus the readers became interested enough to dive into the story, became educated about the reality and mulled over the issues.

One of the best examples of *New York* capitalizing on this principle was its contribution to putting the spotlight on misconduct and corruption within New York's criminal justice system.

When serious rumors about "dirty" sitting judges in New York began peeping up from the sewers of organized crime and corruption in the early seventies, Clay ordered up a cover—an absolutely stunning story by dogged investigative journalist Jack Newfield called "The Ten Worst Judges in New York." Not only did it enumerate the "dirty" justices—by name—it also included the reasons why they arguably deserved to be so dishonored, whether it was routinely showing up to the bench inebriated and falling asleep during the trial, or having dinner with "friends of Michael Corleone or Tony Soprano" once too often. By putting the actual names of the judges in the magazine, it got people's—and lawyers'—attention. It also helped lead to the development of a special independent prosecutorial team appointed by the governor, and the eventual indictment of sitting judges and even a district attorney.

It was the very "frivolity" of *New York*—and its subsequent deliverance from the boring label of "serious journalism"—that attracted so much attention and so clued-in an audience that enabled it to do significant work. In fact, one of my better journalistic efforts at *New York* was a major story on the special prosecutor appointed by the governor to clean up the mess.

Before I get carried away in a tsunami of institutional and personal self-congratulation, let the record show that the special prosecutor's efforts in cleaning up the criminal justice system were valiant but incomplete. Few heads rolled, and, at the end of the day, it was unclear that the system was perceptibly more noble and antiseptic than before the attack of the journalists.

Fully reporting a story and even following up on the uncovered criminality and injustice is not the same thing as actually removing the issue or solving the problem. In our vanity fairs of self-congratulation, we journalists go to great lengths, what with our Pulitzer Prizes and even house awards, but the parade of social injustice, economic disparity, and political and corporate corruption proceeds apace. Sometimes when we blow our own horn, we are doing little more than playing with ourselves.

CLAY'S AMAZING AFFINITY and efficacy in finding an engrossing magazine approach to issues that were tough as well as confetti that was candy could sometimes make you uncomfortable. At one point, I worked on articles for *New York* called "The Mafia at War," which was an illustrated history of the internal cataclysms of organized crime. It was also a "one-shot," which is a big special issue of a magazine sold as a special edition and for a high price. Well, it turned out to be a national bestseller, and so as its principal author, I was asked to trek off on a promotional tour to Boston, Chicago, San Francisco, and Los Angeles.

To be truthful, I was anything but the magazine's principal investigator about organized crime. That delicate job belonged to Nicholas Pileggi, whose solid journalistic work and carefully constructed books fueled Hollywood products from "Goodfellas" to "City Hall." I greatly admired his story-telling skills but there was also something else about him that is hard to explain. I guess it is this: a lot of adjectives come to mind when thinking of the essential character of journalists but for some reason, the word "classy" is not high on the list. But with Nick, that was exactly the word that came first to mind.

Nick had other commitments. As a single man, I took the challenge of being weeks on the road with equanimity, even enthusiasm. It may in fact have been this trip—at the age of about 27—that first sparked my apparently unquenchable appetite for five-star hotels that rages on even today.

Despite the luxury, however, at times the promotion tour for *New York* was nasty. I could have used Nick's mastery of the mafia world. For, after I had spent a day in Chicago doing sunrise plugs with Sally and sunset photo-ops with Sam, I was taken on the second afternoon to a studio where I had been told I was to be interviewed for a documentary on organized crime by a well-known local producer. As it turned out, I was met by a lawyer of the ethnicity you would expect a lawyer to be who worked for Chicago's organized crime syndicate. He quickly startled me by complaining about "The Mafia at War," which he had judged to be libelous to all Italian-Americans. I responded that our portrayal of those who carried guns and happened to be Italian-Americans was not false because they actually carried guns, and proudly bragged about their ethnic linkages and alliances. But he was very vehement about his position and, had I been at the age I am now, I would have been frightened, but I was too young at the time to understand how "offended" he really was.

He went on to say that maybe one could get away with this kind of journalism in New York, but one definitely could not in Chicago and therefore that "this trash" would not be distributed in Chicago. What was more, he recommended that I get out of Chicago soon. He was not making idle threats for, at that time, many of the trucking companies in Chicago were owned by people who were sympathetic to other people who really did not approve of journalism that shed light on organized crime.

I hustled back to my downtown Chicago hotel room, telephoned my boss and asked him what I should do.

Replied Clay Felker, founder of *New York* magazine, not delaying more than a couple of beats, "I think you ought to get out of town as fast as you can."

I did, and right away. I canceled the remaining Chicago appearances and flew on to my next stop: sunny, beautiful Los Angeles, where I not only felt warm, but safe. If there was a mafia there, they did not know about me or care. They were probably too busy chasing starlets.

Looking back, there is obviously no question that I was threatened in Chicago but at the time, I would rather have forgone the honor. Nonetheless, it just goes to show how powerful journalism can be if it took a stand and went after entrenched interests. If it could shake up the deeply engrained fortress of a century-old crime syndicate, then imagine what it could potentially do to our political and economic establishment, and, more importantly, to shake out of the mind of an individual reader the accepted conventions of our society that may be against our best interests.

> Do you want to have excitement in your life? Then work for a hot magazine edited by a very hot editor and hold on—but sometimes for dear life!

Clay concentrated on the elements of a magazine that made people want to pick it up. He knew that all successful magazines have a unique identity and a title that is conveyed, at least at first glance, through the cover. Clay preached to us all that cover lines and headlines are ultimately at least as important as story text, for no matter how much time you spend researching and writing and rewriting and polishing a story, if you slap a headline or title on it that is unengaging, no one is going to read it. Only a minority of people read and absorb the full text of the piece, anyway; many more skim the title and captions and move on. So Clay's policy was to craft headlines and spotlight pull quotes and photos that conveyed a clear sense of the story, and enticed the reader to dive in.

IN MY CAREER, I have encountered many ethical breaches, and often, in well-reputed places. Ethics issues are the number one unaddressed issue of the news media profession.

When I was first hired at *New York* magazine decades ago, the magazine was so new that it lacked a stalwart advertising base and thus it could not pay its employees very much or hire too many of them. This led to the assemblage of a mostly female staff, as it was still the early stages of the women's liberation movement and women resigned themselves to being paid less than men.

The result of this at *New York* was that Clay was able to hire many women of tremendous drive, competence and brain power—Elizabeth Crow, who later became a top magazine executive at Gruner & Jahr and the editor of many women's magazines, launched her career as a *New York* secretary; Judy Daniels, also hired as a secretary, went on from *New York* to become the editor of *Life* and *Savvy*; and Gail Greene, who started as a humble reporter, became one of America's most outstanding restaurant critics, as well as a bestselling novelist (*Blue Skies, No Candy*—edited by her then-husband Don Forst).

I know I have left many out—but there were just so many notable women editors and writers. There were plenty of super-women at *New York*, though in the beginning, they were super underpaid. Even so, from that time on, it seemed to me, the role of women in the news media grew splendidly. Today, the media business, though far from perfect, is probably as good as any, and better than most, in opportunities for women. Yes, there are still problems, but the general progressive tenor of the media culture reinforces the proper ideal of fairness for all.

At *New York* in the early seventies, the feminist revolution was really getting into gear. Within just a few years, the magazine—with the help of young Glora Steinem, a staff editor—was to launch *MS. Magazine*, a feminist monthly. But in other respects, the feminists that Clay hired were somehow exceptionally feminine-looking. The office could have been the studio set of a *Vogue* photo shoot, as it was later to become the breeding ground for *MS.*, the first mass circulation feminist magazine.

In fact, the staff's gender balance became so skewed that one day, the great Dick Reeves, who had been the *New York Times* City Hall reporter until Clay lured him away, showed up at the office, surveyed the scene and said, "Clay, you have too many women here to put out a magazine in a city that has both male and female readers! You have to hire some guys!"

So I jokingly credit Dick for jumpstarting my career because it was not long after that I was hired.

But the truth was that the women of *New York* were essential to Clay. One of the most famous women that Clay brought on was Gail Sheehy, who also—surprise—got her journalistic start as a secretary. While at *New York*, Gail wrote a number of special pieces, among them the previously discussed "Red Pants" which not only made her famous but increased her market value tremendously. She soon had a book deal and penned the runaway bestseller *Passages* which sought to identify the predictable stages in men's lives.

Gail was an extremely ambitious and hardworking young woman, which was partially what made her such a good reporter. There is really no substitute for plain, grind-it-out hard work in journalism.

For *Passages*, she conducted more than a hundred interviews, and one day, asked me if I would be willing to sit for one as well. I figured she was interested in me for several reasons. In my mid-twenties, I was on the young side to be a "senior" editor at any magazine. I was also single, okay-looking (maybe ... by a (very) charitable estimation) and a somewhat mercurial guy, which for whatever my faults ensured I was not boring. So I said, "Sure, Gail. Why don't you come over for dinner and we'll talk for a couple of hours?"

Not that I figured I would be able to contain her interest for that long, but she was, after all, the known Significant Other of Clay Felker. And so it stood to reason that by giving her whatever time she wanted, I would avoid an insult not only to her, but also to Clay, who hired me. I liked my job and I liked Clay. Besides, as a journalist, I feel there is a particularly warm place in Hades reserved for those in my profession who resisted interviews!

There was a caveat though. I agreed to the interview on the one condition that Gail would, as they say in the news business, put significant enough "shade" on me so that I would not be recognizable in the final product. If I was going to tell her the truth, and that was the plan, I did not feel I could talk candidly about my mother, my father and my ordinarily pathetic relationships with women if I felt that people afterwards would come up to me on the street, point their fingers, laugh hysterically and then fall down, and perhaps die from laughter.

Gail (I had thought) agreed to this stipulation and so she came over for a meal and we talked. She left happy, and I went back to my life.

That is, until one December night, when I took a young woman to dinner. As the overwhelming forces of amour, vino and fate would have it, we ended up at her cute and nicely decorated place for the evening. The conversation was animated and pleasant.

"Oh, by the way, Tom, I saw your profile in this new book I just read! It was really weird, I must say. I didn't know you had to overcome all those family problems, and I really think you are a lot better-looking than she made you out to be."

I was enjoying her company so much that it did not even occur to me what she was talking about. I said something silly about how much of an honor it was for me to be included in John F Kennedy's *Profiles in Courage*, to which she laughed and said, "Tom, I know you're not in that book. You're featured in *Passages*."

My heart sank but I halfheartedly attempted to play it off. "Whatever would make you think that I'm in that book? I'm not even sure what it's about, to be honest with you."

"Tom, it's so clearly you in that book. You know you don't have to pretend with me! And it was written by Gail Sheehy, the famous writer with whom you work at *New York*."

My heart was pounding unhappily, angrily. "Do you have a copy here?"

"Sure," she said, and she got up from the couch to fetch it. Her brow was contorted in instant puzzlement as she brought it back to me. She did not understand the reason for my sudden mood change.

I started to read it, and I do not know whether I had too much to drink or not enough, but with each passing word, I descended deeper into despair and rage. After I had made it through a page or two, I looked up and said, "I have to leave. But can I take this book with me? I will buy you another one."

"I guess so, but what is wrong? Did I do something to anger you?"

"No, you didn't do anything. Gail Sheehy is a colleague of mine, and I agreed to be interviewed for her book only if I was significantly disguised in the published edition. I guess you would concur that there is no disguise."

With that, I stomped out of her apartment and onto West End Avenue. I was furious and I would have walked out naked, even though it was one of those perfectly brutal December nights in Manhattan. The city was in the bitter grips of a silent but determined snowfall. As I walked home through the gathering storm, I started reading and then re-reading the passage in *Passages* about me, and as I did so, I dismembered the book page by page (as if dissecting a diseased animal), depositing various chapters in various trash cans and refusing to even look for a cab. While I was truly furious, I was even more disillusioned, for it was then that I realized that there was no assurance that any promise a journalist offered would be observed as a matter of professional ethics.

I later came to see that Gail justified this out-ing of me (and others) with a disclaimer in the introduction of the published book, after, of course, she had interviewed us. It admitted that her sources had asked to remain anonymous, but trying to alter the professions of the sources and to change their geographical location "in an effort to avoid any possibility that a reader might recognize them" turned out to be difficult: "...The occupations that people choose and the places they live are too intimately linked with the personality that explains them and the fabric that shapes them," she wrote. "There is no such thing as a precise equivalent." Thus, she concluded, she would only change the name but not the identity.

And so I, Tom Plate, was presented to the world as "Tony," the man whose genetics in "a sort of do-si-do [had] caused him to come out short-legged and porky and also cursed with the kind of skin suitable for illustration in medical texts of the permanent ill effects of acne vulgaris." Nice, eh? (Dear Gail, I would rather have preferred it if you had described me as resembling "Red Pants"!)

Other details nailed the identity down to a certainty. "Tony" was a man who had gone to an Ivy League school and had written a book on the arms race; a man who currently was a freelance writer who had just released a new book on the mafia; and so on. Well, she sure had her facts right.

This, among other things, is why I was completely identifiable to all who knew me, superficially or otherwise. This is why they suddenly knew some of the painful details of my relationship with my family that I would have preferred to keep private. This is why when Gail asked me almost twenty years later if I would sit for her new book in the stages of men's lives, I politely declined, as much as I respected her talent.

Looking back, I think the idealism and arrogance of youth made this incident perhaps more painful than it should have been, but again, on hindsight, it was a very good lesson to learn early in my career and life: never trust a journalist unless you have something on him/her.

> There is no body of ethical rules within the profession of journalism that *must* be followed, just as there is no method of enforcing sanctions against those who violate standard ethical practises. Forget this at your peril.

But, let us forget about it. Gail was and is a real talent. I wish her continued success—but no more interviews!

HERE WAS THE WEEKLY working ritual at *New York*:

On Mondays, Clay would chair the story conference in a room with some secondhand sofas and run-down chairs. Clay was always (delightfully) feeding everyone—box lunches were always brought in, usually from some trendy café.

These meetings were important for three reasons. One was that the great Tom Wolfe would sometimes attend. He was as fun to meet as his work was to read. He was also one of the politest of living legends you would ever encounter—but perhaps too polite! He would never turn down anyone who had a strongly-felt story they wanted him to write. You would call him up and he would agree to do it. Weeks would go by and—surprise!—no story. That was not because he was irresponsible, but because he was too polite to say no to any editor, and because he was horribly over-committed. (Tom was always every editor's first choice for almost any story.)

The second reason these Monday meetings were vital was that they got everyone into the same space in the same time period. This was not so easy to do—maybe only Clay could have done it, with Milton Glazer hovering, too. Believe me, many of the young editors and writers in that room were dynamos. I joke today (to my students at UCLA) that if you look back on the *New York* magazine masthead of the early seventies, almost everyone on it is more famous (certainly) and richer (certainly) than I am. They were asked to accept assignments from the best known magazines throughout the world. But they would rarely miss one of Clay's Monday-morning, catered lunches.

The third value—beyond the obvious of consensus-building and direction-finding among the staff—was to be able to see Clay's directional editing skills. He had a charming way with talented, creative but neurotic designers, photographers, editors and writers that added up to a combination of Tyrannosaurus Rex bullying and Big Daddy coddling. His interaction at these meetings also demonstrated a truth about this magazine: this magazine was, notwithstanding the small but talented staff, all about Clay.

To illustrate, Milton Glazer, the great Push Pin Studios guru, would answer this way when asked by outsiders about the organizational structure of *New York*: "For starters, you see, we have this dictator...."

> Remember: never underestimate the insecurity of the person above you. He or she may have the fancy corner office and designer furniture and expansive expense account and monster boss-of-the-world title. But they

are likely to be as insecure as anyone and, given how much they have to lose, perhaps more insecure than most of us. Recommendation: always handle the person above you with special care.

Another way of describing the organizational architecture was to propose (as managing editor Jack Nessel often would do) a line like this:

```
x x x x x x x x x x x x
- - - - - - X - - - - - - -
```

The lower-case "x"s represent all the editors who are arrayed in a single horizontal line without any real hierarchy, and then the capital "X" represents Clay who would run left and right along the line like some crazy man. As one of the magazine's best editors, Jack Nessel, would put it: "The most influential editor is the one who talks to Clay last, ideally at the moment just before the decision has to be made."

These representations would apply as well, it seems to me, to virtually all relatively small-staff size magazines that hoist a Hitler or Eva Peron at the top. As for Jack's suggestion that Clay would change his mind a lot, well, it is true—he did, and this did drive us nuts. At a wonderful celebration of Clay two decades later at the Waldorf Astoria Hotel, written tributes were collected and framed into a booklet. Mine went like this: "Clay made working at the magazine fun. That's why it was so much fun for the ... readers. But Clay could also drive you crazy. I think I am still recovering." – Thomas Plate, editor of the editorial pages, the *Los Angeles Times*.

MAGAZINES ARE INHERENTLY and properly the product of the will of the editor. You cannot (well, maybe you can, but you should not) fault the boss for changing his mind, even if Clay's mind resembled a rugby team changing room more than a manicured garden of planted decision.

But in a weekly magazine, at some point, a decision had to be settled on and stuck with. The time issue is even more daunting when editing a daily newspaper, of course. Magazine editors might have a hard time being able to stay on top of a daily. One does not have enough time to change one's mind that often.

A free-flowing weekly like *New York*—with little more than the boundaries of Manhattan island as its central conceptual framework—required the constant hovering of a single sensibility. This is where having a dictator comes in handy. A magazine as lifestylized as *New York* cannot be run by a committee—it can only be run by egomania and will power.

Like any strong editor, Clay worked for a kind of communal relationship with his readers. He felt he could read their minds, and sense their wants and needs, and ease their pains. That was to suggest a constantly shifting sensibility—a small boat on a turbulent sea.

The editor's methodology for communing with readers was to spend at least as much time with people outside the office as in it. A typical daily routine for Clay would be an elegant breakfast meeting at either his spacious (by Manhattan standards) East 57th Street co-op apartment, or at some chic café spot. He might or might not get to the office before 11am or so. By 1pm, he would be at an expensive restaurant with a writer or a designer.

I noticed that when he left at night for a dinner party, he would often take the Third Avenue bus uptown instead of a cab. I asked him why the bus and not the cab, not to mention the limo.

In a cab, he said, you cannot see anyone else, except mistily through the window. In a bus, you can see how people are dressed, what they are reading, and even what they are gossiping about. An editor needs to get out of the office and find out what is going on—not hide behind the desk and make believe. An editor is both a judgment maker and a reporter.

One day, he called me into his office. He said he wanted to speak to me about something.

What about?

Your expense accounts.

Oh, God! I must have done something wrong. "What's wrong?" I asked. I was more than surprised; usually the total sum of my expense account at week's end was piddling: they reflected inactivity.

"You've got to get out of the office, Tom. I don't want my editors sitting at their desks over lunch having a conversation with their tuna fish sandwich. I want them to get out, meet people, get into the mood of the city—get energized, Tom! GET OUT THERE!"

I was happy to. But this was the first time an editor had ever called me on the carpet for low-balling on expense accounts. And it would be—trust me on this—the absolute last!

SINCE WE DID NOT REALLY HAVE a formal editorial conference room, we pack of editors would stand around an old unwanted ancient architect's table and, in sort of a college brainstorming session, come up with arresting language that would glue the eyes of the reader to the magazine like flies to fly paper. Clay would often look to me for cover lines. This was one of my (honestly, few) strengths. When I would come up with one, Clay would laughingly say, "Now that's the cliché we were looking for!" Praise with a funny put-down is sort of the ultimate compliment in Manhattan.

Six years after the magazine's founding, when the magazine became tremendously successful and had money for an actual fancy conference room, both the creative process and the magazine became more formal in tone and tonality, and I think the language of the journalism became a little less interesting. So my (wholly unsolicited) advise to anyone starting a magazine is this: whenever possible, keep the atmosphere casual, even somewhat recklessly informal; it is more conducive to free thinking and creativity. A formal conference room is the kind of corporate church in which the prime vestment is a business suit, and the lead song in communal hymnal is the protection of thy ass. Fight it, worship instead that free form atmosphere. Tangential thinking is not always a bad thing in the magazine world; but thinking outside the box is easier when there is no box. Most conference rooms are box-shaped, right?

Clay knew that all journalism is a mediated reality and his pitch was that the editor needed to make it a compelling, interesting, passionate reality. Not dull. Again, this is not a point generally taught in journalism school, save, surely, one: at this writing, Clay was director of the Felker Magazine Program at the University of California, Berkeley, which on the whole is easily one of the best journalism schools in the nation.

I hope he is passing along one particular point that he instilled in me: that, for a magazine, you do not need to have an absolute separation of the church and state in a magazine—that allegedly impermeable firewall between the financial and the editorial side. Publications are commercial; they must make a legitimate product and a legitimate profit. To paraphrase the late Sir David English, the legendary editor of the London-based *Daily Mail*, "If the editor-in-chief keeps his hands entirely out of the retail part of the store, then the likelihood is high that the entire operation will be taken over by those who stock it."

But again, this real-world model is not given to you in many journalism schools. What is generally taught instead is some fairy-tale version of a *New York Times* model. Maybe that is because one of the leading journalism schools in the United States is the Columbia School of Journalism, which is located in New York City and has a faculty that banners former *New York Times*, *Washington Post* and *Wall Street Journal* personnel.

The *New York Times* has been a very special newspaper with an extraordinary family behind it, and so serious problems will inevitably arise in attempts to replicate it or offer it up as anything other than the specific exception that proves the general rule. Over the years, the family was both willing and financially able to maintain the editorial quality and expenditures at a certain level even when times were tough. Most newspaper corporations are publicly traded—as *New York Times* is now—and thus want to keep profits up and expenditures down to protect against stockholder revolt. Until recently, though, the *New York Times* was almost sui generis.

I would like to close with a final observation about *New York* magazine. For all its flaws, superficiality, invented reality and commercialism, it is important to note that the formula that Clay concocted in turn spawned a magazine that was avidly looked forward to by more than 300,000 people each week. In New York, the most sophisticated, media-saturated city in America, to create a publication that people anticipate with almost as much delicious delight (if not more so) as much as they do a new episode of "Friends" or "Seinfeld" or "Desperate Housewives" is saying something. In this way, for the period of time that Clay ran *New York*, he really had in his hands a special magazine that stood out even in so frenetic a city as New York.

Ordinary journalism cannot reach or move people at the level of great sex or great music but, at its best, good vivid journalism can create a common focus that tickles the mind and the imagination at the moment it appears. And therein lies its value—not eternal value, but real contemporary worth.

And so in its own way, *New York* did (and perhaps continues to) perform, though its current crop of very talented editors and writers will surely understand my original-sin bias and loyalty, a laudable public service: it interests people in the issues, and thus offers an engaging, literate antidote to rampant indifference.

I HAD DRIFTED AWAY from the close family staff atmosphere of *New York* and into the solitary single-male writer's life in Manhattan. My own peculiar brand of institutional ADD had started to kick in and somehow I just started losing interest in the magazine.

This was mainly not anyone else's fault but mine. It was still a very good magazine; I just had lost interest in it. But—on second thought—perhaps Clay, whom I consider a good friend today, and whom I will always find fascinating, was partly to blame as well.

My endless personal insecurity was certainly not helped by the boss's habit of inviting Aaron and his girlfriend (the very delightful Sally Keil) out to his vacation place in the Hamptons virtually every weekend—but not even once, my then-girlfriend Lesley and me. Why? Had Gail convinced Clay I really was that ugly?! Was Lesley—a brilliant New York University law student and one of the sweetest persons in the world—no Pamela Tiffin? Who knows? And why did I care? Clay was entitled to his own weekend life; I was hardly the only staffer ignored.

I don't know why I cared but I did—deeply. Perhaps it was a sense of competitiveness with Aaron; perhaps it was the hurt that I felt it was causing Lesley. Perhaps I was insanely neurotic. Perhaps I liked Clay too much. But the fact of the matter is that when an editor seeks to create a warm family atmosphere with the staff, being asked to leave the dinner table before the dessert is served can be devastating, especially when your best friend is never excluded from the sweets.

I know, this was juvenile on my part. Whatever; irrationally, I started to drink, heavily—which I tend to do when I am unhappy; and then I started to resent my boss, foolishly and unwisely.

One day, I arrived at the office in Manhattan's East 30s at around 2:30am—but not that late out of lethargy or hangover but after spending all morning and lunch working on a special story about a hard-charging prosecutor for the magazine. Clay arrived at the building at the same time, saw me, and figured I had spent the night drinking. He even said that to me. I was so hurt and so devastated, I simply replied with a positive nod of my head. I wouldn't dignify the intimation with the truth. I was odd this way when I felt I was being wronged. I would just tune out and say, in effect, the heck with it.

I took refuge in writing. And so I wrote two more books for Simon & Schuster. One was a book about American policing with trailblazing top cop Patrick V Murphy whom I admired; another was a study of professional crime called *Crime Pays*! I also knocked out a novel titled *The Only Way to Go*. I thought it was terrible. In fact, it was terrible. But a major New York publisher published it anyway. If you read it, you would probably agree that it was ... terrible.

I lived in Manhattan with a Burmese cat named Mr C and a Tonkinese cat named Ruffian. To pay the rent, I did a lot of magazine work. My book, *Crime Pays!*, garnered a measure of critical notice and *Playboy* editors asked me to go down to the Caribbean to do a story. It was not exactly a difficult assignment to accept and *Playboy* was—and still is—exceptionally good and decent in its treatment to writers. Most people do not know that. I sent back some photos of young Caribbean women—and the editors wanted me to return to do a full shoot. But I was too full of myself as a young writer to imagine how I would lower myself into photography (pornography? I'm not that judgmental, and many years later I was to make friends with Hugh Hefner, the magazine's founder; I liked him, actually. He is very un-phony for a multi-millionaire. And his number two, Dick Rozenzweig, is a prince.).

In fact, during these late twenties years at *New York*, I was discovering a side to myself, as you might with yourself, that might be called tabloidian. Maybe there is a little bit of the tabloid inside all of our souls. That is why serious New Yorkers will read the *New York Times* in the morning but then, on the train ride home at night when their brains are fried, run their eyes over *The New York Post*, a terrific "we-have-no-class-and-we-are-proud-of-it" tabloid.

The tabloid of my soul allowed me to partake of the frivolities of Clay ("Milton, it's only a magazine") Felker. For *New York* magazine was more tabloidian in content than *Newsday*, the Long Island daily that was a tabloid in size but not in heart or soul.

One of *Newsday's* best editors was Don Forst, who sported a gargantuan tabloidian brain in a diminutive frame. Don was the kind of top editor a young journalist dreamed of becoming—irreverent, extremely comfortable with innovation, and funny as hell. He was to provide the next turn in my destiny.

It was through him that my media voyage was to take me to Los Angeles, but it might have stayed in New York, had I been a little more avaricious. One of my freelance outlets was, in fact, *New York*, which had been hit by a cyclone. Its name was Rupert Murdoch. To make a semi-long story as short as a snippet, Clay was basically pushed out the window and Murdoch gained control of the magazine. Clay was quoted as saying, "Rupert raped me!" And that was how I first met the Great Murdoch—with this terrible turn of events burning somewhere in the back of my mind.

During this period, the city was experiencing mysterious midnight fires in abandoned neighborhoods of the metropolis. Alien invaders landing on dry patches and sparking fires? Not exactly. But to get the full story, I received permission from the New York Fire Department to live for a week in a real fire house. This meant you got a bed, and you got to chip in to the daily food jar and got to eat some of the best home-cooked food in America. Believe me, all the clichés about firemen are true: they care for one another like family, they are in tremendous physical condition (remember the sexy firehouse scene in "Sex in the City"?), and they are—by and large—true heroes.

In the course of the research for the article, I was not only to go out on many midnight runs to put out fires, but in one of them, I was permitted (against regulations probably) to don a fire hat and gear, and enter a burning building. I did this only once, but a staircase fell on me that one time, and I almost got crushed and hence, did not go in again! But I was glad to have done it once. I would not exactly call it a jump-the-midget moment but it was true grit magazine reporting.

The story of the firemen was powerful. It told of how greedy or desperate landlords were hiring arsonists to burn down inner-city buildings for the insurance money when no tenants could be found. It was the New York Fire Department's job to put the fire out and arrest the firebugs.

The story was titled "Why Brooklyn Is Burning," but before it ran, I received a pleasant call from the magazine inviting me to join the editors left behind after the Great Clay Felker Bloodbath. Imagine my surprise when I walked into the conference room and there was Rupert himself. This was like the second week of his ownership.

"That's an excellent story on the arson-for-profit racket in Brooklyn, Tom," he said. Rupert is properly thought of as the consummate businessman. But the journalist's printer's ink runs in his psyche as well. Some of his publications today are simply outstanding, like *The Times Literary Supplement*, published out of London, which may be the most intelligent periodical in the English language. Some are simply hilarious and sometimes ludicrous, but always extremely well-done, such as the London *Sun* and the *New York Post*. Others, like *The Australian* and *The Times of London*, have their critics and their admirers. Frankly, in various meetings, especially those involving his brilliant Chinese-born wife whom I would run into at Asia Society conferences, I found Rupert easy to like, but then again, I was never one of his employees.

Rupert looked at the other editors, who were all of the female persuasion, "What have we got right now for the cover?"

The response was that it was about great sidewalk cafés.

Rupert looked at me. I knew what he wanted me to say, because he knew I was not dumb.

Here (if I wanted to have become editor of *New York* more or less on the spot) is what I should have said: "That's an excellent cover concept. It is sure to have wide readership and will attract advertising. It's *New York* magazine at its best. But, since Brooklyn is burning, and since probably most of those cafés will still be in business in two weeks, why don't we go with the city-burning-down for this week's cover before there's nothing left of Brooklyn, and then the Café Society story for next week, when it will still be as fresh as morning coffee?"

That was what I should have said. What I did say was, in fact, nothing.

Rupert looked at me slightly in disgust. I did not blame him. He gave me an open shot on goal and I would not even kick the football. Clearly, I was not the man he wanted.

Question: Dr Freud, why did I not pull the trigger?
Answer: Maybe your subconscious agreed with the architect.

Journalism that fails to engage people runs the risk of irrelevance; journalism that only entertains people degrades the value of serious purpose. And so locating an Aristotelian ethical mid-point on this precariously balanced plane of existence is the true art of responsible journalism. But—please note—such effort is no task for the scientist but for the artist. It is less achieved through measurement than instinct.

Famous People – and Me!

Taiwan's Annette Lu: A strong-minded woman who says exactly what's on her mind—and I do like that!.

Hong Kong's Tung Chee-hwa: A warm, sincere and lovable human being who had all the wrong stuff for a politician.

Japan's Keizo Obuchi (center) and his wife Chizuko: Obuchi was a fiendishly hardworking man who was to pass away months later of a heart attack from, doctors said, working too hard.

South Korea's Kim Dae Jung: A man who conveyed a sense of destiny (in this pre-election photo) that many fellow Koreans shared.

The late American choreographer Martha Graham: As elegant in person as in her dance designs.

America's Ronald Reagan during an interview at the Oval Office: Thank God Reagan's people were taping the interview too!

Prince Charles, also called the Prince of Wales.

Playboy empire founder Hugh Hefner: Though nicknamed by some of my students the "Prince of Darkness," he is actually a very generous and thoughtful man.

Singapore's Lee Kuan Yew: The man who was generally misunderstood in the US but otherwise is well appreciated around the world.

Singapore's George Yeo: One of modern diplomacy's brightest political minds.

America's Bill Clinton visiting with *Los Angeles Times* editors: Before meeting a group, he would memorize the names of everyone in advance—something I could never do!

Ireland's John Bruton in the prime minister's office in Dublin: A very thick skin is almost the most important quality required for this roughhouse job.

Australia's long-running Foreign Minister Alexander Downer: Utterly incapable of giving a boring interview.

Robert Kuok, one of the richest men in Asia, with his amazing son Ean: The family owns the *South China Morning Post* in Hong Kong, the Shangri-La hotel chain and various other businesses in the region.

Britain's John Major (and Pulitzer Prizewinning journalist Bill Tuohy, then of the *Los Angeles Times*) at 10 Downing Street: The incumbent prime minister sensed that the political end was coming soon with the ever-clever Blair hovering ahead waiting to eat him up!

David Laventhol (center), then publisher of the *Los Angeles Times*, looking at Carlos Salinas, then president of Mexico. "You can't change the religion," Dave would always say.

What my staff at *Newsday* really thought of me: When I left for the *Los Angeles Times*, they put up this electronic announcement for all to see in Times Square, New York!

ATHLETE'S CHOICE   AGFA ◆ FOTO-LAB ◆ AGFA

Chapter Four
London Calling:
Good Newspapers Don't Have to be Dull

As I said before, there is a little bit of the tabloid in all of us. We gossip around the water cooler or whisper to others (or even when just swishing around the dirt within our minds), especially when someone else loses a job (are we really sad?) or gets a promotion (and if it is not us, then we are really mad!) or goes through a divorce (couldn't happen to a nicer couple!).

Tabloid newspapers and magazines can be big money makers. They do not necessarily have to be skuzzy, though many are; they do not necessarily have to make up stories out of whole cloth, though many do; and they do not necessarily require you to compromise your integrity, though that was always the risk.

Two of the best lively newspapers anyone could hope to work for were *The Los Angeles Herald Examiner*, which (alas) went out of business six years after I left it for a markedly non-tabloidian job at *Time*, and *The Daily Mail*, which remains one of the strongest English-language newspapers in the world, though it is not in quite the same league as it once was under a gentleman to whom you are about to be introduced.

I wound up working for both because of the long-standing affection and mutual admiration between James G Bellows (Jim), the editor of *The Los Angeles Herald Examiner*, and David English, then the editor of *The Daily Mail* and by wide acclaim the greatest British editor of his generation. I was the happy recipient of their mutual admiration. Decades before, Jim had been the editor—in fact, the last editor—of *The New York Herald Tribune*. David was then a hungry young journalist from London.

David, who died in London some years ago, believed strongly in what he semi-seriously termed "trans-Atlantic journalism." The American and British brands of journalism, he believed, were enough alike, and yet just enough different, that one could jet across the water, sit down at an editorial meeting on either side, and before long fit in, contribute well and learn a lot from the exchange experience.

David had benefited from just such a personal exchange-student deal at *The New York Herald Tribune*. He worked the night copy desk, the wicked vessel through which all the stories to appear in the paper the next day were routed. At night, the pace of the editing could become frenetic. An import like David from London would ordinarily find such a job hard going but David was anything but an ordinary journalist. Under the pressure of the deadline, he was an absolute maestro.

At the night copy desk, David was special fun to watch. He was a knowledgeable photographer. His mind was lightning fast, his instinct as keen and his story-angle talons razor sharp. Perhaps his greatest editorial gift was his exceptional clarity of vision. His mind worked like a computer that knew what program would work best and he was happy with his employees if they gave this "human computer" exactly what it wanted (and was very outspoken in anger when the desired result was not forthcoming).

Personally, David was an absolute charmer and a bit of a rake. It was through Jim Bellows that I was to meet David and he became perhaps the single most important mentor in my professional career—and that is saying something because I have been so lucky to have several excellent ones indeed.

> You undoubtedly have heard much about the impact of mentors and probably a lot of it seems like hype. But do not make the mistake of underestimating the mentor factor. It can be huge in your life if you are lucky to find the right one and wise enough to let it happen.

HERE IS HOW my career happened to turn tabloidian, for an entertainingly bizarre period of time, anyhow.

Two years after I had left *New York* magazine, I received an intriguing offer from Jim Bellows and Don Forst, respectively the number one and number two of *The Los Angeles Herald Examiner*, to become the troubled paper's editorial page editor.

Offers from "troubled" publications, whether *The Los Angeles Herald Examiner* or *Family Weekly* or whatever, are especially attractive. New employers of such publications look for a "fix-it" capability and an insatiable appetite for innovation in their hires. That was where I usually came in.

The offer from Los Angeles was so welcome because I had, at that point, gotten weary of the freelance life in New York. The romance of not having a single or direct supervisor, of working twenty hours a day for four days straight and then not working for two weeks, had reached the point of diminishing returns. I wanted to get a job like a semi-normal person, if I could somehow manage to fool the world that I was semi-normal.

Don Forst, a wonderful editor with a wicked sense of humor, who was also only semi-normal, had been a colleague at *Newsday*. He was familiar with my work and recommended me to Bellows, who was a newspaper editor of uncommon flair for the great headline, the great writer and … let's face it … the flop.

As mentioned, Jim had been the last editor of *The New York Herald Tribune* as it died and had unsuccessfully tried to revive *The Washington Star*. Now he was being asked by the Hearst Corporation to revitalize Los Angeles' slow-dying *The Los Angeles Herald Examiner*. That he would do— for a time anyway. In the end, it died nonetheless. Up against the powerful and well-entrenched *Los Angeles Times*, what chance did Jim or anyone else really have?

I did not worry about corporate successes in those days; I worried only about personal failure. So I soon warmed to the task of revamping the paper's editorial pages and put together a whole new staff.

HIRING THE RIGHT PEOPLE is perhaps the hardest and most artful job in journalism (and probably anywhere else). When you go wrong, you often have to live with the mistake for months, if not longer; and when you go right, you wake up in the morning and cannot wait to get to work.

If I had any particular talents in journalism that were better than average, it was the ability to write a snappy headline; the capacity for recognizing, recruiting, nurturing and promoting talent; and perhaps the imagination to design non-boring editorial and opinion pages (the list of negatives is much longer—let's not go into that yet, okay?).

The hiring game requires a good nose, a measure of personal charm, and the ability to avoid conceit and insecurity. You should try (and try hard) to hire colleagues who are at least as smart as you. Hire dunces in order just to feel safe and secure in your job, and they will pull you down and eventually their mediocrity will pull the rug out from under your job. But hire the highest quality (and the funniest people, if possible) and you would have an office environment that would make you want to go to work every day and produce editorial pages people would want to read.

Jim and Don gave me a relatively free hand to hire a small staff at *The Los Angeles Herald Examiner*, a daily broadsheet that had lost its greatness long ago. Hired as editorial page editor, I came aboard and realized quickly the editorial pages were so bad, I could not make them worse. So with the new team, we made them better very quickly. Once again, it seemed, the more space an employer gave me, the more likely I was to handle the job well.

In a matter of just months, everyone agreed that our small staff was doing a great job. The number one paper had more people (ten times as many)—and they were very good people indeed—but we managed to hold our own.

Though the team was small, we had great people—a particularly great one was the late Sarai Ribicoff, a Yale graduate and niece of the late Connecticut senator. She was brilliant, won major national awards and was a dream to work with. Had she lived a full life, I tend to believe she would have wound up somewhere at the level of her generation's Meg Greenfield, the late great editorial page editor of *The Washington Post*, or Maureen Dowd, the op-ed diva with whom I was later to work at *Time*.

Life is not fair, John F Kennedy used to say, who was himself gunned down, and a decade and a half later, so was Sarai. A year after joining *The Los Angeles Herald Examiner* staff and writing some amazingly insightful editorials, she was gunned down by a robber outside a café in Venice, California. A young woman who had given passionately with her heart and soul to the cause of all minorities, even as she was born into one of Connecticut's most prominent families, she had perished while not even resisting the robber's efforts to tear off a piece of costume jewelry of value only to her.

When I arrived on the crime scene around midnight to identify the body, all life had left her, and she was no longer the Sarai we all knew because Sarai was everything life was meant to be. I asked the police for a moment to be alone to stare at her because probably as her boss and (perhaps, in my mind at least, as her first professional mentor—we had hired her right out of Yale) I had grown to care for her so much and so I wanted to be able to remember my last look at her forever. The cops were quite good about this, but, alas, in minutes, the media started to arrive (and God, how one hates the swarmy media when one is on the other side of the firing line), and then our executive editor Mary Anne Dolan showed up, noted how shaken I was, and suggested I back off and let her deal with the press. I was more than happy to do so. I walked away from the crime scene numb and crawling with fear about everything; my insides went to pieces.

It was only many months later that I realized how much a young person of such enormous talent changes you. It relates to a story I make my UCLA students suffer through today. Call it the "Puccini Theory of Life."

It goes like this. Either one is a true genius or one is not. I know I am not; are you? Perhaps you are—perhaps you have the celestial talent to compose arias that move listeners to tears decades or even centuries later; write magisterial novels that haunt readers' souls through eternity; or in a singular moment, have the scientific insight to change the course of physics or genetics. That would put you on the level of Puccini.

I am not on that level so I tell my students this: Maybe you are but perhaps you are not; so slow down, catch your breath, study hard but also enjoy life, respect your family, spend time with your loved ones. Only if you are a Puccini should you presume to require every minute of your waking (and perhaps sleeping) life in solemn devotion to your art. So let us stop stressing, become a good person, take the ups and downs in stride, and stop acting as if we were Puccini.

Alas, with Sarai, the world may have had some kind of Puccini in the making. We will never know. Her killer—one Frederick Thomas, 22—saw to that. He was sentenced to life imprisonment a year after the 1980 killing. Ironically, this man—from a minority group—murdered one of America's youngest journalists who from the outset of her career was determined to help minorities obtain fairness from American capitalism. Thanks to this murderer, however, there is now one less Puccini-like voice to be raised on their behalf.

Did I go too far with the Puccini analogy? Maybe, maybe not. A few months after Sarai's death, I was at an awards ceremony in Washington but I was not an honoree—the late Sarai was. I was there to pick up her Loeb

Award for the best economics journalism in America. This annual honor invariably would go to some veteran journalist at *The Wall Street Journal* or *Forbes* or *Business Week* or *The New York Times* or whatever. It had never gone to a Hearst paper, much less *The Los Angeles Herald Examiner*. But Sarai had won it, at the age of 22, little more than one year after graduating from Yale—and just after she was killed.

I recently re-read the tributes that appeared in her honor, in Yale publications, and in the Congressional Record. It was all familiar to me but I had forgotten all about the startlingly intense letter of recommendation I had written for her as part of her application for a Rhodes scholarship. I will not bore you with the exact language but looking back now, I see that Sarai was an exemplar of what every young good journalist should be, not only because she was so caring about the issues but also because she was so scholarly about them. Sarai was, really, the original "deadline scholar," and living proof of the essential value of a superior education in order to pursue a proper career in American journalism.

I am sorry, folks, but I cannot tell a lie. A bachelor's degree from some semi-joke school is just not going to hack it unless you want to remain a hack. Sure, chase all the ambulances you want, if that is all you want to do with your journalistic career; but if you want to chase history or the undulations of the US prime rate or a major social trend with anything approaching actual understanding, you need to be well educated, you need to study hard (and harder and harder).

American journalism all too often skates over the issue of requiring higher education for its reporters and editors. If the major redeeming value of the news media is its contribution to political debate and the informing of the public—this, in the de Tocqueville sense of the press being essential to democracy—then each year, this worthy goal becomes ever more difficult to realize if the issues are getting harder and harder, and the journalists, on the whole, are not getting any smarter. American journalism needs more Sarai Ribicoffs, not fewer.

STILL ON THE TOPIC of smart young people. Another wonderful young hire at *The Los Angeles Herald Examiner* was the multilingual Teresa Watanabe (who eventually worked her way up the journalistic career chain to top jobs at the *Los Angeles Times*). Her editorials on stereotyping Asian-Americans won major awards and her fabulous personality won her legions of friends.

Then we had the extremely capable Connie Stewart (we stole her from *The Des Moines Register*, an excellent paper, and she is now an entrenched editor at the *Los Angeles Times*) and local-boy-makes-good John Hollon, now an editor with Crain Communications.

Thanks to all of the above, we garnered the Best Editorial Award three years running from the Greater Los Angeles Press Club. Frank Dale, the kind-hearted publisher of *The Los Angeles Herald Examiner*, ordered up a house ad to run in the newspaper that pointed out, delightfully and self-servingly accurately, that "winning three first place awards in a row has never been done before in the 23-year-history of the club."

One extremely interesting staffer was Gina Hearst. She was the sister of fellow heiress Patty Hearst, also the granddaughter of publishing magnate William Randolph Hearst. Patty became famous in 1974 when she was kidnapped by a young revolutionary group, and, while in captivity, joined her kidnappers in robbing a bank. She was convicted and went to jail, but a nationwide "Free Patty" campaign led to her receiving a presidential pardon.

Her sister Gina was much lower profile—more quiet, quite beautiful. But I have to say right off the bat that I did not want to hire her. She had been pushed on Jim Bellows by Hearst headquarters in New York City, and then he had pushed her off on me. I insisted that the department then go one-up in staffing because I had a huge bias against the sons and daughters of rich families. Having been educated at Ivy League schools (but—my defense!—I was a scholarship student), I knew the rich only too well and generally despised those who had more money in their pockets even before they could spell "pockets" or count to 25.

As it turned out, I was happily wrong about Gina. She alone caused me to revise my bias—somewhat. Hardworking, honest and a team player, she invariably gave much more than she received. As a result, in later years, I was to try to take a far more nuanced view of the rich and tended to treat every individual as unique.

You might be surprised, by the way, at how minimal was the corporate interference of Hearst in the editorial page line. New York would send out these generally awful "Hearst" editorials—we used to call them "The Chief

Speaks" (that is, William Randolph Hearst, Jr)—which Jim was forced to start on page one. The first time I got one of these editorials, I asked Jim what I was supposed to do with it. He replied that I could throw it out if I wanted to—which is what I usually did.

But at one point, the issue of the release on parole of Patty Hearst came up and I must say while New York/Hearst lobbied Jim and me heavily to run a "Free Patty" editorial, Gina, Patty's sister, never said a word, not one. Ordinarily, Jim and I would have defied the corporate "request," just for the hell of it. We were both pretty hireable so what the hell? But because of Gina, and her alone, I felt differently about the issue and told Jim so. I think, actually, he was relieved that I felt this way because the pressure from New York to run such an editorial was understandably intense.

Corporate pressure from New York on the editorial page was much less prevalent than I had anticipated. Robert Danzig (Bob), in Hearst headquarters in Manhattan, was the head of the Hearst Newspaper Division and it is true he would sometimes telephone me directly. There were two reasons for this. One was that he and Jim were like a constantly quarrelling couple and after a year or so, Bob simply gave up trying to have a civilized conversation with Bellows who was often in a rage about corporate under-funding of the challenge to *Los Angeles Times*. The second is that Bob and I liked each other, in part because Bob genuinely liked our editorial pages—and was delightfully unshy about calling me and saying so. So, instead of feeling corporate pressure, I felt corporate support.

To be sure, I was not stupid. When the Patty Hearst pardon/freedom issue surfaced, I realized it would relieve pressure all around if *The Los Angeles Herald Examiner* were to take an upfront position in support. About this position, I had few moral qualms. Patty was not exactly a threat to the community or a likely candidate to ever again brandish a gun in a bank. Sure, her wealth and connections got her legal appeal a measure of attention otherwise unavailable to most people but so, what else is new? I decided to take Gina out to lunch and there I told her what we planned to do and asked her for some background on the issues—figuring that she would know much more about them than anyone, except possibly Patty. And that was how the *Herald* was to publish the single best-informed, non- knee-jerk "Free Patty" editorial in America.

Sure, a lot of people called me and Jim sell-outs. But I knew where the decision had come from—it came from us; I also knew that NYC/Hearst Corporate had been under a lot of family pressure and they only passed some of that on to us. Direct corporate interference in editorial pages is greatly overstated, in my experience, though hovering daily. My best advice is to keep changing your phone number and the locks on your doors!

I loved working with Gina and the rest of the team. As a result, the editorial pages had been enlivened and enriched (author says modestly). Meanwhile, I was having a great time, so were Don and Jim, and I got to work with Teresa, John and Sarai—but with each of them, for differing reasons, not long enough. The whole point of the above? Life is definitely worth living when you are allowed to live your office life with young people of talent, commitment and—how shall I put it?—charming goofiness, with which I easily fit in.

Oh, yes, I did meet Patty Hearst, but only once. She seemed nice, actually, not as shy or nice as her sister—but definitely no menace to society. I think her being released from prison while continuing to report to the parole board was the right decision for America to make. Of course, there are a lot of people in our prisons who are not Hearsts who ought to be out, too. But life is not fair at all, alas.

Just ask those of us who loved Sarai.

> With whom you get to work is at least as important as where you get to work. Without good and challenging people around you, you will sink like the "Titanic," emotionally as well as professionally. If you are going to be allowed to personally hire those with whom you are to work, try to get a sense of who they are before you commit them to being where they are Monday to Friday. Having fun and competent people as office colleagues is worth ten per cent of your paycheck ... at least.

ALTHOUGH I GOT ALONG with almost all of my colleagues, I hit it off exceptionally well with both Don and Jim, because they hired me precisely for the purpose of getting new impact from the pages, and they were anything but afraid of stirring up controversy. At places like *Time* and later the *Los Angeles*

Times, it was almost always my experience that in response to controversy, people typically jumped under their desks and said, "Oh my God! What did we do wrong?" This attitude would surface whenever we ran a piece that was the slightest bit controversial. Imagine that. Why must a good newspaper or magazine be dull?

To their great credit, Don and Jim had brains that were hard-wired in just the opposite way. They understood and accepted that a certain and unavoidable percentage of decisions in the news media was destined to be inherently controversial because journalism is news always in a great huge hurry. Journalism is little more than history put down as a terribly rough first draft as journalists scurry to process fast-moving events and coherently present issues that are sometimes immensely complicated and almost impossible to simplify. With deadlines looming, misperceptions, distortions and even blanket errors are ever present.

Even so, Jim, who generally played the newspaper game as well as anyone does, and Don, who absolutely got a chemical high off outrageous controversy, would welcome someone trying to work with a controversial topic and they would not distance themselves from the mess if and when an ensuing storm broke. This was in stark contrast to later experiences at both *Time* and *Los Angeles Times*. Generally, it was a very lonely moment when one sticks one's neck out for a controversial story and then has to brave the resultant fury alone, without a scrap of institutional support to speak of. As John F Kennedy wisecracked after the infamous Bay of Pigs fiasco: "Failure is an orphan; success has many fathers." (Okay, so the comment was not originally Kennedy's, but that in itself makes the point.)

A GOOD NEWSPAPER not only need not be dull, it need not have to do bad to be good either. *The Los Angeles Herald Examiner* looked to take controversial positions in the community in an effort to differentiate its product from the number one and to provide the community with a service by not Xeroxing the *Los Angeles Times* on every issue—or even on many. The *Los Angeles Times* was a formidable national and international newspaper (it still is) but its heart was not in Los Angeles, and the brightest metro desk reporters would only feel rewarded career-wise when they were promoted to the national or foreign desk. In other words, for the most part, reporters who remained in Los Angeles to cover the city (local news) were not regarded by upper management as future stars unless they were very young, or there were special circumstances; conversely, reporters who escaped from local assignments were winners. The logical conclusion was that the *Los Angeles Times* valued its foreign and national coverage more than its local coverage, which was true; but it also suggested that the paper tended to under-value readers in those areas of the community that were not so much interested in international trends or national issues as local issues such as crime in the streets, police corruption, racism (police or otherwise) and the inadequacy of city services.

Moreover, because the *Los Angeles Times* paid its staffers well, few staffers lived in any of those Los Angeles communities where those issues were paramount, and many traveled nationally and internationally, and had aspirations to live elsewhere as was reflected in the *Los Angeles Times* coverage.

In my later years as an editor at the *Los Angeles Times*, I found very few career journalists at the *Times* who did not fit this stereotype. One was Janet Clayton who even educated her lovely daughter at an inner-city Los Angeles school. She understood the real Los Angeles as well as she understood the *Los Angeles Times* whose staff she joined immediately upon graduation from the University of Southern California. When I was to leave my position as editor of the editorial pages of the *Los Angeles Times* in 1995, she was my successor and I was happy for the paper because of it.

But in the late seventies, an African-American woman had about as much chance of becoming a top editor at the *Los Angeles Times* as a PLO leader had of heading the Jewish Defense League. It was, with limitations, a great paper but it was a white paper, and that gave the cagey Jim Bellows—the paper's top editor—the opportunity he was seeking.

It fell into his lap one morning as he was looking over the newswire. Spotting a little story from City News Service (a sort of local Associated Press), he came over to me and showed me the little item. One had to read it twice to get it. Stripped down, it went like this: police, responding to a utility company's request, visit an address in a low-income neighborhood of Los Angeles in an effort to collect a late bill; woman (black) opens the door with butcher knife in hand; two cops (white), armed, pulled their guns, order her to drop knife; she refused, they shot her, Eulia Love is dead. End of story.

What do you think? asked Jim, looking at me.

Story of the year, I answered, especially if the *Los Angeles Times* ignores or buries it.

They will, said Jim. Off he went into the newsroom, launching the story of the year: how a pair of white cops, armed with guns, shot down and killed a poor black woman unable to pay a utility bill—and she was armed with nothing more than a knife.

Bellows ratcheted up the news side, sending as many young reporters as we had, which was not many, out onto the streets of Los Angeles to get this big story. (Don Forst would liken the deployment force of *The Los Angeles Herald Examiner's* city room to that of the Afghan guerillas fighting the army of the Soviet Union, that is, the *Los Angeles Times.* Bring out our big guns, he would joke, as a big story was breaking: "Snap, crackle and pop.")

On the editorial page side, my little staff would crank up an editorial every other day. Eventually, the *Times* noticed all this and began covering the story, which meant, eventually, that the Los Angeles Police Department noticed and began a true investigation. In other words, the little paper pushed the big paper into doing its job. Bravo, Jim!

GOOD PEOPLE make for good jobs. The importance of a pleasant and engaging personality to motivate those around you (especially neurotic, creative talent like yourself) cannot be underestimated. I was up to my ears in the arduous redesign of *The Los Angeles Herald Examiner's* decrepit editorial pages and tired beyond belief, but when Jim (Charm Inc.)—Don had by then left for another Hearst paper, in Boston, called *The Boston Herald*—asked me to captain a small team covering the Democratic National Convention in New York City and the Republican National Convention in Detroit in 1980, I did not hesitate for a second. Even though I was being pulled off one job midstream, so what? This was a great opportunity and because of the team environment Jim was creating in which we all were pulling for a happy common goal (embarrass the *Times*, at all times!), why be a sour puss? Besides, he knew how to reel in my ego: he asked me to captain the team.

So I went off to Detroit for the Republican Convention and wrote some pieces, and, frankly, some of them were damn good. But they were nothing as compared to the work done by my colleagues, including the award-winning journalist Rick Du Brow whose columns on television were widely read in Los Angeles, political reporter Linda Breakstone, superstar gossip columnist Wanda McDaniel and Los Angeles-based editor Mary Anne Dolan who packaged everything back at the home office so well.

We worked together as a team and the result was better than average by far. You see, almost all the clichés about teamwork in newspapers are true—the teamwork cliché being less true in magazines.

One day, I received a wholly unexpected phone call. It was from Tom Johnson, the immensely likable publisher of the *Los Angeles Times* (later on to head CNN News), arguably the better paper than ours by far, but inarguably the only profitable one. Out of the blue (he had spoken to me but two or three times since I took up *The Los Angeles Herald Examiner* job), he telephoned to say that he thought our little team did a better job than the monster-size team fielded by *Los Angeles Times*. That was some moment for me! I responded to the genial publisher of our competitor by using a line I heard from Ted Sorenson, John F Kennedy's legendary speechwriter, who once taught a foreign policy seminar at Princeton: "Your compliment is unarguably excessive but who am I to argue?"

A supportive word of that quality from a person of the caliber of Tom Johnson makes so much difference to life. People sometimes say when given a compliment: "Just put it in the paycheck." I understand the sentiment; people have families to feed, mortgages to pay out, sports cars to finance and maybe even vital charities to support. But not everything can be measured out in dollars and cents and stock options; true life is not just bottom lines but special moments, special people and lifelines to inspiration. Besides, journalism is not the place for you if money is all you want out of life.

Now, I would like to introduce you to the most unforgettable journalistic character I have ever met. His name was David English. He is, extremely unfortunately, dead now. But when he was alive, he almost defined life as a journalist—and he practically defined the meaning of newspaper life, which is a special (if inherently limited) way of living.

He was the editor of *The Daily Mail* of London, a large circulation (about two million; by contrast, the *Los Angeles Times* today is less than a million), mid-market, quality tabloid. He was also a monumentally high-impact aerobic mentor for me.

Some definitions here: A quality tabloid is different from a sex and violence rag sheet. There are plenty of the latter types, to be sure, but quality tabloids can thrive too. Probably the most obvious example internationally is *Le Monde*, the Paris-based paper that is a tabloid in size but whose content is at least as excellent as the best broadsheet. In America, probably the best example of a superior tabloid is *Newsday*, the Long Island daily that over the decades has been a serious and substantial newspaper. (Whether it will thrive on journalistically under the new management of the Tribune Corporation of Chicago remains to be seen.)

In London, *The Daily Mail* (which its proprietors described as a "compact" instead of a tabloid) aimed for a mid-market readership and a very large circulation. Its direct competitor in the United Kingdom was *The Daily Express*. Under David's editorship, *The Daily Mail* was to surge past *The Daily Express* and become the dominant mid-market compact in Great Britain.

His exceptional talent notwithstanding, Sir David was hardly without his critics. John Lloyd, the *Financial Times* editor, once put it well: "Under editors such as David English ... and Kelvin MacKenzie, tabloids such as *The Daily Mail* and the *Sun* created a culture in which editors, and even writers, deliberately created the mental worlds they wished to project on their readers, then told the reporters to find the facts to fit them to. Some rarely or never met the politicians and other public figures about whom they wrote [as if] scared of diluting the purity of their disgust."

The criticism is entered here for perspective but I do think it is a bit overdrawn. Fleet Street is Fleet Street, an avenue of vicious competition and broken dreams. David was, for most of two decades, simply better than the competition operating in that special intense environment. What was more, David was a prodigious behind-the-scenes reporter, calling members of parliament and even of cabinet to chase down stories or confirm putative exclusives. As for averting the eyes of the politicians whose public images they concoct, I do not know about the editors of the *Sun* (a deeply silly if highly entertaining paper that cannot hold a candle to *The Daily Mail*, even today), but David was a tireless socializer, party-goer, high-level snooper and visitor to politicians' lairs. Indeed, as editor of *The Daily Mail*, he called on Prime Minister Margaret Thatcher at 10 Downing Street, the prime minister's official residence, so often one might have thought him a member of cabinet. But David was first and foremost a journalist and that means, among other things, maintaining some measurable closeness to reality.

David used to date his friendship with Jim from the night Jim sauntered over to the night copy desk of *The New York Herald Tribune*, where David briefly labored, with the inevitable cigarette dangling from the Ian Fleming cigarette holder, and bluntly demanded to know who had penned the headline the previous day on a story about Brooklyn, which yet again wanted to secede from New York City.

Most of the night copy editors cowered but what they did not anticipate was Jim's delight with the headline. Journalists sometimes forget how vitally important are great headlines (or, as they called them at *Time*, "titles"). A correspondent can spend days (even weeks) on a story and editors (and sometimes lawyers) can devote endless hours to manicuring the final product (and making it libel proof as well as bullet proof)). But after all this effort, the copy desk, often operating against the insanity of the deadline, will slap a headline (or title) that fails to do justice to the editorial product by not engaging the instant attention of the reader.

The angle of the story in question—that the borough of Brooklyn, always threatening to break away from Manhattan in order to maximize local control, was really, really serious about it this time—was captured by the headline: "Brooklyn: Not Just Whistling 'Dixie' ". This was perfect—bingo!

So when Jim (scarcely able to hide his enthusiasm) inquired as to who wrote it, someone raised his hand and said "I did," but with a distinctly English accent. Jim was totally taken aback. "Who are you?" he asked, forgetting. "My name is David English," was the reply.

Jim was amazed that a Brit could come in and, in the space of a few weeks, capture such a silly nuance of American social life, history and culture in one super, nifty touch. Suffice it to say they became fast and good friends immediately. Jim was to regard David as the greatest newspaper editor he had met outside of the US; for his part, David was to liken Jim to the Civil War general who, though vastly outnumbered by the Army of the North, would lead an insanely bold charge up the hill, and sometimes capture it, against all the odds.

And so when Jim—this is now years later after the golden years of the late lamented newspaper, *The New York Herald Tribune*, which died in the late sixties—heard that David was also to be in Detroit leading his *The Daily Mail* convention team, he suggested I look him up. But I had no idea what to expect. I had no idea he would be so amazing.

The organizers of the Republican National Committee had ensured that the foreign press corps were far away from their American counterparts. So, looking for Mr English, I meandered my way over to their cramped quarters and after some time, located David and introduced myself.

David was not especially tall, perhaps my height of five feet eleven inches. But he was elegant in a conservative business suit, blue tie and white shirt—very British indeed. He always possessed (and it was a quality that almost overwhelmed you whenever you were in his presence) that thermodynamic twinkle in his eyes that bespoke of unexpected story ideas, a little bit of mania, a great deal of charm, a ready snap of wit and perhaps a wicked conspiracy or two!

"You know, David," I said, "I don't know what you think of this proposition but I'm stationed with the Hearst newspapers over in the American camp, and we have so much more space and many more desks than we can ever use. By contrast, you seem pretty cramped here in the cage of the foreign press zoo. I know if I were in England, having to cover a Labour Party convention, I wouldn't want to hang out with American journalists; really, they wouldn't know much that I didn't already know. But you English, on the other hand, would be able to help me understand the politics and nuances of what was going on in a way that I could never fathom by hanging out with mere Yanks.

"So, I don't know whether this appeals to you or not but if you want to move your people in with us, we could hang out together, and you could read our copy, since you're not in direct competition with us. There may be some quotes or lines you might like to use. If so, please be our guest. We would take it as a compliment."

David, to my surprise, laughed, thought a few seconds and then said to his team, "Come on, everyone. Let's go hang out with the vulgarian Yanks!"

So that is how *The Daily Mail* jumped across the pond, so to speak, and moved in with us, however temporarily, for the convention.

I became instantly drawn to David's charm and energy, as did almost everyone who has ever met him; and we all had a wonderful time covering Ronald Reagan's presidential nomination.

Now, nominating conventions are not what they used to be, perhaps; invariably, there is little drama these days, with the ticket pretty much decided during the primary season and thus the reporters had to splash about like fish out of water to manufacture drama and stories. It seems to get more and more like this every fourth year—very dreary.

Even so, conventions (especially a Democratic one, because the delegates tend to be younger and the parties more fun, even slightly wild) in effect become huge journalistic reunions. It is absolutely amazing how little social/sexual trouble I managed to get into at these things; there must really be something terribly wrong with me! Fun-type trouble was always so easy to find, especially at allegedly serious political conventions.

The Reagan convention of 1980 (sorry to date myself, but this was when I was ... er ... 24 years old ... please trust me) was actually pretty interesting. There was a struggle for control of the party's central ideology and though Reagan, the former Republican governor who positioned himself as a rock-ribbed magazine cover conservative, was the slam dunk choice for the top spot, a bit of intrigue surrounded the vice presidential slot. At least the press made it into an intrigue; what other story was there?

The early favorite was former CIA director, and career diplomat and politician George H Bush. But certain elements of the party's rightwing thought him soft and wishy-washy, as if almost a (dreaded) "moderate." Others felt he lacked stature. Thus, a movement began to draft Gerald Ford who had lost four years before to Jimmy Carter in a squeaker. Brokering the effort was Henry Kissinger, the foreign-born former secretary of state. He was pitching the deal to both Ford and Reagan as a kind of "co-presidency."

David liked the idea immediately and thought it would fly. No surprise—in Europe, a separation of the head of government from the head of state is common, but it is not in America, because the two were as one. "It won't fly," I said to David. "It's an un-American idea. It's too European. The whole reason America came about, remember, was to be unlike Europe."

Mystery swirled around who would be Reagan's running mate. I still thought it would be Bush. He was the perfectly rational choice—smart, safe and competent, if lacking sizzle. But for sizzle, the Republicans had the Gipper. That was why this otherwise perfectly rational convention would make the perfectly rational choice for number two.

The day before the nominee was to be chosen, I decided to shake things up a little and so wrote an "authoritative" lead opinion essay about why the nominee had to be George Bush.

I then had to endure a few tense moments, and a bit of David at his competitive best (worst?). For, Bush's chances seemed to fade as the moment of decision neared by the hour. When I walked into the press box that afternoon, David was sitting there reading my lead piece bannered across the top of the Los Angeles newspaper, shaking his head, scoffing at my call that Bush would be the number two on the Reagan ticket—as if I were the second coming of the village idiot.

"Good God, Tom! When Jim realizes what you have done to spoil his otherwise splendid reputation, he'll fire you! But don't worry," he smiled wickedly, "I'll hire you anyway, though at a much lower cost, as your value will have been so vastly diminished!"

I really was out on a limb in absolutely proclaiming Bush the inevitable vice presidential nominee. Fortunately, however, the prediction turned out to be bang-on correct; and when finally the news came at the eleventh hour that, after all the back and forth, Bush was Reagan's man, I tried not to glow too obnoxiously (but this was tough for me, what with my ego!).

David came round to congratulate. I tried to be gracious and humble. But Wanda McDaniel, then our wickedly resourceful society reporter, said afterwards that I looked like a cat that had swallowed about only a thousand canaries. Rick Du Brow, our TV critic, laughed so hard I thought he might wind up in the hospital.

This was definitely a major jump-the-midget moment in my life.

Well, hey, David had, after all, been needling me all day about my "ill considered" George Bush column. (In 1991, David threw a luncheon for me in London and asked me whether Bush or Clinton would win the 1992 presidential race. When I said Clinton, David again suggested that he worried about my sanity. But, after another correct political prediction, he learned to listen just a little bit more carefully to the Yank! After all, I wasn't always just whistling "Dixie," was I? Three years later, in London, David was actually asking me for another prediction: whether Tony Blair would ever become prime minister. I said yes, certainly. The rest, as they say, is history.)

I RETURNED TO LOS ANGELES totally full of myself after having met David and having had such a good time. I also returned with a personal invitation from the editor of *The Daily Mail* to come to London as a guest journalist. He envisioned me working as Visiting American Editor, writing pieces and organizing projects. I would stay for a month or two, using much unused vacation time and some sabbatical, and relying on the graciousness of Jim Bellows, assuming he would react positively and give me leave.

I was surprised how warmly Jim greeted the idea. If I had not known better, I might have thought he was trying to get rid of me! He was very supportive and, flattered that David would covet one of his top editors, offered to have the paper cover my transport costs as well as proffer some expense money. I could not have asked for a more generous and understanding man to report to.

Later, I was to realize there was a hidden agenda here, and even much later, I was to realize there is almost always a hidden agenda when a corporation is especially nice to you.

> There is no Santa Claus, Jim Bellows used to say to me. I never realized what he meant until it was too late. But you should—before it is too late for you. He is right: there *is* no Santa Claus, at least in the corporate media world.

I WAS TO LEARN A LOT in England. I learned, for one, that British editors placed a higher premium on having fun than their American counterparts. For example, in London, it is not unprecedented for a hoax to be openly perpetrated by one newspaper onto another. Indeed, it is often a coveted feather in one's cap when one is able to pull it off.

The best example I know of this trickery concerned an editor and a pompous columnist from a rival paper. I had befriended a British editor whom I came to adore. He was later to become a top editor on Fleet Street, then the generic name for the competitive British newspaper industry. I offer the following story as a Fleet Street legend but there surely is more than a little truth to it. It was told to me by a friend and "reliable source" (oxymoron) who was a prominent editor in London.

The story goes like this. My friend was editing a major British paper and everything was going well, but he was looking for a special angle to play.

One day, a great big opportunity fell into his lap. It was a typically rainy London morning, and in trots the excited features editor of his paper—let's call her Samantha Tillingham—asking for a word with the editor-in-chief. "Sir, I know we rarely deal with freelance writers but a young woman who is clearly outstanding has presented herself in my office. She has a particularly unusual idea for a feature that I think you'll be sorry to have missed."

If you are in the newspaper business, you would know that no editor-in-chief appoints a features editor who has seriously suspect judgment. So he said, "Of course. Bring her in."

A few minutes later, a vivacious and obviously bright young woman strode into the boss' office. The editor-in-chief, aside from being instantly overwhelmed by Michelle's stylish entrance, was, as a seasoned newspaperman, interested to see what else she had to offer. Once they were all settled down in chairs, Samantha turns to Michelle and said, "Ms Jones, I'd like you to share with Stewart your feature idea. It's so original and you deserve full credit for coming up with it."

Michelle smiled sweetly and said, "Thank you for your kind words, Samantha. I'd be happy to. I should start with the fact that I'm a sociology major at Radcliffe, which as you know is the women's college at Harvard University. As this Fall will mark the beginning of my senior year, I've recently spent a lot of time mulling over possible topics for my thesis, and I've settled on the employment sociology of Pigalle, the red-light district in Paris. I plan on taking an ethnographic approach—meaning, living amongst my culture of study—and so I've taken a job as a stripper in a club there. I'll be doing serious research, including interviews with the strippers, proprietors, and patrons of the district.

"In designing this project, it occurred to me that this experience could produce a pretty funny piece of journalism. You know," and then she scribbled across the air in front of her an invisible headline: " 'American Businessmen in Paris Frequent Sex Clubs, Buy Crummy Cheap Champagne, Pay a Thousand Dollars for It, Get Drunk, Fall Down and Put It All Illegally on Their Expense Accounts.' Might you possibly be interested in a story like that?"

Stewart shifted a little closer to his desk and said, "You mean the story 'I Was a Teenage Stripper in Paris and My Very Hot Lap Dances Were Paid For by the Corporate Accounts of America's Business Elite'?"

Michelle smiled ever-so-sweetly again and said, "Exactly."

It was the editor's turn to grin. "I would love to have that story."

Stewart's thought was that all Europeans, generally speaking, absolutely loved it when Americans fell on their faces. This is exactly why Jerry Lewis was always more famous in Europe than he was in America. The bulk of his act centered on being a bumbling American idiot. Europeans regarded that career-long ploy a credible portrayal of the American character and thus reacted to it with more enthusiasm than Americans did.

So Stewart said, "I'm very interested in your story, Michelle, but I can't officially authorize the assignment because you don't have a prior track record as a journalist. It wouldn't be proper to give you an advance or—"

"That's okay, Mr Editor. I just wanted to know if the story was of interest to you."

"Let me put it to you this way, young lady. If you write this story, I personally will read it."

Michelle, being a bright girl, figured she was way ahead of the game at this point. She had engaged the keen interest of one of Fleet Street's most brilliant editors. "That's all anyone can ask for."

After the niceties and the goodbyes, Michelle took leave of the two journalists, who then looked at each other and kind of giggled. Wouldn't it be great if ... but they figured they would never see Michelle again. Her story was too good to be true.

The end of the summer arrived and, much less predictably, so did Michelle's article. Stewart, as promised, read the piece personally and the next day had Samantha come by his office.

"This is one of the funniest damn things I've ever read, Samantha! God, those Americans are obnoxious—what boozers and lechers! What great stuff! Let's get our Paris photographer to get some pictures of Pigalle and we'll make a big splash of it—a banner across the top of page one and splash the whole shebang across the centerfold. This is going to be great! Let's do a television promo too."

When the story ran the next week, all of London loved it. It was the one story everyone was talking about.

A few days later, Stewart called Samantha into his office and asked, "Where is young Michelle now?"

"She's about ready to leave Paris and head back to Boston."

"Have her stop off in London, on our tab, of course. I want her to do another story. We'll pay the extra airfare and put her up at Claridge's. Tell her we're pleased as punch with the piece. Don't forget to pay her double for it."

So Michelle arrived back in London and shortly thereafter, met with Stewart and Samantha once again in the paper's offices. Michelle appreciated the newspaper's prominent display and promotion of her exclusive on Parisian strippers, not to mention the generous payment for the article, but said she had not one new idea and had to return to Harvard soon. But Features Editor Samantha had an idea—did she ever! She said, "Stewart, look at Michelle. Does she remind you of any famous person, perhaps a certain highly esteemed American actress?"

Stewart looked at Michelle for a very long moment. "With her hair done differently and with makeup done just right..." He laughed out loud. "Perched in the corner of a fancy hotel suite with the lighting strategically arranged, some facial lines added, indeed a total makeover, and some proper distance kept, Michelle is a quite passable ... (Hollywood star's name deleted for legal reasons)!"

Samantha chuckled and looked at Michelle. "Young lady, you are about to become the centerpiece of what I hope will become one of the most successful and therefore notorious hoaxes ever perpetrated on Fleet Street."

Three days later, a famous (and famously pompous) columnist of a British newspaper received a telephone call from Samantha masquerading as a representative of a famous American public relations agency. "Mr Peter Alston Harrington III (not the columnist's real name, though it might have been!)," said Samantha, "I have a wonderful opportunity for you but I can only speak under the condition of the strictest confidentiality."

This columnist, like any journalist, was always eager for a scoop and so he quickly said, "You have my solemn word as an English gentleman."

Samantha wove her wicked tale of deception. "There's a famous American actress coming to town this weekend. She has a total abhorrence of the media and almost never does press interviews, but she has been here many times and has since come to regard you as perhaps the world's greatest journalist. She's always wanted to meet you and said to me just this morning that if you would be able to see her Sunday morning, confidentially, she will grant you an exclusive interview, but only under strict conditions of secrecy. If word gets out that said actress is in London, her weekend will obviously be ruined by the paparazzi, an outcome which she would understandably like to avoid."

The columnist, being exceptionally pompous and self-important, did not even think to doubt Samantha because he shared the same high opinion of himself! "I am so honored to meet with this person, and I'm sure I'm as big a fan of her work as she is of mine. Would it be out of line for me to ask, Madam, the name of our actress?"

"I'll tell you her name," Samantha said quite seriously, "but you must not breathe a word of this to anybody. You cannot tell your editor, your wife or even your best and closest friend. As an esteemed veteran of the British newspaper business, you know how quickly stories spread here, and we simply cannot risk this news getting out."

"You have it on my honor as an English gentleman that I shall not breathe a word of this to anybody."

Samantha, trying very hard to remain serious and in control of her desire to burst into laughter, said, "Very well. It is so-and-so who will be here, and she wants to talk with you about communism in Hollywood. Apparently, there is a real Malibu-based colony of actual Reds running the place. Far more than anyone realizes. Most of the studios have commies in them, actually."

"That's an incredible story!"

"Yes, it is. This famous actress wants me to tell you that you may quote her by name, but you may not publish the story or tell anyone that she was here until she is well out of town."

"Completely understandable. This great lady is taking a great but noble risk in speaking out on this. What courage!"

"Yes, she is a great and noble lady. And her admiration for you simply cannot be described. It is at 9am on Sunday morning that she wishes to see you so please come promptly at that time and we will take you up to her suite."

"I will see you then."

"I will thank you in advance for maintaining your confidentiality. Oh, and one more thing, please don't be late. Our star wants to make sure she has a full hour with you."

"I shall be there at nine on the dot. What did you say your name was again, Miss?" the columnist asked.

"Sa—Sarah Foxworth."

"Very well, Sarah. I shall see you in the lobby of the hotel on Sunday morning at nine. Goodbye for now."

"Goodbye, Mr Harrington."

The eager columnist, true to his word, arrived at 9am on the dot. It looked as if no one else in London knew about the hoax. The only moment the whole ploy almost unraveled was when the columnist unexpectedly asked what film the famous Hollywood actress was currently shooting. Stewart had hired a flatmate of Samantha's to play the part of Sarah, as Samantha could not risk being recognized, but they had not thought of everything; and so "Sarah" had to manage something or other about the star's old films that sufficed to kill time and occupy the pregnant answer space until, finally, they reached the front door of the magnificent suite at the top of the winding staircase.

"Sarah" quietly entered with the columnist in tow, and there, in the far corner was someone who looked almost exactly like the famous Hollywood star. The "star" waved her hand and coughed into a Kleenex. She then swallowed very deeply and eked out in quite a hoarse voice, "Please don't come too close. I have a very bad cold and I don't want you to catch it. There is a wonderfully comfortable sofa over there right by the door."

Thus commenced the monologue for which Michelle had so very competently choreographed: a detailed confession by the "actress" regarding her amazing knowledge of the closet communists hidden and planted and thriving in the nasty studios of Hollywood, and their real and bold plan to bring down the United States by poisoning the minds of the masses with extreme leftist ideas.

The next morning—with the "star" safely out of town and back at Radcliffe—there atop the front page of our star columnist's unfortunate paper was a headline that went something like this: "Communists in Hollywood Studios Undermining American Values, Says Famous Actress!" What followed was a very widely read exposé detailing how the conscience-stricken star could no longer keep silent about who was really running—and ruining—Hollywood, and America. The famous actress, in an exclusive interview with the world-famous columnist, portrayed the motion picture establishment as a virtual network of Leninist cells out to undermine traditional American family values and capitalism with their insidious mass entertainment laden with ultra-liberal values.

Meanwhile, another newspaper of the same chain ran (that very day—imagine!) an equally shocking story: "Scotland Yard Said To Be Probing Astounding Hoax of Hollywood Impostor and Crestfallen Columnist." Of course, the revelation came as a great embarrassment to the famous columnist and his newspaper.

The rest of the European newspaper world's reaction was not so muted. In fact, it was noisily amused. For when the perpetrator of the hoax showed up for his regular Monday night dinner reservation at a wonderful high-end restaurant and jazz club for politicians and media mavens, all the journalists and politicians in the room stood up for a standing ovation.

In other words, it is perfectly acceptable in some press establishments to play a hoax on a competitor—and even more okay if you could get away with it!

> Having fun in journalism is a requirement; the business doesn't pay enough to compensate for boredom. Remember the great Oscar Wilde's maxim: Life is too important to be taken seriously.

THIS IS THE SENSE OF fun and play that infuses much of Western journalistic culture, though not so much in the United States. Even the quality press in England—such as *The Telegraph* and the *Financial Times*—turns a tolerant other cheek at this genre of harmful but delightful pranks.

Unfortunately, this spirit somehow tends to sink like a rock when you cross the Atlantic pond. I mean, really, imagine if I had done something like that while at *Time* magazine or *Los Angeles Times*. I would have been called upon the carpet by my betters and written up in a professional journal as a poster boy for a journalistic unethical practises act.

It is this sense of fun and playfulness that is an especially telling difference between American and British newspapering. That is why, on the whole, I always looked forward to a British newspaper in the morning, even the ultra cosmopolitan *Financial Times*, and less likely so for the average American one. I realize that I am branding myself an unpatriotic defector, but I am happy to make the argument for the slight superiority of British over American journalism. I shall explain in time.

> If you want to experience the full possibilities of newspapering, do try for a "David English" fellowship at a foreign newspaper or magazine. You might even try working there for a few years. After all, David did exactly that at a New York paper and the experience worked well for him!

GREAT EDITORS CAN bring out the best in writers who otherwise might not be so great. David did that for me. Find a mentor like him and he can do that for you—and you will find that you can do little wrong. Great editors will sometimes take chances with writers when others will not.

Great Britain at this time was undergoing one of its periodic political party convulsions. The Labour Party, which until the rise of Tony Blair had been out of power for years, was threatening to split in half.

The political convulsion was typified by a story concerning a troubled middle-aged man in Northampton, England. His father had been a fervently loyal member of the pro-union Labour Party, and so was his son. But something had been eating away at the latter even as the former went to Heaven utterly undisturbed in his view that Labour was almost always right and the Conservatives were almost always wrong. What was eating him was one of the most mentally destructive of all intellectual emotions: profound doubt about one's chosen course in life.

Ordinarily, this story would have been assigned to a highly experienced Fleet Street journalist—not to an imported American guest from Los Angeles like me! But gifted editors like David always had the good sense to plan ahead—and the penchant for calculated risk-taking.

In a few weeks, a new political party in Britain was to be formed: a Third Force, as it were. It would neither be very leftwing nor at all conservative; it would, indeed, be somewhat centrist, and sensible. It was to be called the Social Democratic Party.

The troubled man's name was Tom Bradley and I was assigned to work up a print portrait of why a lifelong Labour Party member with a family tradition of fierce, blue-collar Labour Party loyalty would suddenly turn his back on it all.

In writing an in-depth profile, one key is spending as much time with the subject as the subject will allow and your deadline will permit. The Bradley family was as middle class and middle of the road as any American family in Iowa. But perhaps because I was a (relatively) innocuous American journalist (as opposed to a meat-eating British one—and, believe me, those Fleet Street journalists are anything other than vegetarians!), the family allowed me and my wife Andrea to spend, more or less, an entire weekend with them.

The key to a profile may be in telling detail, that is to say, detail that tells the story without you having to explain it didactically. In this case, for this story, I luckily had an inside source, a Deep Throat, as it were. For this story, about this Labour-defecting member of parliament, that key source was to be Bradley's pre-teen son. He became my secret sharer.

I generally always get along very well with young people (it was the older ones whom I tended to run into difficulty with) and the son was an exceptionally sensitive 11-year-old soul. As I chatted him up, I had the deep sense that he knew the key to his Dad as no one else did.

So I puttered around with him, playing catch-ball in the backyard despite a nasty February winter, and letting him show me around the family's prized outdoor possessions which included the typical English backyard greenhouse.

During a quiet moment inside the warm living room, with his parents out of hearing, I was able to take him aside and ask him, rather point blank (never ever try to con a young person, be as straight as the proverbial arrow; kids can see spiritual aspects of character that we older people often cannot):

when was the first moment he suspected his father was very upset? The answer was memorable: when winter ended and Dad did not replant the gladiolas in the greenhouse. At first, I did not understand; then—drum roll—I did.

In England, gardening is not just a pastime; it is a national passion, like cricket. Every year this kid had been alive, he had observed (and perhaps quietly admired) his father's horticultural rite of spring. In would go Dad, his Dad, like seasonal clockwork, into the greenhouse with the trowel, in with the new bulbs, in with the proper fertilizer.

Not this year. This year, the son told me, there was no greenhouse effect at the Bradley home in Northampton.

"I knew something must have really been bothering father for him not to be planting. Spring was coming. He would always plant just before spring."

And it was this little story that began the profile—a story of a father whose mind was elsewhere, a story about a man who was at a turning point in his life, a story about a politician who was so deeply troubled that the habit of a lifetime had to be put on hold.

> Journalism is generally most convincing when the writer leaves her or his ego and enters another's. Okay, this observation may be less true for political opinion columnists, but even for them, the use of telling details can make an argument far more convincing than mere emphatic assertions of the "I."

"It's absolutely brilliant," said David. "How did you know the gardening anecdote would be so perfect a beginning?"

I did not; it was just instinct. Then again, my instinct always told me: go with your best stuff. The Case of the Unplanted Gladiola was the best anecdote—might as well put it near the top.

A few days later, David summoned some of us into his office. "Our American guest has written us a fine piece on a defector from the Labour Party, Tom Bradley. We need a proper headline that's worthy of the tip-top effort." David explained that the article was to run in the features spotlight on the day of the official announcement of the new "third way party."

One top editor offered: "The Defection of a Labour Party Loyalist."

David said nothing. That meant, not good enough.

Another editor: "Portrait of a Defector."

None of those headlines made David's cut. Again, David said nothing.

I understood the problem. In a headline, David would always look to spotlight the emotion of the story.

I dug deep into my own emotions, having lived the last few weeks in Mr Bradley's own whirlwind of emotions. Finally, it came to me: "The Night Tom Bradley Couldn't Take It Anymore." As soon as I said it, David said, "That's what we want. Let's go home."

On another night, I was working late with him on the Backbench near Fleet Street, in what was then *The Daily Mail* home office—it has since moved to another (much lovelier) section of London. Backbench was the famed horseshoe working table where the next day's front page started to come together.

We were all staring at a fabulous picture of Lady Di. And she was staring off intently and concernedly into the distance at a horse and a well dressed equestrian who, the story was to reveal, was about to be thrown rudely off the saddle. David wanted the picture on page one, of course, as the equestrian was none other than Prince Charles himself, and the story was about how the heir to the throne of England had been unceremoniously thrown off his horse. We struggled and struggled to find the right headline for the horse-play picture. Finally, it came to me. How about this, I asked: " 'Be Careful, My Prince'." Then, and only then, did David smile. "Good night, gentlemen. That's what we want."

Headline writing was one of my few genuine talents. At *Time* magazine a few years later, we were all stuck trying to figure out the cover lines for an amazing story about a man named John DeLorean, who had designed and marketed a famous luxury car, married a famously beautiful woman, run into financial trouble, and then, incredibly, been arrested by narcotics agents for cocaine trafficking. I came up with the head that was finally used—but only after a couple of wines at lunch. I submitted it to the editor, Ray Cave, who came to my office, after seeing my suggestion, with a very rare word of praise: "No one in this building could have come up with that. No one."

The cover line for the DeLorean cover story on how a cocaine problem had led to the catastrophic failure of his business beneath a picture of DeLorean himself was: "The Bottom Line: Busted."

I am not sure what sort of talent headline writing really is. It is not that important, really. It does not cure cancer, ease any sort of reading or learning disorder, nor clean up polluted rivers and oceans. It is just, well, journalism, which means it is not that important. It is the ineffable capture of a particular moment or the lassoing of a confluence of events in time, whether in words, pictures or sounds. My own sense would be to liken headline writing to the opening tableau in a very old TV series titled "The Adventures of Superman." So strong was Superman, you see, that he could pick up a piece of coal and crush it in his hand with such force that the coal was transformed (somehow) into diamond. At *Time*, they were to call me "Mr Head." I was certainly no Superman, to say the least; and I was not a very good editor at *Time*, as you will see, except, though and curiously, with heads, or, as we were to call it at the magazine, "titles."

The two months with David at *The Daily Mail* seemed more like a year, but only because I was savoring every minute of it. It was the experience of my then-relatively youthful career. Andrea had gone with me to London for the ride and we camped in the tiniest of a furnished flat in the elegant Mayfair neighborhood of London. I had a better time of it than my wife, however, because while I was cavorting on Fleet Street, Andrea had very little to do in the bleak England winter once she had put the finishing touches on our book, *Secret Police,* and shipped it back to Doubleday, our New York publisher.

Perhaps one of her finest don't-mess-with-me moments in London came one night at a gala dinner party at David's townhouse in Westminster, a section of London not unlike Georgetown in Washington that was geographically and socioeconomically much closer to parliament than to Fleet Street.

David loved dinner parties that were anything but sedate and mannered affairs; and I was to attend none more like them until I was to work at *New York Newsday* and found myself at the thrust-and-parry dinner parties thrown by the energetic Ed Koch, then mayor of New York.

Any excuse for a party was good enough for David and Lady Irene, his wife and a former English actress, and so as my stint at *The Daily Mail* was coming to an end, David figured, why not throw one for Tom and Andrea?

Well, David got more than he planned for this particular night because he had not met anyone quite like my wife before. She was no knee-jerk feminist, for that would have presented David with too easy a target; rather, she was more like a Margaret Thatcher of the Left if the then-prime minister were portrayed in a movie by the fiery actress Salma Hayek whom Andrea then looked most like.

Mrs Plate, like Thatcher, you see, was not a lady for easy turning.

After plenty of good food and a whole lot of wine, the decibel level at the party rose to hysterical heights, especially when David launched into a full-bore attack on American feminists as inveterate male-haters. Andrea, as I said, was not a doctrinaire but she was not having any of David's Tory demagoguery and dug her five-foot-one inch frame and heels into the thick Scottish wool carpeting in the drawing room. Back and forth went the argumentation, Andrea repelling each of David's assaults with precision and energy, leading the room of perhaps eight couples to divide themselves into warring gender camps.

The quarrel inside the townhouse was so noisy, but delightfully so, that no one could hear the telephone ringing, which, we were to learn in a few minutes, had been ringing urgently for some time. It turned out that, back in Washington, then president, Ronald Reagan, had been shot and taken to the hospital.

The caller to the townhouse was the wonderful Peter Grover, deputy editor of *The Daily Mail*, a veteran journalist and an iconic Englishman to love. I had taken to him as a temporary father as I had to David as an older brother. With his boss hosting the dinner party for me, Peter had drawn late duty back at *The Daily Mail* office.

Extremely frustrated that the phone was not being answered, Peter then dashed off a note to David, and summoned a car and driver to take it to Westminster with all due haste.

The arguments were still raging in the drawing room, now suffused with the combined odors of cigars, cognac and expensive women's perfume, when suddenly someone shouted, "Wait, someone's at the door, I think."

Silence surfaced with the suddenness of an earthquake and stopped everything cold. No one moved. Now we could hear the pounding clearly—and it was frantic.

David jumped up, went to the door, opened it, and was greeted thus: "Mr English, this is a note from Mr Peter Grover. He has instructed me to ask you to read it and then wait."

David unsealed the envelope and peeled open the note, which read: "David, President Reagan has been shot. True extent of injury yet unknown but he has been taken to hospital, it is said urgently, and surgeons are said to be about to operate. It would be helpful if you could return to the office, and Mr Plate, too. But if both of you cannot, then the one person I could really use is the American. [signed] Peter."

Weeks later I was to marvel over the note. Only someone who had worked very closely with David, only outwardly the most secure of egos, would know how insecure he was. This is true of almost all the very creative and successful people I have known.

I once analyzed a problem for my good friend Lesley Stahl, of CBS' "Sixty Minutes." It led to a mantra I believe in as much as anything else I have learned in life. Lesley, the first time she heard it, said to me, "That is the best piece of advice I have ever gotten; if I had had it earlier, I could have minimized some difficulty." That piece of advice was this: never ever underestimate the insecurity of the person above you.

No need for David's enormous skill at the office in a moment of high drama over the attempted assassination of an American president? Peter understood the insecure mentality of the "person above him" very well indeed.

David grabbed his coat, quickly but elegantly (and with a characteristic dramatic flourish) explained to his guests the urgency of the moment, grabbed me by the arm, and said, "Let's go."

In the car we sat for minutes without speaking as the rain pounded the pavements of London and the top of the Mercedes. I was trying to imagine what use David would try to make of me. I could see his mind working, trying to lay out a clear picture of what could be done to remake the paper within the 90 minutes we would have to do that when we arrived at *The Daily Mail* office.

My guess was that rather than ask me to edit English newspaper copy —a tricky task on deadline—he might ask me to write a "splash" piece either for the centerspread (the big two-page display area at the very middle of the paper, like two swing doors opening) or for page five where "analysis" pieces tended to appear. Quite un-humbly, and characteristically so perhaps, I had told David two weeks ago of winning an award from The American Society of Newspaper Editors for my analytical "splash" pieces written in the preceding year on the Democratic and Republican Conventions where we had first met.

Suddenly, David, with the pieces of the puzzle fitting together, turned to me and, with the rain pounding even more ominously, said, either as a challenge or as a threat, "Okay, Mr Deadline Writer, now we shall see just how good you are!" I had to laugh. Was the guy an original or what?

To be truthful, I do not think the piece I wrote in 40 minutes was all that great. In fact, David and I almost argued over it when he first proposed the theme: that American celebrities are particularly prone to murder attempts (John Lennon, etc.) because the very attempt confers fame on the otherwise anonymous and insignificant perpetrator adrift in America's culture of fame.

I had objected to that for two reasons. One was that I put political assassinations in a separate category from the entertainment target, and two was that before I had left Los Angeles, Jim Bellows had said, "The only thing about David I might need to warn you about is that there may come a time in London when he will ask you to do or write something that you don't want to do or write."

That very moment had arrived, and I was expecting the worst, for I had seen David's temper flare and a pretty sight it was not. But David surprised me, as with the nimbleness of a ballet dancer, he shifted on a dime. "Okay," he said, well hiding his probable exasperation, "then let's look at your way."

I approached it from the standpoint of America's culture of guns.

Even today, I am not sure who was more right or wrong. The piece was not very good. Maybe it would have been better done David's way. But you had to stick with your gut, especially when writing on deadline in a crisis.

The next day, I mentioned to Stewart Steven, the associate editor of *The Daily Mail* who generously agreed to share his office with me for the two months in London, that I was not happy with it.

Stewart shook his head. "Tom, it's in the paper," he said. "That's all that really matters."

That was an interesting way of looking at it—"It's in the paper." Or, to put it as Clay Felker might have, it was only a newspaper/magazine ... (so don't take it so seriously?!).

For all the uptight, stuffy tendencies Americans delight in attributing to our former colonizers across "the pond," it is often us Yanks that could really afford to take it down a notch or two—and particularly in the newsroom.

It is not some genetic defect that made American editors and publishers unwilling to have a little fun in the business but rather that in America, news is business and more or less only that—and a very serious activity at that.

Increasingly, American publishers are required to achieve high profit levels—especially now that so many media companies are publicly traded on stock exchanges.

British newspapers are under comparable pressures, to be sure, but somehow the rich British tradition of press lords, the cut-throat competition and the insane Fleet Street environment keeps their journalism vibrating at a higher energy level.

I imagine (in my most pessimistic moments) the main difference between American and British papers to be like this: American newspapers are like banks—they gather and store a valuable resource (information), and pride themselves on disseminating it seriously and fairly to those who have access to it (their readership); British newspapers are like a noisy party—they are rife with people having too much to drink and too much to smoke, and chattering far beyond the limits of good taste. They imagine their readers to be guests at their party.

I must say that the American model remained unquestionably superior in my view until I had the pleasure, as you now know, of serving as a guest editor at *The Daily Mail* of London, a paper known for its Conservative leanings, sharp political coverage and broad appeal to the middle class, especially to women. I did not find the transition from working in a quiet bank to working in a virtual Las Vegas difficult but it was a transition that definitely required a paradigm shift.

Those who are fortunate enough to embed themselves for a time in the lively revelry of the British newspaper tradition are never again able to blindly accept the solemn tenor of its American counterpart. There is method to the madness of the British method, though no one should underestimate the measure of madness. Even so, their way is often so much fun.

The Los Angeles Herald Examiner could be fun. An illustrative example of this came one day during my tenure as a deputy editor of *The Los Angeles*

Herald Examiner. A famous writer, who also shall go nameless, had penned the paper's rather renowned gossip column for quite some time. Now, gossip columns by their very nature run against the grain of "serious American newspapering" because it is not necessarily reality, but instead, what everyone is saying about everyone else.

The crusty old curmudgeons of the US press had realized one day that other folks liked to be entertained (even if they did not), so they begrudgingly began to allow gossip in the paper, just as long as it was clearly labeled for what it was. This practise, incidentally, is found throughout American newspapers and most readily on the opinion-editorial page, where overt opinion is allowed in the paper precisely because it is clearly labeled as such.

British papers, on the other hand, unabashedly weave subjectivity through their copy and find no need to label the obvious. (American papers vigorously deny the existence of opinion in their news stories, but of course, complete objectivity is an illusion and a delusion.) In a metropolis like London, where eight to nine major dailies thrive, partisanship serves as the very foundation of a publication's identity, with the rare exception.

So, back to our story about the gossip section and a famous writer. As a deputy editor of *The Los Angeles Herald Examiner* paper, I occasionally was asked to look at gossip items before they went to press. This was a very wise thing to do, particularly in the case of the famous writer under consideration, because not only was he a wildly imaginative (!) fellow, but he had been trained in the British tradition, where almost anything goes (that is, if a story item cannot be conclusively proven to be false, it may just be true—and thus is inherently and imminently publishable). So, as I read over what he was proposing to publish that particular day, I spotted a particularly racy item and asked, "Hey, shouldn't you make an extra phone call to verify this?" I'm not one to cringe at the sight of extremity but his gossipy assertion was exceptionally wild.

The writer looked at me for a moment, as if he were taking pity on an ignorant soul, and then reposted, in a flawless British accent, "Dear Mr Plate, many a good item can be ruined by that extra phone call."

This exemplifies the gaping differences in both methodology and standards that exist in America for gossip writers and more "serious" columnists. In short, the Woodwards and Bernsteins of the world are usually required to have several sources for significant revelations, while for gossip columnists, the standards are much more, well, flexible. The same distinction is true, to a degree, about the difference between the American and British newspaper mentalities. What gossip columnists can get away with in America is significantly less than what is allowed, even encouraged, in British newspaper houses. To further illustrate the difference between the varying approaches of the two countries, let me juxtapose two experiences I encountered as, respectively, the editor of an American, and then of a British, newspaper.

One morning at the struggling Hearst paper, trailing as it was in the shadow of the mighty *Los Angeles Times*, I arrived bright and early at the office to the sound of the great Jim Bellows, the top editor indeed, bellowing out to me, "Tom! Good Lord! Look at page two!" This was what we called our gossip page.

I immediately figured that the commotion had something to do with the gossip column, as it was, dare I say, the only interesting thing on page two—and on some dark days, in the entire paper. I became even more certain of the source of the trouble once I recalled that the previous day all three top editors were out sick—which meant that no one with any real editorial authority had signed off on the column before it ran. So I reluctantly slipped into my office and, cringing slightly, grabbed the paper on my desk.

There, shouting out from page two, was one of the weirdest headlines one would ever get to see: "Hit a Pet!" Next to that was a picture of the cutest little dog ever, and then the caption: "Are you having trouble sleeping at night because the dog in the alley thinks he's the night watchman? Has the cat next door made your favorite petunia bed his personal potty? Hit-a-Pet can help! No more frustrating exchanges with pet owners who just don't care. Hit-a-Pet takes care of all of your furry problems. Call us and you'll soon be sleeping free and easy through the night. Squeamish about using our service? We take care of pet problems quietly and under the cover of darkness. And we take Visa, Mastercard and American Express. Just telephone us at 213 237 7000."

Jim shouted at me through the wall, "Tom, call that number, I don't have the nerve."

I dutifully dialed it. A ring or two or three, and then the human voice representing the institution said: "*Los Angeles Times*, how may I help you?"

By then, the *Los Angeles Times* (our competition) had been absolutely flooded with outraged phone calls from pet lovers and animal rights organizations alike. It was two hours until the next opportunity to remake the edition so I called my counterpart at the *Los Angeles Times* to formally tender an (almost sincere) apology for all the trouble our troublemaking gossip columnist caused. In addition, being the serious, ethical American paper that we were, we of course published a formal apology and publicly retracted the item, as well as reprimanded the writer.

Well, I did not reprimand him (I thought the gig was absolutely hilarious but, then again, I had worked a bit on Fleet Street!) but I think Jim Bellows might have. Or maybe he did not. I was not actually present at the session but my guess is that the writer, who had worked on Fleet Street for many years before, and Jim, who as you know admired David, probably laughed privately over the hit-a-pet contretemps. I bet Jim warned him not to do anything like that again but had to try hard not to die laughing.

The truth was, the "Hit a Pet" stunt was damn funny. It was the kind of gleeful absurdity that you rarely got, or more accurately, was not permitted, in American newspapers. In America, you were virtually guaranteed a spanking from the boss for even attempting to pull off something like that. What dull lives of quiet desperation most US journalists live!

Meanwhile, in london, on the night before I was to return to Los Angeles, David invited Andrea and me out to The Connaught—one of the world's most delightful hotels—and offered me a permanent position at *The Daily Mail*. What a charmer!

As David was such a wonderful leader and an inspiration to work with, it was a tempting offer. Indeed, if I had not been married to Andrea with our home base still in Los Angeles and had not felt great loyalty to Jim, I would have accepted the offer from the man who was arguably the best newspaper editor in the English-reading world.

But I did feel deep loyalty to Jim. Whether he was or was not the world's greatest editor, and whether or not he really was such a great newspaper "savior," he had not only resurrected my newspaper career but had allowed me to go to England for two wonderful months on a sort of field study, and so I felt I owed it to him to go back. I am loyal, to an extreme fault.

So I left London in a great mood. I had just completed something worthwhile in which I had contributed, and I was heading home to share.

Just a few weeks after I was back on the job, Jim resigned and almost instantaneously, Mary Anne Dolan ascended to the editorship. I was getting vertigo. I thought at first that my ears were affected by a rare and protracted form of jet lag but the truth soon became all too apparent. I immediately went to see Frank Dale, the publisher.

Frank had been a major contributor to the Nixon Campaign, had received in return a minor ambassadorship to Geneva, and had been a main owner of the Cincinnati Reds, the baseball team. I liked Frank. He had been very good to me. But he was not always a tower of strength and resistance in a storm. Don once likened his character to that of a bar of ivory soap floating in a warm bath—nice but mushy and falling apart after only a half hour in even moderately perfervid waters.

"Frank," I said, "I'm kind of confused here. I've worked for you for almost four years, I've won major awards which makes me think that maybe the editorial pages have been pretty good, and I obviously enjoy the job. And, to be honest, I have enjoyed the honor and privilege of working for you. You are a kind and warm man.

"Here's my problem. I go to London, I come back, and suddenly, Jim announces he's leaving and two hours after the announcement, you've already chosen a successor. Doesn't the company want to agonize over the decision for a few days, if only to give me the impression that the decision had been carefully thought through and that I have been carefully considered? If it's a level playing field and she gets the job, then that's fair and fine, and I'm loyal to her for as long as she needs me.

"But, because as far as I can tell, it took you a total of two hours to not only recuperate from the loss of one of the best newspaper editors in the country but appoint his successor..." It was then that I stopped and thought for a minute. "Frank, Jim's resignation was a surprise, wasn't it?"

"Oh yes," he said.

I continued, "Well, if it was a surprise, Frank, then is it so immediately obvious that Mary Anne is more qualified for the job so that there is no question about it—not even a two hour-plus pause just to make me not look like a fool?

"You know, Frank,"—and here I really began to dislike myself because I was losing control and getting mean—"David Shaw, the media reporter from *Los Angeles Times*, has been calling me all day. He wants the lowdown on why I wasn't chosen as the next editor. I'm trying to stay loyal here but I'm kind of rocked by the rapidity with which Jim's successor has been selected.

"I'm not saying that Mary Anne isn't a qualified choice or even a very plausible one indeed; hell, she may be twice the editor I am! But what I'm troubled by is that I'm getting the impression I wasn't even fully considered.

"For that very reason alone, I'm uneasy enough about the reality here now so as to be tempted to quit. With full disclosure of an exit interview with Shaw."

Hearing that, Frank got visibly nervous. He blubbered and blustered and then finally said, "Okay, Tom. The truth is that while you were in London, Jim and Mary Anne came to me and presented a fait accompli in the virtual form of a kind of contract for her that guaranteed that in the event of Jim's resignation, Mary Anne would become the next editor-in-chief."

I was incredulous. "You signed that?"

He said, "I had to."

"What do you mean you had to?"

"If I didn't, Mary Anne was going to leave us for a position at ABC News and we just couldn't afford to lose two top editors at once."

"So you submitted to blackmail, Frank? I could have just as easily called you up myself from London and said, 'Frank, I'm going to stay at *The Daily Mail* unless you promise me X, Y and Z promotions upon my return.' Is that the kind of person you want running your paper? Jesus, Frank. That was stupid."

"You of all people know how Bellows can get, Tom."

"Yeah, I know how Bellows can get. But you are the publisher and CEO of this paper, Frank, and you should have held firm and said, 'When the time comes, Mary Anne, you'll be very seriously considered as a strong candidate for the head position, but as the publisher of *The Los Angeles Herald Examiner* and as an official of the Hearst Corporation, I need to keep my options open.' I mean, suppose word got out that Jim was leaving and then someone very qualified from the *New York Times* or *The Wall Street Journal* came along and expressed interest in the job. Would the sellout to Jim and Mary Anne seem like such a smart idea then, Frank?"

There was no answer he could possibly give me that would rationally explain what he had done. I went back to my office, which happened to be right next to Jim's, and I stared at him for a moment as I walked by, but he would not meet my gaze. The two of us were so close that we car-pooled to work nearly every morning. This night, he had no way to get home except with me. That evening's drive from downtown to the seaside in Santa Monica was the quietest, coldest drive I have ever sat through. My heart was broken.

When I pushed Jim to answer the question of why he had chosen Mary Anne for the job without telling me, he mumbled something about how they had worked together for years at *The Washington Star*, not to mention *The Los Angeles Herald Examiner*, how he was so comfortable with her. But the question about which I was still greatly puzzled was unaddressed: why hadn't I been told that the decision had already been made and formulated behind my back?

I am far, very far indeed, from being perfect but I do have a big heart—for better or for worse. In journalism, that might just be a mistake. The career of journalism is sensational at breaking hearts. Especially if you are a fool, and especially if you are a loyal fool … which is the silliest fool of them all. And that is me. I do pray may it not be you.

> The notion of a "trans-Atlantic journalism" is perhaps more fanciful than factual. But it is true that a handful of talented editors have made the leap from London's media world to New York's with grace and good effect—though notably less so in the opposite direction. All the more, the practise of established US journalists taking temporary mid-career jobs in very different media cultures needs to be encouraged. There must be some way to get the journalistic profession to break out of its stifling provincialism, no?

Chapter Five
Time Pressures:
The Businesslike Bureaucracy of Quality Control

EMOTIONS OFTEN RULE the decision-making process, as may have been the case in *The Los Angeles Herald Examiner* succession melodrama; and emotions often rule in your reaction to a decision that goes against you.

One day, Steve Smith, a senior editor from *Time* magazine, telephoned me at home in Los Angeles to invite me to interview for an editing vacancy. When he raised the issue of how quickly *The Los Angeles Herald Examiner* had moved, and asked if there was a story behind the story, and I hinted vaguely that there was, he said, "That's what I thought. Why don't you come see us? There may be a job here for you."

> Big media institutions are basically all alike—unhappy in their own way. I never lusted to work at *The New York Times*, as tremendous a newspaper as it is. It just seemed like I would be more of an appendage than a necessity. My own sense is that the larger the media institution, the less the enjoyment one should expect. But *Time* magazine seemed like it might be an exception.

I jumped at the chance, thus filling my need for revenge—and my need to feel truly wanted! (Wouldn't you do the same in my shoes?)

Years later, Steve went on to become a top editor at *Newsweek*, and then at *US News and World Report*. He was smart, charming and funny. In personal appearance, before he spoke a word, with the suspenders and the clipped haircut, you would almost expect a British accent. I always liked Steve, because even during the tensest times at *Time*, he could make you laugh.

Time was gracious in the invitation, putting me up in a fine hotel and arranging for a fancy luncheon at which I would meet a top editor and we would decide whether to proceed or call it all off.

I booked myself into the hotel the night before, ordered room service, and tried to settle in for a nice rest. I wanted to look my best for the interview—

The magazine's journalistic standards were high, if highly stylized. For example, *Time*, in the eighties at least, would not always let the facts get in the way of an institutional preconception, despite the existence of a terrifically talented research staff. The consequences of these deeply engrained institutional perspectives—really, a genetic inheritance from founder Henry Luce—were at once profound (in the case of the Ariel Sharon libel trial, to be discussed) but sometimes relatively harmless.

On one notable occasion, Henry Anatole Grunwald, well on his way to becoming the editor-in-chief, was holding down the BUSINESS section one week as a senior editor. A correspondent in the field came up with a hilarious little story but too trivial to bother recounting here. The point is that the story was so funny, though, that it was almost too good to be true. And you know what—well, it turned out, really, not all that true. But it was funny as hell, and when one writer recounted it at the BUSINESS section's weekly story-conference, everyone started doubling over, including Grunwald, whose intellect was generally fiercely intimidating.

This time, Grunwald was laughing too. So then there was a silence. Then he broke it, looking at the department's chief researcher directly in the eye, and said, "My suggestion would be not to check this little story too carefully." She got his drift. For this little Portobello mushroom of a story, the magazine's fact-control mechanism was disabled.

Time was its own world. You spent more of your time at the office than at home, and there were consequences and casualties. Not many people at *Time* had been married only once; most had consummated second and third marriages with people they had met on the job—and sometimes in the office.

There was nothing insidious about this. When you put boys and girls together in a submarine-like atmosphere and send them on a search-and-destroy mission each week (our enemy: *Newsweek*, and to a lesser extent the *New York Times*), given all that pressure, and the closeness of the quarters, and the quality of the people involved, things will and do happen. And that was how God intended it, no?

This is especially the case when you had booze around the place. At the end of every week at *Time*, liquor carts would come rolling around laden with free booze, and you could have drinks on the job without reprimand and in fact—with management sanction. Not infrequently, one drink led to another drink, and then one drunk led to another drunk, and before you knew it, you would not be going home to your place, you would be going home with the cute new stud writer from *The Kansas City Star*, or with the stunning ex-model copy girl, or whatever. (Boys with girls, girls with girls, boys with boys—I can't say enough about my open-mindedness! I really don't care what people do in their private sex lives, do you?)

There was nothing really wrong with all this messing around; you could state as an absolute ethic the separation of business from pleasure, but like prohibition, you have to be realistic. On one particular August night, however, this alcohol-induced atmosphere nearly prevented *Time* magazine from coming out. And, as luck would have it, this occurred during my temporary stewardship over the NATION section.

At the time, I was pretty excited about being in charge, I must say. Since I did not realize I was in over my head and had no idea what was to happen, I was not daunted or intimidated in the slightest. I was too dumb for that!

My freshman hubris was enhanced by the fact that my first night as commander of NATION led to the magazine closing at around 11:30pm—a full three to four hours earlier than normal. A staff writer named Ed Magnuson—whom I used to call Mr Mag and whom I grew to greatly respect—added to my feeling of omnipotence when he came to see me on his way out that night. He chirped, "I want to pay you a compliment, Mr Plate. I've been writing in this section for too many years and I can't remember a week when we ever closed the magazine before midnight. Good night."

Well, that just motivated me to continue on my not-a-care-in-the-world track. The second week at the helm I did almost as well and by the third week, I managed to even improve my new standard of closing the section early. I was getting the reputation of being a fast gun—not a top gun, but a fast one! Which is to say, I may not have been the most precise of editors—in truth, I sometimes wrote and edited like a madman with a bad case of ADD, or perhaps like a fugitive worried about staying a few steps ahead of the law—but whatever, I did move copy along.

Some of the writers and most of the researchers appreciated the hell-with-it pace of this new bishop from the West Coast who nudged the cattle faithful into their appointed pews without much ado. But, in retrospect, I was probably too quick for *Time*—my bad, as the athletes say.

Then, during my fourth or fifth week of running the ship, something really extraordinary happened. The incident was to become known (in my mind at least) as "The Week *Time* Magazine Almost Didn't Come Out."

It was about 10pm on a particularly work-crazed Friday night, when I finally had a brief moment to sit back in my chair, take a breath and fantasize about how much more relaxed a daily newspaper was by comparison!

Well, not ten seconds of solitude went by before there was a knock at my door. I was not startled. This, after all, was *Time* in its issue-closing hours. Something always went awry, though usually it would not turn out to be that big a deal.

"Come on in!" I barked, probably. Sometimes my impatience over being interrupted was all too evident, especially to nice people.

The chief researcher quickly entered. She was exceptionally skilled with detail, possessed an encompassing grasp of the magazine, and was awesomely effective in the home stretch on Friday night. I liked her a bunch.

"Tom," she said, "There is something funny going on."

"What's that?" I said.

"None of us have gotten any checking copy back."

That meant that the acting editor-in-chief—the actual editor-in-chief was in Maine on vacation—was not approving any copy.

"Well, maybe my copy isn't any good," I said. "Maybe he is having problems with it and is too kind to want to raise questions and is fixing each one himself." As the new man amongst *Time*'s accomplished editorial wizards, I was still insecure about fitting in and so I had doubts and worries.

She shook her head. "No, that's not it. I went over to the WORLD section and they haven't gotten any copy back either. No one has."

The WORLD editor then was a brilliant news media man, an accomplished former *Time* foreign correspondent, and quite elegant and likable.

Well, this acting NATION editor from Levittown/Hicksville did not really know what to do. But there was only one thing to do, and so I said to the chief researcher, "Well, let's go see what the problem is."

The corner offices on the twenty-fifth floor of the Time-Life Building at Rockefeller Center were always reserved for top editors.

How the "copy checking" process worked is simple enough. On the desk of the top editor on duty each night was both an inbox to which all copy that had passed the senior editors' checkpoints was taken by young copy clerks for final approval, and an outbox for the copy boys and girls to fetch what was finally approved and put it into production. Today, of course, this process is entirely computerized, but, back then, in the mid-eighties, it was somewhat paper and pencil.

It was with no small sense of foreboding that I walked down the long paneled corridor to the corner office facing Sixth Avenue and Radio City Music Hall, for it had never happened that checking copy just did not come back. Never.

When I reached the corner office of the acting editor-in-chief, I took my second deep breath of the evening and then jiggled the handle on his office door. It was locked. I knocked. No answer. This did nothing to ease my anxiety.

I asked the chief researcher to summon a couple of her staffers in case we needed extra hands and also to locate security keys to the office. The chief researcher knew where they were, of course; she knew virtually everything about everyone and everything in the building.

With her on the case, the door was unlocked forthwith, and I walked into the office alone and shut the door behind me. On the walnut sideboard, the TV screen flickered eerily, without sound. A bottle of vodka sat on the desk—a totally empty bottle of vodka would be a more accurate description. And there, in the inbox, was a sky-high pile of untouched copy.

But the outbox was absolutely empty.

And then I heard something that stopped me in my tracks. I cocked my head for a moment and then detected a faint snoring sound around the desk. Following it by ear to its source, I saw a crumpled up figure of a man curled up on the office floor.

It was the top editor. Drunk. Prone. Snoring. One hundred per cent not sober and asleep on the floor.

While there had always been drinking wherever I had previously worked—and I had taken many more than a few drinks myself from time to time in my life—this was a new one for me. The no-brainer in the situation, though, was the ticking of the clock and the stationary production deadlines; in other words, if someone did not do something, the magazine would not come out.

Since I did not have any better idea of how to react, I reacted instinctively—I grabbed all the copy from the inbox, methodically initialed each piece of it with a "TP," and then deposited it in the outbox. I then carried the box to the copy desk and told the copy clerks it had all been officially approved and to rush it into production. I then asked the chief researcher to call a taxi, have someone escort this once-awake editor to Bellevue Emergency and have him screened for alcohol poisoning. He was clearly in a collapsed condition, well beyond the average drunk.

"Have one of your staff stay with him," I suggested. "If Emergency says he can go home, then make sure he is taken home to his wife. But under no circumstances is he to be left alone at the hospital."

I had spent more than one night at the bedside of a famous or semi-famous colleague who had drowned himself in alcohol. During their bedridden collapse, they were only vaguely aware that you were there, of course; but when they sobered up, they would have a subconscious memory that someone had actually cared for them in their hour of major embarrassment. I drank too much myself over the years, but somehow I had always avoided falling over into the gutter, or into an emergency room. Maybe if I had taken the extra negative step once or twice, I would have worked on reducing my drinking sooner in life and with more resolve.

It took several researchers to pour him into the taxi, but they succeeded and off they sped. Bellevue indeed admitted our editor for alcohol poisoning and he stayed there for two days to work through the effects of the massive dehydration his plunge into the abyss had triggered.

Well, at least the magazine got out—as Clay had said to Milton: "In the end, Milton, it is only a magazine."

Upon returning to the office on Monday, I was immediately summoned to the office of *Time's* top editor, now back from Maine. I was half-anticipating an official reprimand for so readily approving all that copy that night, as I had no real authority to do so.

But then, the editor said, "Thank you, Tom." I opened my eyes for a moment and stopped cringing. "I know what happened on Friday night. It was a serious situation indeed, and you handled it well. We would have gotten the magazine out somehow, but, thanks to your quick thinking, we got it out on time."

Then came the silence where I was supposed to say humbly, thank you, and leave, but I was worried about our friend, the editor. Drunk that night or not, I sort of loved him. *Time* can be a very metallic place, and this guy was as warm as a cozy fireplace in the middle of a harsh snowstorm.

I said, "Well, what about our troubled friend? He's a nice guy and he's been very good to me. I really feel for him."

The editor-in-chief said, "Right now, he is en route to an alcohol rehab institution where he will reside for a month or whatever. He will then stay out of this building for at least a few weeks, and when he returns, he will do so only under the condition that if he ever has one drink or evidences even the faintest smell of alcohol on his breath, he will be right then and there fired and forbidden to work here again."

"You told him that? Gee, isn't that a little harsh?" I said.

The fallen editor in question was truly a good guy and he had been warm to me from my first week—and not everyone at *Time* had been so warm.

"The harsher thing would be to do nothing about it," said the editor. "We all in life will have friends who drink too much, and since we love them, we don't want to ruin their fun by saying anything. But true friendship morally compels us to tell them that they drink too much and need professional help. And they ought to get it. If they don't get help, there is no way you should remain their friend. To simply stand by and watch a friend self-destruct is not an act of true friendship."

That was a lesson I had not learned until I came to *Time*. Over the years I had been too lenient with the drinking habits of others, not to mention with my own. I have subsequently applied the *Time* editor's rule of thumb in other workplaces and added this lesson in my university teaching. But still, taking a hard stand against alcohol abuse, especially in a bastion that positively promoted social drinking, can be very difficult, because the line of unacceptability is often made invisible by the live-and-let's-party custom of the engrained corporate culture.

> All jokes aside, if a friend is drinking too much, compel him or her to get help, otherwise you are not being much of a friend; and if it is you who are drinking too much, well, be a friend to yourself, be your best friend, in fact, and get professional help!

And engrained it certainly was at *Time*. It was everywhere.

There is another example. It was near midnight one Friday when all of a sudden there was this enormous floor-shaking thud! I ran out my door and into the office of the chief researcher across the hall.

"Did you hear that?!" I asked.

"Oh, yeah," she said offhandedly. "That's just [so-and-so] falling over."

"What do you mean?"

She sighed and briefed the virgin newcomer about *Time's* true ways.

"[So-and-so] is probably our top writer, but he likes to drink. On Fridays, he usually starts with beer at around 11am or noon, and then at around five, he eases into the good Scotch. But don't worry Tom—he knows exactly how much he can tolerate. He always waits until after the researcher finishes checking the last details on his story before he'll take the last half tumbler and keel over."

She looked at me and smiled like a happy nun making the novice priest wise to the ways of the world, adding hilariously, "And that's how we sometimes know the NATION section has closed. By the thud!"

I was both amused and shocked. "You just leave him there on the floor?"

"No, no. Staff security have been trained to pick him up, take him to the elevator, prop him up in a cab and then call his wife to tell her that he's on his way. She's been through it a thousand times. It's no big deal."

This was all a bit much for me, actually. I spent too much of my time drinking—though not until graduate school did it become big-time, and steadily thereafter. But I never thought a place with as pristine an image as *Time* would turn into a scene out of The Front Page.

Upon joining *Time*, my first instinct was to go with the (gin or vodka) flow. But I could sense this wasn't going to work, especially after I had been moved into the NATION section (ostensibly a promotion). Ron, the wonderful editor who had interviewed me for the initial hire over lunch, called me into his office one day. He said, "Your new job, well, I once had it too. It's hell. So, you have a choice. In a year, you can be a total lush; or, you can be totally sober. But I can tell you, on that job, there is no middle ground. At least, there wasn't for me."

Another senior editor assigned to NATION—very smart, a better editor than me by far, and more years on the job—seconded Ron's advice. He stared right into my eyes, and said, "I don't drink any more, either."

I was stunned. "Only Perrier," he added.

For the next year or so, he and I become known as the Perrier Twins.

We may have been boring but we were always sober.

ONE MORNING, IN THE WEE HOURS of the Friday closing, I staggered from exhaustion toward the couch, packed my briefcase and started grimly toward the elevator bank. I had not an ounce of energy left in my mind, soul or body; virtually every story had to have major late-night surgery. At 11am or so, as I was dropping copy off in the routing box, a veteran editor looked at me with sympathy and asked what was wrong. I said, "So many problems ... too many problems." He said, "Well, NATION is all problems. You're really in the middle of it there."

I sure was that night—and boy, did I need a drink!

Moving ahead of me toward the elevator bank, also with about the speed of a backlash of taffy, was a very famous Time Inc. editor. He had just finished up his chores for the evening—a nice run for him from noon to 4am. In his hand—grabbed from the company stash as he left—was a bottle of fancy scotch.

Now here was the brilliant editorial mind, pulling down at least a million a year in salary and bonuses, snatching a bottle of booze from the editorial department Friday night liquor cart. Was he going to start sipping in the limo home? Was he afraid the home bar was barren? Had his wife banned all alcohol from the home? What was the significance of this scene?

IT IS POSSIBLE TO DRAW TOO MUCH from these stories of substance abuse amongst the ranks of a top US media organization because similar behavior can be found almost anywhere else in the US employment scene—although and of course this is to say nothing of the mores at today's *Time*. In fact, there is almost certainly less of it now. This is because the latest generation of journalists is far more health conscious than my generation. They eat less and eat better, drink either less or more healthily, and work out more.

Still, anesthesizing pain with alcohol is not entirely an irrational act and will always be a practise disproportionately common in the businesses where bloodstreams are pumped by deadline pressure. When you are "inside the deadline," you are eye to eye with the abyss—the abyss of having to make decisions where the probability of their being wrong is exponentially reinforced by the rapidity with which those decisions must be made.

What adds to the pain is that the best journalists are idealists—if with a cynical eye. They want the entire human race to go to heaven, even as they suspect many political leaders (and some journalists, usually editors) are sure to go to hell. But they never stop hoping, and they never stop trying to contribute.

A LACK OF FAIRNESS can be crystallized even into an institutional culture that on the surface stands for fairness.

When I was at *Time* magazine as a NATION editor, it became apparent that the place was permeated by sexism. For starters, the structure of the staff was such that the vast majority of the researchers and fact-checkers were women, while the vast majority of the writers and editors were men. It was therefore the men who made the important decisions (and the most money), and the women who did the housework.

As I was hired from the outside and thus was thought to be more susceptible to change and innovation, the top editors put two recently hired young female writers in my section, thinking I would have no problem with this. They were right—up to a point.

Each week, I watched drearily as these women were left at the bottom dregs of the writing assignment list; invariably, the top stories went to the established top male writers. What made it worse was that half the time, by the end of the week, the lower-tier stories were squeezed out of the magazine, anyway, and so the women were becoming understandably frustrated.

I was frustrated, too, because I thought they were good writers, and one by the name of Maureen was just plain excellent. So I kept trying to advance their cause, which was difficult because trying to make any slight change at *Time* was about as easy as trying to rewrite the US Constitution. Still, I kept my eyes open and argued their case whenever I could. Perhaps this was because I had come from Los Angeles—or perhaps because something inside of me had a great respect for women. This was probably due to my relationship with my late mother—but who cares?

One particular cover conference (they were usually scheduled twice a month) offered the perfect opportunity for me to make an idealistic fool of myself. More often than not, cover stories were driven by news events. This meant that some inescapable event occurring the week before publication would make it onto the cover as our lead story.

But every so often there would not be anything especially crushingly newsworthy, and so we would make plans to work up a preconceived cover on a not so timely topic, like the latest Tinseltown femme fatale or modern art trend or teenage obsession. At this particular conference, we were playing around with the possibility of working up a cover story on the latest model and one smart editor said, "You know, we haven't had any women on our covers that aren't arguably bimbos"—he did not exactly use that term because he was too polite and elegant a man for that (especially now that he was totally into sobriety)—"we ought to try and highlight some women of professional accomplishment."

At this course in its institutional evolution, *Time's* political leanings were still establishment oriented, so there wasn't exactly a very broad lens through which to view many possibilities—and therefore we dredged up the name of Jeanne Kirkpatrick, who was then serving as the US Ambassador to the United Nations. Appointed by Ronald Reagan, she was having a delightful time indeed lecturing Third World Marxists on what they had done and were continuing to do wrong (this was of course a rich mine to farm!). Her dramatic performances, given the Cold War spirit of the times, went over well, especially with establishment Republicans.

Everyone agreed that she was a solid choice, though not an inspired one; and so then the issue became who was going to write the story. The usual top writers' names were thrown out, and at that point, as I had been feeling the pain of the two young writers in NATION who had never gotten a major story, much less a cover story, I had had it. So I spoke up, "How about throwing one to Maureen?"

There was a silence of long seconds. It was as if I had proposed some axe murderer for the cover spot in *Time's* "Person of the Year" issue.

Finally, a veteran *Time* journalist, who had occupied all the top editorial positions at *Time*, spoke up. For a second I thought he might have been joking, because he was a brilliant, urbane man—though someone who had never really been out of the *Time* cocoon after graduate school—but when he sort of smirked and without chuckling, said, "Oh Tom. The girls aren't ready for a cover story yet!" I sensed he was serious.

Many in the room laughed and snickered, but I had not found it funny and could not laugh about it. I was no saint by any means—you know that by now; but this was just too much. As I shuffled back to my office after the conference, my head sunk down into my chest because I knew I should have had the balls to say that Maureen was a better writer than 80 per cent of the magazine's current male staff and that all she needed was a chance to prove it.

The Jeanne Kirkpatrick story would have been the perfect trial run for her because the story did not have to run next week and thus we could exercise all the editorial control required, though I did not think much would be needed, because Maureen was brilliant and, indeed, a more engaging writer than most of us. Plus, it would be a woman writing about a woman, and there was a certain real attraction to that coupling as well. So I was not only disappointed in *Time* when they assigned the story to someone else, but I was disappointed in myself. I felt I had let my two young women writers down because I had not fought hard enough for what was truly the right thing to do.

> Remember the "jump the midget" story? I guess what I am trying to say to you is that at the end of the day you will have more regrets about yourself if you did not jump it than if you did. Sincerity is no justification for restlessness but, then again, why wimp out?

A FEW WEEKS LATER, I had Saturday duty, which at NATION meant you went in and tied up any and all the loose ends, and assigned writers to cover a big story, should one break.

That particular Saturday, a gifted male writer was on duty. Also in the bullpen was the young Maureen.

About mid-morning, a story having something to do with an interest-rate change at the Federal Reserve popped up, and the assignment ordinarily would have gone to the male, who was, of course, senior to Maureen, and who was as well a terrifically nice and gifted guy. But as it was Saturday, and I had absolute reign on the section, I brought the two of them into my office. "We ought to do a full page story on this and get on the development as soon as possible," I said.

Then I said to the excellent male writer, "Ordinarily, I would hand it to you and Maureen would understand that. But would you mind if just this one time we gave it to her? She's had nothing but lollipop stories to do since she got here, and I think this would be a good chance for her to stretch a little. You'd be able, of course, to look at what she produces and make sure that her writing is up to it." Which I knew it would be.

At the time, the writer, whom I liked immensely, took it well, but I found out later that it did not go over so well with some of the other top people. (Although, by contrast, Steve Smith, my immediate supervisor—who was a half dozen years my junior—very quietly congratulated me for having given Maureen a chance.)

But the young women's cause was not otherwise something that I had a lot of support for, and so I felt a bit like a black sheep walking in *Time's* halls for weeks after that.

Not long after this dismaying incident, I got a phone call from Arthur Gelb, who was then the colorful and legendary deputy managing editor of *The New York Times*—a real power and a very smart guy. I picked up the phone and said, "Arthur! How are you doing? What's up? You giving me your job? Hey, we could switch for a few years! You come here and shake things up, and I go there and shake it too."

Gelb was what New Yorkers called a mensch. (What does this New York Yiddish term really mean? I don't know, really. Perhaps it connotes someone who was a cross between a genius Albert Einstein and a madcap comic.) Over the years, I had become very fond of Arthur—though I had never wanted to work at *The New York Times*, bizarrely.

"Hah!" he retorted. "Listen, Tom, there's something I need to ask you, sort of confidentially. Are you alright with that?"

I liked Arthur; he had a great sense of humor and he liked my work, although he thought I was a little weird—which was odd, because he was weirder than even I was! One reason for our easy relationship is that once he had described me as a "real character," which, the way I took it, would be like Groucho Marx saying to you: What a comedienne you are!

"Sure, ask me anything. You know that, Art."

He got straight to the point. "We're interested in hiring someone who works for you."

"Uh-oh," I said. "Who?" The truth is, I thought it might be William A Henry III, our brilliant media and theater writer.

"This is about Maureen. What do you think of her?"

"What do you want her to do for you?"

He said, "We'd like to start her like we do anybody, you know, mentor her through different types of assignments. But we eventually want to phase her into doing political color pieces."

What do I do? I was hired by *Time*; I was being paid by *Time*. What was I to do? Was there a serious ethical issue here?

Perhaps if I had not had that history of unpleasantness with *Time*, and had not been told that "the girls" were not quite ready for a cover story, I would have felt more loyalty towards the publication and tried to screw up the deal. But given the fact that I really liked Maureen a whole bunch and felt that she was not being treated fairly where she was, I said, "Arthur, I probably should tell you that Maureen has a drug problem, is constantly late and we have to rewrite everything she writes, but I can't in good faith do that. I think Maureen is an exceptional talent and her potential is phenomenal. Hiring her would be one of the smartest things you've ever done. You'll be immortal."

I think he was a bit stunned by the strength of my endorsement.

"Really?" he said.

"I haven't had a single major or minor personality problem with her, Art. There was one time where I edited one of her pieces and she didn't like the way I did it, but she came in and talked with me reasonably about it, and by the time she left, I thought she was more than half right, actually—maybe a lot more than half. She's very easy to work with and tries very hard. She could be a superstar, Arthur. I'm not kidding."

He said, "Well, I guess that does it, Tom. We are going to hire Maureen Dowd and make her a star."

And they did. And as of this writing, she had become, and still is, a star.

The US news media has a special moral obligation to practice what it preaches. When it does not, it morally forfeits the right to its phenomenal constitutional protection under the First Amendment. But it must be said that, these days, women are probably less oppressed than in many other professions.

In reality, women were anything but a liability at *Time*. In fact, it was only when they were ignored or even marginalized that the magazine would tend to get into serious trouble.

No better example ever surfaced than the famous libel suit against the magazine initiated by Ariel Sharon. At the time of the writing of this book, he had been stricken by stroke and had plunged into a coma after serving as Israel's prime minister; during my tenure at *Time*, he was one of the government's cabinet ministers.

In a terrible 1982 incident in Lebanon, Christian forces had entered an Arab refugee camp and massacred many of the residents. The attack was in revenge for a prior attack on Christians. It was a horrible tragedy.

What was even worse was the allegation that Minister Sharon had known in advance about the intended massacre and had in effect either given his consent or looked the other way. The allegation led to an official Israeli government inquiry, with the focus on Ariel Sharon. The defense minister was now under a cloud of suspicion.

Time reported Sharon's involvement more as fact than allegation. In response, Sharon sued the magazine for what he called a "blood libel." The case was tried in a New York court and, in the end, the jury ruled that the magazine had in effect been sloppy if not irresponsible in its reporting.

What was interesting to me at the time was the magazine's arrogance not only during the trial itself, when it acted as if the very fact it had been sued by Sharon proved conclusively that he must in fact have been a war criminal, but even after the jury had rendered its finding that *Time* had been less than diligent in the pursuit of absolute truth in a situation in which the magazine's allegation was—let's face it—so heinous. *Time*, in this internationally famous incident, exhibited, it seemed to me, two traits of note.

The first was that it had got into trouble, in the first place, when it printed an allegation that its fact checkers were unable to nail down as fact. That was the first problem. In this case, the magazine's top editors simply ordered a "policy override." This occurred when its powerful editors simply made an editorial call they believed to be important and consistent with the magazine's overall political line.

The second issue was that in the past, a measure of anti-Semitism had plagued the magazine's image, especially in the founding years of Henry Luce —a double-helix inheritance that *Time* had never managed to completely escape. So, for Jewish and/or Israeli readers, the accusation against Sharon, as unpopular as he was in many circles in the US for his harsh anti-Arab line, seemed to fit into their perception of the magazine's inherent bias.

My own sense was that if in the eighties the magazine did retain a measure of anti-Semitism, it was more deeply embedded in the unconscious ghosts bouncing around the corridors of power at *Time* (probably with bad hangovers) than in the minds of the current editors. Certainly, none of the top editorial guns there ever publicly espoused anti-Semitism (more likely would be a sexist utterance)—and the staff was almost all-white then.

Whatever, policy overrides can only occur when the magazine's fact-checking researchers are in effect told to have a drink, take a hike, look the other way and chill out. This would happen only occasionally but it did happen. In most instances, the override was harmless. The magazine might have a truly funny story to tell—whimsical and unimportant but a delicious delight. And so an editor might say to the researcher or fact checker on the story something like: "Hey, this is a fun story. Let's not fact-check it to death!" Everyone would understand what was going on and follow suit and, frankly, was it the end of the world?

The Sharon libel, however, was of a far higher order of journalistic felony. *Time* had in effect unplugged its rock-solid system of fact-checks and balances in order to arrive at a fact set consistent with a pre-determined instinct.

Indeed, when I was to launch my syndicated foreign-affairs column ten years later, I was to pay for fact-checking out of my own pocket to be sure that *Time*-level quality control was maintained. My columns might be misconceived or just plain wrong; but they would try never to be wrong on the facts, dates or sequences of events. In fact, researchers at UCLA who review my columns before they are sent out for publication employ the magazine's time-honored red-check system—the columns' stated facts were underlined in red for checking against objective, verifiable sources for confirmation.

To me, *Time* unplugged was ethically wrong. Worse yet, the rank lack of contrition from Higher Authority during the libel trial (Sharon versus *Time*) only compounded my sense about a magazine that in so many other respects was quite admirable.

I had no direct hands-on control, no say whatsoever, on this story—I might as well have been working at *Newsweek*. But when I was to leave *Time*, at my going-away party, something happened that was to suggest, to me at least, the strain under which top management had put itself due to the libel case—but more on this later.

I have to add another very personal observation. At this point in its history—the early eighties—*Time's* researchers were almost all females: brilliant, dedicated, hardworking and in almost every respect, women. All the top editors at *Time* then were men. My belief—and it is no more than this—is that the Sharon story would never have appeared in the libelous way that it did had the gender staffing of the top editors corps and the researchers corps not been so clearly sexist, and where, therefore, such a power difference existed. This instinct is not inconsistent, of course, with my perception of the way in which "the girls" were treated, even if they were promising writers. Of course, since my time at *Time*, the magazine has greatly improved itself in this regard, as we all have (I hope). But for too long, *Time* was shamefully slow on the uptake on this issue.

If you are guessing, my only child is female.

I CRUISED ALONG FOR A FEW MONTHS and it seemed to be working well enough. I was given good assignments and occasionally, I even excelled.

In journalism, writing headlines is a special and difficult art. Few have it; most want it. My own overall editorial skills were on the whole uneven. I seemed not to have the even temperament and capacity for concentration required to copy-edit stories at a continually machine-precise level. Frequently, I would start reading them, get bored, drift off and then forget what I had read. Today, this syndrome would probably be diagnosed as ADD. Maybe that is what I had. Or maybe after the first year at *Time*, I started to get bored—not because *Time* was inherently boring but because Tom got all too easily bored even at a fine magazine like *Time*.

On several occasions, a top editor would ring me up and ask me, basically, what the hell I was doing with a certain story. I could not tell him I had lost interest in it, could not concentrate, or was watching TV. *That* was not the correct answer. Usually, I just fumbled back some dorky response. The truth was, I probably had been watching TV. *Time* magazine's NATION and WORLD sections tended to close late—I mean 2 or 3am on Saturday mornings! Sometimes, I would be waiting there for a late piece of copy staring at something or other on TV.

My problem is—as I've mentioned—that I consider myself a 10- to 12-hour wonder. That is to say, for half the day, I am probably a reasonably talented American media man, but after 10 to 12 hours, I start to fade, fast. Alas, 14- to 18-hour days were common at week's end, and it was typically after midnight that some key decisions would go down. In other words then, the moment of the magazine's maximum need would often coincide with the moment of my most diminished capacity. There was theory behind this editorial Stalinism—a method behind the madness. The idea was to keep the magazine in the control of as few hands as possible. Too many cooks might spoil the broth. But we "senior editors" certainly paid for the honor and privilege in flesh and fatigue!

My predecessor had a different solution, I was told. The soon-to-be-famous Strobe Talbott, a former deputy secretary of state in the Clinton administration who at this writing was head of the Washington-based Brookings Institution, would take leave of the office for an hour or two and go watch a *kungfu* movie at some Times Square movie house, as it were. I was too insecure to do that—instead, I would watch TV right in the office and buckle myself into the chair.

One of the shows on NYC cable in the wee hours of the morning was called "Midnight Blue." Basically, it was godawful, but it was pioneering—a cable-TV sex show. Almost everyone on it was unappealing and infected by some common skin disease, and the show itself was lame. But it was a lot better than the "Tonight Show" or some re-run, because it was new and different and weird—and tasteless.

Better for me, perhaps, but not for everyone. One of our talented women writers huffed in one night to tell me how tasteless it was for me to be watching this show and how offensive it was to the section's women. It had not occurred to me that anyone had noticed or that my office viewing habits were a public issue. But I was embarrassed and shocked that I had offended anyone. I turned the TV off and never watched that show again—at home or in the office.

A few thoughts on workplace offices: At some point in your career, you will be offered a private office, and told it is yours. The truth is, it is not. It is not yours (you were simply the temporary occupant of it) and it is not private (dozens of fellow workers are going to be trekking in and out of the place during the day, sniffing around). There is no privacy in the workplace; there is no such thing as a private office. (Just ask Bill Clinton!)

Further note: My current UCLA office looks something like an advertisement for an import-furniture emporium. But that is a lot better than how it looked when it was handed over to me.

In revolt against how badly the average hardworking professor is rewarded and weakly perked, with shabby offices and so-so compensation, I shipped out all the weary institutional furniture they offered me, whipped out the latest VISA card that had just come in through the mail, and tore off on a highly focused pro-office shopping spree. The mission: To create an office of beauty to the eye, so as to transform the hard and mundane life of the worker bee into the inspired life of the artist-unique. To create beauty, one needed the challenge and inspiration of beauty all around one. The idea of the office as a cave of beauty is as a retreat from visual mediocrity.

My first best office in my career might have been at *New York* magazine. I really had no (private) office there. Everyone was thrown into large rooms, bull-pen style; even the top editor had an office that was only two-thirds of an office. The walls went up eight of the twelve feet—meaning private conversations were difficult—but Clay, the editor-in-chief, wanted it that way. He wanted his most important top editors, whose desks were near by, to hear the details of his conversations with writers, illustrators, photographers and even backers.

My favorite desk amid the happy chaos of *New York* was that of Michael Kramer. He was our hard-charging City Hall reporter. Ivy League-educated as he was, he was a character right out of some B-grade movie, with a fast-talking manner and an even faster mind. Instead of throwing old newspapers out, he would pile them up on his desk until he was barely visible. Asked about throwing them out, he would answer by saying: "Where's our library?"

My first serious office desk came with *The Los Angeles Herald Examiner* job. I insisted on a private office but the ramshackle newspaper building offered very few, none with air conditioning. Thinking quickly, Jim Bellows had graciously offered to give me his adjoining conference room which I had ungraciously accepted on the spot.

Time's office was elegant, in a corporate sort of way, but without individuality; and it was not very private. CBS offered nicer digs—a gorgeous corner office with a view up Broadway toward the park, past one theater marquee after another. In the course of time, the *New York Newsday* corner office, on 48th Street and Third Avenue, was at least equally gorgeous and bore some of my trademark collector's items from prior jobs. At the next stop, I inherited the office and furnishing from my predecessor Anthony Day, an elegant and eloquent thinker who ran the *Los Angeles Times* editorial pages for many years.

But it was not until UCLA that I gained entire control of my office, converted it into a sort of office den, and felt it to be my own. Of course it is not; it is merely a haven insulated from it all, thanks to the generosity of the good taxpayers of the state of California in their firm support for the idea of public education for all. And what a good idea that is, office or not.

CHIEF EDITOR RAY CAVE put me in charge of PUBLISHER'S LETTER—an assignment that was every editor's nightmare. As the new kid on the block—and thus the lowly placed Indian on the totem pole—I was put in charge of the half-page in the front of the magazine (or "the book," as it was called) that trumpeted some aspect of the magazine's grandeur. It might be about how the Jerusalem Bureau landed an exclusive interview with Arafat, or how the Washington Bureau reported the cover story on the president's political battles or the appointment of a new editor.

One problem with PUBLISHER'S LETTER was the collective egos of the people being featured and interviewed: *Time* staffers. It was funny when you thought about it: Here were professional journalists—of a very high caliber indeed—who for their paychecks were hunting down politicians and other public figures and almost defaming them at times. But when the shoe was put on the other foot—even when they owned the shoe store!—they would howl like babies if the slightest editorial nuance suggested anything other than heroism and sainthood.

In any new job, you will be given a task that no one else wants. This is the price you pay for acceptance into the group. Then, when the next new warrior comes into the tribe, you move up a notch and get to off-load the lower-rung chore.

Aside from this, Ray Cave tried hard to be good to The Outsider. This kept my spirits up as I sought to become a fully accepted member of this new family. For one thing, he asked me to start up a new section called COMPUTERS.

In preparing for a launch of something new, I generally worked better by taking a set of simple guidelines, going off by myself and rolling the various options over in my brain, and letting the creative juices stew, and then produce the proposal. Having to work with and through a committee when innovation is the primary goal but backside-protecting is the overwhelming hidden agenda only adds to the burden of creation; and when singularity is the aim, having the patience to permit inferior views to marinate long enough for their inferiority to befoul the air takes the project in the wrong direction.

Now, isn't that pretty obnoxious? I know, but that was how I really think—and how I work best.

Alas, *Time* was nothing if not one big committee (as are many media joints), though at the time it had one big exception: Ray Cave. He was an authoritarian who ran a tight ship. His father had been a military man; he was his father's son. The answer he usually required from us was: "Yes," with the tonality of "yes, sir."

When the authoritarian is very sharp, as was this editor, it is possible for you to work well with him/her. You just have to be fast, precise and right. You cannot relax and you have to deliver; but if you meet the autocrat's standards, you can survive and even thrive. I liked working with him because he made fast (and usually correct) decisions, was very straight with everyone (sometimes painfully so), and played no favorites. He did not invite certain favorite editors out to his East Hamptons country retreat on weekends and leave the others behind, as one of my past bosses had been inclined to do (very demoralizing to the uninvited). He kept his private life to himself and was thus equally fair—and sometimes close to mean, though absolutely never malicious—to everyone.

He had two major traits that were of great value to the magazine and the staff. One was his extreme decisiveness. This is hugely helpful for a weekly or daily newspaper—somewhat less of a necessity for the more leisurely monthly magazine editor or a book editor.

The other was the gift of a true photographer's eye. Before he had become *Time's* top editor, he had for years served as the number two to the fabled editor of *Sports Illustrated*. On Fridays, we would congregate in the editor's conference room and look through the "selects." These were pictures on exhibition for the top editor who would personally select each and every one for the magazine.

For Henry A Grunwald, a picture was usually a problem, an obstacle: it reduced the amount of words available to tell the story. But for Cave, photographs were essential keys to unlocking readers' imaginations. Grunwald made sure that *Time* maintained a high literary and intellectual standard; but Ray brought the weekly news magazine into the twentieth century of visual appeal. For Marshall McLuhan had been right all along: it was the visual (TV) that was to become the mass media king, not the printed word.

I REALLY AM NOT ENTIRELY SURE WHY, even today, but as *Time* went on, as it were, my editing skills seemed to get worse. I got increasingly bored, lost my focus, could not locate my zest, and began not caring. This process took about 20 months—and after many weeks where my days only ended after 20-hour shifts.

Without a doubt, my editing skills were thinning but I just could not figure it out. I could not quite understand why. It was bewildering, to say the least. This bothered me so much that several times in the prior months, I had thought seriously of walking into the editor's office to confess bafflement and failure. But I did not; I kept believing that it would be only a matter of time before the old all-star pitching form returned. For some reason, however, it never did. I kept throwing pitches out of the strike zone—and sometimes even over the protective batting cage!

I spoke to my wife Andrea, in a guarded fashion, about the problem. She had been working as a researcher at *People* magazine, a few floors above *Time's* central command where I worked. She was brilliant, but did not like her job either. Like mine, her superiors were first rate, she said, as were almost all her colleagues.

A graduate of Berkeley and University of Southern California Annenberg, Andrea was also a former child actress. She had lived in Hollywood as a well-employed young mini-star from the age of 6 to 13. During that time, she had met many legendary stars and historic icons, but with the occasional exception of great talents such as Barbara Stanwyck, Rod Serling, Alfred Hitchcock and Bill Cosby, she was greatly under-impressed by the environment. She had seen too many so-called "stars" off the screen to be too impressed with this materialistic culture of celebrity. But *People* magazine was practically a weekly press release touting these people and, in the end, the stupidity of it all became too much for her. Another issue was the weekly celebrity magazine's grindingly impersonal editorial process. Finally, *People* closed each magazine mid-week, at which point she went home, collapsed, spent, angry over the stupid star worship; by contrast, *Time* closed on the weekend, at which point I was the spent jellyfish. And so our optimal points never overlapped.

Marital difficulties seemed to be looming. Andrea soon resigned her position to take up a freelance writing career which included writing the brilliantly reviewed *Pretty Babies*, a realistic book about being a child actress in America. *Variety* praised it as the best such book then written.

Andrea sympathized with me and understood that I could never stay loose enough in that tightly-woven structure to show my best stuff, and that I had over-estimated my versatility and permitted the hubris of my sizable ego to get the upper hand over a proper humility.

But it never dawned on me that the organization would come to the conclusion that it had little use for me at all—even as, at the same time, I was reaching the conclusion that I was not what they wanted.

ONE DAY, THE PHONE RANG in my twenty-fifth floor office at the Time-Life Building at Rockefeller Center.

"Can you come see me?"

It was the voice of the editor who had declaimed that "the girls" were not ready yet for a cover assignment. It was the voice of the one editor who, during the job interview process almost two years ago, had voiced the question: "But do you think you could save a cover?"

I had reasonably answered, then, that I wasn't sure but there was only one way to find out, wasn't there?

The door to his office down the hall opened and he motioned for me to come in. As I passed him, he looked pointedly at his secretary as if to suggest he did not want to be disturbed.

He invited me to sit down. But I remained standing.

The editor settled behind his desk and stared out at the awesome but oft-cold Manhattan skyline. Then he let out a deep and prolonged sigh. "It just isn't working, Tom. I'm sorry."

My stomach dropped a foot. My self-esteem crashed through the twenty-four floors of the Rockefeller Center building and landed below.

"We tried," he said. "We really wanted it to work. We really did. Believe me, we really wanted it to work … But … it isn't."

He sighed pointedly, as if in misery. I tried to hold on to my composure.

"You've got to be very frustrated here," he said. "You are very astute and you have a million ideas. We probably can't implement any of them and the editing positions here don't play to your enormous strengths."

"When do you want me to leave?"

"Whenever you want. Whenever. Heck, if you like, you could switch over to the writer's side and try that out. That might work."

But the invitation seemed, well, without enthusiasm. Working 20-hour shifts as either a writer or editor seemed senseless if the organization was basically—and perhaps quite properly—pessimistic about my prospects.

I went back to my office, closed the door, locked it, sat at my desk, and stared out at the skyline. It seemed colder than usual.

I sobbed, as quietly as I could. I did not want anyone to hear me. After all, there is no such thing as a truly private office.

> When you decide to leave, or when they decide you should leave, you should probably do it as soon as conveniently and mutually possible.

There is no sense delaying the inevitable.

ACTUALLY, MAYBE I DID KNOW something like this had been coming. Indeed, I had been warned even before I had moved back to New York that this job might not be ideal for me. Skip Shearer, a *Parade* magazine veteran, had graciously thrown a farewell dinner party in Los Angeles just before Andrea and I left for New York.

His sons, Cody and Derek Shearer, showed up, as did the latter's wife Ruth and good friend Strobe Talbott. What I did not know was that Strobe, who then worked in *Time's* Washington Bureau, had held the very same job that I was being hired to fill—a senior editor position in the NATION section.

I always liked Strobe, always admired both his directness as well as his skill with indirection and nuance. He had been marked for greater things at *Time* but instead had gone on to greater things than *Time*.

"Tom, you are absolutely going to hate that job. I know you well enough," said 'The Strober,' as he was often called at the magazine. "You're a terrific editor but psychologically, you won't be able to take it—just sitting there and sitting there hour after hour. I know you; it will drive you nuts. The hours are very long; it's very bureaucratic; it's just not you."

But inherited hubris (somewhere on my paternal grandfather's side, pre-World War One in Germany, was a "Von Platt"—yes, it is unbelievable but true ... it must have been *very* minor royalty indeed!) is the genetic over-ride of wise self-knowledge. I took the job anyway. Forward to New York, follow your destiny.

But I should have listened to Strobe. He is a very smart man—and actually a caring one.

In my mind, the Strobe Talbott success story, at *Time* and thereafter, was a glittering intellectual exception that proved the rule. The rule is that too many journalists occupying high media decision-making positions were under-educated. They were smart, hardworking and (mostly) extremely honest; but they had not acquired a requisite level of professional education adequate to the task.

I can recall cover conferences with *Time's* top editors at which, for example, the question would be whether to do a cover story on the monetary policies of the Federal Reserve Board, then headed by Chairman Paul Volcker.

For the first couple of these meetings, I was pretty quiet and rather in awe of the oral facility, indeed extreme cleverness, with which the editors bandied about terms like "prime rate" and "Fed discount rate." But at the third meeting, I began to suspect that there was less deep knowledge here than met the ear, and so, during one lull in discussion, I told a "yield curve" joke, but no one got it. I raised the issue of whether the "marginal analysis" employed by the Fed branch in San Francisco to make a stunning policy point contradicted the Fed in Washington; and very few knew what I was talking about. The reason: I had studied some graduate-level economics at the Woodrow Wilson School (the very school from which the giant Volcker—the wizard tamer of evil inflation—had also graduated); and while my economics professors did not give me A's (it was my weakest subject—so boring!), I did take those courses, I did pass, and I did at least grasp some essentials. This did not make me anything but semi-literate in economics, but at least it was something.

In my own blowhard view, serious journalists, whether or not they go to journalism school—news media people such as top news magazine editors, editorial page editors, nightline staffers, PBS and NPR (Public Broadcasting Service and National Public Radio) journalists—ought to have at least a decent master's degree from a good public policy school, an international relations school, or some economics program. The issues of the globe are getting too complicated to permit our journalists to remain so indifferently educated.

How quickly the *Time* deal changed! In the beginning months, all had seemed so effortless; but by year two, I was starting to drown.

Even before I was told "it was not working," I had started what I had hoped was a very quiet search for a new job. On one level, that was not too difficult in New York, a city of rampant print journalism. Secretly (I had incorrectly assumed), I had been talking with CBS which then sported a full-fledged magazine division; with the *New York Times*; and with the founders of *Manhattan Inc.*, a monthly to be launched in less than a year.

Confidentiality is difficult to achieve in the tightly-woven Manhattan warren world of print journalism, a field populated by well-compensated professional gossips. I realize in retrospect that *Time's* top editors probably knew about these employment change chats. Maybe they had not liked them? Maybe they had expected total loyalty even from an employee who perhaps did not figure prominently in their future. All I can tell you is, once you start negotiating for a new job outside the organization you are in, it is only a matter of time before that organization finds out.

Of course, every organization insists on loyalty from their workers; every organization has its own ego. It wants to conquer you but once you are conquered, then it may lose interest in the investment in you. In this current age of corporate takeovers and "labor mobility" (that is, layoffs and buy-outs), it seems wise to take organizational appeals to loyalty with the proverbial grain of salt (and one stiff shot of vodka—or whatever is your preferred poison).

THE *NEW YORK TIMES* WAS SERIOUS about hiring me but, as was its accustomed way, was moving slowly. CBS needed an editor-in-chief immediately, as the current number-one had accepted the top job at *GQ*, the men's magazine owned by a famous US media company. *Manhattan Inc.* offered me the job of founding editor for what was *then* a very good salary in New York ($100,000), but the proprietor was making me nervous for a number of reasons. I began to worry (perhaps unfairly) that he really wanted to run the magazine himself. As he was putting his own money into the magazine, that would be his right, of course. But I knew I was the kind of person who worked better with more space in which to operate rather than less. Perhaps I would not be the best editor for that magazine after all (in fact, in the end, even though I was formally offered the position, Jane Amsterdam, a highly regarded young journalist was to take the job and boy, did she dazzle!).

You need to be very careful when changing jobs—more careful than I was. Perhaps I should have waited for the *New York Times* to come through, as then number two Arthur Gelb said it would. I respected the *Times* and liked Gelb, who was one of those productively neurotic editors who knew how to get a laugh while getting it all done.

Patience is almost always a virtue when negotiating a new job, but emotion often gets the upper hand on objective calculation. The value of a job can depend not only on the monetary compensation but the freedom one is given and the personality of the supervisor. When CBS first called to inquire of my availability, I had an image of CBS that was like that of *Time* —successful and powerful, but perhaps more like a factory than a family. As it happened, the top vacancy at CBS was for the editor-in-chief of *Family Weekly*, the Sunday supplement, since renamed *USA Weekend*. It was no *Time*, but the job being offered was the top spot.

At some point in the life of every ambitious journalist, that kind of trade-off decision will inevitably materialize: take a top job with a second-tier publication or stay where you are in the premier organization. As I wrote to my colleague Shelby Coffey, then at *The Washington Post* but later to become editor-in-chief of the *Los Angeles Times* (and thus, one day my direct supervisor): "*Family Weekly* may be more like a leaky Boston Whaler than an ultramodern luxury liner, but at least I get to be the captain of my own ship."

Shelby was later to tell me that my note had struck a chord in his own heart. Having worked for *The Washington Post* most of his adult life in hopes of succeeding Benjamin Bradlee as the top editor, he had begun to wonder if it would ever happen; and so, when the Times-Mirror Corporation came a-courting, and eventually offering the top job first at a Times-Mirror newspaper in Dallas, then in Los Angeles, he had started thinking: so, well, do you want to be captain of a ship or not? If the answer is yes, then if you decide to wait for the *New York Times* to open its pearly gates to your ambition, you had better be prepared to dig in for a very long wait.

For those of us who are less patient than that—which is to say all those of us who have functional ADD (that is, most journalists)—we look for a reasonably good top editing opportunity to come along, we then look it over as objectively as our emotions permit, and then ... jump the midget!

Time WAS NOT PUSHING ME out on the street. In fact, Cave himself had not had the stomach to deliver the bad news. When he returned from vacation, he assured me that I had as much time as I needed to cut the best deal I could.

You could not ask for much more than that from an organization into which you were not born and for which you were not ideally suited. In a sense, they were doing me a favor by simply stating that I was miscast in a position that in effect was no more than a glorified copy-editor. Well, maybe the job was more than that—but not a whole lot more than that.

Had my outside marketability been weak, the organization probably would have found something for me. They knew that the transcontinental move from Los Angeles was a big decision for the family. They were "not throwing me out on the street," as the managing editor Ray Cave had put it after I was told by another top editor that it just was not working. Ray could be so gruff, but at bottom, he was a deeply caring and sensitive man. Even after I had left *Time* for CBS, we enjoyed a bunch of happy lunches together.

Thus, when I was able to tell *Time* that I had accepted the *Family Weekly* position and would leave as soon as they would permit me, I received a kind and thoughtful note from Henry A Grunwald, then *Time* Inc.'s editor-in-chief:

Dear Tom,

We were very fortunate to have you with us. Good luck in your new job. Remember this about yourself: the larger the job, the better you will do.

Sincerely, HAG

"THE LARGER THE JOB, THE BETTER YOU WILL DO." Good advice, from a wise man of the media. We are not all cut from the same DNA cloth. My late father-in-law—a brilliant man, though a misguidedly convinced Marxist to the very end of his life—worked well only in a confined space with duties as clearly drawn as a blueprint.

That was not how I worked—and perhaps not how you work either. We make life more difficult for ourselves when we ask ourselves to do everything and be everything when no one can do everything and be everything. This self-imposed pressure is self-destructive. One does not have to be able to do everything in order to be successful. I hope you do not learn this the hard way and break your own heart.

USING THE "HAG" STANDARD, I would say the reason I probably could have claimed an "A" grade at *Newsday* was because Dave Laventhol had understood that the more room an organization could give Weird Tom, the higher the performance level. I was given the op-ed page ball and told to run with it.

I give myself only a "B" at *New York*, mainly because my neurotic emotionality prevented me from being at my best with Clay, who himself was a bit of an immature (if terribly talented) flake himself.

At *The Los Angeles Herald Examiner*, where I worked with Jim Bellows and Don Forst, my grade was probably an "A", partly due to the fact that they knew me well enough to give me an immense barnyard of space in which to operate and partly because no one could have possibly made those editorial pages any worse than they were before I showed up!

My *Time* grade was at best a "B–," with an "A" for effort but a "C" at best for performance. I just could not get up enough air/speed to effect a take-off because I could never manage to get out of the hangar.

Similarly, I was attracted to the *Family Weekly* job not because of the prestige (there was not very much, despite the association with CBS), but because the largest job in any organization is the number-one spot.

In that role, you are on the high wire all by yourself and you (and fate and circumstances) make or break your performance. As one of the Flying Walenda brothers once put it, reflecting on his brothers' famous Barnum and Bailey high-wire circus act, "Real life is when you are up on the wire. All the rest is just waiting for that moment."

The problem with *Time* for me—leaving aside my many imperfections—was that the job required too much waiting. It was a "receptor" position. I did not mind being a catcher on the baseball team if the pitches are coming at me every other five seconds. But life in slow motion required, at this time in my life, more self-restraint, patience, and inner personal tranquility than I could field.

Of those three qualities, I was zero for all.

I remember my very last Friday at *Time*. It was like 1 or 2am (not unusual), and I was finishing up, fussing with the last piece of copy. My usual practise was to stroll out of my office on the twenty-fifth floor of the Time-Life Building—at that time of the night, I was more like sleepwalking—to drop the last of my senior editor-approved stories off for processing. The

Washington Bureau was usually the first to finish up, in part because some of the correspondents wanted to go out drinking; and also because the bureau was in the same time zone, of course, as the headquarters in Manhattan. The latest and last correspondents to sign off on copy (all stories had to be checked for factual accuracy and nuance by the correspondents who filed them) were on the West Coast. They lived life three hours earlier and we had to stay three hours later for them.

As the number two in NATION, I had to wait for the West Coast "comments and corrections"—"C and C's", as they were called. And you know how much I liked waiting! I began to develop a visceral hatred for everything West!

But even as this was my last day at *Time*, and all I wanted to do was to run out of the building and head for CBS, where I would have a bigger office, a larger salary and almost no one to report to, nonetheless, it was not my way to run unceremoniously out the door. If I could offer *Newsday* and Dave Laventhol six weeks, I could offer *Time* six more hours on a Friday night, if that was what it was going to take to finish up the job properly.

I will never forget the look on the face of the top *Time* editor that night as I dropped off the last piece of copy sometime near midnight. I leaned on the counter where the copy intake chute was located and put a new title on the story. I did not see Jason, then the top *Time* editor, who in effect had recommended that I leave, looking over my shoulder. He read the head I had put on the story, looked at me, and smiled. "Pretty good," he said.

After I had been at CBS for but a few days, *Time* threw me a fantastic going-away party at the famed restaurant "21". The editors rented a private room, with an open bar. The most unforgettable moment came during the toast-and-roast period, toward the end.

A well-respected *Time* writer tried to stand up. It took a bit of doing but finally he made it to the elusive and invisible balance beam known as standing. "I just want to say," began his foreshortened oration, "that in all my years at *Time*, the only senior editor who would talk to me for more than five seconds about the ethical implications of a story was Tom Plate. He was the only one." Then, as he tried to raise his hand in a toast, he fell over. Several less-inebriated editors caught him just before he hit the floor. It was nice for once to be at a drinking party where I was not the first to fall over!

Until perhaps recently, *Time* magazine has been America's most famous and influential weekly journal. In many respects, it set the standard for American journalism. To be inducted into the position of senior editor, as I was in the mid-1980s—during my thirties—was to be elevated to a relatively high rank. At the same time, to work at *Time* is to place oneself in a highly unusual and complex professional environment. The magazine is one of the weirdest—and most wonderful—places I have ever worked.

Keep in mind that it was then a bit unusual for an outsider to start working at *Time* as a senior editor—the magazine preferred to ratchet its own people up through the ranks. Big, successful institutions frequently try to deceive themselves into thinking that they would benefit by an infusion of outside blood. This is counter-intuitive. The blood transfusion rarely takes place because in fact, successful institutions are especially skilful at resisting change, in part because they have been wildly successful doing things their own way for so long. But it is fun to bring someone in from the outside and see what happens—the institution has little to lose. If the experiment works, it shows the organization is open to change; if it does not, it will prove the place was already as good as could be and change was not needed. In my heart, I did as well as I could, and tried as hard as I could.

Maybe that was why they blew an unnecessary bundle on the "21" farewell blowout.

> Large established institutions will not be trifled with. They can state that they wish to be reformed from within but what they mean by that is that they will not cede control of the reform to anyone who is not an insider. You can fight this institutional "religion," if you wish, but unless you are yourself the Pope, the institution will expunge you before you manage to accomplish much. Ignore this truth at your peril!

Chapter Six
With CBS: Where I Wished
Spanking Were Back in Fashion

IT WAS MY FIRST DAY as editor of *Family Weekly* and it was terribly exciting. I paid a courtesy call on the publisher, Patrick Linskey, and then went over to the CBS corporate office to pay a courtesy call on one of the top executives.

In front of his large office suite was a waiting area where I waited. But someone was already ahead of me and she was, you guessed it, waiting too. She had been waiting about a half hour, she said, as she had been asked to show up for a job interview; but no one had come out to greet her, even though she felt there was someone inside the office.

She was in her mid-twenties, looked like a cover model for *Cosmopolitan* magazine and, as far as I could tell, had no surface imperfections whatsoever. I would say she would be hired, if what the big CBS executive wanted was a gorgeous model who had an Alabama accent.

I proposed to her that she should simply knock and go in. I knew this guy and he was anything but a stiff. Standing on formality was not his thing. On the contrary, he was a happy-go-lucky bloke—like a riverboat gambler; funny as hell, and, I told her in a whisper, extremely dashing, especially for a corporate type.

Energized and inspired, she knocked on the door and pushed it open. "Mr-[so-and-so]," she sort of shouted out, in a sexy stars-of-Alabama-whispering screech.

The door swung open more quickly and widely than we had anticipated. The two of us could only see the lower half of the executive's body and the back part of that, as it were, was unclothed; and two legs of the female persuasion wrapped around his back in the well-known architectural tryst of passion.

He looked up over his desk at Miss Alabama (but fortunately not at me, whom he could not see). "Oh, sorry to delay you," he said. "Can you wait 10 or 15 minutes more? This won't take any longer than that."

Gosh, was I ever to like that man!

As did many women at CBS.

WELL, HERE WE ARE. We made it to the captain's deck. We are finally numero uno. So what was it like?

Let me give you the upside first—and there were many of them.

The most hilarious was surely when a Hollywood agent was trying to pitch Demi Moore for the cover of *Family Weekly*. Although *People* magazine it was not, *Family Weekly* actually had a circulation that was much greater. As the Sunday supplement to more than 300 newspapers around the country, its theoretical circulation was more than 30 million; *People's* was much less than a third of that. So for an established star with a new movie or for a putative star looking for big-number exposure, landing on the cover of *Family Weekly* or, of course, *Parade* was a big deal.

"I can set you up for a lunch with her. She's so gorgeous!" enthused the Hollywood agent, talking rabidly.

"What's her name again?" I asked. We had recently had Harrison Ford on the cover. He was promoting a new film. We also had in hand a very nice profile of Diane Lane, who struck me as an actual actress.

"Dem-me More," said the agent, accenting both names.

"Dem-me seems like a weird name to me," I said. I had to laugh. In college, my best friend's girlfriend was named "Sigourney." When she first announced it, I laughed out loud. "With a weird name like that," I declaimed, in huffy Princetonian, "you'll never go anywhere." But the gal from Sarah Lawrence College was very self-assured. "I am going to be a famous Hollywood actress," Sigourney Weaver firmly replied.

"Forget the name. She was a smash in 'Blame it on Rio'," the agent said.

"Right, the one with no boobs—she had the hair over them, right?"

A pause. "She's had them done since."

"That's nice."

"You can see them ... after dinner."

Now it had gone from lunch to dinner. I decided to stay with Diane Lane. I still think she is the better actress, don't you? What I am not in doubt about, though, is the need for a firm line of separation between journalists and the entertainment world. Too often, it is almost wholly corrupted, by sex and money.

So, what's new, eh?

THIS IS WHAT IT WAS LIKE to be the editor of a magazine with a large circulation. It was no *Foreign Affairs*, no *Time*, no *Newsweek*. But it was something, a very real thing, and I was happy and lucky to have the job. If you do go into journalism, at some point, you are going to want to be the captain of your own ship, whether it was the QE-2 or a plebian 30-foot cabin cruiser.

Every publication that has been around for some time offers the editor some kind of leverage, though the kind of leverage is different with each publication. For a news magazine, the leverage is credibility. (I remember a famous and ambitious US senator at lunch at *Time* being asked by Henry Grunwald what would be the one thing that would serve to jumpstart his campaign for the White House. The southern politician, Ernest Hollings, snapped back in a short drawl, "Getting on the cover of *Time*.")

Well, credibility was not something *Family Weekly* could offer anyone, but massive circulation was. After *Readers' Digest* and *Parade*, *Family Weekly* had the largest circulation of any magazine in America. With that circulation, I figured I might be able to leverage anything. So I shot for the moon. It was 1984, Ronald Reagan was running for re-election against former Carter vice president Walter Mondale, and so I pitched to both warring camps the following deal: an exclusive interview, and on successive weeks, their pictures on the cover of a generally non-controversial magazine that was on the coffee tables of more than 13 million homes every weekend, with an estimated total readership of some 30 million (using an average of 2.5 readers per household). What was there not to like?

Well, I was still waiting to hear from the Mondale camp (which lost almost every state in the union in Reagan's re-election gallop) when I heard from the White House. Within two weeks, the president's handlers had accepted the deal—an interview for a cover; and two weeks later, I was in the Oval Office, all by myself, tape recorder in tow, alone with the president of the United States, the leader of the Western world, the former B-movie actor and former governor of California—oh, and two staff aides standing inconspicuously to the side, praying that "The Gipper" would not say anything too ... er ... messy.

In fact, the White House staff had insisted that the interview last no more than twenty minutes and that the questions to be asked be submitted in advance. I was not happy with either condition but I submitted them anyway, for I was being offered a one-on-one interview with the president in the Oval Office and such encounters were the rarest kind.

My good friend Lesley Stahl, who had married Aaron Latham, had been a CBS White House correspondent for years and had not once had a one-on-one with any president. Even when *Time* landed such an Oval Office session, a half dozen top editors would pile into the limousine to constitute the team—so big a deal it was. But for this event at 4pm on a Thursday afternoon, though, it was just little old me, my tape recorder and my half dozen prepared questions.

Beforehand, I had told the White House staff that I was concerned that the president might tear off on a tangent at, say, question number three, and the twenty minutes would be up, and I would be stuck with a "cover story"—much desired and indeed needed to justify the "cover" picture of the president—that was a pathetic three questions long. The Reagan staffers instantly promised that they would ask the president to be sufficiently brief in his replies so that all six topics would be covered and the end product would not look so thin.

They had but one request: the questions had to focus on domestic, social, and family issues. I replied that, given the title of the magazine and the fact that it was a magazine that would go to more than 13 million homes, not to mention the fact that the demographic concentration of these homes tended to be not coastal but heartland, sunbelt and middle-America, why, yes, I could do that without selling out my soul.

And of course I submitted the same set of questions to former vice president Walter Mondale (and I was still waiting for a reply).

Walking into the Oval Office to interview the president of the United States is not like walking into the state motor vehicle office for a license renewal. The history, the aura, everything about it was awesome.

My students often ask me if I ever got nervous when interviewing VIPs. I respond with a "never, except for the solitary exception of the White House interview with Reagan." Not that he was some Albert Einstein and I felt intellectually inferior to the task or that he was a cold, aloof, intimidating personality. It was just that when you walked into the Oval Office—where John F Kennedy worked and Eisenhower worked and Lyndon Johnson made his blunders and Nixon did his plotting and Carter did his malaising—you would feel the awesome aura of the place—a little scary, though a great honor and thrill to be within it.

A few things happened that afternoon that I did not expect. The first was that though at first, Reagan was kind of laying back, even cold, he warmed up within minutes. He then shooed the gaggle of photographers— who were getting their forty-second photo ops—out of the room, asked my art director to leave after he had gotten a few more shots, and warmed to the conversation.

Also, I was surprised that the president was so well programmed—or, perhaps, so in command of the material—that he was able to speed through the half-dozen questions so efficiently and breezily. Very quickly, the twenty-minute mark came up. What did I do? Say thank you very much, Mr President, I have to leave now for my tennis lesson? No, no, no ... stay in the room as long as the president is in the room (remember the earlier Clinton-in-Davos story) and keep firing questions until someone hauls you out on your ear.

The problem was, I was out of prepared questions, which meant that this was another one of those wonderful jump-the-midget moments! I looked up at the ceiling, the wall, the Oval Office furniture, scouring my inner consciousness for off-the-wall questions and, thank God, it happened. I managed to come up with a few, such as, "Mr President, we read that your daughter Patti Davis recommends that a couple live together before actually getting married? I was wondering, as her father, what do you think of that approach to marriage?"

What came back, with astonishing speed, was pure Gipper: "Well, I'm just sad that spanking is so out of fashion now!" And it went on like that—for another fifteen minutes. I served up big fat off-the-wall folksy social-issue questions (prayer in the schools, etc.) and the president would hit them out of the park. He was obviously enjoying himself so much that when we hit the forty-minute mark, an aide came out from leaning against the doorway to call a halt. "Mr President, we're running a bit late." Reagan got the hint, stood up, shook my hand, and wished me well. "I enjoyed it," he said.

I strolled out of the Oval Office feeling like a Pulitzer Prize-winning champion. After all, I had an exclusive question-and-answer with the president, and it was all here on tape, inside the very tape recorder in my very hands. Or, was it? I looked down at the tape recorder and I must have turned white or something, because the White House aide asked me whether I was feeling ill. I replied by saying, do you have a gun I can borrow? He looked at me with alarm, suggesting I not use the word "gun" in the vicinity of a president who had already been shot once. I said, no, for me, I want to shoot myself. I showed him the tape recorder; the pause button had been pushed down. Nothing was on the tape.

The aide saw the problem and laughed. Not to worry, he said, we taped the whole thing. What, secret taping in the Oval Office! Now I thought I had an even *better* story, but the truth was, if you looked at the official picture of the interview, you would see a whole bunch of wires openly raveled around our chairs, so that some electronic device was obviously operational. So shut up, I said to myself, they are saving your bacon.

Then, he said, "When do you need the transcript?" I replied that I should be hearing from the Mondale Camp very soon, so... the aide interjected, "When is your flight back to New York?" "Tonight at 8pm," I replied. "Fine, we'll have the transcript done by then—how many copies do you need?"

I was incredulous that a forty-minute interview could be properly typed up, packaged and gotten to the airport! But as I was padding toward the gate for the flight to New York at National Airport, there it was, the presidential sentry—the overcoat, dark glasses, funny little insect-like instrument and wire hanging out of his ears. "Mr Plate?"

I nodded. "This is from the president of the United States." I opened it on the plane. Inside it were two typed copies of the interview, a copy of the original tape, and a signed portrait of the president. Looking back, I realize that one major key to the relative political success of the two-term Reagan presidency was the efficiency and competence of his staff. Heck, in the Carter administration, there would have been no interview; in the Clinton administration, they would have lost the tape!

A week later, I received a call from a White House staffer, wondering how I thought the question-and-answer went. "It was a terrific interview," I said. "How did the cover picture turn out?" "To be honest," I answered, "not so well." The photographer had been my art director who had pleaded with me to let him do the cover shoot. Foolishly (whether because I was a nice guy, or a pushover, or both), I agreed. But the contact prints were mediocre. Then the staffer said, "We can give you ten minutes next Wednesday, if you want to try again with someone else." "You betcha!" I said.

So we asked Sigma, the rightly famous photo agency if they had a photographer who wanted the job. What do you think? Even ten minutes alone with the president is a photojournalist's dream assignment. The photographer we agreed on was to later tell this story: he gets a call the afternoon before the 10am–10:10am shoot from the White House; President Reagan suggests, says the aide, that the shoot be outside, on the little porch behind the presidential desk in the Oval Office, so that instead of the usual boring shot of the chief executive signing some legislation, you have the president outside, in the lovely backyard under a Cherry Blossom tree, as spring is in the air.

It was a great concept, of course. But the problem, as the photojournalist recalled it, was that, while spring was in the air that afternoon, dark storm clouds were in the air the next morning. The sky was so ominous and gray, it was as if God was really angry at the world, but especially at photographers planning an outdoor shoot that morning.

When the photojournalist was ushered into the Oval Office at the appointed time, Reagan looked up, sadly, and, referring to the severe overcast, said, well, I guess we will just have to do the usual—boring shots of me behind the desk.

Resignedly, the Sigma ace then began to set up his equipment inside and started clicking away; but then, just as it sometimes happened before a major cloudburst on the US East Coast, the sky split open as if God was shooting down a message. The entire back porch was illuminated like a Hollywood set and the president, despite being in his seventies, jumped up, caught the eye of the Sigma man, ran out on the back porch, relaxedly leaned against the Cherry Blossom tree, and for all the world, looked as cool a cowboy as the West had ever seen. Not ten seconds later, the sky fell in like a tidal wave from the heavens, but somehow, the photojournalist managed to click through a dozen or so shots.

Back in the New York office, had I not known the full story, I would have imagined a leisurely outdoor shoot in which nothing was rushed, except for the fact that ten of the twelve rushed shots were out of focus, one was okay and the last one was magnificent: a beaming Reagan, with the beautiful blossoms behind him, smiling out at the world from the cover of *Family Weekly*, from the kitchen tables and coffee tables of more than 13 million homes. The triumph of the image, the re-election triumph of a politician who knew that in this visual age image is substance, and ultimately the triumph of the hoofer-entertainer who knew what his audience wanted and was determined to give it to them, especially if he wanted to sell tickets.

Oh, and I am still waiting to hear from the Mondale people.

WHILE I AM IN this political mode, let me say that I consider myself a card-carrying member of neither the Republican nor Democratic Party. I would not axiomatically trust a member of either of them with my daughter for a single weekend. But certain individuals transcend partisanship and make themselves so likable, you forget momentarily that they are in part but fronts for a certain assemblage of vested (monied) or ideological (narrow-minded) interests. This is the way the American political world is and there is nothing anyone can do about it, except to enjoy those aspects of it that are most enjoyable and accept the imperfections of all political systems ever conceived. It is a truism to suggest that the best definition of utopia is a state of political being that does not exist.

George Bush Sr, for example, was a very different kind of person than his then-boss in 1984, President Reagan. Bush's reputation for Yale aloofness daunted me one day during that same 1984 campaign as my wife Andrea and I drove from Boston to spend a few hours with the vice president.

We were greeted at the Bush compound in Maine by a most likable lady: Barbara Bush. My wife is a former Berkeley radical and daughter of a once-Marxist City College of New York lecturer, a quite brilliant man. But she took to the next First Lady of the United States like, well, I would have said, like a fish to water, except Andrea is not one for fishing. In the fish department, she likes hers cleaned, nicely cut and neatly served at expensive sushi restaurants.

After I had interviewed the vice president, he and an aide invited Andrea and me for a run up the Kennebunkport River in his fancy "cigarette" fishing vessel. Andrea, a relatively short woman, looked at Barbara, and Barbara pulled her off to the side as we were walking toward the dock. "You don't have to go with him," she said.

Andrea looked at me. "You can go if *you* want."

I looked at Bush. "Mr Vice President, I don't think Andrea wants to go."

Bush looked at Andrea. "It's perfectly safe, a little windy perhaps." In fact, the winds were all but howling, and Andrea, I knew, was imagining flapping fish inside the boat struggling for their lives but losing them with blood-covered hooks in their mouths.

Barbara looked at Andrea with a hard stare, as if to say: stand your ground, don't be bullied by this bully. In fact, Mrs Bush may have said exactly words to that effect.

Andrea looked at me. "Go if *you* want, I'll stay here with Barbara."

A fishing run up the Kennebunkport River would last at least an hour. I knew from having done my homework that an upriver fishing expedition with the vice president was one of the central elements of the Kennebunkport charm offensive, whether for visiting VIPs or for journalists skeptical about whether the golden-spooned vice president had the common touch. I realized that as warm and intelligent as Mr Bush had been during the hour-long interview, the fishing expedition was simply part of the co-optation process.

I politely declined the offer, and explained that Andrea and I always came as a "two-fer," adding that I always stayed close to the girl I brought to the dance.

Mr Bush smiled, turned on his heels and headed to the "cigarette" with his aide.

Mrs Bush turned to Andrea, corralled her with an arm hug, and said, proudly, "Young lady, you are the first person ever to turn him down. I applaud you."

One liked Mr Bush a lot, but his chosen mate in life was something else.

Family Weekly was a fun job, I have to say—not important, probably, but interesting, entrepreneurial, inventive. Plus, I had a wonderful publisher with whom to work.

Here is what I mean. Not everyone at *Time* was stuffy or slow-moving; many of them were not, to say the least, any of these things. But compared to Pat Linskey, the publisher and CEO of the magazine, and the man who hired me from *Time*, they seemed practically cadaverous.

Pat, memorably, was a big noisy Irishman with a heart as broad as the sky, an appetite for a drink as deep as an ocean (immensely befitting his national heritage), and a healthy attitude toward editors that bordered on the reverential without the slightest bit of wimpishness. He knew that he knew about the business side of things and wanted his editors to know more about the editorial side than he did; he would ask questions but would almost always take "no" for an answer. This is what you want from "the power"—the person to whom you report.

Family Weekly was sort of Avis to the Hertz; and the Hertz was *Parade*. It made a lot of money. Pat had heard through the grapevine—probably through his outgoing editor-in-chief, the late Arthur Cooper—that *Time* was not working out so well for me and calculated that I could be lured to a less prestigious publication via the glory of the number one spot under conveyance and via the greed-appeal of a better money deal.

He was right on both counts. I had always wanted to be the captain of a ship, and while *Family Weekly* was not exactly the second coming of the *Queen Elizabeth II*, it was a lot better than a leaky rowboat (well, actually, it was leaking, but more about that later).

Moreover, the top spot was coming open as the incumbent, Arthur Cooper, was about to be offered the top job at *GQ*, a magazine he had wanted to work at for decades. When the job was actually offered to him by *Conde Naste*, Arthur accepted and then recommended me highly to CBS and to Pat, whom Arthur greatly respected for the same reasons I would come to respect him.

Art Cooper had telephoned me while I was still at *Time*, asked me out for a drink, and told me what was up. He also said Pat would be a dream to work with. This was a key point.

There is nothing in the world like running your own magazine. Being editor-in-chief is not like any other position. I had been a number two, a number four, number eight, and number 212! And the top spot is twice as demanding intellectually and physically as the number two job—as well as twice as exhilarating: yes, it was "life on the wire," and I suppose, in one sense, every job prior to this one was "just waiting."

Benjamin Bradlee, the editor, for decades, at *The Washington Post*, used to argue that one key to an editor's success was being able to work under and with a great and understanding publisher boss.

Pat Linskey was certainly no Katherine Graham (publisher of *The Washington Post*), as he would be the first to agree. He was not born rich, he was anything but patrician and he had no social connections. But in one sense he was like Graham in her relationship to Bradlee (but not to *Newsweek* editors whom she had ruthlessly tossed out like a two-year-old car on a whim). He respected his *Family Weekly* editor and allowed me as much space in which to operate as possible. You will recall the sweet note from Grunwald when I left *Time*. When very high-level people like a Grunwald or a David English take the time out of their frenetic lives to focus on you for five minutes and make a trenchant observation about your strengths and weaknesses, it is probably a good idea to burn the thought on your brain, if not on an arm-band and carry it around.

I mention Pat in part to contrast him with some of the people I was to encounter when disaster was to strike *Family Weekly* about 18 months after I took the top job. (Lucky guy, eh? Timing is everything in life, and sometimes mine was *terrible*.)

In real life, disaster can be another word for a corporate takeover. They may call it a "friendly" takeover or whatever—but it is always unpleasant and/or it is always treacherous. So the story I am about to tell is designed not to settle any scores—I have none to settle and could not be happier about the life that I have had and the opportunities that have come to me. I tell the true story only as a guide to others who may face a similar crisis.

IF YOU ARE WORKING at a company facing a takeover by another company—however friendly the acquiring force appears to be—the probability (though not certainty) is that you will lose your job, possibly in an ugly way. So start looking for a new one immediately; better yet, any time you take a job, ask yourself—is this company stable? Would it offer me a contract for two or three years if I asked for one? Always test those waters before taking the job, because remember, as I've said, you're at the point of your maximum leverage

BECAUSE PAT LINSKEY WAS SO MUCH FUN and gave me the room to maneuver, I was determined not to disappoint him. *Family Weekly* had started to go south profit-wise before he came on as publisher—and long before he hired me from *Time*. Together, we would save it from extinction. Or so we thought.

Pat knew he wanted me for the editor's job the minute we met. Because I was at *Time*, he feared, I guess, that I might be some kind of Princeton or Amherst stiff. The truth was, my origins were as his—hard-scrambling escape from the lower middle class, mostly via hard work and more hard work and some luck and genius mentors. And so we got on famously and worked our butts off. The result was that for almost two years, *Family Weekly* was probably editorially competitive with *Parade*.

Family Weekly, despite the name, was in effect a general interest monthly. That is to say, it was a magazine driven neither by the news—as in a newspaper or a news magazine—nor by some clear formula (*Motor Trend* or *Cosmopolitan* magazine), but by the sheer willpower of whoever was the editor, and his or her staff. Hence, rather than requiring a savvy but quick as lightning response to the ever-changing news, the magazine required imagination, flair, wit, and superior writing and photography—plus a lot of advance planning. The staff strength was much smaller than a newspaper's and so the esprit de corps needed to be tighter.

In 1985, when it was announced that Gannett, the giant US newspaper chain, was purchasing *Family Weekly* from CBS, the following commentary appeared in *Advertising Age*, the lead professional (and gossip) magazine for Madison Avenue. It appeared in a column by James Brady, who was famous for having edited or worked at high levels at a number of top publications. I include his commentary not only because it is entirely self-serving, but because it has the additional virtue of being true.

He wrote: "In the backwash of media acquisition such as Gannett's takeover of *Family Weekly* from CBS, you wonder what happens to people. Tom Plate, *Family Weekly's* editor, resourceful and energetic guy with time in [publications such as] *New York*, *The Los Angeles Herald Examiner* and *Time* magazine, gets high marks from newspaper editors who run *Family Weekly* every Sunday. Plate's done editorial wonders for the Sunday magazine."

What Brady was in fact saying was this: why not treat people with dignity, rather than as disposable parts?

I probably was, in fact, a pretty good editor of that magazine. In my twenty months there, the magazine's articles were picked up by the wire services, TV shows and other publications at least as often as our competitors'. But I also had a great staff—from the whip-smart Kate White (who went on to be the top editorial diva of *Cosmopolitan* magazine), to the moody but brilliant John Tarkov, to the quiet but deep David Granger, who was to become the editor of *Esquire*.

In fact, I recall an event years later in honor of Clay Felker, where Brady, looking dapper as ever in his tux, introduced me to the always-affable Walter Anderson, the long-reigning editor of *Parade*, as if we had never met. At the time, I was editor of the editorial pages of the *Los Angeles Times*.

Brady had said to Walter, a gentleman editor of the highest order and the shrewd editorial steward of that giant circulation magazine for decades, "Have you ever met Tom Plate?"

Walter had replied, "Met him? He beat my brains out almost every week when he was at *Family Weekly*."

That tribute was far more gracious than precise, but I will take it, especially on behalf of the late and not adequately lamented *Family Weekly* staff, crushed by the Stalinist forces of the takeover.

But while Tom Plate and his staff got the credit for the improvements to the magazine, it was the publisher who let those improvements happen. That is to say, it was Pat Linskey who purposely created the spacious environment in which it was possible for wildly neurotic editors to do their thing. Those of us who have had the honor of running a large circulation or influential publication need humbly to reflect that we are toast unless our supervising publishers are gold standard.

GANNETT, ONE OF THE WORLD'S LARGEST media companies, made more money than the mafia but its newspapers, with rare exceptions, would never make it to the Journalism Hall of Fame, if there were one. That, in any case, was not the corporate goal; the goal was to make money while publishing newspapers. The organization is successful as a business precisely because its suits (that is, the company's dispassionate money managers) watch like hawks over every penny of expenditure (which puts a lot of stress on the editors); because they tend to be ruthless (which Wall Street of course adores); and because editors are on the whole second-class citizens in that particular culture (as in very many other corporate media cultures these days).

As do so many changeovers in life, the takeover occurred because of money. Indeed, most, if not all, takeovers or media sales are about money—more rather than less (that is, greed). Takeovers are not primarily about "improving the product," though the press release will inevitably state so, or combining "synergies to optimize consumer value." It is always much simpler: just follow the logic of the money if you want to understand what is happening to you as your life down-clutches into a shambles.

In this case, the key money issue was the price of CBS stock. It was at this time so low that Ted Turner, founder of CNN, thought he had enough cash to buy enough of it to take CBS over and make it into a kind of a commercial network as well as a cable network. As Turner approached the CBS gate, the network's sentries shouted "barbarian approaching" and began to start buying back their own CBS stock, which increased the stock's value. But before too long, CBS began to run out of cash and thereupon organized a series of fire sales by unloading non-core assets (CBS was not about to sell "Sixty Minutes") in return for cash, which was then to be used to buy back more stock until, depleted and exhausted, Barbarian Turner retreated back to the jungle of Atlanta, home of the Braves and CNN corporate headquarters.

Among the non-core assets were CBS Toys, Steinway pianos, and *Family Weekly*. We went on the market for about $50 million and Gannett in the end paid about eighty per cent of that for full ownership.

When the deal went through, I was still under contract with CBS but I knew my staff were in big trouble when a top Gannett official telephoned me to invite me to a reception for Al Neuharth, the top Gannett-teer. After the reception, this short man with the extraordinary ambition—and dressed in his trademark sharkskin business suit—came up to me and said, "Tom, welcome to Gannett. We're happy to have you. I'm sure you'll do well with us."

With that, I knew my goose was cooked. When you are a member of the team being bought up and the buyer welcomes you on board as if an equal, smell a rat. As Jim Bellows once put it: "The problem with Al is that you never know where the suit ends and the shark begins." Moreover, I had been tipped off by a true friend, David Laventhol, at one of his East Side Manhattan parties. "Watch out for those Gannett people" was how he put it, in his typical laconic style.

You should understand that whenever a media property is sold, the new owner will want to make changes—usually major. New owners will want their own editors and will want to put their own stamp on the product. You could be a Rhodes scholar (which I was not) and a Pulitzer Prize winner (not me) and they would still want their own man or woman reporting to them.

I did not really blame Gannett for that. They paid good money for the magazine ($40 million was a fair piece of change in 1985) and it was theirs to do with as they wished. Al Neuharth was a tremendous innovator and deserved great credit for creating *USA Today* and, in the process, for developing new graphic and packaging techniques that almost overnight became cloned everywhere in the States, livening up our otherwise dull-looking newspapers. Moreover, a larger-than-life figure like Al the Shark had managed to attract and keep highly respected journalists such as John Quinn, who had come from Providence. Hey, was I so great that I could dismiss Al as nothing more than a shark when in fact he was a newspaper whale who changed the ocean tides (for better and for worse, to be sure) of American newspapering?

I just felt sorry for my staff—almost all of them were much younger than I—and what they had to go through. Most, though not all, would be fired; I would probably land on my feet—I was not the world's greatest editor but I had a respectable track record. I also had a two-year letter of commitment from CBS. But for some of the kids for whom *Family Weekly* was only their first or second job, they had nothing. I felt really terrible for them.

IN THE REGRETTABLY LENGTHY LIST of personal habits of mine, near the top was the fact that I would often get too close to my staff, care too much about them, worry too much when they broke up with their boyfriends or girlfriends or ran into money problems. One lesson I was never to learn as a manager of editorial talent was the need to keep my distance, to not get so involved. But I could not help myself. Perhaps because I myself came from a small dysfunctional family, I thought of the workplace as a sort of substitute family. I truly believed that it was important to care for the people with whom one worked. Whether the net result of a family atmosphere was to produce a superior product, only my former bosses and readers can tell you. But I was incapable of doing it any other way—even up to today.

A TOP GANNETT OFFICIAL—I won't mention his name because this is not a get-even type of book—invited me for a chat over dinner in Washington. He brought along his fabulous wife, who struck me as an excellent judge of character—which was probably why she was there! I liked her but not so much her husband.

At one point, she asked me to go into some detail about my working relationship with the publisher Pat Linskey. I said it was ideal—"he rarely interferes." She said, "I think you're probably not going to like to work with my husband, then!" I looked her straight in the eye and said, to her not him, "I don't see how it can work then. When I am crowded, I tend to underperform." Returning to New York City, I realized, sadly, that *Family Weekly* and Tom Plate were history. The magazine would be reborn as something else and I would go somewhere else.

While I was still under contract with CBS (I was not stupid enough to leave *Time* before getting a written guarantee from CBS) post-takeover, my staff had no such lifeline. Linskey and I talked this over, and Pat, who could be brilliantly blunt, politely informed the Gannett people that a staff rebellion was brewing, and that without some kind of severance package, the editors were going to walk out. This would mean that there would be no magazine next week or the week after or the week after that and that would mean everyone—all 300-plus newspapers—would blame Gannett for the hole in their Sunday package.

Pat Linskey was very street smart. So maybe he had not gone to Princeton. (I once took him to the Princeton Club for lunch and when the check came for signing, the waitress gave it to me. Pat commented—and I would never forget this, and how poignant this was, because basically we both came from similar socio-economic roots —"Tom, why do you think she was so sure I wasn't a member?"). But I would rather have him in my trench fighting the Bad Guys than many an Ivy Leaguer I can think of. In the end, Pat basically extorted from Gannett eight weeks' severance pay for the young staff, who were extremely relieved to hear the news. Eight weeks' pay meant zilch to Gannett but it meant everything to these good young journalists (for one, it could cover months of rent on their cramped New York City apartments).

This was a very stressful period, and when I am under stress, I tended to drink alcohol, because it would make me feel better (up to a quantitative point). But this was only my second takeover experience: the first was back at *Long Island Newsday* when Times-Mirror (the parent corporation of the *Los Angeles Times*) bought out the Guggenheims and Otis Chandler. The head of Times-Mirror had flown in from Los Angeles to make personally certain that the transition was handled well and that people were treated properly. And they were. In fact, Dave and his team not only survived but triumphed, producing record profits and winning many Pulitzers and other major awards.

But this takeover was a toughie, and I began taking major doses of Dalmane (a serious prescription drug for physical pain) in the office to kill the mental and psychic pain. I am not sure the staff was aware of my deep pain. But Pat probably was—and felt terrible about the whole damn ordeal.

At one point, I telephoned my designated point of contact at Gannett to tell him how miserable I had become.

He said, "Have a drink and relax. You're secure with us. We want you to come down to headquarters and work with us on the magazine."

I said, "John, with all due respect—because you are a well-admired editor—but I'm not coming." I knew that would be a problem for them because they had no one there who knew how to produce this kind of magazine.

There was silence at his end.

So I continued, "I'm under contract with CBS and I'm staying here in New York." I had not said—though I wanted to—that only Pat Linskey could have made my job at *Family Weekly* so enjoyable, and only he could have inspired me to come up with some great cover stories, simply by *giving me as much psychological space as possible*. With whom I work—the *person*—is more important to me than the *organization* for which I work. I rarely believed in organizations but often (too often?), I did believe in individuals.

Finally, John said, "How long does the CBS contract run?"

"Until the end of the year—three more months."

"What if we were to extend it for three months? Would you come down here and show us how to put three issues out?"

Three months' pay for three weeks' work—not bad.

That's a fair offer, I said. But what about my wife? I have to leave her back in New York?

No problem, he said. We have a hotel we put visitors in.

I asked its name.

He said some place or other that I had never heard of (my wife and I are hotel snobs, especially Andrea).

I said, "You don't know Andrea. She's not going to stay at what's-its-name. Forget about it."

I was not lying. Andrea will do a lot of ordinary things—today she is a professional social worker. We are not rich. Her father was a socialist intellectual. But staying at anything less than a five-star hotel is just not in her makeup—and good for her!

John said, "Where would she like to stay?"

I suggested the Four Seasons Hotel. I told him she had stayed there before, and that she liked it very much indeed.

He paused, sighed and then said in a low voice, "Please don't run up the bill too much, ok?"

I laughed. "John, I'll be down there to help you for three weeks. I'm almost happy to do it, but, to tell you the truth, I might have done it for free, had you not cremated my young staff."

He paused, then said, "It's not personal, Tom. It's just about budgets and money."

I thought: *There's something wrong about the norms of a culture in which people so often come in second.* I think I then said something like: "John, either we are editors who have an ethical responsibility to our readers and to our staff, or we are only profit-seeking businessmen." Or maybe I had not said anything at all.

I went down to work with the Gannett editors. They were nice people, not Martians. But the overlords tended to be profit-seeking businessmen first, and journalists second. I had not gone into journalism to make money; I went into it because I thought it was important in a democracy like America's.

When the three weeks were over, I returned to New York City. In the mail box was a letter from Sir David English, whom, as you know, I adored. I think this note snapped me out of any possible return to Dalmane. It read: "I can only imagine what you are going through. But don't take it personally. Gannett is well known for screwing good editors."

Friends are terrifically important when the going gets tough—not just when you are flying high. I was moved by David's letter. Here was the greatest editor on Fleet Street and he took time to worry about me. This one letter must have saved me from thousands of dollars of therapy.

To be sure, its central message was not entirely fair to Gannett, a huge US newspaper chain with many hardworking publishers and editors. Some Gannett papers today run my foreign affairs column; some Gannett-teers I count among my best friends and finest professional colleagues. When Gannett fired most of my staff, I knew it was not personal, it was just business—it was the corporate American way. This is why, whenever you are negotiating for yourself with a corporation, you have to look out for yourself; probably no one else will.

Oh, by the way, Andrea enjoyed the Four Seasons Hotel immensely, especially the white chocolates on the bed every night!

IN RETROSPECT, IT WAS A blessing in disguise: *Family Weekly* was so much fun, I would have stayed for ten years had the magazine not been sold out from under us. If I had stayed on and not moved, I would never have had the chance to work in Manhattan as an editorial page editor and start on an exciting new chapter in my life.

I should have known the end was close at hand, though. Just six months before the secret sale, at a CBS Magazine Division retreat in Key Biscayne, Florida, a top corporate executive from CBS Higher Authority had flown down to deliver the keynote address. At the end, he proclaimed yours truly to be the "Hottest Young Editor" in New York. For hours afterwards, I glowed.

Only *later* did it hit me: my days were numbered. Corporate big shots believe that speech to be given primarily to disguise other thoughts. A compliment such as that—in front of a cast of hundreds—would not emerge from the goodness of the corporate heart (puh-lease!), but out of some corporate deceit. What a fool I was again!

> Snobbery in your selection of journalistic jobs may not be in your best interests. In the course of your career-span, there will be but a limited number of number-one editors at *Time* or the *New York Times*. If you pine to have the experience of being number one—to see whether you

are up to the challenge—and an opportunity comes along that is arguably less than first-tier, you are probably better off jumping the midget than staying in line and waiting...and waiting...and waiting...for the job Godot. Life, I am reliably informed, is short.

Chapter Seven
New York Newsday: Another Fabulous Start-up, Another Journalistic Lease on Life

SOMETIMES, I AM TOLD BY FRIENDS, I can be charming; but sometimes, I know, I can be obnoxious. I don't mean to be, to be sure; I just am, sometimes—well, at least I hope, only sometimes.

One of those times, for sure, occurred about a year after I joined *Newsday's* big start-up adventure in New York. The Long Island giant launched a valiant effort to develop a full-fledged New York City edition in the mid- to late-1980s.

New York Newsday was spawned by the vision of *Newsday* CEO David Laventhol—the guiding light of the Long Island-based paper for decades—and by the enormous profits generated by the near-monopoly newspaper company on the island.

It was not quite a wholly separate, independent newspaper; rather it rotated into orbit like a very large moon around Saturn—that is, around its mother, *Newsday* on Melville, a former farmer's pasture on Long Island. As a practical matter, the New York paper picked up and re-formatted the mother paper's national and international coverage, and its editorials, in order to focus entirely on the affairs and issues of the five large boroughs of the city of New York and its roughly eight million people.

New York Newsday's editorial pages were central to the effort because they aimed to give the paper a very loud, clear and intelligent voice in the political affairs and debates of the city. This meant that the first and founding editorial page editor of the New York edition—and that was yours truly, in 1986—would have to go to daily battle against the major-league pitching of the *New York Times*, the *New York Daily News* and *The New York Post*. This was fierce, fast and sometimes Machiavellian competition—and none of those papers took any prisoners. They were out to beat you, to beat you badly, to let you know it, and to watch you bleed on the curbside.

As I got caught up in the helter-skelter pace of competing against these three formidable newspapers, I began hectoring my boss on Long Island to speed up the pace of the mother ship's editorials which we were to use in the New York edition. Since we were to concentrate on the Big Apple, we could not in our offices on Third Avenue in Manhattan write our own editorials on the president's latest folly or some foreign intrigue and were dependent on Melville to do that part of the job. Timeliness was to us on Third Avenue the essence of the competition. To put the matter more or less prosaically, a daily paper was not a weekly.

But ordinary bucolic life out in the shady, leafy suburbs is rather more leisurely than in the bump-and-go grind and competition of pressure-cooker Manhattan. I found myself constantly hassling, cajoling and irritating Long Island with my constant, unremitting pressure to "speed things up." If something important happened on Monday about which something of substance needed to be said, I wanted it said in *New York Newsday* on Tuesday—not on Wednesday, not to mention Friday.

A fair point but sometimes an irritating one and as it happened, my boss on Long Island was one of the nicest, wittiest and most considerate gentlemen I had ever met or even could hope to meet. His name was Sylvan Fox and not only was he a fox in the sense that he was very smart, he was also a fox in the sense of being a very special colleague in the journalistic jungle.

It all came to a head one day when I was summoned out to Long Island for a sit-down meeting with the mother *Newsday's* editorial page editor Fox and *Newsday's* dynamic publisher Robert Johnson. Although I was in daily communication with Melville via a conference call to go over what each side aimed to do that day and I was often on the phone with Fox who was the American version of Noel Coward for his invariable wit, I rarely journeyed out to Long Island myself. It would give me the shakes, to be honest. I had too many bad memories of growing up there, I guess. As I have said, I loved and respected *Newsday*, but its environs threatened me.

The showdown meeting held in the publisher's spacious office was immediately tense. I was taken aback by how unfriendly the environment was. I began to think I was going to be fired or at least reassigned.

The Long Island editorial page editor (and in effect my immediate supervisor, if not my effective boss) was the first to speak: "We have to straighten this out." Johnson was sitting to the side, watching.

"Straighten what out?" I said.

"Tom, you are getting on my nerves. You have become a royal pain in the ass."

"I don't feel that way about you," I said, weakly.

"Well, I feel that way about you!" he said, loudly.

I said I really did not understand, and, in a sense, I really had not. I knew there was growing friction between us over the timeliness of the editorials, but in all other respects I thought of our relationship as a virtual model of cooperation between Long Island and New York, which on the news side suffered nothing but tension.

The editorial page editor continued in this manner—that I was making too big a deal out of the timeliness issue, that I had become a royal jerk (which I probably had), and that things could not continue this way.

"Why are you constantly pushing so hard this way?" he said.

I was a little shaken but answered as calmly as I could: "Because we need very snappy, up-to-date journalism in the New York paper. If we do not have that, others will."

"Do you actually think people choose their newspapers over when editorials appear?"

"Over time, yes, probably. It's part of the paper's total image and personality. If editorials are unimportant, then why have them at all? Fire the staff and expand the sports section and the hell with it."

Fox explained that rushing editorials was a prescription for intellectual mediocrity, or what he called, not unfairly, "television journalism"—the quick, knee-jerk, thirty-second microwave reheat reaction where there is hardly a moment's actual deep reflection.

I answered by saying I accepted that description of a lot of electronic media commentary and that *Newsday*, as a class act, would not want to dumb down this way. But my fear was that waiting an extra day or two to publish an editorial on Thursday that would have been more or less the same as the one we could have run on Wednesday meant that we would not only be a day late but a dollar short as well.

"That may be your view," retorted Fox, "but it is not mine. And it's not what I want."

Suddenly Johnson, sitting quietly to the side and having said nothing thus far (which was not his custom), broke in: "But it is what I want."

Fox was completely thrown off balance, stunned.

"Tom wants it, Sylvan, because I want it."

"Oh," was all the ashen-faced editorial page editor could say.

For once, wisely, I said nothing. Game, set, match. At almost all American newspapers, the ultimate power lies with the publisher. *Newsday* would have more timely editorials; Tom would get what he felt was needed in New York; and in six months, Sylvan Fox was to retire after decades of distinguished journalism at *Newsday* and the *New York Times* where he once won a Pulitzer.

I returned to Manhattan in the *Newsday* limo, never so sad in my life for winning.

If I could choose between being a Plate and a Fox, being a fox would win hands down.

A YEAR OR TWO after that episode, I was asked by Long Island to re-design the Sunday commentary section, titled CURRENTS, which featured a long, *Economist* magazine-style "super-editorial" every Sunday. This "super-editorial" would be exceptionally well researched, thought out and written. While it was my concept, it was under the management of Sylvan's successor, James Klurfeld—the paper's former Washington Bureau editor—that the innovation was carried through exceptionally well.

I have always been amazed that the "super-editorials" done by my Long Island colleagues never won a Pulitzer Prize for editorial writing though I am not much in awe of Pulitzers.

IT HAD STARTED at *New York Newsday* with a phone call from the godfather of the mother *Newsday,* Dave Laventhol.

"Tom," said Dave, in his quiet, slow-moving, laconic tone. "Remember how you liked *Newsday* when you worked there right out of graduate school but just hated Long Island? Well, since you are such a terrific editor, we've decided to create a whole new newspaper in New York City just so we can have you back—this time as editorial page editor. It will be called *New York Newsday* and we want you to be one of its founders."

What could I say to that? And what could I say to David English writing to me from London: "I do hope you will make *New York Newsday's* editorial pages aggressive, controversial and provocative, and break out of the paralyzing blandness that grips the American press in this area to the point of anaesthetizing paralysis."

I agreed with that and I was determined to make the paper's editorial pages the most responsibly exciting in the greatest city on earth.

New York is a very special place, of course, and as a media man, it is not far removed from something akin to—I have to say—a news media maven's haven. The politicians are larger than life, the pace is fast and furious, and the journalistic competition feral. Believe me, competing against the *New York Daily News* and the *New York Post*—not to mention the *New York Times*, *New York* magazine and *The Village Voice* (a tremendous weekly)—is not like preparing for junior prom. These editors and reporters are fast on the draw and even quicker to pull the trigger. It was an ideal job, what with a great boss, a great staff and a great city.

Dave's vision was, however, not only ambitious but enormously complex. In effect, the New York paper, with headquarters on Third Avenue and 49th Street in Manhattan (initially), would be the spanking new baby in the *Newsday* family. But, like most new babies, it was not only the object of everyone's adoring affection but, at times, of everyone's unadoring annoyance. It cried a lot, needed its diapers changed often, and—rather like New York itself—was not always a model of deportment or civility.

The chief news executive of *New York Newsday* was Don Forst, a delight to work with if you were obviously on his side, but one tough cookie if he thought you were not playing ball with him. Our relationship was near-perfect: he rarely made a suggestion for an editorial and he never made a senseless suggestion. And, he was funny as hell.

But his relationship with his superiors at *Newsday* headquarters on Melville, Long Island, was rocky, to say the least. In part this was because of the very nature of the tricky Laventholian structure: it required editors who were competing against their counterparts at the likes of the *New York Times* and the *New York Daily News* to take orders (theoretically) from editors who were running a newspaper in the relatively tranquil suburban environment of leafy Long Island with little direct competition.

In addition to the inherent structural tension, personality clashes exacerbated things. Don was not one for backing down; and Long Island editors in general were not ones for taking chances (why should they—the mother ship was making millions every month in profit).

Before too long in the great *New York Newsday* experiment, the city-island friction got so bad that Don started to refer to *Newsday* headquarters on the island as "Mel-Vile." At one point Dave himself would sometimes have to fly east to spend quality psychiatric time with both sides to calm everyone down and remind all that we were all on the same team.

Don had often held my hand, psychologically speaking (he probably understood me almost as well as my long-suffering wife who was world-class in this and other respects), and I would always try to return the favor by holding his. This was easy for me to do not only because I liked Don a lot but also because my own personal relations with my *Newsday* counterparts on Long Island were generally good. They understood what I was up against, were unfailingly helpful, and they rarely criticized. They supported all my hires and one year even submitted my editorials as *Newsday's* official candidate for the Pulitzer (editorials on the New York City mayoral race).

The truth was that Don needed the tension with Mel-Vile to keep himself edgy and competitive. Like the tennis great John McEnroe, he adopted an abrasive style to stay at the top of his game. I do not know whether the Long Island editors ever understood that but instinctively, more than consciously, I did. And so almost every day, Don and I would take fifteen minutes out of a pressure-packed day to take what Don called our daily "serenity walk." Don was not wanting in exercise, mind you; even later on in his seventies, he would work out during lunchtime instead of having lunch. He could pass off as a very trim 50-year-old, even today. But Don, like many media people, lacked inner tranquility. Patience was not at the top of the list of his virtues. Neither was tolerance of mediocrity or editorial bureaucracy.

An editorial accountant once intruded on a tense major-story planning meeting to complain that his budget advisory memos had gone ignored and Don, enormously irritated, advised the bean counter to leave his office or he would cut off his tie. When the accountant inexplicably persisted and returned with his sheaf of budgetary printouts, Don opened his desk drawer, pulled out a pair of scissors, bounded out of his chair and, before the startled bean counter knew what had hit him, scissored off his corporate-looking tie.

The accountant never ever returned to Don's office—nor did any other member of the mother *Newsday's* financial department. In the insanely competitive print media environment of New York, a totally sane editor may not exactly be what the doctor ordered. Really terrific editors are generally not all there, to be perfectly honest.

THERE IS ONE undeniable advantage of working in the media: boredom is not in the job description. One reason is the kind of people with whom you work, including charming politicians—though the shrewd and successful ones can often create big trouble for journalists.

Let's face it. American politics is inherently messy—even dirty—and politicians are rarely saints. The campaign system is more devilish than angelic. Yet we journalists often act as if we are vessels of virtue in a dirty sea of corruption. Life is more complicated than that and we journalists swim in the same muddy, over-warmed seas as everyone else.

Politicians were always trying to pimp journalists. And we journalists were always seducing and then abandoning them after we had used them up or exposed them. It is a silly game that has little to do with making America work well.

In fact, some of the most remarkable and complicated human beings you could ever want to meet in life are politicians. But dealing with them is a fine (or maybe not so fine; maybe crude?) art that is never an in-depth instructional topic at journalism school. Yet the interaction of politico and journalistico has got to be arguably one of the more significant human interactions in a working democracy, not to mention in aberrational psychology!

One notably colorful politician was former New York City mayor, Ed Koch. Ed was every bit as engrossing, charming and obnoxious in the flesh as he was on TV. There was very little difference between his public persona and his private one.

I was at my desk at *Newsday's* Third Avenue New York City office one morning when I received a call from Ed. It was 7:30 in the morning. The odds of the calls that came in this early from someone in charge of something important—that is, New York City, New York state or the entire country—were considerable. Either that or it was a reader in Queens complaining about an offensive editorial cartoon (an "offensive" editorial cartoon—oh, my!) or the non-delivery of the paper (and the operator simply put the irritated caller through to me because I was the only one around!).

When the phone rang at 7:30am that morning, I asked myself, "Do I feel lucky today? Should I pick this up or not?" On this particular morning, I was feeling lucky—silly me—and so I picked up the phone. It turned out to be none other than the irrepressible mayor of the self-characterized "greatest city on earth"—Mayor Ed Koch.

But boy, was he angry! He had, unsurprisingly, read the morning's lead editorial demeaning his management of the city's social services department and he wanted to tell me about how wrong we were at *New York Newsday*. What followed was a perhaps fifteen minute-long excoriation that began something like this: "Tom, this is the dumbest editorial I have ever seen! Only somebody who really doesn't understand New York could have written this. I can't believe *Newsday* really thinks this. I thought you all were better than this! Why are you peddling such trash to the people of New York? Have you no pride in what you produce and disseminate to the public? You guys oughta go back to Long Island and stay there. You just don't get New York!"

This is what you got from the mayor of the city of New York when his top was blowing off tornado-style! Ed was willing to make the call, though, precisely because he understood that my nose did not easily get out of joint. The political and journalistic worlds were rough, tough and blunt. I knew the mayor well enough to know that he did not intend his diatribe personally. He was just upset and worried about his public image.

This would happen often enough and what I would usually do was sit on the phone and wait until he paused for longer than it took to catch a breath, and then say, "I guess you don't feel strongly about this issue, Ed."

And he would invariably laugh in acknowledgment.

Then I would say, "Do you feel better now? Stress relieved somewhat?"

And he would laugh again.

Then I would suggest that at any time he wanted to blow off steam at a staffer or anyone, to just pick up the phone and blow it off on me. I was only half-listening most of the time, anyway. And I was used to it. Part of the job of the news media as official messenger is to take the blame—it comes with the territory.

That morning, Koch had paused and then said, "Hey, by the way, there's a new Woody Allen movie opening tomorrow. Why don't you and I go see it, afterwards we'll go for Chinese? Bring Andrea, if she can make it."

In other words, it was not personal. This was Koch's style and it was a style that was impossible not to enjoy.

Andrea and I soon became guests at Gracie Mansion, the New York mayor's official residence, as did the other three editorial page editors in New York. More often than not, Koch would introduce Andrea and me to the other guests by saying, "While Tom is not Jewish, ladies and gentlemen, Andrea is. And she bears the distinction of being the only Jewish woman I know who has a daughter named Ashley, which is about as goyim (White-Anglo-Saxon-Protestant) as you can get." Koch would then feign utter exasperation. "Andrea, when are you going to face up to your ethnic heritage and accept your Yiddish tradition?"

(Though ethnically and thus technically Jewish, Andrea was about as "Jewish-looking or acting," whatever that might mean as, say, Barbara Bush. Besides, it was a distinction without a difference: I am German/Irish/English but I was born and raised in New York. I am an "honorary Jew"—just like any other New Yorker who is comfortable with that appellation.)

And then everybody would laugh because, more often than not, the opera stars, artists, and political and media figures sitting around the table were also Jewish. But even if they were not, they laughed just the same. Koch somehow always made it funny. Andrea and I grew to like him, even as his political fortunes in New York sagged. We got to like him too much, in fact.

One of my saddest moments, personally, was when *New York Newsday* decided to endorse his opponent, David Dinkins, in the Democratic Primary of 1988. To make matters worse, the decision was primarily my doing.

New York, the world's greatest city had gotten extremely tense and nervous, especially over relations between the Jewish and African-American communities, police violence against African Americans, and the epidemic of crime being committed by black youth. The entire emotional, urban uptight scene was captured well in Spike Lee's film, "Do the Right Thing."

As is typical in politics, the number one, that is, the mayor, unfairly bore the brunt of the blame for a problem much greater and complex than one person could instigate or fix. But precisely because Koch liked to put himself in the center of any and every storm—or, if there was no storm, he would create one (if Koch could be likened to a sport, it probably would be roller derby or Australian football)—he would get the heat whenever the political weather boiled over.

Newsday (both the New York and Long Island editions—they were both branches of the same tree but the bigger branch, or the trunk, really, was Long Island) was the only New York paper with the balls to endorse Koch's primary opponent—David Dinkins, a career politician, the city's most prominent African-American establishment political figure, a skilled tennis player, and a very nice guy (a claim about himself Koch would not make). The problem was that the two pairs of balls in question were mine and my publisher's. In effect, it could be said that I betrayed Ed Koch. And self-interested betrayal is, alas, at the heart of the relationship between politicians and media people.

Let me tell you the story. First, we must review the mechanics of the newspaper endorsement process. Basically, the way it works is that candidates come in for an hour or so and answer the policy and political questions put to them by the publication's editorial board. It is a true ritual in several senses— including the true if sad fact that often the endorsement decision is a done deal before the candidate's appointed meeting but nonetheless a superficially open-minded rendezvous luncheon (usually) is considered a requirement of the process. Candidates know this. Some would come in who were slam-dunks to be endorsed. Others who knew they had no chance for endorsement would come in anyway, some hoping for a better shot the next time, if there ever was one. It is all just part of the fabric of a politician's life and the interview routine helps newspapers and magazines determine the tonality of their endorsement editorial or lack thereof. Both sides know how important it is.

Politicians depend desperately on the media to flourish. And the media depends desperately on politicians to provide hot copy. It is ultimately a symbiotic relationship. There is no doubt that Ed Koch's relationship with Tom and Andrea Plate, my wife who was now pregnant with our first and only child (Ashley Alexandra), was primarily driven by the fact that Tom was editorial page editor of one of New York's daily newspapers.

Despite that friendship—indeed, all friendship aside—it was vital that *New York Newsday* make the proper endorsement. At that time, we were convinced that Koch, a three-term mayor looking for his fourth go-round, had had enough. It was enough; he was enough; it was time for change. Although he was brighter than his opponents by far, he was also becoming increasingly shriller in his public attacks and quicker to condemn than ever, and he was obviously totally fatigued by the job. Who wouldn't be? I don't know how he did it; I could never have done it.

In the parlance of politics, the threads on the tires were well worn. His main opponents were David Dinkins, a member of the city council, and two other local politicians. Only Dinkins, based in Manhattan and the only minority (African-American) in the race, had a real shot at upsetting Koch. And the key battleground would be the vote in Queens, a county of New York City lying between swanky Manhattan and suburban Long Island.

Ordinarily, a politician in New York would be far more concerned about an editorial page endorsement in the *New York Times*, with its vast influence among the upper-income and better-educated tier of residents, and the *New York Daily News*, with its huge circulation everywhere (about 90 per cent or so of all New Yorkers looked at or read at least one newspaper each day, in part because of the omnipresence of public transit, a fortunate infrastructure all but missing in places like Los Angeles).

But neither the *Times* nor the *Daily News* had a particularly strong concentrated circulation in Queens. *Newsday* did, precisely because the home paper was based on Long Island and the county of Queens is contiguous with the county of Nassau, the westerly edge of Long Island proper. Its New York edition, for which I was the editorial page editor technically reporting to the editorial page editor out on Long Island, was very popular in Queens. We sold well there and had some clout. In fact, more copies of *Newsday* than *The New York Times* were sold in Queens; the *Times* basically had a circulation of significant concentration only in Manhattan (and was spread thinly across the greater metropolitan New York region and of course the nation).

Koch's campaign people had calculated that Dinkins would run strong in Brooklyn, with its large African-American population, and thus Koch would need a strong vote from Queens, with its huge middle-class white strongholds (think the fictional TV character Archie Bunker) as the offset. So his courtship of everything *Newsday*, including me and Andrea, was assiduous, whether he could in his heart tolerate us or not (Andrea probably yes, her husband probably no!).

Aside from Dinkins and Koch, a highly intelligent white politician Richard Ravitch was also running. He had everything going for him except the one thing—there was no way he could win, ever. You could endorse him if you wished, but if it was important for New York City voters to show Koch the door because he had stayed long enough, because his intemperate remarks were exacerbating race relations, and because the city needed a new face to scream at, blame everything on and vent over, then voting for this very nice but very unelectable third man was a wasted vote. The only way to get Koch out was to vote Dinkins in. There was no other way. The winner of the Democratic Primary for Mayor of the City of New York would become the next mayor (the Republicans were weak and disorganized; there was no Rudy Giuliani yet). And the winner of the Democratic Primary would be the candidate who carried the borough (county) of Queens. And, as bizarre fate would have it, the newspaper that was strongest in Queens (though in no other borough) was *New York Newsday*.

From my Manhattan office on the thirty-ninth floor of the sleek dark-brick red midtown office tower, I made that pitch to my betters on Long Island. They included Robert (Bob) Johnson, the University of Michigan Law School graduate who was then the publisher; James (Jim) Klurfeld, the crack Syracuse University journalism school graduate who was editorial page editor; and a terrific Long Island-based editorial board which included Carol Richards, the deputy editorial page editor. Because they were all intelligent and well-informed, they expressed serious concerns about Dinkins who obviously was no mental giant—no second coming of Thurgood Marshall. But he was a very nice man, a New York City patriot knowledgeable about the city, and the only candidate in the race with a chance of sinking Koch.

I came on strong (if a bit over the top): "If we want to be a big player at the big table making the big bet, Dinkins is the play for us."

Obviously, this was the "'jump-the-midget" moment for me—do you play it safe or go for the big hit?

Bob Johnson listened very carefully. He was the most wonderfully receptive boss for an activist editorial page editor to work with. It was not just that he was very smart, he was also decisive. Unlike so many corporate climbers who wanted only to protect their backsides and let others make high-profile decisions that if, well, in the end do not work, could potentially cause a fall, Bob reveled in the action.

Both Bob and Jim were willing to take a calculated chance for the purpose of making a positive and helpful contribution to the mayoral race debate, as well as putting *New York Newsday* on the map as the new big player in New York politics, especially as the *New York Times* had wimped out and the *New York Post* had jerked its knee and endorsed Koch as the candidate who would most appeal to its core readers: blue-collar workers who were fed up with the city's welfare atmosphere, homelessness and crime.

Bob, Jim and I had already agreed that we would endorse Dinkins because Koch's time had expired and Dinkins was the only horse in the race that could edge Koch out of Gracie Mansion. And this was all decided and agreed before the endorsement interview. Nonetheless, we still had to do the interview with Koch. Admittedly, the unannounced pre-decision was not fair to Koch but it sometimes happens in the media that minds have been made up, as ours were about this race, and there was nothing anyone could do about it, though in a way, this time, it was sad.

Koch was brilliant at the endorsement interview at our Third Avenue office. We had heard all the answers before and there was that screw-everyone-who-doesn't-see-things-as-clearly-as-I-do edge that infects incumbents re-elected many times over; but Koch being Koch, he was never boring.

That session, however, sealed the deal, even though our minds had been all but made up. And so the *New York* editorial page editor escorted him to the elevator. There was an uncomfortable silence. As the doors opened, an aide moved to keep them from closing and the mayor had a chance to turn to me and ask, almost plaintively: "Tom, do I really still have a chance with *Newsday*?"

I could not tell him that we had all but decided to endorse Dinkins—without losing my job. So, YES, I lied. I said, "We haven't decided yet. It's still an open question. You have a chance."

This is the problem, of course, with having developed—or at least accepted—a sort of personal relationship with the politician you cover. US journalism requires you to be detached emotionally in order to remain as objective as possible. When the doors closed behind the mayor, honestly, I really felt like a total jerk.

Our endorsement of Dinkins led to his carrying Queens in triumph and thus edging out Koch for the job. The overall city margin was very small; the *Newsday* endorsement was obviously crucial.

Koch was finished with elective politics. I have not seen Ed Koch, who showed up on numerous TV and radio shows, ever since. But I think I owe him an apology. I should never have gone to the movies with him as long as I had that job.

Dinkins went on to become a reasonably ineffective one-term mayor. In the short run, though, *Newsday* clearly benefited from the new prominence gained by the bold Dinkins endorsement.

THE FALL OF KING KOCH which led to the rise and almost immediate fall of David Dinkins also led to a most unusual development: a Republican mayor of New York, a hugely Democratic city. But this was not just any Republican; it was former federal prosecutor Rudolph Giuliani.

As a newspaper editorial page editor in a major metropolis—in my case, with *The Los Angeles Herald Examiner*, *New York Newsday*, and the *Los Angeles Times*—you get to meet and greet almost everyone. In some instances, you come to know them very well indeed and are happy that you do.

In the United States, it is virtually impossible for any reform to succeed without the aggressive backing of a strong metropolitan newspaper. The mayor or the police commissioner or the chairperson of the Municipal Reform Commission would need as many allies as possible and a serious newspaper—in both its news coverage and editorial position—is absolutely essential to put wind into the reform sails.

Perhaps there are one or two instances of reform efforts succeeding despite the indifference or opposition of a major newspaper, but I am not aware of them. The entrenched forces need to be scared and, for better or for worse, there are few forces like a newspaper that can bring that kind of heat. For instance, at *The Los Angeles Herald Examiner*, relentless news coverage and repeated attacks by the editorial page about the Eulia Love killing by police had convinced Los Angeles citizens that they had a problem. The *Herald* carried the campaign until the much-better financed *Los Angeles Times* finally rose to the challenge of challenging the police department. Another example which happened many years later showed how tremendous media noise had led to the establishment and empowerment of the Christopher Commission on Police Reform which helped put the Los Angeles Police Department on the tracks of modernization.

Another factor that could contribute to promoting reform is an aggressive prosecutor and one of the best ever was the US Attorney for the Southern District of New York—Rudolph Giuliani. Riding a cascade of high-profile cases, Giuliani promoted the image of the fearless fighter against organized crime, drug trafficking and official corruption. Although a Republican, Rudy is a genuine New Yorker—in-your-face, direct, smart, abrasive, not always politically correct (thank God!) but extremely resilient in a crisis. He was not yet the mayor of New York City when we first met but you could see he was going to be. You could also see that, with proper fortune, he could become even more than that.

Rudy and I had liked each other when I was at *Newsday* and he was in the federal attorney's office as a razor-edged prosecutor of official corruption and organized crime. All Republican and Democratic politics aside, there is something refreshingly real about him. He was not stupid enough to fight the tide of public opinion on every issue, but when he digs in his feet, establishes his ground and starts to hit out at you, there is no tougher fighter in political America. The country was to see what true grit really was in the immediate aftermath of the 9/11 catastrophe.

When New Yorkers rejected the nice but ineffectual Dinkins for a second term in 1993 and rewarded his opponent Giuliani with the job, I was by then in Los Angeles where I was the editor of the editorial pages of the *Times* there. On a nostalgic trip back to New York, I had arranged to go by City Hall for a chat which led to an exclusive published interview.

Rudy was his usual delightfully combative self from the moment I entered his large office. He greeted me warmly, enthusiastically. First thing out of his mouth: "Hey, Tom, if you had still been at the helm at *New York Newsday*, I know you never woulda endorsed Dinkins that second time. He is a nice man, mind you, but incompetent, for a second term."

Well, he was right. In fact, just before New York City's mayoral election in the fall of 1993, I had sent a confidential note to a top Times-Mirror official back east who helped oversee the *New York Newsday* operations. I wrote: "Do you think *New York Newsday* should endorse Rudy?"

The answer came back, scrawled on my own handwritten note: "No! Why replace one vague, lost soul with another?!"

That was a very poor judgment on Rudy who struck me as outstanding presidential human material, but the *New York Newsday* endorsement issue was out of my hands. Besides, I was having enough problems in Los Angeles. But I do believe that this top newspaper executive's main problem with Rudy was mainly that Rudy was a Republican, not a Democrat. And that was sad: a good leader is not bad just because he was not a Democrat; conversely, a bad leader is not good just because he was a Democrat. I would love to see Republican Rudy as president of the United States someday precisely because he would do a great job. At the same time, I would love to see Hillary (Clinton) as president as well, because she would, I think, do a great job, too. If I had to choose between them? Well, Rudy. Why? Because I know him much better.

RUDY-LIKE QUALITIES of directness and even abrasiveness were ones I cherished in my own staff. Just as I had been permitted to hire my own staff at *The Los Angeles Herald Examiner*, I was given the same measure of freedom by the mother *Newsday* on Long Island. They had allocated fifteen open slots and the editors never once interfered.

Well, almost never. I received a call once from the head of editorial hiring. Stan Asimov, brother of sci-fi guru Isaac, was a very nice guy and an editor's dream—supportive but straight. When your nose had to be shoved at the budget line (because you were way over it), however, that was what he would do.

"Tom," he called me at my desk in our Manhattan *Newsday* office, "I don't mean to interfere but you've hired six new staffers so far and not one has any regular newspaper experience."

"I know, Stanley," I responded. "That's because we're not putting out a regular normal conventional newspaper. This one is special."

Stan admitted he did not get it.

I explained: "New York City is an intensely print-oriented culture. People not only read on average 1.2 newspapers per day but they read *The New Yorker*, *The Village Voice*, *New York*, the local neighborhood weekly and who knows what else—especially when they are prisoners of mass transit, whether bus or subway or cab. For the purposes of market differentiation then we are better off providing the sense of a well-manicured daily magazine instead of a scruffy newspaper."

In the end, *Newsday* on Long Island bought that argument. We hired young talent from *Vanity Fair*, *The National Law Journal*, *New York* and other magazines. It was not until we got to the twelfth or so hire that someone came on board with a true blue newspaper background—and we were happy to have her, if only for balance!

With a relatively intimate staff of a dozen or so, we worked to create an atmosphere of peers—even a college of hardworking cardinals—rather than a corporate platoon with an inherent hierarchy. The process of writing and editing editorials at *New York Newsday* demanded that everyone was more or less equal and that everyone had to go through the same editorial control gauntlet. No one was above peer group editing, not even the boss.

One day in the inter-office mail, halfway through my four-year stint at *New York Newsday*, I received an unexpected note from Dave. It was the kind of note that made your week—or month: "Every day when I pick up *New York Newsday*, your pages leap out—interesting, opinionated ideas; crisply done and to the point. What you are doing is a key part of this great adventure! Dave L."

> This is management by inspiration—and management inspiration leads to staff perspiration.

I responded to that note, whether he wanted me to or not (until recently,

when I finally wised up, I had never met a memo I did not respond to!), by making a few points:
1. To create something from nothing, you need a strong initial plan and design, supported through thick and thin by top management.
2. You needed subtle, supportive backing by mother *Newsday* on Long Island and this we in New York received in spades from Sylvan Fox, my director-supervisor, who was a gem and then too, from his worthy successor James Klurfeld.
3. You needed quality staff.
4. You needed the right city for it—most important!
5. We here in New York have been able to build on *Newsday's* preceding reputation that lent itself to being taken seriously. This was a big help in a city of serious people.

NO MORE SERIOUS AND REFINED a person existed than Frederick A O Schwarz Jr. Fritz Schwarz (of the FAO Schwarz Toy Emporium) was a law partner at the top tier firm Cravath, Swaine & Moore. He was the city corporation counsel (that is, chief official lawyer) and in the late 1980s, served as chairman of the New York City Charter Revision Commission. About ten years later, the *New York Law School Law Review* gave over its entire issue to a narrative and analysis of New York City's successful charter revision reform written by Fritz Schwarz and Eric Lane ("The Policy and Politics of Charter Making: The Story of New York City's 1989 Charter," *New York Law School Law Review*, Volume XLII, Numbers 3 & 4, 1998, see especially pages 966–972).

"This is a long story," Schwarz and law professor Eric Lane wrote in the sweeping law review essay, "reflecting ... the importance of editorial board endorsements." Schwarz then explained the vital and healthy role of major city newspapers in helping raise public support for political reforms that are by their very nature powerful threats to well-monied, well-entrenched special interests. In their narrative, Schwarz and Lane gave particular attention to the roles of the *New York Times* and *New York Newsday*, at the time the two most serious newspapers in the metropolis. In the end, both *Newsday* and the *Times* endorsed the controversial charter reforms but as Schwarz and Lane wrote, "*New York Newsday* came out first."

Remember my silly little competition in college with the *Harvard Crimson* over which paper would be first to oppose US military involvement in Vietnam? As I say, this time competitiveness thing is either in your blood or it is not.

This law review article sometimes appears on the required reading list for my course. Students need to understand that newspapers and to a lesser extent magazines, at their best, have a huge responsibility to make democracy work. That obligation is not discharged by simply exposing official and political corruption—there is plenty of it and it is not hard to find but that is not the whole of the civic story. There are very many dedicated professionals who give to civil life far more than they get out of it in terms of the usual compensations. But does the news media do enough to build these policy warriors up as it does to tear the bad ones down? Schwarz was one of those noble warriors: he tried to make civic and political life better. For that worthy effort, he had the *New York Times* and *New York Newsday* behind him. I was proud to have had a small part in that. In retrospect, I only wished I had done more of this sort of thing in my news media career. Then I would have truly merited the First Amendment protection my profession is accorded by the Constitution. But often, my profession and I do not.

Nonetheless, whatever part *New York Newsday* had played in the charter reforms, it was the result of great team effort. No truly successful editor is an island unto herself/himself especially when editing a product that met the public eye every day. My team was as good as any I had or would ever get to work with. In addition to street smarts, solid literary taste and an inspired work ethic, they did not take themselves all that seriously, did not take me all that seriously (perhaps in part because of my unbroken rule that the pages had to be completely finished by 5pm so that I could catch my heartthrob, MTV-VJ "Downtown" Julie Brown on what was then a hit show, MTV's "Dance Party"), and they would generally always say what was on their mind.

And team candor is precisely what you want as a supervisor. Sure, we are all human and praise and compliments can really make our day, but with staff, what you do not need is to be told only what they think you want to hear; you need them to tell you what they really think.

A hilarious example of how well my staff did this candor thing is their fabulous but unexpected farewell gift presented to me at my going-away party.

A week before actually starting a new job in Los Angeles, the editorial pages staff of both Long Island *Newsday* and *New York Newsday* organized a gala goodbye. There were the usual insincere speeches ("You'll never know how much we will miss you") and a few jibes (my good colleague James Klurfeld joked that I probably invoked the name "Dave" when in direct argument with Long Island far in excess of any reasonable statute of usage!—and he was right, fencing with Long Island often scared me, though they did not know it, I think!) but at this party at least (this was not *Time* magazine), no one fell over drunk.

But the best part was to come at the end. They presented me with a picture of the 42nd Street/Times Square tower. The picture had been taken a few days before. The "zipper"—the electronic news flash that *Newsday* actually had leased for its own use—flashed: "GOOD RIDDANCE, TOM PLATE!" That picture still hangs proudly in my office. My staff, truly, had learned to say exactly what they thought!

Years later, Sir David English once saw it on my office wall and remarked that it may well have been the single best going-away gift he had ever seen and to be sure, he had seen more than a few. "Too bad you don't have the original negative; you could blow it up ten feet high."

Here was my *New York Newsday* happy-exit strategy. Recall that I greatly respected the *Newsday* organization and when I left *Long Island Newsday* more than a decade before, I had offered several months' notice. I believe they never forgot that.

This was a different deal, of course. The father of modern *Newsday*—Dave Laventhol—had been elevated to the position of president of the parent company, then Times-Mirror, and then had been asked to take on the second job of publisher of the *Los Angeles Times*, the flagship paper of the publishing company. And he wanted me as his Los Angeles editorial page editor—so I was not defecting but rather, moving to the mother ship.

But I wanted to leave *New York Newsday* with a legacy it deserved. To this end, I had sought to hire a very good mix of people for the editorial pages that more or less mirrored the diversity of New York itself.

In the greatest city on earth, that was not hard to do, and *Newsday*, with its liberal civil rights and equality tradition, was a supportive environment.

In fact, in general, the news media business probably does as good a job as any business in advancing women and minorities. It was still far from perfect, to be sure, but precisely because the media business does an avalanche of reporting about discrimination and economic inequality, it is probably more keenly aware of the problem than most other institutions.

In journalism, I have met many more sexists than racists; male editors of my generation were far more likely to drag their heels, as it were, at a woman's prospects than at a black's or a Latino's. Indeed, if anything, the news business tends to suffer from a severe case of political correctness—the disease that inhibits the honest evaluation (and thus sometimes produces unavoidably, the negative assessment) of an employee precisely because of his or her ethnicity.

I certainly do not wish to make the case for sainthood in my own attitudes toward minorities and women. But it is a historical fact that when I left *New York Newsday* for the *Los Angeles Times*, I had teed the succession issue up to my publisher so that he had the delightful dilemma of a choice between a black man and a woman who happened to be Jewish (Patricia Cohen, who was to morph into a *New York Times* staffer before long). Whatever the choice, he could not go wrong: they were both well qualified and exceptional human beings. In the end, he chose the man—Ernest Tollerson—and so when I left the newspaper, my successor was in fact a minority. And he did an outstanding job, as I knew he would, because he was talented and he worked hard as a key member of the team.

When my time came at the end of my tenure as editorial page editor of the *Los Angeles Times*, I also tried to tee up the succession question to my publisher whom I greatly respected. But this time the management did not have to choose between a minority and a woman. The publisher got two for the price of one—an African-American woman. She handled the job with distinction for seven years (I had had six), after which she returned to her first love—news-side reporting.

THE PROBLEM WITH what you are about to read in the following few paragraphs of praise is that basically I agreed with it. Not the personal praise—that was silly—but the sense that Los Angeles was beckoning with a great job and a tremendous challenge in a fantastic location—on the fringe of the Pacific Rim, Asia, China, India and the geopolitical center of the world.

For me, for Tom Plate, read: pseudo-intellectual—running editorial pages of a major world paper with a substantial staff was, from my perspective, quite possibly the best job in journalism.

The telephone started to ring in my Manhattan apartment the morning the story in the *New York Times* announced the appointment.

"Yes?"

"You're the king?"

The voice was unmistakable: that gravelly grounding of merriment, dinner party troublemaking and paternalistic paranoia was uniquely Felker's.

"Hi, Clay, what do you mean?" I stumbled back.

"None of us at *New York*—none of us, Tom—could have landed that job. That's what you have to understand. Many of us wouldn't have even been considered. None of us, except you, could have gotten it. In the end, maybe we're just not serious enough people for it. But with Princeton and your arms race book and all those serious little magazines you read that hardly anyone else has ever heard of, you're just perfect for it. I know you've had your troubles with drinking in the past, but … this is a good moment. Enjoy it. None of the rest of us could do it, I can tell you that."

Was that gracious or what, eh?!

Then Jim Brady, the novelist and Madison Avenue journalist, telephoned, and fairly screamed: "You're number one! And there is no number two! You're the king."

I think he might possibly just have used that line once or twice before with others. I lapped it up nonetheless. If you cannot accept Jim Brady for what he is—a helluva nice guy but a (most likable) con man like everyone else on Madison Avenue—then you cannot accept life!

Most surprising of all, perhaps, was the note from Tom Johnson. Recall that he had been publisher of the *Los Angeles Times* when I was slaving away at the lesser *Los Angeles Herald Examiner*. When news of my *Los Angeles Times* appointment surfaced, I received this note from Tom who had been pushed out of the *Los Angeles Times,* but then had smartly moved on to become president of CNN: "Most of the happiest and proudest moments of my life are of working with the people of the *Los Angeles Times*. [But] I also wish you and I could have enjoyed a longer association. I had thought of you [for the job you are getting] long before." Wow!

And so it went on and on like this. Calls from the mayor, former colleagues, people I barely knew. Well, it was a very good job—being editor of the editorial pages of the *Los Angeles Times*, a newspaper with revenues of more than a billion dollars a year and a circulation about on par with *The New York Times*. West of Chicago, it was the biggest paper in the United States.

Perhaps the niftiest congratulatory note I received came—but naturally—from Sir David English, recently knighted by the Queen. From London, he wrote: "You must be careful, Tom, not to let the power go to your head. I hope that I myself have set you an example in this matter and I will be available for advice and guidance whenever you feel the corrupting influence at work!" Was I capable of keeping my head from expanding to the possibility of sinking the Titanic? Ordinarily, yes ... but I would have at my side in Los Angeles David Laventhol, who knew me better than my own father and who would not let me make a fool of myself.

New York definitely was the big leagues—with possibly the most amazing politicians and personalities on earth—and here I was, moving to Los Angeles. I was not surprised therefore at Jack Rosenthal's (then editorial page editor at the *New York Times*) sweet note which nonetheless managed to take a swipe at "provincial" Los Angeles: "Dear Tom, Congratulations on your new job. However, what I do not understand is, having proven to everyone in town that you can hit major-league pitching, why would you then want to go back to Triple-A? Warmly, Jack."

THE *LOS ANGELES TIMES* JOB was, however a titanic job, and I looked forward to the challenge. The title was "editor of the editorial pages." When Shelby Coffey, the editor-in-chief of the *Los Angeles Times* telephoned me at *New York Newsday* to offer me the job in 1989, the first question I asked was whether the duties included the Sunday opinion section as well as the daily opinion-editorial page and the editorial page.

"Right," he had said, "the whole ball of wax."

Only the important women in my life—wife Andrea and daughter Ashley—seemed downcast. In particular, Andrea loathed the prospect of leaving Manhattan, which (dirt, crime and congestion notwithstanding) she adored and she did not like the notion of putting all our chips on the shoulders of Dave Laventhol who had ascended to the publisher's job at the *Los Angeles Times*—and hence the job offer to me. She reasoned that if anything happened to Dave, I would be left alone to float on the West Coast which offered a scandalous paucity of print opportunities, outside of screenwriting. By staying at *New York Newsday*, even if the paper folded, it would be easier to move laterally to a great paper like the *New York Times*—or to some magazine or book publishing house.

I agreed with her reasoning, but I viewed it as alarmist: what could possibly happen to Dave? We have nothing to worry about. But we did...

> Before taking a huge career jump, even to a terrific job, take a day off, walk on the beach, and make some mental notes. Use Pentagon worst-case scenario analysis—imagine the most terrible thing (aside from death) that can happen to you. What would be your back-up plan?

Chapter Eight
The *Los Angeles Times*: The Responsibility of a Major-League American Newspaper

SEEING THE SMOKE broke my heart. Driving at 95 miles per hour along the Santa Monica Freeway heading west, I was heading as fast as I could towards the city's affluent Westside from downtown. This was in 1992, the year of the great Los Angeles urban riot.

Downtown was where the *Los Angeles Times* and City Hall and other municipal landmarks were. But it was also close to the troubled neighborhoods of Los Angeles that were rich in poverty and poor in hope, whose residents were once described by a past publisher of the *Los Angeles Times* as not "our kind of readers," and whose individual rights were honored by the Los Angeles Police Department more in the breach rather than the observance.

These neighborhoods were now mostly in smoke and as I high-tailed away from there, it came to me with a heavy thud what a failure the American establishment had been in reducing injustice and increasing fairness. You could blame it on genetics as much as you want or turn your back resolutely on the facts, but the misery of America's inner cities was a reality that could and would explode at any time. Here it was now: reality sending smoke signals to our conscience that whatever the degree of poverty and discrimination and hopelessness elsewhere—whether in Asia or Africa or wherever—a heckuva lot of it was right here in America's own cities and unless it was reduced, the implosions and explosions would continue throughout our history.

> The closer—geographically speaking—the main headquarters of America's leading dailies are to the real and serious social, economic and political problems, the more impotent they appear to be in actually helping address and solve the issues.

It struck me hard—so hard that I almost wanted to turn back and spend the night on the floor of the *Los Angeles Times*—that so much inner-city misery existed just a few blocks from America's leading newspapers. Here were the *New York Times, The Washington Post* and—yes—the *Los Angeles Times* opining about poverty in the Third World and corruption in Europe and the international monetary system; yet here, in their own backyards, was misery and depression and chaos about which none of their journalism had done, effectively, very much. And I personally felt some guilt for that too. I had been in establishment American journalism for long enough.

EDITORIAL PAGES EXIST for a number of reasons. One is that at some newspapers they provide the publisher/management with a kind of millionaire's playpen in which to lay out management views—and, if you like, in the democratic spirit of openness, provide alternative views or even civic leadership.

Another is to make the news pages look less opinionated by comparison. Allegedly, you see, the news pages of American newspapers contain only dispassionate facts and exclude actual opinion. This is a dodgy proposition, of course, (what about passionate facts and dispassionate opinion?). But this absurd assertion is reinforced when one is able to showcase opinion pages that expressly and noticeably showcase pointed perspectives. The idea, of course, is that the rest of the newspaper is strictly factual and objective. Of course, nothing is quite that simple.

I was brought in to the *Los Angeles Times* to reinvigorate the "opinion" dimension of the editorial pages. This was tied to other reasons. The department was teeming with "issues." The first was that many *Times* editorials seemed, at least to me, to be knee-jerk liberal restatements of views that had been repeatedly stated over and over during past decade(s). "Stale" was one word for it and "stale" had two downsides: a declining (or reclining, as in sleeping) readership—why bother to read editorial pages if you knew what the positions were beforehand?—and enormous pressure on the publisher.

This greater pressure on the publisher stemmed from two main sources. One was the existence of a very conservative board of directors whose views were a lot closer to Barry Goldwater's at his worst than Bono's at his least liberal. The other was to complicate the paper's efforts to attract new readers, especially in Orange County, the rich and growing suburb south of Los Angeles, whose residents were increasingly turning to the rising *Orange County Register* as their primary daily newspaper.

In an effort to regain lost ground, the *Los Angeles Times* had set up a well-funded Orange County bureau for its suburban edition. To that end, in our conference room, we would plan our editorial page with Orange County editorial writers on the phone line—they were patched in on a conference speaker phone and sometimes even a San Fernando Valley editorial page editor would plug into the conference call, too. It was the most complex editorial page system in America. Naturally, I loved it.

But to make matters more complicated, there was an unsolvable political problem. In general, the inner-city people of Los Angeles deemed the *Los Angeles Times* "too establishment" and perhaps even slightly conservative, which clearly it had been (until the rise of Otis Chandler in the 1970s); but, in contrast, Orange County, which until relatively recently was viewed as the conservative stronghold of the state, tended to view us as too liberal, even leftist.

My predecessor did not have to worry about any Orange County editions, but I did. Under Dave and Coffey, the circulation effort was prioritized and marketing considerations understandably began to influence editorial thinking. The pressure on the editorial page therefore was to maintain the integrity and consistency of its views without needlessly turning off potential readers who were less liberal if not conservative. This put tremendous pressure (unprecedented at the *Los Angeles Times*) on any new editorial page editor who inherited, on the one hand, a staff from his predecessor that was decidedly liberal, while reporting, on the other hand, to a publisher and editor who were ordinarily exceptionally cautious by nature and geared up to worry about Orange County's post-Goldwater sensibilities.

It was only in retrospect after a month or two on the job that I began to understand why Editor Shelby Coffey (when he first telephoned me at *New York Newsday*) had then described my hiring as "highly confidential." He had said: "Let's observe Kremlin rules of secrecy." Then he added: "We do feel very good about you. We like the play of your mind. We like what you have been doing at *Newsday*. Given the range of your interests and experience, you might be the ideal person for reinvigorating the editorial pages here." Wow, did I ever fall for it! (Fools rush in where angels fear to tread…)

Always look before you leap: sometimes an apparent promotion can prove a rendevous with trouble.

What would you make of such incidents as the following which occurred early on?

Incident number one: A few weeks before the hiring was announced, I had dinner with a long-time member of the editorial board. The dinner had been suggested by Higher Authority. The aim was to see whether this person found me suitable. In effect, I was being interviewed for the job by someone who was then to become a titular subordinate. It was bizarre. This person turned out to be otherwise a wonderful human being and a good journalist but for the editorial pages, he was probably miscast from the beginning.

Incident number two: On my first day at work, the publisher called for a meeting in his conference room to announce my appointment. Before I went into the meeting with him, he said to me: "Have you got yourself under control?" He knew my ego; he knew me well. I said I did. But when the meeting began to announce the change, one of the editorial writers (whom I had never met previously and who knew little about me) stood up to denounce the occasion. When the editor asked him to sit down, he replied, testily: "Is this a meeting or an announcement?" The editor replied, rather astutely, not to mention coldly: "I guess it is an announcement."

The editorial writer—at this writing he was a superb weekly print commentator on the news media—offered up his poisonous peroration, notwithstanding. It was, actually, partly brilliant but also very emotional and quite implicitly insulting, in fact. (I think I never told Andrea about it as she had always opposed my accepting this job and telling her would only have reinforced her generally dismal estimate of my ability to sniff out trouble beforehand.) The gist of it was that oh, my predecessor was a saint and I was the devil and now we would go from a principled editorial page to an unprincipled one.

I was shocked, hurt and somewhat angry but, later, when asked whether the staffer should be instantly transferred to Outer Orange County, I declined—something told me he would prove an excellent editorial writer (which he indeed did).

Perhaps in retrospect, I should have gone back to *New York Newsday* the next day. I had noticed that Bob Johnson, the publisher there, was keeping the position open. Perhaps in case I hated the new Los Angeles job? Perhaps he had known something about the Los Angeles situation that I did not? Perhaps I should have returned to where I came from. But—fool that I am and always will be—there I was, the captain who wanted to feel what the controls of the tanker would be like.

I do not know what you would have made of these incidents. But as it turned out, I did not make too much of them and the slightly bumpy start notwithstanding, I carried on with the job.

The next day, I went through the office to visit with every staffer individually. Perhaps what I should have done was to fire everyone and start over. But I am not the firing kind (It hurts, badly. I hate to do it, even when it was warranted. And I have never ever fired someone I hired, because ... hey, who hired her/him? Besides, I hated being fired myself!) and I wanted to keep everyone that I could even if emotionally it took a big bite out of me. Well, this mistaken decision wound up taking more than a bite. It undermined my happiness immensely.

Not everyone was hostile, however—not by far, thankfully. I stopped in the office of an opinion-editorial page editor who happened to be female and black. Before I could say anything, she blurted out: "I don't know what your agenda is. I have no idea actually, but I support it. I sure wasn't getting anywhere under the previous regime. I can't do any worse under you. You have my unconditional support." Well, this was at least some kind of positive response! Six years later, this talented young woman editor was to become my successor as editor of the editorial pages. Deservedly so. I was happy for her.

This staffer's rise in the department was a good thing indeed. It turned out I had a kind of minorities problem. Just a few weeks into the job, in late November, I was given the memo of annual pay raises approved by Higher Authority. The only two staffers receiving nothing at all—zero—were not white.

I was so alarmed in fact that I wrote a memo on the problem to a member of Higher Authority. In part it read: "There's a ... potentially volatile compensation question that I want to bring to your attention ... At the end of last year, when I inherited the staff, I was told I also inherited the salary raise recommendations ... But it turns out that the only two staffers who did not get any merit raises at all are [minorities] ... I have a recommendation if you want it."

A member of Higher Authority then called me in to submit to me that an issue of this magnitude and sensitivity should not have been put into a memo. He was absolutely right but sometimes a memo like that is the best way to draw attention to an issue that I feared was not being prioritized and to make it very clear that this curious omission was a large issue for me. Well, to make a long story short, the rocket got proper attention. The minorities in question (whom I liked a lot, actually, each for different reasons) got raises.

The next day, another minority staffer asked to see me. She was a fabulously gregarious woman with very pronounced views. "I think you should know this. I was preparing a lawsuit for race discrimination against the *Los Angeles Times*," she said, "but when I heard you were coming, I decided to hold off. I checked you out. You have a good reputation with minorities and women. And you endorsed David Dinkins, the only New York City paper that did that, right? So I think I will wait and see."

She never did file a lawsuit, but I was shaken up by the fact that I was moving into such a racially charged atmosphere at what was supposed to be one of America's most liberal newspapers—and no one had told me anything in advance! (Of course, if they had, I probably would have chosen to stay in New York!)

You see, a vast majority of the staff was white male. Many were smart and talented and committed to excellence, but they had unknowingly knitted themselves into what appeared to those excluded as a tacit club that relegated anyone who was not in the club (that is, women and blacks) to secondary status. Moreover, the White Boys New Republic Knee-Jerk Club (as I privately called it) had been in place for so long, everyone in it figured that they had tenure and that they really did not have to answer to anyone.

I was to discover what these boys were like a few weeks into the gig. A white male editorial writer said something that could arguably be construed as racist. I knew he certainly did not mean it. In the deeply-rutted atmosphere of the White Boys New Republic Knee-Jerk Club, it was probably the kind of offhand comment that would surface from time to time at the ritualistic 9:45am editorial board meetings and would have gone unchecked. But Mr New York Newsday was in town now and it was a new game.

After the meeting, I spoke privately with the writer who was a true gentleman and otherwise a fine man. None of us is perfect and we all are capable of saying the wrong thing (especially me). But in the context of the only recently dropped lawsuit and the rapidly developing environment of political correctness, some sort of administrative action had to be taken.

I also told Higher Authority about it, and said I would simply issue an oral reprimand and put in my file a private memo about the incident in case it ever happened again. It did not. The writer not only verbally apologized to the offended staffer (an African-American woman), but he penned me a personal apology, too. As I say, he was otherwise a true gentleman.

The editorial pages atmosphere at the *Los Angeles Times* was impossibly acidic for those who were not members of the White Boys New Republic Knee-Jerk Club. This meant, mostly, women and/or people of color. This had to change. And it did.

> The more established and successful an institution, the harder it will try to resist change of any major kind. If you are brought into such an institution as an agent of change, make sure you work out at your health club daily to build up your endurance and control any proclivity to reach for the vodka in the many moments of stress!

WHEN ONE JOINS a successful and powerful media institution, whether the *Los Angeles Times* or *Time*, one enters the deep waters of an entrenched tradition. It is like encountering a huge historic harbor with its own low and high tide schedules, and ecological resistance to storms that would otherwise blow lesser structures over. There are huge under-the-sea tides and even weird, outsider-eating, deeply embedded sea creatures. I also came to think of these institutions as a huge tanker which would take days to launch forward out of the harbor and then sometimes even longer to turn completely around. By comparison, *Family Weekly* and to some extent even *New York Newsday* (which was after all "new," whatever the "Mel-Vile" restraining influence) were like twenty-foot runabouts that could be turned on a dime.

Not the *Los Angeles Times*. Envision a huge ship that did not immediately respond to the touch, which meant that the captain had to be always on guard for possibly threatening titanic icebergs—not to mention crew mutinies!

I cannot say that I went onto the captain's deck unprepared. In fact, I had been reeling with all sorts of self-involved phobias about what would hit me at the *Los Angeles Times*. The job put me at my desk at 7am (I would leave my wife and daughter every morning at 6:15 and get on the freeway from Santa Monica to downtown) and for the first few years at least, I rarely left my desk before 7pm. There were usually three to five unbreakable appointments each day and the weekends were never entirely free.

I am told my successor found the job so tiring that she once fell asleep at the wheel of her car (no damage caused to her or the car, thankfully!). My guess is that my predecessor survived for as long as he did in part because he had a gifted number two (which is always very helpful) to whom he delegated mightily, and in part because he put in as close to a nine-to-five shift as he could manage. I was either not that smart or not that efficient.

When I left the job after almost six years of the immensely interesting grind, I was, as the articulate and astute Shelby Coffey, the editor-in-chief put it, greatly "relieved" to go. I was totally exhausted—emotionally, physically and spiritually.

Yes, I am a bit weird and as you will see later, I do not wear black socks, but I lasted a half dozen years.

But more than fitting in, there were battles every day in dealing with corporate interference, supervising the editorial cartoonist and dealing with a staff inherited from my predecessor that were absolutely enervating.

CORPORATE INTERFERENCE in the decisions of the editorial page came to my front door rather early in the game. Dave Laventhol, the publisher, and Shelby Coffey, the editor-in-chief, would do all they could to either shield their editorial page editor from the direct hit or to deftly maneuver in whatever little space they had. They knew that with a largely inherited group of editorial writers who were on the whole more politically liberal than the Democratic National Committee, Tom Plate would soon be toast if the executive suite added to it with constant interference.

They both did the best they could. With his prior experience as *Newsday's* publisher and CEO, Dave was perhaps the more skilled dodger-and-weaver than either Shelly or (most certainly) me. The truth was, though, that I did not mind corporate efforts to influence the editorial page as long as those efforts were above board and honest. What was grating were the slick operators who thought this New York born-and-bred to be somehow born yesterday.

Actually, as long as the attempt was not intended to take decisions out of my hands, I even welcomed corporate input. One top executive—they called him the "silver fox"—often called on me with suggestions and input which were usually quite informative and never ill-willed. There were others, however, whom I would never have even risked lending my car to and who steered clear of me, working through intermediaries out of deference to appearances.

Sometimes the interference was more poignant or comical than unsavory. One day a top corporate official came into my office unannounced, asked if I had a moment to spare (no, but, of course, yes), flung himself on the couch, took a deep breath, and looked me in the eye with a faint flavor of the beseeched. A somewhat long pause, then: "This is about saving my job." That was a pretty attention-grabbing beginning.

"How can I help you save it?" I figured that was my best response.

The corporate big shot explained that a regulatory issue affecting a major utility in the state was brought to his attention at a recent board meeting by the CEO of that affected utility. "I know nothing about the merits of the issue but he's a good guy, he always sounds reasonable, and he controls the board and therefore my job," said the bigwig.

What did the bigwig want?

Just hear him out, he said, he respects you and he just needs someone like you to hold his intellectual hand. "Can you do that?"

I said I could. And I did.

MOST OF THE TIME I was shielded from upper-division pressure mainly by Robert Erburu who was the CEO of the company and, in many ways, a saint and a very classy man. He took so much of the heat from the company's conservative board of directors that it was extraordinary that he did not burn up like Apollo 13.

One day, the political pressure did trickle down—or so I thought. When I realized I had thought wrong, I really had to laugh.

It was sometime during a lunch hour, and the chairman of Times-Mirror, then the parent corporation of the *Los Angeles Times*, came sauntering in, as innocent as could be for all the world to see. Ordinarily, I might have called 911 and proclaimed the presence of an intruder. But in this case the intruder was none other than Franklin Murphy, Erburu's predecessor, who was a very special man indeed.

For starters, he had been an absolute legend at UCLA. As the chancellor there for decades, he lifted this Westside Los Angeles public university out of commuter school mediocrity into a world-class research university. His legacy was so revered that the most beautiful part of the campus is the Franklin Murphy Sculpture Garden—a few acres of paradise, an undulating lawn populated by striking sculptures by Rodin and other greats. After leaving UCLA for Times-Mirror, he insulated the newspaper from the very-conservative board of directors like a one-man defense line of a Superbowl team. If ever the tremendous pressure got to him—for some of these trustees made the late, iconic conservative Barry Goldwater seem like Kofi Annan—he never showed it. Or did he on this one day? He had burst in, and then sort of threw me off balance by asking: "Whom are we endorsing in this election?" (Yes, he said "whom"!) And then he came to the side of my desk, kneeled down, and took out a notepad.

His question, I thought, was, were we endorsing the right candidates? But that was not the question. The question, as it turned out, was: for whom should I, Franklin Murphy, vote? The reason for the question: Franklin was going on vacation for three weeks and wanted to send in his absentee ballot by mail. So, for whom (*not* "who"!) should he vote?

In other words, instead of telling the editorial board what to do, he wanted us to tell *him* what to do. This was because he respected the integrity of the basic process by which we reached our decisions (that is, a process that was impartial and corruption-free; jobs and future favors were not being exchanged). In a sense, he was saying: I may be the chairman of one of the world's leading media corporations but I'm so busy, how would I know for whom I should vote in the 63rd Judicial District?—but you, the *Los Angeles Times*, you know, right?

So he ticked off his choices based on the page proof of our forthcoming THE TIMES ENDORSES page on his to-be-mailed-in ballot. Isn't this charming?

Newspapers can and should be thought of as community assets. The idea that they are institutions outside of the environments in which they exist is a severe delusion. The failure of newspapers to use their influence for the public good is a moral abnegation.

ANOTHER PERK OF THE JOB lay in the inherent possibilities for carrying out your civic duty, if you were working at a responsible newspaper and had its support. After a few years of returning phone calls and actually trying to be warm and interested in people, my office became a bit of a gathering place for police chiefs, school reformers, city officials, and all sorts of civic types. A lot of what happened in that office never made it to the editorial pages. A lot of what I did was behind-the-scenes.

A school reformer once phoned me in despair. The usual coalition forces of bureaucrats and union officials were blocking the implementation of a much needed innovation. The blockage was a manifestation of the larger, classical problem: entrenched interests versus the public good. I counseled him to take a few days off and visit his mother in Palm Springs. I then arranged to host two luncheons at the executive dining club.

At the Wednesday meeting were the reformers and their allies; at the Friday one were the resisters and their allies. It was important to have the "angels" come in for lunch before the "devils." Once word got around that the reformers had first crack at the editorial board of the *Los Angeles Times*, fear overcame the resisters. When Friday came, they were almost literally shaking.

With the reformers and their allies, I was interested in only one issue: what was the one thing they wanted done that might re-charge the reform process? Then, with the resisters, I had only one question to which I wanted a straight answer: why are you (bad guys) opposed to this innovation? It turned out that by Friday, roughly around noon, the resisters had changed their minds and had become wildly supportive of the reform. The result: one reform, zero editorials, and new life for the school reform movement.

In this way, a newspaper, civic-minded and properly engaged in the public interest, could become a community resource. On our better days, this is what journalists ought to be doing.

THE SECOND MAJOR WORRY was the issue of supervising the cartoonist. But my fears proved to be unfounded. I had a lot of problems—and enemies—in this job but none with Paul Conrad.

"Supervise a cartoonist" is quite the wrong phrase, to be sure. It was more like trying to supervise a python without becoming its dinner! And "editorial cartoonist" was not quite the right phrase to sum up Paul Conrad. Editorial "Force Majeure" would be closer.

By 1989 Conrad had already won three Pulitzers and was viewed as the reigning guru of US editorial cartoonists. You may recall from my youthful days at *Newsday* that I adored the editorial cartoon genre and used as many of them for which I could plausibly find space.

But even if I adored editorial cartoons, I rarely found the artists themselves so adorable. Some were outright nasty; all were major egomaniacs; only a few were major talents; and very few were gentlemen or "gentle-ladies."

My expectation therefore is that three-time Pulitzer Prize winner Conrad would be as much fun working with as frolicking in the shallow end of the pool with piranhas. This phobia was based on some prior experience at another newspaper about which I would prefer not to elaborate!

But in Los Angeles, in the end, instead of staying at the top of my Excedrin-headache list, Paul went to the very bottom. He was a genius, for sure, but also a total professional. And—for a cartoonist—he was so easy to work with. Notice that I said, "for a cartoonist." I recall once asking a friend of mine who was serving on the board of the Los Angeles Philharmonic whether the justly-famed maestro Essa Peka Salonen was easy or hard to work with. My friend replied: "For a conductor, relatively easy." Pause. Then he said to me: "But notice that I said 'for a conductor.' "

When managing creative people, many distinctions and nuances must be allowed. This was not like managing, oh, accountants, if you will. Wildly creative people—like three-time Pulitzer Prize winners—are by nature mercurial, temperamental, easy to offend, and prodigiously hard to love. But Paul—or "Con," as many called him—was the Michael Jordan of cartoonists. Even on a bad day, you knew you were in the presence of greatness.

Con's office was next to mine, and he would generally catch me for approval of the day's cartoon before I headed for the offices of Higher Authority for the 11am "sales presentation" meeting (selling the line-up of the next day's editorials to the bosses). Often enough, this was an easy chore. Con did not become America's most decorated editorial cartoonist because he had a low batting average. But problems would occur when he produced the rare dead fish (something that did not work) or a Titanic (a cartoon which, if published, might rock the paper unwisely).

Here is the "supervising" dialogue I developed for the "supervision" of a creative giant.
1. If the cartoon was superb, I say: "That is a very great work of art."
2. If I thought it was somewhat unfocused, could be improved, missed the point altogether or would trigger thousands of subscriber cancellations, I say, simply: "That is a great work of art."

If the latter, Conrad would invariably reply: "What? You don't like it? What's wrong with it? Gee, I think it's just perfect."

To which I would say something like: No, I *like* it. In fact, I just said that it was a *great* work of art, etc. Around and around we would go until Paul would slink back to his drawing board. But by the time I got out of the Higher Authority meeting in the late morning, Paul would invariably propose a revised approach, and invariably it would be a better editorial cartoon.

Then there was a third option. One morning he showed me the outline of Iraqi dictator Saddam Hussein bare-assed, mooning the world. The graphic architecture of the dictator's bottom was bold and unmistakable and yucky. It was an edgy idea, but graphically it was something better designed for a small London literary magazine than for a family paper. If I had been the publisher or editor of the paper, I probably would have let it run, anyhow, because I basically believe you hire or fire the cartoonist, not micro-manage his or her work. I knew however that if I let it go in the paper, by 6pm or so, someone from Higher Authority would be on the phone, ordering me to yank it, and the staff would be scrambling for a substitute editorial cartoon to put in its place. Why put them through that if I knew that this was exactly what they would be put through?

I told Paul that the bared-ass cartoon was not going to fly in a family paper. He bitterly complained (and, understandably—his conception of his job did not include the obligation to make readers feel comfortable).

So I produced option three: do you want me to show it to Higher Authority? Most times the invocation of this option would prompt him to sigh, withdraw into his office like a wounded dog, and come up with something else. But he had strong feelings for this cartoon. So I walked it down the hall, put it on the desk of a High Authority, and waited for the inevitable phone call. An hour later, the phone rang: "Thanks for showing it to me, Tom. Pull it."

Fortunately, option three was rarely necessary. Conrad was a great communicator, not a petty anarchist. But his cartoons were sometimes too strong for Higher Authority (maybe the way you get to be Higher Authority was to play it safe?). Pretty soon, the Conrads were moved off the editorial page (where their presence might suggest official sanction) to the opinion editorial page (where it could be said by upper management that they were just "another view"). But eventually after five years Conrad was moved off the pages as a staff regular altogether. It made me sad but in the end it was done; and I knew it was going to happen.

Nothing, and indeed no one was forever at a newspaper. But he was one of the all-time greats. Indeed, I doubt that the adjective "genius" readily applies to anything or anyone in journalism but if an exception can be made, it should apply to an editorial cartoonist of the rare caliber of a Conrad.

IN A WAY, Dave had warned me about the *Los Angeles Times*: "It's a little weird that the *Los Angeles Times* would have a publisher who's from outside the building. It's also a little weird that it would have an editor long identified with *The Washington Post* [my direct boss Shelby Coffey]. But it is very weird at this place for the editorial page editor to be an outsider—and from New York. This is like a 7.1 on the Richter Scale here in this long-insulated environment. You need to know that coming in."

But did I really listen?

I guess a lot of people were resentful. I was thought of as some East Coast weirdo, not a proper and loyal careerist at the *Los Angeles Times* who would put his or her professional life and heart and soul into the further construction of the building's cathedral of achievements. Moreover, I was the guy who had run the editorial page of the late *Los Angeles Herald Examiner* that many years before had committed oh-so-many perceived blasphemies, among them endorsing infamous Proposition 13.

In fact, on about the second or third day on the job, veteran opinion-editorial page editor Robert Berger had informed me that the *Los Angeles Times* people were wary of me because they thought of me as a bit "quick and dirty." By this it was meant that there was a touch of the demagogue in me—as exemplified in the endorsement of Proposition 13.

Well, maybe. You decide. Here's the background on the controversial Proposition 13:

The landmark statewide ballot measure had sought to restrict the ability of the government to raise property taxes to levels unendurable by many middle-class families. The mighty *Los Angeles Times* had opposed it with everything it had, but while its editorials were learned and well-researched, their tone was condescendingly avuncular—as if only the *Los Angeles Times* knew what was good for California. By contrast, *The Los Angeles Herald Examiner* had endorsed it with what little clout we had. Our editorials were direct, frank and deliberately in-your-face and anti-establishment. We were not smart enough at the struggling *Los Angeles Herald Examiner* to propose to know with certainty what was best for Californians but we did know that in a town so long dominated by one newspaper—the mighty *Los Angeles Times*—a little intellectual and public policy competition between the editorial pages could not help but be a good thing for civic debate. Ultimately, after all, editorial pages do not vote but they can illuminate issues and help voters work through the complex arguments, and weigh the pros and cons. If *both* Los Angeles papers were on the same side of such an important question, how would the intellectual unanimity contribute to civic discussion?

Even so, I was initially leery of endorsing Proposition 13, in part—to be truthful—because of the solid intellectual structure of the argument made by the competition, which was then under the steady hand of *Los Angeles Times* veterans Anthony Day and deputy editorial page editor Jack Burby. As much as the unrelenting tone of intellectual superiority made my skin crawl, the central theme of putting the government in a tax straightjacket would inevitably trigger the famed Law of Unintended Consequences and prove harmful to the state's infrastructure and educational system and so on, and perhaps prove irreversible. These were not trivial arguments at all and they deserved to be pondered.

My boss Jim Bellows, a thoughtful editor, was troubled too about the position *The Los Angeles Herald Examiner* should take. Then came the epiphany which happened when Jim asked me to join him at a luncheon for the two of us hosted by the Los Angeles Board of Supervisors. It was at this lunch that my stomach turned from a reasoned and enlightened editorial page editor into a foaming-at-the mouth editorial page demagogue.

The members of the board of supervisors—the most powerful political entity in Los Angeles—were, almost to a man (and the board comprised only men then), disdainful of any counter-argument, contemptuous of easily understandable voter fears about continually rising taxes that were actually taxing some people out of their homes, and utterly confident that their view would prevail and that Proposition 13 would be defeated handily.

It was a performance of breathtaking arrogance—an arrogance that the editorials of the *Los Angeles Times*, in their tone at least, mirrored. Well, no surprise there: the *Los Angeles Times* was part of the Los Angeles establishment. Let me tell you this: if you want to have influence on public policy and have a choice between being editorial page editor of a major American newspaper, or serving as a journeyman congressman/woman, there is no contest—the former is more influential.

After the luncheon, on the ride back, Jim, who could read me so well, was silent until we got to *The Los Angeles Herald Examiner* parking lot. We were lost in thought and perhaps Jim had been watching me out of the corner of his eye.

"Well, what do you want to do?" he asked, quietly.

"Let's screw 'em," I answered. "Who the hell do they think they are?!"

Jim paused. "I guess I agree."

Afterwards, I paid a visit to Frank Dale, the paper's publisher, to obtain his consent on this controversial view. Frank, a warm man, had worked for Richard Nixon and was a high profile Republican. He was not exactly hard to convince that *The Los Angeles Herald Examiner* should endorse an anti-tax measure, especially with "the liberal" *Los Angeles Times* so obnoxiously in opposition.

Thus, this was how *The Los Angeles Herald Examiner* came to make the most outspoken arguments in favor of Proposition 13. I believe we may have been the only major newspaper in the entire state not to oppose it. In the end, of course, the voters of California passed the measure overwhelmingly (and our page garnered the Best Editorial award from the Los Angeles Press Club for the editorial series on this controversy). After this incident, my staff and some colleagues would jokingly refer to me in public as "the father of Proposition 13." But the joke was pretty lame: *The Los Angeles Herald Examiner* may have been in sync with the mood of the people but you could take all the influence of our editorial page, put it on the head of a pin, and still have room left over for an elephant. I doubt we changed seven votes, but by opposing the *Los Angeles Times* (rather than simply supporting Proposition 13), a lot of people began to pay attention to us and to look at us as a strong voice in loyal opposition to the establishment which was the *Los Angeles Times*.

A LOT OF PEOPLE also resented David Laventhol, the new publisher, and Coffey, the new editor, in large part because they came from the outside. Together, the three of us were pagan infidels inside the holiest of holy cathedrals.

Dave's own editorial mantra was "quick and deep." By this he meant journalism had to keep pace with contemporary society and also, not be stupid or dumbed-down. Dave liked his fellow journalists smart (with a master's degree from Yale, he had no intellectual insecurities) but unpretentious, and slightly bold (though always amenable to being reined in).

The *Los Angeles Times* was indeed a real tanker and many years after we all had left our jobs there, Dave was to comment on our struggle to reform the *Los Angeles Times*: "You can't change the religion. You can try but it's not possible."

But that was exactly what we were trying to do when we came on board in the late eighties. The whole floppy, impossible paper—once dubbed "The Whale" by *The Los Angeles Herald Examiner's* page two gossip columnist—needed to be made over, Hollywood-style, into a modern, cosmopolitan editorial product while maintaining the high international and national standards inherited from the 15-year publishing tenure of Otis Chandler. The paper had to beef up on the coverage of the greater Los Angeles area and improve on its editorial pages, as elsewhere.

Generally, most newspapers believe the key to their survival is their local coverage, a level of detail and a specificity right down to which

CNN and Fox News and NBC cannot routinely go. The result was that, in trying to change this ("the religion")—as if converting a Vatican *Time* to a fast-paced reformational *The Economist*—we made a lot of enemies. Fortunately (or otherwise), all three of us had huge egos, unwarranted and limitless self-confidence, and a shared vision of an appropriate "Vatican II" reform plan. (In fact, I even proposed that we created a West Coast, US version of *The Economist* which we would insert as a free magazine in the Sunday paper and market commercially on the news-stands and via subscriptions.) Then the terrible West Coast recession hit like a ton of bricks and many new ideas were put back in the freezer—where they remain today, frozen).

At the same time, a serious American newspaper could scarcely ignore the increasingly globality of the world. In some respects, for California, the decisions made in Beijing, Tokyo or even New Delhi have more of an effect on the average *Los Angeles Times* reader than what happens in adjacent West Covina or Sepulveda. To this end, Higher Authority launched WORLD REPORT, a weekly special section that displayed the great strengths of the *Times*' foreign correspondents splendidly. I loved it. Alas, as the California recession ground on, the section vaporized into nothingness as we had to cut costs everywhere.

On the editorial pages, we tried to offer readers more of a West Coast editorial offense, as it were, without being too offensive. Half-conceding Europe to *The New York Times*, we began to offer a more consistent look at Asia, especially Japan, and cultivated a young editorial writer who was fluent in Japanese and vitally interested in the issues.

For all this, my gut feeling though was that we were still not doing enough in the Asia direction. The *Times* of Los Angeles was too much of a mirror of the *Times* of New York, the generally accepted gold standard for the US newspaper profession. At one point, I looked to run a regular column on Asia but there was little out there that would work right away.

Several years into that reform, though, enough had been accomplished that other journalists elsewhere in the nation had begun to notice. One of them was Howell Raines, who invited me to New York to have lunch with him after it had been announced that he was to succeed the wonderful Jack Rosenthal as *The New York Times* editorial page editor.

Some of America's most outstanding journalists—James Vesely of *The Seattle Times* comes to mind, so does the late great Meg Greenfield of *The Washington Post*, and others—are editorial page editors. Opinion journalism is at once the most marginal of newspaper priorities—its staff always shunted to the side—and the most essential. Great newspapers can offer great leadership, especially when the nominal political leaders are not that great.

I HAD ALWAYS greatly admired Howell's passion for journalism, a quality that seemed not always in abundant supply at The Old Gray Lady, as the East Coast *Times* was nicknamed by its critics. When his appointment was announced, I deemed it a great day for editorial page journalism.

At lunch I was to see that *The New York Times* had indeed chosen a good editorial page editor. While very self-confident, Howell, at least around me, was anything but arrogant. He was almost humble (especially for a *New York Times* man!) and wanted to know things such as how I was able to make the letters to the editor so current (we had a terrific editor and we accepted email messages as well as faxed letters—then an innovation and we were perhaps the first US paper to do so).

He wanted to know how the twin feature I created—COLUMN LEFT/COLUMN RIGHT—was doing. I said that the feature could be better but that it was the best I could do given the *Los Angeles Times*' aversion to standing opinion editorial columnists, such as the *Los Angeles Times* had then in Friedman, Safire and Dowd.

He asked how we managed to keep the editorials so relatively punchy and short given my reporting structure. He knew that I was sat on by Higher Authority, whereas in the East Coast *Times*, the editorial page editor reports only to the publisher, not the chief news editor. His was a superior system. We agreed that too many cooks spoil the broth.

And finally, he asked how I liked Los Angeles. "You did such an outstanding job at *New York Newsday*," he said, and now my head was really *swelling*! "We could never understand why you didn't come with us rather than go to a second-rate city like Los Angeles."

I responded that I had not been asked! He said something like, you could have just walked into the building and been hired. Well, maybe (maybe not!).

I thought about all this for a few seconds, looked at the ceiling and the walls, as I am wont to do when I actually have to make a decision. "Howell, you will be an outstanding editorial page editor ... maybe the best in the paper's history. And you don't need me. You have loads of talent over on 43rd Street. But Dave Laventhol needs me. In truth, he is the main reason I am in LA."

He had one more thought for me to ponder. Was I happy with the editorial page itself?

That was a tough one. I was, and I wasn't. Yes, I thought it somewhat improved because we were, firstly, able to maintain the high intellectual inheritance from my predecessor; avoid the appearance of the knee-jerk; make the language in the editorial more colorful and lively ("snapping it up"); and overall, shorten the length of the editorials—primarily via a page design that placed the editorials across the top (as the *Guardian* of London used to do, and *The Age* of Australia does so nicely today) instead of running them like tombstones on top of each other down the left side.

But then also, no, there was not enough improvement because, well, to quote Steve Isenberg, a top Times-Mirror executive and former associate publisher of *New York Newsday*: "Your pages get the grade of A where they let you be an A, and B where they only let you be a B." Steve was referring to the editorial page itself. And I agreed with Steve, a former deputy major of New York and one of the wittiest people in the world.

I thought of the very kind note I had received from a very nice man named Henry Muller. He was *Time's* top editor in 1991 when a favorable story on the reform and remake of the *Los Angeles Times* appeared in the magazine's press section. I knew Henry well and liked him a lot. When I arrived at *Time*, he went out of his way to show me the ropes and help me stay on my feet. Rather than think of me as a future competitor for the top job, he treated me like a colleague of equals. I will never forget it. And so I had taken the liberty of sending him a private note thanking him for the story while expressing the wish that his own efforts to crank up the magazine for the twenty-first century would not get too watered down, as I feared my own feeble efforts were. He wrote back: "Thanks for your note. Although I did not order up the story on the *Los Angeles Times*, I am very impressed at what you are trying to do. Based on my own experiences here, I share your irritation at people who are quick to criticize any innovation. Best, Henry."

While I had been chatting with Howell, I also wished I had been able to fish out of my pocket a memo I wrote to Higher Authority in 1991, only eighteen months into the job. An article in *The New York Times* had featured a roundup of European editorial commentary about Vice-President Dan Quayle. These editorials—in world-class newspapers like *Le Monde* and *The Financial Times* of London and so on—used colorful language routinely. A German newspaper described the US electoral system as "careless"; *The Financial Times* described Quayle as a "cynical choice"; and *Le Monde* said he was a man who "inspires, rightly or wrongly, more jeers than confidence."

I clipped the article to a memo: "Note that strong language is often the hallmark of strong editorials. Unlike a news story—or even a front page analysis—an editorial needs to use especially colorful language when the occasion is appropriate. As a statement of opinion, it is a helpful tool to use highly opinionated language. Of course, tonality is everything: we are a world-class paper, not the old *Herald Examiner*. But even a major paper, such as *The Financial Times*, will not hesitate to lay it on the line. My job, I think, is to present editorials that use [strong] language ... Thought of the Day Department. Cheers, Tom."

Before I looked up at Howell, I realized I had never gotten a reply to that memo from someone in Higher Authority.

(Well, the truth is, I send too many memos, often to people who were too busy for anything... .)

I looked him in the eye and answered honestly, no, I am not that happy with the *Los Angeles Times* editorial page. But I think the problem is one of structure rather than personality (I was not sure of that myself but it seemed the right and loyal thing to say).

"You mean," he said, "you have two bosses, not just one."

"Correct. You report directly to the publisher, right?"

"Right."

"Then you have the better system," I said.

As it turned out, I was right about Howell's editorial page abilities. When he was promoted to the number one news side position—executive editor—I was elated. Finally, an editorial page editor (a position in which the occupant is sometimes typecast as a hopeless, indecisive pseudo-intellectual) was getting his proper recognition. He was going to be number one.

In the end, alas, the promotion turned into a major disaster. And I think I know what happened. As blustery as he could be, Howell was in fact a supremely caring and sensitive person who caught the infectious disease which was then a pandemic at the *Los Angeles Times*, both the East Coast as well as West Coast versions. It is the dreaded disease of political correctness, which has symptoms such as a jerking knee, intellectual infirmity, narrowed vision and not telling it like it is.

Political correctness is the mentality that says because of decades or centuries of oppression, people of color or so-called minorities cannot be treated as real people but as a human reconstruction or urban renewal project. But they can, and will, stand up for themselves and succeed on their own merit, no condescending "help" needed. Janet Clayton, my successor in this job, may have been a black woman but she brought a helluva lot to the table, as did Ernest Tollerson, my successor at *New York Newsday*, who was a black male and an editor par excellence.

But pampering gets us nowhere; honesty and directness is the only way to go. When we enter the world of political correctness, we begin not to hear things that we should be listening to and not to see developments before our very eyes.

Besides, it is ultimately insulting to the "protected species;" there are plenty of minorities/women/people of color out there who can compete on their own two feet. They just require a level playing field, an occasional pat on the back (as we all do); in the final analysis, they should get the very same treatment accorded everyone else.

Howell perhaps wanted to nurture minority talent too much and thus as Higher Authority, he became a perhaps subconscious foil for political correctness. When a black male reporter was discovered writing fiction and allowing it to be published as nonfiction journalism in *The New York Times*, Howell lost his job and so did the reporter; worse yet, the boys and girls on 43rd Street lost a great journalist in Howell. But such fate will keep on happening until America wakes up and smells the poison—political correctness smells like the environmental degradation it is and it is polluting the American culture and the ethic of merit.

THE *LOS ANGELES TIMES*, like most American newspapers, had a long history of trying to walk down the middle of the road. When I arrived at the paper in 1989, the official opinion of the management, as expressed in the unsigned editorials on the opinion page, was—by and large—standard, bland, liberal. This was not on the whole a good thing. The American press tradition was born out of the assumption that excellence arises as the product of a variegated and rigorously debated marketplace of ideas.

The *Los Angeles Times* editorial pages were of a high quality but low intensity. You learned much from reading them, especially the opinion editorial page, but you had to want badly to learn. With the exception of the daily editorial cartoon by Paul Conrad, the *Los Angeles Times* editorial pages were anything but edgy.

In this respect, they were very much in the muddled left-tilting mainstream of most American editorial pages and this is a pity. The effort to be either all things to all people, for market reasons, or to be "responsible," for reasons of "fairness," does a disservice to the true intensity of the important—and sometimes crucial—issues of political life. It fails to reflect the mortal combat of competing forces and ideologies that ferociously compete for public space and popular support beneath the otherwise civilized veneer of American society. By smoothing over the rough spots of the nation's political landscape, overly "responsible" and "balanced" editorial pages unintentionally paper-over roiling American political realities, as if trying to trowel over a snake pit with gorgeous gobs of white icing.

With Higher Authority's blessings, we set in motion a makeover of the editorial pages that emphasized sharp rhetorical angles and personalization of issues. On the daily opinion editorial page, the staff efficiently launched COLUMN LEFT/COLUMN RIGHT. Bracketing the opinion editorial page on the far left and far right, this every-other-day feature illustrated the further—and sometimes far-out—fences of the national debate. We also added the SUNDAY OPINION INTERVIEW, an in-depth question-and-answer with a scholar, leader or public figure. This added personality to the ongoing debate of issues.

With exceptional energy, the opinion editorial page staff launched a little feature called VOICES, which was reserved for those perspectives that ordinarily would fail to make it to an opinion editorial page because the voicers would lack the usual Ivy League degree or the think tank certification or the insignia of public office. VOICES brought to the *Los Angeles Times* editorial pages the nun who taught inner-city students, the water engineer who had views on our decaying infrastructure, the social worker who was aghast at the lack of funds for our valiant but forgotten vets... Without such an editorial accommodation, what chance would these solid citizens have of seeing their views on a major opinion editorial page?

About two years later, a meeting of Latino community leaders was held at the *Los Angeles Times* office, shortly after the inner-city riots of 1992 that erupted in the wake of the astonishing, innocent verdicts for police officers charged with beating Rodney King. They ripped us (mostly fairly, I thought) across the board for house-on-the-hill indifference. But then someone asked them if there was anything about the paper they actually liked. One community leader spoke up: "I like that VOICES feature." Why, he was asked. "Because we see names there that we recognize instead of people we have never heard of." Later that month, Higher Authority proposed expanding this little feature into a full-page section that would appear three times a week. It seemed like a grand idea to me. And that was how it turned out.

The staff also executed a terrific redesign of the editorial page itself. Editorials were placed in the top half of the page. They also became a lot briefer, crisper and more pointed; in addition, little happy art elements were included almost daily. When the *Los Angeles Times* had something it deemed of huge importance, the editorial could banner across the top of the page with graphic urgency. This is when the "true brilliance," as Dave put it, half tongue-in-cheek, of the redesign was apparent. With LETTERS TO THE EDITOR beneath that, the page beckoned—almost begged—the reader to indulge herself or himself in the issues of the day. The look was so much more inviting than the design of many editorial pages. Or so I thought.

NEWS MEDIA EXECUTIVES pay so little attention to issues of media ethics not because they were fundamentally unethical people, but because they were so overwhelmed every day by pressing decisions and so poorly trained in how to think about the ethical components. Chaos theory rather than conspiracy theory is a better guide to media behavior, if you are looking to predict or explain it.

When my ultra-cynical *Daily Mail* friends in London got wind of the news that I was asked to teach (Mr Quick Judgment becomes Mr Chips, the educator: teaching media ethics—can this be serious?) media ethics as well as Asian media and politics at UCLA, one colleague telephoned, transatlantically to have a good-natured laugh at my expense. "Ethics and the media? How long does your class last? Twenty minutes?!" In fact, as you know, issues of media ethics had churned within me for a long time now.

> Almost nothing is more certain to provoke the acidic skepticism—and gales of laughter—of a true newspaper or magazine editor than the admission that you, a one-time real journalist, have been recast as an educator in the subject of media ethics.

But as the editorial page editor of a prominent newspaper, I felt an obligation to establish some sort of personal and ethical framework. After all, it would be the height of hypocrisy to hold political leaders, corporate executives and other political figures (gosh, even NBA players!) to a higher standard if we in the press did not observe a comparable ethical level of our own.

Without going beyond a pompous pale, newspaper editors—and especially editorial page editors—need to view themselves not just as journalists but as potential civic resources. You just should not hide in your office and insulate yourself from the community you serve.

I came to Los Angeles, as you know, after four years as a New York City editorial page editor. This former position was a very *public* position—everyone in the political and business community knew who the editorial page editors of the major papers were. Public figures from the mayor to the executive director of Lincoln Center to the head of the Dance Troupe of Harlem would visit my office, make their pitch, and sometimes even ask for advise. I felt no ethical hitch there—and always observed the off-the-record courtesy rule.

But when I arrived in Los Angeles, I was to discover a newspaper with journalists who holed up in their big house on the hill, sometimes not even answering phone calls from civic leaders who deserved a bit more respect than they got. After all, who elected the *Los Angeles Times*?

A week at the job, an elected member of the city council—in effect, the metropolis' co-governing body, as the Los Angeles mayor job had limited powers—telephoned to have a word with me. He was to tell me years later that he almost suffered a heart attack when I actually returned his call just a few hours later. This had not been his experience with the *Los Angeles Times* before that.

My habit of returning calls and opening the door for visitors (from the police chief to a congressman to the head of a non-profit organisation) to come in, sit on the couch, and unburden themselves (off-the-record, of course) was deeply ingrained. The sense I had of being the *Los Angeles Times* editorial page editor was not of entitlement but of privilege. Many other editors in America, just as smart (and many, surely, smarter) as I, would have killed their pet parakeet for this job, and I had landed it in part because of luck, circumstances, naked ambition, and Dave. Who was I to act as if I was better than anyone else? And I always tried to remember that.

One of my favorite interlocutors in this—or any other job—was Warren Christopher. On TV, which is the defining mass medium for any political figure of our time, Chris, as he is sometimes called, comes across as drab and dull, but he is rather something else in person.

Before he became secretary of state during Bill Clinton's first term, Chris served in an important civic position in Los Angeles. Various allegations of brutality and corruption—highlighted by the well-publicized and videotaped police clubbing of Rodney King, an unarmed miscreant minority motorist—had led to the empanelment of a special commission. It was to become known as the Christopher Commission, after its chairman. At this time he had been known mainly as having excelled as President Jimmy Carter's deputy secretary of state. The commission's public goal was to offer a series of recommendations to induce the Los Angeles Police Department to launch a long overdue process of modernization and reform. The unstated goal was to create irresistible public pressure for incumbent police chief Daryl Gates, a classic take-no-prisoners cop, to step down. Chris' commission issued a unanimous report about the Los Angeles Police Department that was widely heralded, especially on the editorial pages of the *Los Angeles Times*. But still Gates doggedly held on, by his fingernails.

One day, the phone rang, and it was Chris (this conversation was off-the-record then, but the passage of time now permits its rightful entry into the public record), and this great public servant was plainly worried: "Tom, I don't know how we're going to get him to leave."

I said: "Yeah, I know. He's one tough customer. Maybe you could Yeltsin-ize him."

There was a silence. I could almost hear Chris thinking to himself. He knew I was referring to how challenger Boris Yeltsin had finally managed to force Gorbachev out of power in the Russian succession struggle. Yeltsin had, at one point, literally done such little technical things as cutting off the electric power lines to Gorbachev's office elevator. By analogy, what are the ways in which the anti-Gates forces can edge the incumbent out?

"That's not a bad idea, Tom—to Yeltsin-ize Gates."

"We just need to be patient, Chris, and let time take its course."

I could, again, almost hear the accomplished lawyer and distinguished diplomat breathe more easily. The last thing he wanted to see was a *Los Angeles Times* editorial decrying the commission's ineffectiveness in forcing the incumbent brute out.

That editorial was not going to appear. Such an editorial in the *Los Angeles Times* would have been crudely misconceived. Los Angeles had every reason to be well pleased by the indefatigable work of Christopher and his team of largely lawyer volunteers. Moreover, the news media must start to understand that writing about a problem is not the same thing as solving it and that often true change takes time. We become part of the problem when we are too quick to criticize those who are trying to solve it, and too quick to demand results.

"Thanks, Tom. Let's see if we can indeed Yeltsin-ize him, as you put it."

In fact, the Christopher Commission process did just that; in due course, Gates was to leave the job. Los Angeles became a better place for it.

During the height of the battle, and just after the official issuance of the final report, we received a neat note from Christopher: " ... I want to tell you how much I appreciate the spectacular coverage by the *Los Angeles Times* of the Independent [Christopher] Commission Report. The quality and thoroughness of the coverage exceeded anything in my memory. We had a small party for the staff Wednesday night and the room was abuzz with admiration and appreciation for the coverage in the *Los Angeles Times* ... I know this represented a major commitment of resources and I wanted to tell you of our deep appreciation."

Though a seasoned diplomat, Chris was anything but a gratuitous backslapper. All flattery aside, what the future secretary of state was saying reflected exactly what a famous former New York City reform police commissioner once told me: no civil reform effort can succeed without the firm and implacable backing of the dominant metropolitan newspaper. Without unrelenting media wind in the sails of the reforms, the task is probably hopeless, however noble.

TAKING A CLEAR LEADERSHIP STANCE on any and all important civic issues remains a responsibility of any major publication. But for decades the management of the *Los Angeles Times* took a different view. On the big issues—the endorsement of a president, a gubernatorial candidate, even a US senate race—the mighty *Los Angeles Times* would quietly absent itself and in effect punt rather haplessly.

"Before too long, the general election [in California] will be on us, and we could be in the position of defending anew the old non-endorsement policy," I wrote in a memo (right, I wrote a *lot* of memos—way too many!) to Dave Laventhol, the publisher, and Shelby Coffey, the top editor, less than a year after I had arrived. "In my view, the *Times* should feel free to endorse in any election, primary or general—big office or small—where it perceives a significant reason for doing so ... Its voice should be used to try to help make things better ... Sometimes, some candidates—or ballot propositions—are better than others. We should have no shame in saying so..."

Was I unhappy? I was unhappy with myself for accepting the job without clearing this issue up beforehand, just as I had been less than thrilled to learn after I had been installed at CBS *Family Weekly* that health stories in the magazine that even mentioned the word "cancer" were forbidden by the terms of CBS's contract with those giant cigarette advertisers. It seemed to me that a commitment to First Amendment journalism meant, if anything, that journalism should be as honest as it could consciously be.

I have no idea how Higher Authority put up with me. I was pretty relentless (read: obnoxious) about the endorsement issue. A half year later, I penned anew: "We should review the paper's long-standing policy of not endorsing in races like governor, senator ... and president. It is a safe policy ... But is it what we want? If America is indeed at a crossroads, is the appropriate place for the *Times* on the sidelines?"

Memo sincerity aside, the policy did not change.

I WORRIED ABOUT many things. One of these was a fear that our editorial pages were headed towards doomsville. It was a known fact that editorial pages that do not take a stand on issues of public interest generally become increasingly unread. I worried we were heading in this direction. Newspapers should take a stand and defend it when it comes under attack. And more than that, they should never tell lies.

I felt myself to be in an uncomfortable position, and so I was always agitating. Perhaps at times I crossed the line. But I felt strongly about the knee-jerk wimp-out.

Before long, I became depressed. I even went to see a shrink. A University of Southern California medical school graduate, he specialized in middle-aged professionals. "That place is eating you up," the good doctor said at the end of one session. "The longer you stay, the harder it will get."

The next day at lunch in the executive dining room, a famous physicist was the guest of honor. At one point he asked an editor why so many sections—like CALIFORNIA or SPORTS or CALENDAR—were wrapped in a covering advertising section. One higher-ranking editor answered with a mumble and a jumble and a shake and a bake kind of explanation about the mechanical configurations of the printing presses.

That answer was misleading at best. The real reason was money: advertisers pay a premium for that positioning. Now, I see absolutely nothing wrong with making money by charging profit-seeking businesses a premium for special positions; heck, I was very happy with my healthy six-figure salary (plus annual bonus and stock options) and I knew that the money paying for our salaries was surely not trickling down from the heavens. But I am never happy when a newspaper lies or fails to tell the full story—who would be?

And so, frustrated, I blurted out, at the luncheon, right in front of a member of Higher Authority, (for I could not help myself): "We make more money that way and the hell with the reader."

Was that dumb or what?

That evening, driving home, my phone rang. It was a supervisor. "You should know, Tom," he said, angrily, "that I did not appreciate that comment. You were out of line. Let's not have this again." And he abruptly hung up.

You see, it was okay for a newspaper to pound politicians who prevaricate but for a newspaper, you see, a double standard can prevail. I am sorry, I do not buy it, and whatever my faults—and the heck with them all—this is not me. Newspapers must not lie, in print or otherwise.

> It is vital that you be allowed to personally choose your top deputies. Too often, however, that is not permitted. And so, trouble can, and will, brew.

THERE WAS A PROBLEM with one of my deputies. He was starting to hate me. I think the problem was that, in the final analysis, he felt that after working at the *Los Angeles Times* for some two decades, he could not accept that the top job would have gone to an outsider. To add to his frustration, his position on the editorial page job did not play to his strengths. He was at the very least somewhat miscast. He was extremely knowledgeable about southern California's Latino communities and as a local journalism graduate, had solid skills. He was not however, by intellectual bent, voraciously interested in world issues in the largest sense or about many of the other extremely complex issues that a major editorial page editor must stay on top of.

It was important to constantly remind myself and my colleagues of this: some of the people who bothered to read unsigned editorials in newspapers were extremely smart, dedicated and committed to high standards. In California they ranged from the head of the largest state university system in the world to the major domos at Dreamworks to the director of the latest movie hit to a Nobel Prize physicist at UCLA to the mayor, the governor ... maybe even the president of the country.

Because of his unsurpassed knowledge of the local scene, especially the Latino/Hispanic world, this particular deputy was extremely valuable to the paper but he should have been a top editor in the newsroom, not on the editorial page. Why he was cast in the position that they gave him was a mystery to me. He was an extremely likable journalist but the corporate miscasting put a tremendous psychic pressure on him that must have been unbearable. But because of the management's felt need to have a minority journalist on the masthead—anywhere on the masthead!—he got put into the position he got. Hey, I would be miscast as the sports editor, you know! We all have our limitations.

Several times, I proposed creating a special news side job for him. The longer he stayed in the editorial pages department, the more likely the occurrence of some catastrophic blow-up. In one memo (yes, yet another memo!), I spelled out my views to Higher Authority: "I wish to put into writing my thoughts [on creating a new job for this otherwise talented editor] ... Judging from your reaction to my two previous efforts to do this, I have done a poor job of articulating my thoughts.

"The position would not concentrate solely on minority recruitment, hiring and training. This would be only a fraction of it. The position—of an assistant managing editor nature—would seek to embed at a high level of news management a greater sensitivity to and knowledge about 'new majority' [that is, Latino/black] coverage. Far from a mere window-dressing position, this new position would enhance and deepen strategies and tactics of news coverage. Often, after a discussion with [this star employee], especially when he is critical of a specific failure in our news coverage, I am convinced that, as valuable as he is on the editorial page, his talents could be used at least as well on the news side. The editorial page, whatever its faults, does not want for minority perspective." (More than half of our editorial board comprised minorities or women.)

Higher Authority turned the idea down with very little discussion. I was devastated because I knew that the net effect of sticking with the staffing status quo would eventually prove to be catastrophic for me—and for everyone else. I was extremely worried and on edge.

THE THING THAT kept me going was my loyalty to Dave and a belief that on the whole my presence on this particular job was a net plus. Hey, if I did not actually believe that, why bother?

I kept pushing the envelope. One short (!) memo went: "Are we happy with our editorials? Are they lively enough? Are they what we want? Tom."

I was not happy enough with them. In general, our editorial process had the effect of toning down rather than firming up. The 9:30 editorial conference with the writers and researchers was one obstacle course. (God forbid, for example, that any editorial be proposed that was remotely critical of Latinos or Liberals.)

But the smaller, top management conference at 11am was another mountain. Attending were members of Higher Authority. The point of this meeting was too often to make sure the editorials caused no major ripples or would not complicate the news side's reporting efforts. I think every member who attended was frustrated at one point or the other. In retrospect, I wish I had been stronger, more convincing—but I tried the best I could do at that time. And the best you can do is all you can do.

It was early in 1993 when I received a phone call from David Laventhol who then was still our publisher. "Tom," he said, softly, "Do you think the paper needs to run something special on the whole gun control issue?"

Dave had asked the question because people were dying everyday in Los Angeles, especially on its inner-city streets, due to random gunfire from drug gangs. It was not only scary, the deterioration was getting to be a very bad joke, and the joke was on Los Angeles.

Many of these gangs could not shoot straight. Latino or black or white or whatever, their bullets more often than not would hit babies or innocent bystanders. Either the guns had to be taken away from them or they needed to take regular supervised target practise! I did not mind their killing one another but the death of an unsuspecting school kid or mother was something else.

By that time, I had been the editor of the editorial pages for a few years and my personal frustration with the paper's generally tentative and overly nuanced approach to tough issues was growing to an unhealthy level. Had it not been for my personal loyalty to Dave, I was thinking of looking for another job: the staff I had inherited from my predecessor obviously did not like me and I did not like the editorial page tradition of ducking the Big Ones. Hey, I was a New Yorker, basically, and will always remain that. I'm (thoughtfully—I hope!) argumentative. There is more pushy Ed Koch in me than Mellow Surfer.

And so I answered Dave's question with a little sass. "Yes, we do need to speak out, and really, we should have done it by now. It is a tough problem, and it is one that people genuinely care about. But it's not going to do anybody any good if we merely indulge in some thumb-sucking consideration of this approach or that.

"If we're going to do this, then we must take a high-profile, bang-bang approach to match the explosiveness of the issue. No hedging permitted. Leave the footnotes to the professors. If we're going to speak, then we need to come up with a strong and even controversial statement. Doing anything less would be worse than continuing to remain silent."

Looking back, I realize I was perhaps a little edgier with this exceptional man whom I greatly admired than I needed to be, but the truth was that I was fed up with the paper's wishy-washiness (and especially with my own acceptance of the gray code—I repeat, I am blaming no one more than myself). There was no national security threat to justify the paper's silence on this or any other issue. And people were being shot at all the time by gun-toting lunatics who had very bad aim! In the schoolyard, at the office, in the post office, outside of church! It was clear that America was too gun-crazy for its own good, too immature to handle them properly.

I then made the perhaps blunt suggestion to the publisher of the *Los Angeles Times* that if we wanted to be truly serious and responsible on the issue, we needed to be prepared to focus our staff resources on the achievement of a free-swinging series of editorials that would *take a very strong stand. Period.* The stand was this: almost no one should have real-live trigger-happy guns in their possession.

Unbelievably, we soon got the okay from the editor, ordinarily a most cautious man, and began to write an eight-part series on gun control in America, spearheaded by our staff research team. This was created, through the generosity of Higher Authority, in response to my observation that our editorials sometimes lacked the depth of research befitting the leading Western newspaper of the world's only superpower. And so we created what—as far as I know—was the first research unit of an editorial pages department in any US newspaper. We were able to hire a researcher from RAND, the famous

Santa Monica-based research institution; and another who had worked as a fact-checker for Doris Kearns Goodwin, the celebrated biographer of Lyndon Baines Johnson.

When we were about halfway through publication of the sequential editorial series, our long-standing letters editor came into my office—she was like the Little Old Lady from Pasadena but had the taste, sense and sensibility of Jane Austen—and announced: "Tom, I have some good news and bad news. The bad is that we have already received two or three thousand letters about the series. The good news is that only half of them are against us."

That was one savvy observation from Mary because newspaper editors were well-versed in letter campaigns that were fully and vilely orchestrated by groups with vested interests—and there is no group more vested or interested in the gun issue than the National Rifle Association. Accordingly, a large portion of the anti-*Times* letters was generated by this enormously efficient, powerful epistolary lobby.

What was more heartwarming—as the saintly Mary reported—was that the other 50 per cent of the incoming letters were from individuals writing on their own who felt strongly enough to say: "Thank you for taking a bold stand on an important issue. Even if I don't agree with you, the fact that you've taken a high profile position points the way towards some solutions."

This is, of course, exactly what an editorial page cognizant of the civic implications of the First Amendment should do. It must lead, responsibly, instead of hedge or follow for fear of commercial loss. If the news side is meant to bring you a nuanced, multifaceted view of the world (though it does not always do so), the editorial page should present sharp though richly detailed rhetorical and political angles. But taking a stance can sometimes be a risky business. I was worrying that I might have gone too far about two-thirds of the way into the series when my secretary buzzed me and said Otis Chandler was on the line.

Otis, of course, was the legendary former publisher of the *Los Angeles Times*. During his many years at the helm, he never felt the need to put profit above quality because he believed the two went hand-in-hand. In that sense, at least, he was a twentieth-century giant in American journalism.

He did not call me every day. Or every month, for that matter. Which is why I was so nervous that he was suddenly on the line in the middle of this series. I thought, "Oh my God! Otis is a well-known hunter and gun-collector and he's going to want my scalp for writing a series that calls for gun ownership in America to be scaled back!" I took a deep breath and prepared myself for a shotgun blast. To my delight, the direction of his call went the other way entirely: "Tom, this editorial series on gun control that you're doing is the best job I can remember we've ever done on an issue that should be done right. You lay out the problem and then you offer an actual solution to the problem. I really admire it and I'm glad we are performing a great public service."

Well, yes, I was in heaven—wouldn't you be?

"But," he said, "there's just one tiny little thing."

"What is it?" I said, tentatively. (oh-oh, here it comes...)

"You know, I'm a hunter, and a conservationist. I'm against the indiscriminate use of guns, too, and worked, unsuccessfully, to get the Saturday Night Special banned. But here's a suggestion. There has to be some way for private, responsible citizens to own handguns. Why, up in Alaska, you can be hunting and the Kodiak bear will be on you in a second. Or you can be in Africa and the tiger is in the tree, and you don't see him, and suddenly he jumps down. It's too late for the shotgun. You need to pull out a handgun, like a .44 Magnum. So, you need a hunter's exception but certainly with very tight conditions. Also, licensed hunting guides—properly licensed ones—need to be able to carry revolvers. They operate in very dangerous game country."

"Right, Otis," I got it. I was scribbling notes furiously, carefully. I've kept these notes to this day, of course.

"Then, Tom, for the responsible gun collectors and competition shooters, maybe we can work out some system where they can be checked out of some central library or something; or require owners to register them at least yearly, like cars. But on the whole, I think we have the right position."

I said, more relieved than annoyed by far: "I'll look into it, Mr Chandler. It sounds like a valid point, so there must be something we can do."

"Again," he added, "let me apologize for intervening. If you can't make this exception work, don't worry about it. I do think it is a magnificent series of editorials. I am very proud of them."

Naturally, before I did anything, I hot-pedaled over to the offices of Higher Authority and along the way probably told everybody else in the building from the janitor to the receptionist about how I had just gotten a most laudatory telephone call from Otis Chandler. We eventually won the prestigious California Newspaper Publishers Association award for the series, which I know pleased Otis tremendously. (Actually, if you do not mind my saying so, we won that award three years in a row, though I have great doubts about the validity and integrity of some of these journalism award deals. I'll explain later.)

SOMETHING ELSE HAPPENED to move the *Los Angeles Times'* editorial page into the big leagues. In 1994, the paper's management finally decided to act like most other adult American newspapers and express true preferences when it came to controversial national and major election issues.

For years, *The New York Times* had expressed solid opinions on issues that affected the masses and thus people around the country could reach for the paper to see what it said around election time and other crucial civic occasions. But for decades, people in Los Angeles have not had a major paper that would stand up to the big ones—largely because the *Los Angeles Times* maintained a policy of not endorsing candidates in high-profile political races.

Publicly, the newspaper had justified this by saying that the *Los Angeles Times'* editorial contribution to the community came in its pointed illumination of candidates and issues involved in otherwise obscure political races, like the California state assembly or a local judgeship or a minor statewide race. The *Los Angeles Times* would use its clout to interview the candidates, research the issues and make recommendations that would seek to demystify obscure state propositions, ballot measures, and constitutional amendments. Thus did it perform a great public service. But when it came to the bigger races, Otis had said that Angelenos did not need help with something as intuitive as crossing the street, or pouring a cup of coffee, or choosing the next American president, for that matter. They were just too sophisticated.

Well, not exactly. The real reason behind the *Los Angeles Times'* non-endorsement policy had little to do with such unbounded faith in its readers and everything to do with the politics behind a newspaper. As most papers are now owned by publicly traded media conglomerates, most publishers (the average newspaper "numero uno") report to and represent a board of directors which in theory reports to and represents the conglomerate's stockholders.

Add to this the *Los Angeles Times'* less-than-sunny endorsement history. In 1972, the last time the paper had endorsed in a US presidential race, the editorial board chose Richard Nixon and two years later he had to resign from office to avoid congressional impeachment. Then, in the 1976 Senate race, the *Los Angeles Times* endorsed a Kennedy-like Democrat, John Tunney, over conservative S I Hiyakawa, who then crushed Tunney in a landslide vote. These episodes made the *Los Angeles Times* look not only like a confused newspaper but also as if it lacked much clout to influence events, such as to stop a guy like Hiyakawa, a San Francisco professor of linguistics who would wear a Tam O'Shanter cap and had such a knack for the outrageous statement that sometimes it was hard not to laugh at him even when he thought he was not being funny.

Looking at that crazy history, Otis Chandler, not unreasonably, decreed, in effect: "The hell with it. Let's get completely out of the business of endorsing in these high profile races and we'll just endorse in smaller races that nobody ever heard of." (And perhaps not that many readers cared about...)

Thus, the paper remained painfully and embarrassingly silent during the greater part of my six-year tenure whenever something truly major came up. There was almost no mention of George Bush Sr or Bill Clinton in 1992. Time trod on until 1994 when several unexpected events came together.

The first was that David Laventhol announced that he had contracted Parkinson's disease—this was a 9.0 on my Richter Scale!—and would eventually resign. In addition to contracting Parkinson's, he had been brokenhearted by all the cost-cutting he had to do in the face of the dramatic decline in revenues. I once came by late at night to see him. He was in his office, behind his desk, with one desk lamp lit. Poring over spreadsheets and budget papers sprawled everywhere, this good and decent man seemed deeply troubled. He raised his head, heavy with the weight of corporate-ordered editorial budget cutbacks, and looked at me with what I thought were tears in his eyes.

"What's wrong? What are you doing," I asked.

He responded, wearily, "I'm trying to save the jobs of journalists."

When all this came down—the cutbacks and the Parkinson's and the resignation—I went into a very deep funk. For a few weeks, I kept my door closed and saw as few staffers as possible. I was sick of mind, heart and soul.

First, Dave was the key reason I abandoned New York, which Andrea had loved, for Los Angeles, which she never had; second, Dave's departure would eviscerate my power and eventually mean I would lose one of the best jobs in American journalism—it was just a matter of time. I knew it was inevitable because I had come in from the outside. It would also mean that the possibility of becoming the editor of the paper would go from slim to none. And, three, it meant that once again, my wife Andrea would be proven right—and don't we husbands get tired of this?! "What if something happened to Dave?" she had asked plaintively, when we discussed my move to Los Angeles. I had responded: "What could happen to Dave?" But now the sad question was, what would happen to Dave? The disease had knocked him down and took the fight out of him.

> Jobs that are dependent on one person or one factor are less stable than jobs that have an institutional base. Keep this in mind if you are uncomfortable with risk-taking.

Dave's replacement was a Times-Mirror corporate official. He had spent a good portion of his career at a Texas-based newspaper chain that was never going to win a Pulitzer, but always won over the investors with huge profit margins. Culturally, no arrow was ever manufactured straighter.

When it was announced that he was the replacement, Dave, who knew me well, took me to lunch at the Picasso Room (the executive dining room) and in his special quiet way said, "He's a good guy, Tom, but don't do anything unusual or bizarre or especially original, which you are quite capable of. Don't wear any of your goofy ties. And tone down the hair. Be a straight arrow all the way down the line."

The new publisher was a military man—a former Air Force pilot who had broadened out into a buttoned-down management type, courtesy of an MBA from Stanford. His style was less John Wayne gung-ho than strong-silent-type Jimmy Stewart. He was decent, had integrity, and generally, was charmingly straightforward. I was to learn quickly of his thoughtfulness for others, his quiet but firm manner, and his impatience with excessive detail or briefings that lasted more than five minutes. He was decisive, well-mannered, and precise. For a good period of time, we got on very well indeed.

I tried—as Dave was an old friend—to take his advise to heart. I put the silly ties in the back of the closet, always made sure my hair was combed down and parted straight. But then, for some bizarre and self-destructive reason, I dyed my graying hair jet black, in the style of septuagenarian Asian politicians.

> They say never judge a book by its cover. But some people never get beyond the cover to the book. Personal appearance in the business world—whether to get a job or to hold on to one—is often understated but always understood, if subliminally, as a key factor.

The first time I showed up at the 9:45 editorial board meeting with my newly-dyed hair, I thought my staff was going to die of laughter or shock. (Subconsciously, was I afraid the new publisher would look for a younger editorial page editor to replace me? Was that the motivation for this inept, self-engineered makeover?)

Later, in one of the get-to-know-you meetings with Dick and the other editors, one noticed that everyone was wearing black socks—except for me. While I was not sporting Day-Glo socks or any such, it seemed to me that others in the room kept looking at my socks—and looking and looking. They were probably of a nice floral pattern but certainly not corporate black.

And so I went up after the meeting and said: "Sir, I'm glad we're getting to know one another. Eventually you'll want your own editorial page editor, as Dave had wanted his, and that was me; but I'm happy to stay as long as you want me to. Anything you need or want from me or the editorial staff, please don't hesitate to ask. But there's just one thing that I can't do. And that is, I can't do black socks."

He looked at me as if that thought had never occurred to him. I continued with something like: "I noticed that everybody else in the room had black socks on. I know you or your predecessor didn't order that so it must be part of the unwritten corporate culture. I wish this would come easy to me. But it doesn't. I don't wear them. It's just not in me. I know you are a kind and thoughtful person but if you require black socks out of your top people and all that implicitly comes with it, then we should start looking for something else for me to do at this paper and I know we can work that out. A uniform of any kind that tries to make me fit in won't disguise my true nature. I like to dress a little colorfully. I like to *think* colorfully. That probably reflects my personality and maybe our editorial pages as well. That, I'm afraid, is the bottom line—or at least, my bottom line."

He laughed.

"Conformity is not for me. It requires too much capacity for normality. My sense is that normality is the enemy of creativity."

"By that standard, then, you must be the most creative person here!"

It was my turn to laugh. At that moment I thought of Don Forst interviewing at *People* magazine when I was at *Time*. *People* was looking for a new senior editor and I had recommended Don to *People's* people. Although *People* is a lively magazine of fluffy fortune, it existed in the mainstream of corporate *Time*, with its austere ways. To personally make the point that he was not a black socks type, he showed up for the interviews donning a high white fedora. He looked like Al Pacino in the movie "Scarface." Don did it as a matter of buyer-beware fairness: if you want me, he was saying in effect, you can have me but you have to accept the person who wears this hat.

In any event, a few weeks later, Dick, instead of firing me, surprised me by asking me how I felt about the *Los Angeles Times'* policy of not endorsing in major elections. The question coming as it did from the black socks supremo came out of the blue.

"Well, to be honest," I said, wearing bright red socks, "and I don't mean any disrespect to Dave Laventhol or Otis Chandler, both of whom we all respect, but I have always hated it."

"Really?" he asked, surprised. "Why?"

I said: "Well, I think it takes away from the newspaper's ability to have a positive influence on the course of political events. You don't have to knee-jerkily endorse in every single race but why take yourself out of the presidential and senate races, and automatically have no comment, especially if you have a strong feeling or arguable insight or even stern wisdom that you'd like to share?

"It makes no sense for a major paper with several million readers to de-claw itself before the election campaign even starts. It's also wimpy. We comment on the doings and goings of city council and the mayor; we rap the police commissioner's knuckles for X and praise the County Board of Supervisors for Y, but when it comes to the really big issues, like an election for the White House or the Senate, we zip our lips. It makes no sense. It feels like the ultimate cop-out, doesn't it?"

He said: "You know, I agree, Tom. But you have been living with it for so long."

"Well, that's another story. I live with a lot of things around here that aren't right. If you want, I'll send you copies of two confidential memos on this I wrote a few years back."

"No! Don't send any more memos. Let's talk about changing the policy instead of memo writing!"

I was not sure I had heard him correctly. "Are you serious?"

He said he was serious about no more memos.

I said I meant was he serious about un-wimping the notoriously wimpy endorsement policy?

He averred that he was.

"That would be great. It's not going to be easy to change the *Times'* tradition but I think it's a battle that's well worth engaging in."

I was, well, almost ecstatic.

The political climate in California at the time was super-heated. The state was just emerging from a terrible recession and the incumbent governor was crawling out of the political graveyard—thanks to the nascent economic recovery and an anti-immigrant ballot measure known as Proposition 187. The Proposition was rearing its ugly head and the very competent Dianne Feinstein, the former San Francisco mayor who had become the incumbent US senator, was fighting for her political life against a super right-wing challenger who knew very little about anything but had a lot of money to bank into his political ego account.

The incumbent governor Pete Wilson was widely touted as a sensible conservative—one who was aware of the need for social programs, but who did not let his career slide into the destructible image of a carefree liberal spender. He would have otherwise enjoyed an easy re-election, except for two things that stood in his way. The first was that his first term had coincided with the most severe recession in state history since the Great Depression of the 1930s. Wilson therefore had to manage everything with shrinking resources, and as he cut funding from public schools and so on to make the budget work, the compassionate part of his character lost its sheen and the number of offended constituencies, groups and lobbies increased. The economy, in fact, had gotten so bad that his popularity declined to the point that he became one of the most unpopular governors in state history—not a distinction one wants to have with a re-election looming on the horizon.

A second factor was California's system allowing citizens to make changes in the constitution directly via popular referendum. That is, Californians can put up for a statewide vote virtually any kind of constitutional amendment or policy initiative and pass it into state law by a two-thirds majority vote. In 1994, one measure that got on the ballot this way was Proposition 187, or as it was more popularly known, the "Illegal Immigration Act"—or, in some circles, even better known as the "Anti-Latino Proposition." Wilson endorsed the Proposition and, in fact, made it the lynchpin of his election campaign—a position that incurred the wrath of many in the Latino community.

What Proposition 187 said was that the state of California needed to get tougher towards people who were living illegally in the state, primarily because they were absorbing public welfare funds that were needed to help out legal residents. The measure seemed less a wise piece of public policy than a bolt of anger aimed at the constant stream of unauthorized Mexican nationals flowing into the state. To be fair to the measure, there was a serious component to it, in that the Californian border was unacceptably porous: that is, either there was an international border or there wasn't. On the other hand, it was also a shameful blame game deal, where suddenly we have all these problems because of "them," and if we could just send "them" back where they came from, then all "our" problems would be gone.

The *Los Angeles Times*, a liberal newspaper, took a stance well out of sync with the vast majority of the state's voters and opposed Proposition 187 with the argument that it was hypocritical, unconstitutional, and arguably racist. In more than two dozen editorials we argued that the immigration issue was not one that could be dealt with until the economics of it were dealt with. We cannot exploit desperate Mexican labor that was more willing to work for lower wages than anyone here in America and also at the same time say, "We don't want you, and we're going to throw you in jail and send you back to where you came from."

There was another reason we opposed Proposition 187. The *Los Angeles Times* was extraordinarily concerned with being seen, within the building and without, as politically correct, even celestially across-the-board demographically and ethnically unctuous. We did not say this of course in our editorials. But the fact was that it was impossible to make a joke or a statement around the office that might be regarded as being even remotely non-politically correct. It was thus a very uptight atmosphere.

We were also handed an approved word usage booklet, banning everything from the ugly racial epithets such as the N-word for blacks (banning this from all vocabularies would be a very good idea, in truth) to the aforementioned "Dutch treat" (on the grounds that such use might offend Dutch people ... can you believe it?) to "gypsy" (watch out for the aggrieved Hungarian lobby—it was not exactly goulash!). The only usage issue my pages took serious note of was the "N" word; it was banned from the editorial pages unless it was cleared with me, even if I was on vacation.

This Multicultural Media Disneyland was fast becoming a national embarrassment. The delightfully acerbic critic Christopher Hitchens wrote: "In recent months, the *Los Angeles Times* has become the object of extensive mirth, inside and outside journalism, [for] codifying a new set of amendments to the newspaper's stylebook which guide and shape the use of language concerning 'ethnic and racial identification,' to say nothing of gender and sexual orientation, to say nothing, indeed, of offensiveness, insensitivity, and correctitude in general..." This was in *Vanity Fair* magazine (April 1994), no less. "What [instead is needed], everyday, is the pen of a Mencken or a Lincoln Steffens. What it has settled for is a grand consultative committee, made up of the well-meaning and the ill-tempered, using the language as a chopping block to split the difference between the mostly compassionate and the hotly resentful."

Thankfully, indeed, Hitchens was much kinder to the editorial pages: "In the life of the city, the *Times* acts, or should act, as a kind of daily seismograph. Its editorial and opinions sections—livelier by far than those of *The Washington Post* and *The New York Times*—register the tremors of black

Korean relations; the tension between Beverly Hills and the proposed mass transit system; [and] the rapid growth of the Catholic immigrant vote."

The Hitchens assessment appeared about three and a half years into my editorship. It followed an earlier, equally kind assessment by Joan Didion in *The New Yorker* (February 1990) which was also positive and supportive: "A week after [a news side shakeup], it was announced that Anthony Day, the editor of the *Times* editorial pages since 1971, would be replaced by Thomas Plate, who had directed the partly autonomous editorial and opinion editorial pages for *New York Newsday* and was expected to play a role in doing something similar for Orange County. In the fever of the moment, it was easy for some people to believe that the changes were all of a piece—that, for example, Anthony Day's leaving the editorial pages had something to do with the fact that some people on the Times-Mirror board had occasionally expressed dissatisfaction with the paper's editorial direction on certain issues, particularly its strong anti-administration stand on Central American policy. Anthony Day was told only, he reported, that it was 'time for a change'..."

Later Didion concludes: "[But] the paper's editorials were just as strong under Thomas Plate as they had been under Anthony Day." This was a helpful assessment from one of America's greatest writers, and, at the time, it was greatly appreciated, as you can now imagine.

Both the Didion and the Hitchens assessment need to be reflected on by media historians trying to assess the *Los Angeles Times* of the nineties. One (sub)urban Los Angeles myth had it that Day's day came when it did in 1989 because *Times* editorials had become too liberal; this was not the point; the point was that they had become too predictable. Another rumor was that I was brought in to tone down the liberalism of the editorials. If so, importing an editorial page editor from *New York Newsday*—an establishment paper that endorsed a liberal black politician over Ed Koch—was an odd choice indeed. So was pinning the label "conservative" on David Laventhol, the founding father of *Newsday*, a publication which had under his steady leadership become one of the more unvarying liberal-line dailies in the country. No, the toning-down that had to be done was on the side of excessive knee-jerk predictability, not policy liberality. Didion had it just right—and she wrote her assessment even before the appearance of the grandiose ultra-liberal abolish-private-ownership-of-guns-editorial-series that so fired up the right-wing gun lobby.

Despite these facts, the staff that was inherited from my predecessor was distrustful. About three months into the new job in Los Angeles, I was deeply nostalgic for my pleasant, bright and innovative staff at *New York Newsday* and I was increasingly miserable that I had not been smart enough to accept Higher Authority's hiring suggestion that perhaps a staff purge would be wise. In my foolishness, in my ego, in—yes—the holocaust experience I had witnessed at *Family Weekly*, when virtually an entire staff was machine gunned down by media hoods, and in my smug self-confidence that in the end everyone would come to love me—I did not, could not, and would not pull the trigger. In this case, I may have made a mistake.

> During one especially cursed epoch in American newspapers, diversity training was all the rage. Overnight, diversity experts would come in to teach otherwise adult editors and reporters how to relate to others. On the whole, such training was stupid, condescending and unproductive. We best relate to each other in a straightforward way, as human beings, and without racial, gender or other genetic baggage we might have.

One staffer from the prior regime whom I found infinitely entertaining was the opinion editorial page editor. He had been recommended by me to the *Los Angeles Times* two decades ago and had filled the position with distinction. But he could be a rough bear of a guy!

The critic Hitchens never had to attend any of the multicultural sessions at the *Times*—good thing, for they were an absurd torture. I only managed to avoid having to go because I supervised the paper's most culturally diverse department—by far. I had Hispanic and African-American deputies. Our editorial board was more than half female and white males were in the minority.

While I escaped the training ordeal, my opinion editorial page editor—a brilliant Wesleyan University graduate—did not. He was given to occasional serious office irritations and even eruptions (usually with me—and sometimes with good cause!). Asking him to sit through one of these "sensitivity training" seminars was sure to test his patience. At one session—all were funded and required by the newspaper—the Sensitivity Presenter asked all in the room to recall a personal moment of felt discrimination or stereotyping. Bob was sitting in the back, praying to Jesus Christ (he was actually a devout Catholic) not to be called on. Sure enough, the microphone was passed to him and then he sighed, and then he thought for the longest minute, and then he blurted out: "How much longer are we going to have to put up with this crap?"

The next morning, he walked into my office to proffer a confessional heads-up about his indiscreet rebellion. "You'll probably hear bad things about me from Higher Authority. I just wanted to give you a heads-up."

I did hear from Higher Authority—that morning in fact. I tried to walk both sides of the street—one sympathetic to the need to be sympathetic to diversity and the other to the need to back up a staffer who was sick to death of the political correctness crap. (Privately, I applauded his outspoken candor—remember, I am basically a genetic New Yorker.)

Sensitivity to other cultures, genders, races is a very good thing indeed, but it unfortunately detracted from the newspaper's ability to laugh at itself and see stories from anything other than a politically correct prism. This became ever more apparent when the issue arose as to whom to endorse for the 1994 governor's race.

INCUMBENT GOVERNOR Pete Wilson, perhaps under other circumstances, might have taken a neutral position on Proposition 187 but the basic idea was too popular —and interestingly enough, not just with allegedly "racist" white folks but also with a rather substantial portion of Latinos. They felt in fact that too many illegals from south of the border were soaking up "their" public support and testing the gringos' patience on the larger issue of all immigrants, legal and otherwise.

Thus, Wilson endorsed it and grounded his re-election campaign on it. He knew that there was no way in hell that his Democratic opponent Kathleen Brown, the daughter of the immensely successful governor Edmund ("Pat") Brown and the sister of the dynamic but controversial California governor Jerry Brown, would ever oppose it.

What some critics never understood about Wilson was that his support of Proposition 187 was just politics, and not personal. (The courts, which are all-powerful in the US—recall the US Supreme Court upholding George

Bush's first election as president—wound up throwing the measure out on discriminatory, constitutional grounds. In the end, then, it basically had little effect on anything in reality. It just offered a lot of poseurs a platform on which to posture, whether redneck Caucasian or whining Latino.)

Politically, Proposition 187 did transform the 1994 election into an unseemly circus. It pulled Wilson out of his political grave via the nasty anti-immigration sentiment that tends to sweep like wildfire through otherwise open-minded California from time to time. In fact, once Wilson explicitly pinned his re-election onto the measure—one that the *Los Angeles Times* clearly opposed but that many people, including many Latinos backed—the polls began to pull him ahead of challenger Kathleen Brown, who was an extremely fine human being but an amazingly poor campaigner.

And if the election of 1994 did not present enough controversy in and outside of the *Los Angeles Times*, a California seat in the US Senate was also up for grabs. And was it ever being grabbed at! There you had incumbent Senator Dianne Feinstein running for re-election against the Republican challenger Michael Huffington who had two huge assets: a lot of money and a brilliant wife named Arianna ... who had not yet divorced him.

When the male Huffington appeared before the *Los Angeles Times* editorial board, this presentation was laughable. But again, Huffington had a whole lot of money to spend and the roughly $40 million he pumped into campaign ads made this important Senate race, which should have been a shoo-in for Feinstein, suddenly and dramatically too close to call. Feinstein, who even Republicans agreed had done a very solid job in the Senate, could lose her seat to a guy who had $40 million burning a hole in his tuxedo pocket and who wanted to buy himself a Senate seat.

My nightmare scenario was that the *Los Angeles Times* would stay true to form—and Lady Dianne would go down in flames. Does an editorial page editor have some measure of responsibility to the people of California and to see his or her newspaper used for the public good?

Here was what Higher Authority heard from me, over and over: Dianne Feinstein needed all the help she could get in this race. She was in trouble. The polls showed her behind that multimillionaire. The *Los Angeles Times* should endorse her and it should do it soon.

Higher Authority said: "We don't have a problem with that but we can't endorse her and then ignore the gubernatorial race. If we endorse Feinstein, then we have to endorse Pete Wilson, too."

"Look, both you and I know that Wilson has identified with Proposition 187 for Machiavellian reasons, in part anyway. If we endorsed him, then more than a few people will think we are hypocritical and/or inconsistent. I mean, we've made such a big deal about opposing Proposition 187 already. I think it will undermine our authority if we endorsed Wilson."

"The problem with just endorsing Feinstein, Tom, is that we'll look like an all-liberal paper that just jerks its knee and endorses Democrats." In Orange County, which then was mainly conservative, the *Times* was viewed as ideologically ultra-liberal. "And as for Wilson's merit as governor," he added, "Let's face it. Which one has made the better case in this race?"

"Sure, Wilson has," I said, "but that's because Kathleen Brown hasn't made any case at all. The case for Wilson is we know he can be governor without getting arrested for making people laugh too hard."

And history will eventually conclude that Wilson was actually a very good governor, arguably the best since 1990.

"All right then." Higher Authority thought for a moment. "Let's do a moderately tepid endorsement of Wilson in which we say that we feel his support of Proposition 187 was very ill-advised and then we can write full blast woo-woo endorsement for Dianne with all the bells and whistles."

"Is that what I have to choose from? I have to endorse Wilson and Feinstein or I get no Feinstein?"

"Right, that's your choice." Higher Authority sort of laughed.

"Okay ... but ..."

"I know. You've got some people on your editorial board who will be very upset because Wilson's not a liberal, he's a Republican."

"One of them is going to go through the roof." I actually pointed to the ceiling, shooting an imaginary rocket in that direction. "And I mean, through the freakin' roof!"

"I'll handle him," Higher Authority said. "Don't worry about it."

"Are you sure? Because I know I cannot handle him. Either you do it—you need to have lunch with him like once a week for like forever—or he will blow up the building."

"I will handle it."

"Only you can do it."
"I will handle it. Relax."
But he did not handle it. And the building almost blew up.

To make a long story short—perhaps no one could have handled it. It got out of hand, with the end result, about a year later, that the position as the editor of the editorial pages went to a minority (highly qualified) and I got to become a foreign affairs columnist.

An informal, internal Latino employee coalition "somehow" became convinced that I had masterminded the decision to endorse Wilson, whom the coalition viewed as the second coming of Hitler. I became white toast.

The inside story was that I was eager to leave the *Los Angeles Times* but hoped to be able to write columns for it, though perhaps with an office on another continent. Therefore, what was needed was a way to take the pressure off Higher Authority, which had the power to anoint me a columnist, rather than blame Higher Authority, which had the power to make me mincemeat.

Two things happened. For my part, I had lunch with a member of the informal Latino coalition. He wanted to know how the paper could have possibly endorsed that "racist pig" Wilson. I explained that the decision was entirely mine (which was ridiculous, of course), that I had in effect brainwashed Higher Authority, and that no one should blame him, everyone should blame me, because I was the Great Satan the caucus was looking for.

"You mean," he said, "that the Wilson endorsement was planned for months, that you did it, and that you sold it to [a member of Higher Authority]?" He got redder and redder in the face.

"That's the story. It was all my doing."

The next day the anger shifted from Higher Authority to me. Now I was the baddest of the bad gringos. I had engineered the endorsement of the more competent candidate for governor, while helping break the ban against endorsements that would have deprived the hard-pressed Feinstein a boost.

The day after that, someone in Higher Authority visited me in my office. He looked me in the eye, said I had done a good job for the last six years, but that a minority had to be put in my job—white guys were out.

I said I hoped it was a certain person who was actually qualified.

He said, yes, as I had been suggesting all along, it is she. Then he asked me: "Do you want to be rich? You know I can do that? Do you think you have a column in you? If so, you're a *Times* columnist."

"Do you have a preference? Am I a writer or am I a 'richer'?"

"You send me more memos than anyone—you must be a writer!"

"Do I get to keep my editorial page salary?"

"Yes."

This was going to work just fine. "When can I start?"

IN RETROSPECT, HIGHER AUTHORITIES, scrambling against this Latino revolt, made the right decision. They saw some serious flak under their left wing and decided that their mission was not to protect me but to protect the newspaper—and themselves.

I would come to make this a lesson for my students: that it was always to be the case that the perceived greater good of a corporate enterprise will require individuals to walk the plank. In the face of all that Latino fury, how important was one semi-dumb middle-aged white guy? Not very.

When all hell broke loose, however, I was more than happy to take the fall. The editor had a tree to hold on to and I did not. As for the publisher, he kept his job, but I did not keep mine. A few weeks after the re-election of Wilson (by a gazillion votes) and the election of Feinstein (by a relative hair's breadth), I sent the publisher a memo (right, oh God, another memo!): "These past weeks [this was summer 1994] have been a helluva week for both of us ... But I want to say that...

1. Newspapers will eventually wither away and die if they are bland, cautious, boring. Quality by itself is not enough. Success requires quality plus pizzazz.
2. This past week [of controversy over our endorsements] has been terrific for the paper. At the stands, our editorial pages are being talked about ... This is our future or we have no future.
3. The paper gets high marks for its extraordinary class in publishing the bitter dissent by [a top-ranking Latino editor]. Everywhere I go, people say: "That was classy." I'm glad we did it.

4. The opinion editorial dissent also nails down our continuing commitment to diversity in all the best sense of the term ... [we have] a dozen minority staffers ... in this department ... Just look at the multicultural composition of our editorial board, whose decisions you ... sign off on 99 per cent of the time.
5. Hold your head up high, *Los Angeles Times*. You have a lot to be proud of and if this paper does not flinch from making the tough calls, if it does not wimp out, if it does not run from controversy, it will have a great future, whether it's printed on the world's most expensive paper, or on an absurd electronic tablet, or somewhere out there in as yet undefined cyberspace. Or so I think."

The next day the Higher Authority responded with a handwritten letter. He did not respond to notes very often or so quickly (probably because he received so many): "Thank you for your kind note. Given what I've been going through lately, it was most welcome ... You should know that I have not once had doubts about whether we did the right thing."

I had held this pressure-packed job for almost six years already. As you know from reading this book, six years is a long time for Plate. Nobody owed me anything. Generally speaking, nobody owes anybody anything.

POSTSCRIPT: Life is so short that I wish more people would smile instead of wail. What the Latino coalition at the paper could never understand—mostly because I was never invited to explain it to them—was that the endorsements were not about Wilson. He was going to win no matter what we did.

The endorsements were about saving the Senate job of a woman who was clearly qualified for the job and who deserved the endorsement of a newspaper that had otherwise editorialized passionately and frequently on advancing women in politics and improving the quality of our politicians. Feinstein was a poster girl for both those goals. But some people at the *Los Angeles Times* seemed not to understand that.

You can decide whether I was ethical or not but the fact of the matter is that when we woke up the first Wednesday in November, Feinstein had won the election by a sliver. Did she win in part because of our editorial? Maybe,

maybe not. But would she have slid by without all the help she got? Why risk it?

The basic fact of the matter was that we made a difference to the people. And that is what newspapers are supposed to do. Remaining silent in the name of political correctness is an abnegation of civic responsibility because it excludes the contribution of reasoned debate from the decision-making processes.

Oh, by the way, Feinstein is still in the Senate, with powerful seniority, and with the respect of her colleagues and the media. Huffington is nowhere. Neither, alas, is Wilson. He was a good man, though with flaws like the rest of us. Moreover, the last I heard, no mass deportations of Mexicans from California have yet occurred. There never will be any.

But that truth will not stop politicians from trying to be re-elected by whatever means necessary. This is the American way, after all.

ONE OF MY LAST ACTS was to write—yes—a memo. I was really unhappy. Sure, I'm sometimes neurotic and an egomaniac but does that make me a bad person?

My general sense of the paper was that—despite major innovations—it remained less engaging than what we all wanted. Perhaps because of the devilish influence of Sir David or perhaps because of my rough-and-tumble New Yorker experience, I came to the view that at bottom the *Los Angeles Times* was boring and that the Felker (and Fleet Street) philosophy was right: what good was it—no matter how good it was—if people were not compelled to read it? So I wrote the following about the newspaper's Sunday opinion section, a section that was good but needed to be more compelling.

The memo was to another member of Higher Authority: "We need to keep pushing OPINION closer to the edge. It's the one place in the paper that needs to showcase political controversy—to latch on to the latest intellectual firefight. Pieces that merely state the obvious—'it's a complicated situation, and it's likely to get worse'—have no place in this section, unless they're by Kissinger (!). The overall Sunday paper is so solid, thoughtful, responsible, and serious that there needs to be at least a refuge for the slightly cranky, in-your-face-provocative, leading-edge noisy piece. I think readers have a desperate thirst for responsible controversy. Let's give it to them."

This was from deep inside me.

And this came back from a member of Higher Authority. It was short: "TOM: NO!" [Signed, someone from Higher Authority]

OKAY, SO I STEWED, boiled, inner-raged. (Didn't someone once say that sometimes over-reacting is healthy?)

In the end, I guess I just gave up. I guess I just lost heart. In the words of my immediate boss, I was, yes, "relieved."

Around this time, I had received yet another letter from Sir David, who had recently visited Los Angeles. In part, it went like this: "I do hope I shall have the pleasure of meeting [your daughter] Ashley next time. I am a grandfather now and extremely good with small children. I shall teach Ashley how to speak with an English accent, which will improve her chances in life immensely ... Great seeing Jim [Bellows] again too. I went out to his house and had a wonderful session with him in which he launched a tremendous attack on 'diversity'. He asked me to stiffen your resolve to stand up to the bureaucracy and establishment mentality of the *Los Angeles Times*. It seems to be that you are doing that quite satisfactorily..."

Perhaps I was a year ago, but that was then, and this is now. Ultimately, I was defeated. It got so bad that at one point, an editorial was planned for the front page without my knowledge. More than a few people in the building thought this deeply disrespectful. After the editorial appeared, another different top official of the corporation asked me privately for a run-down of the reaction of readers to the front page editorial. It was an opportunity for me to complain, to gripe, to whine—but that was not my style. So I answered carefully and objectively. I said that our top letter-getters tended to be on subjects such as the controversial illegal immigrant issue and on the California economy. I submitted that the front page editorial was gorgeously written but it did not advocate any specific policy and this was not controversial.

I added, perhaps far too self-servedly, but, honestly: "Five years or so ago, when I came here, I thought the *Los Angeles Times* editorials, as a group, too predictable, too long, and too 'one hand/other hand.' Today, I think they are better—shorter, with a real bottom line most of the time. But, like you, I think they could be better. They will be."

I did not expect the response I received. This Times-Mirror executive scribbled this lovely note back: "I agree with all of this, except I think the editorials are much better these days. I just love a good scrap, and to skewer phrases with a twinge of innocent malice. Devilishly, Your Friend____"

I liked that. Especially the devil part ... wasn't that nice?

I WAS THRILLED with the new career turn. I had thought of a second career when in the first two years at the *Los Angeles Times* I taught a few classes at Santa Monica College and UCLA—pro bono. But UCLA would never have wanted me had I not had a quality professional degree from a well-regarded graduate school.

Little did I know three decades ago what unexpected doors the Woodrow Wilson School diploma would open. As it turned out, it was a good thing I did not take Ben Bradlee's sincere advise to heart. He may have been spot-on about the irrelevance of higher education to US newspaper work, (a pity, of course) but the newspaper world is not all there is in the world—to say the least—and few things are sadder than newspaper people who think so.

> In the old days, the average worker might go three or four major jobs in his working lifetime. Nowadays, she or he may go through several different careers. Therefore, you have no idea how much your higher education will do for you decades later—or in what area. My view is: get it while you can, though it is never too late, even in your forties and fifties, to get it. Just get it.

As a result of that teaching stint at Santa Monica and UCLA, it was easy to move away from the *Los Angeles Times* and toward some new twilight zone of combined academics and journalism—an almost perfect marriage. I then suggested to Higher Authority that perhaps I should make way for a successor—and we had a very plausible one who was right on the scene and raring to go—and when Higher Authority asked me what I would like to do, I pressed the case for an international political column.

The idea came in two stages. One emerged instantaneously with the resignation of Dave Laventhol at the end of 1994. It led to conversations with elements of Higher Authority about The Next New Thing. The other came in early 1996 when we were refining the concept of the column.

The day before, Japan's prime minister and the American president had met in a hotel on Santa Monica to try to tamp down serious political differences between the two important countries. *The New York Times*—3,000 miles from lovely downtown Santa Monica—put the story on page one. The *Los Angeles Times* had the story well inside the paper. This was hard to understand. Which was the closer paper to Japan? Was Asia important to America, not to mention the West Coast, or what?

The explanation for the mystery was bureaucratic. Coverage of the US president, it turns out, is the exclusive purview of the Washington Bureau. Even when the president journeys to the backyard of the paper's headquarters, where some 200 allegedly competent journalists are on hand for deployment, coverage had to be detailed out of Washington.

The problem this time—in early 1996—was that the Washington Bureau did not view a summit meeting in Santa Monica between the heads of the world's two largest economies important enough to send a correspondent 3,000 miles to cover. As a result, the *Times* had a little story inside one of the sections written by a journalist with little preparation to handle the story. Afterwards, I spoke to a member of Higher Authority, who offered the above lengthy explanation. My response: "I just gave up."

Thus, I plotted to design—and to write—my own column on Asia. I raised this option many times with Higher Authority, hoping that the idea would stick. One day Shelby came to me in the hall and said: "Dick and I are getting excited about your column. It would be our first political opinion editorial column since Joe Kraft. That's good lineage for you!"

Despite obvious differences in editorial temperament, we shared the view that the readership for these pages was on the whole extremely educated and knowledgeable, and that these pages were important to maintaining the paper's overall credibility and community profile. Even so, he recognized that the new publisher would require his own editorial page editor eventually and this was as good a time to move on as any. "You've had one full senate term," he once said of my six-year stint. "And you've served the paper well."

I was getting excited about the column project, too. This was the one job in the news media I had never had—and it seemed like a very good one.

And so, when my end was imminent, one member of Higher Authority asked another how I was feeling about moving on. "Relieved," said one.

That was spot-on. I was not only relieved to be moving on spiritually and professionally but even geographically. The private office offered up by the *Los Angeles Times* in the headquarters building, I never used; UCLA offered me not only a full-time appointment but also a lovely office overlooking the magnificent central quadrangle on the campus. From there, for the next five years, I was to teach courses on public and media ethics, and on the news media of America and Asia to gifted young people, many of them Asian-born or Asian-American. After the paper was sold to the Chicago Tribune Co., the column migrated to international syndication, where it lives on today, as does the university teaching at UCLA.

In truth, I was not only "relieved" to be leaving the *Los Angeles Times* but ecstatic about developing a new career as a university professor, international lecturer and foreign affairs newspaper columnist. When UCLA offered me a full-time position in the communication studies faculty (with a secondary appointment in policy studies), I began to believe there might truly be a God somewhere up there who actually liked me.

> To the extent that you can control or at least shape the change in your life, change on the whole is good, necessary and replenishing— it can resurrect the body and mind and spirit!

Take a look at this witty letter, which arrived in my *Los Angeles Times'* inbox halfway through my six-year tenure as *Los Angeles Times* editorial pages editor. Its author was Peter Goldmark Jr who was then Times-Mirror vice president for Eastern newspapers (that is, *New York Newsday, Baltimore Sun, Hartford Courant* etc.), a former top aide to New York City Mayor John Lindsay and New York Governor Hugh Carey, and one of the acclaimed architects of the New York City bankruptcy bailout in the seventies. He was also—as we say in New York—a mensch: he was as funny and playful and endearing as anyone could be.

I had written to him in despair, asking whether journalism had been one huge career mistake for me. He wrote back to me in his job as president of The Rockefeller Foundation in New York: "Vell, dahlink, long time no hear from you. Are you in the wrong business? Fundamentally, as we say in particle physics, yes—as in the small future of newspapers. And you know it. But, as we say under the general theory of relativity, compared to what? Seated aboard the good ship *Los Angeles Times*, where you have reinvented, reinvigorated and at long last reified the editorial pages, the decline will be so slow, so majestic, and evanescent as to seem like a transition—even in faltering Southland.

"What is the right business? It's a little to the left of the right wing and a little to the rigorous side of the right stuff. It is to prepare us for the next paradigm shift. What this shift is or how the old paradigm got Alzheimer's and got lost, and why the period between paradigms is so frustrating and undefined, is too dour a subject for this snappy little note. Suffice it to say that when it comes to paradigms, shift happens.

"... We miss you in the lurid islands of the Gotham Archipelego."

ONE DAY, I received a call informing me that I had been invited to serve as a Pulitzer Prize juror. This role was much coveted and a big deal in the news media world. The invitation came from Columbia University, home to the venerable school of journalism, under the signature of Seymour ("Sy") Topping, a former *New York Times* top guru.

I told Higher Authority that I was planning to decline the honor—I did not like the Pulitzer process; it was sometimes corrupt. At first, they looked at me as if I had lost it and perhaps I had. But in the letter to Sy, I explained my reasoning: "There are few people in our profession who command such respect and esteem as you. I would like to decline the invitation, however, at least for this year. Recent controversies concerning the final selection for newspaper Pulitzers have raised disturbing questions about whether the winners are in all cases the product of a pure merit process. I have found some of the Pulitzer board overrides of the judges' recommendations deeply disturbing."

There is a story behind this letter. Very few people know it because the US media rarely reports it, but the Pulitzer Prize process—which is to the US news media what the Nobel Prize committee is to international diplomacy, physics, literature and so on—was arguably as ethically flawed as the Florida state federal election vote-counting method was in the year 2000. You see, with the Pulitzers, before the final winners are chosen and announced, there sometimes occurs unseemly last-minute jockeying among the Big Powers (like at the UN Security Council), including, especially, the *New York Times* and *The Washington Post* and so on ... so that no one is embarrassed and everyone gets a little bit of the stardust. But the end result does not always reflect who is the best in each category.

I wanted no part in this. At their ethical worst, how were the Pulitzers categorically different from a rigged TV game show?

This was one reason why some enlightened US editors three decades ago established a competing set of top national journalism awards under the auspices of The American Society of Newspaper Editors (ASNE). They were launched in 1981 and the process was structured so as to be politics-free and merit-based. It was little surprise that a decade and a half later, when I went to my betters to ask if I might write Sy a very polite letter that nonetheless turned down the offer to serve as a Pulitzer juror, only one of them was sympathetic—and that was Dave, who had been one of the founders of the ASNE awards. But no one in Higher Authority forced me to serve. I was proud of the *Los Angeles Times* for that.

My refusal hardly makes me a candidate for sainthood; many honest editors of conviction and integrity have served as jurors. My refusal was based on a loathing of a process that in some ways was as questionable as any that we newspapers slammed on our editorial pages. Indeed, the "appearance of impropriety" is a phrase we used frequently when actual criminal or ethical impropriety cannot be asserted. By not serving, I felt, the "appearance" of impropriety was averted.

In ethics, appearances can indeed count as much as reality. Consider the issue of the wall of separation between advertising and editorial. In British journalism, this separation is not viewed as holy and there are few pretenses about what journalism is: it is the business of selling newspapers (or magazine or air-time). That was why my British friends were reduced to a puddle of hilarity at the thought that "their" Tom would waste his time teaching a phantom subject like media ethics.

That was not the case in America where the wall of separation between advertising and editorial was a "Berlin Wall" of sorts, separating the church (pure-as-the-driven-snow editorial) and state (dirty-hands commercialism).

This wall was not to be breached; the "Berlin Wall" norm still rules. Outsiders who enter the US media business not fully suffused with such norms will get burned. (Some of them should enroll in my classes at UCLA first!) That was what happened to Mark Willes, who was the head of the corporation that used to own the *Los Angeles Times* (and, for a stretch, was its publisher as well) after I had left for UCLA—and after Schlossberg had left.

Mark—a former cereal executive at General Mills—was in general a hated figure at the *Los Angeles Times*, not only because he was an outsider (that alleged defect was one with which I could identify and sympathize with!) but also because he was from an alien culture—the hardcore giant corporate world in which basically anything that was not indictable was ethical.

US media norms—at the higher levels of quality journalism, that is— operated differently. At least they have so far. Over the long run, such normative differences will weaken. But until they do, they remain a considerable force to be reckoned with. Willes had little idea of what he was getting into when he unilaterally decided to breach those norms with a cute little side deal he and his cohorts cooked up with the proprietors of the Staples Center, the beautiful sports place in downtown Los Angeles (not far from the *Los Angeles Times* building).

As part of the opening week celebration, the *Los Angeles Times* on the editorial side had put up a special issue of the Sunday magazine devoted totally to the new sports arena. In itself, nothing was wrong here. But few if any on the editorial side knew that the business side had secretly jumped into bed with Staples by agreeing to join forces, sell advertising pages together and split the profit. Under the ethical norms of a major newspaper, such secrecy was an admission of doing something wrong—for if there was nothing wrong with such a business arrangement, why keep it secret? This business deal had no effect on the editorial judgment of the *Los Angeles Times*. The writers wrote what they were going to write and the editors edited as they were going to edit without having to endure business side pressure. But the secret business side arrangement created the appearance of impropriety.

There was another problem. For many observers steeped in the "Berlin Wall" normative tradition prevalent at high quality newspapers like the *Los Angeles Times*, it was hard to imagine that at least one of the top editors did not know of the arrangement. Either they knew and were culpable, or they did not know and were incompetent; either way, the paper's credibility was shaken. Worse yet, one top editor's main office was just a few dozen steps away from those of all the key business people. Under the theory that no office in a business as big as the *Los Angeles Times* or *Time* is ever really private, how plausible was it that no one knew anything besides the business people?

I had left for UCLA by then but people would ask me whether under Dave, such a Staples-*Times* project would have been hatched. This is just my opinion, mind you, but I do not think it would ever have gotten to first base ... hell, it would not even have gotten out of the dugout!

In the end, Staples and other problems led to the downfall of Willes, the corporate boss, and editor Michael Parks, who was to slide over to the University of Southern California to become the director of the journalism program; and in a sense it paved the way for the sale of the paper to the Chicago Tribune Co. in early 2000.

Long before that happened, Mark Willes—who was both CEO of Times-Mirror as well as the publisher—had asked me to join him downtown at the *Los Angeles Times* for a series of luncheons that were in part simply friendly get-togethers (I liked his directness and his willingness to try new things; I didn't like some of the new things he tried though, such as raising company profit levels by killing off *New York Newsday*—earning him the unwanted sobriquet, "cereal killer"!) and in part a subtle job interview. Mark wanted his own editor (as all new proprietors do), and I seemed like someone with whom he could work.

In my own way, I tried to explain the cultural difference to Mark in our sessions. But obviously I did not get the message across in a way that he could absorb. I liked Mark, notwithstanding everything, but I live by the unbreakable tenet: don't look back.

As it turned out, it was a good decision in a number of ways. Two years later, the Staples deal exploded on the US media landscape like a newspaper Watergate. Had it not been for UCLA and the column, I might have been there and wiped out. It is better to be lucky than good.

> To operate successfully in an alien environment, attention must be paid to the norms of conduct required of major actors in that environment. By transgressing them, you run a considerable risk, especially in an environment like the news media, in which secrets are especially hard to keep covered up.

I am glad I decided to stay at UCLA, a place anyone could love. After all, despite Mark's flattering interest in me, he did pull the plug on *New York Newsday*, a near-great newspaper. Why, in a democracy (and arguably the most important, if sometimes the most infuriating one on earth) would you kill an honest newspaper if you could possibly avoid it? The answer was simple enough: doing so raised the stock price, made the company look healthier, and made Mark look the better manager. In our market system, what is the logical quarrel with that?

It was a year after the plug was unceremoniously pulled—and after I had returned from yet another trip to London—that I felt the need for some religious redemption.

On the return from London, control of the editorial pages had passed to Janet Clayton, the number three, as planned. I had called her to congratulate her from London, at this exact planned distance, as I had suggested to Higher Authority. I wanted to do it from afar for I tended to get emotional if I was not careful and I wanted her day of glory to be magnificent and unsullied, as mine had not been, as you may recall. We all get a few moments of glory—why not let her have hers?

Dave Laventhol had lost his baby—*New York Newsday*—and I had lost my establishment perch—being the editorial pages editor of the *Los Angeles Times*. A lot had happened in a year.

I was eager to start the column. It was the one thing in my career I had never done. This would be a signed column. Nothing would filter the viewpoint expressed except for my own internal filters acquired through genetics and experience. If I made errors, I would be happy to confess to them publicly, especially as I would be admitting to what I thought, in contradistinction to what the corporate consensus thought. On this point, my successor totally agreed with me. In her view, the column on Asia and America would be better if the distance between the *Los Angeles Times* headquarters and where I wrote my column was greater. Avoiding groupthink would be the key to its uniqueness (besides, she knew I was fed up with meetings!). We ended this discussion on an inspirational note and the column was to run on the *Los Angeles Times*' opinion editorial page for about five years—not long, perhaps, by some standards but not bad by the standards of the *Los Angeles Times*!

ALL I NEEDED NOW was some denouement with the sage himself and so, David Laventhol and I arranged to sneak away for a weekend of gambling and drinking at nearby Las Vegas. The sage did not know it, but the weekend coincided with my birthday. This was the man who had hired me at *Newsday* (Long Island and New York) and the *Los Angeles Times*. I very much would like to think he went three-for-three in terms of performance, but that is something for others to judge.

There was one moment at the spectacular Sports Book, the glitzy—and legal—sports and racing betting parlor at Caesar's Palace, that struck my heart. Dave, while at his former journalistic den of iniquity at *Newsday*, had contributed to the "experts'" horse racing prognostications with a daily contribution in the *Newsday* sports section that was bannered as "Clocker Dave." Outside of *Newsday* people, few knew it was the editor himself tapping out the touts.

So there we were at a Vegas hotel betting parlor, downing Heineken after Heineken and losing money. Well, actually, *he* was losing money—and the thing was, he was taking it all seriously. I figured half the horse tracks around the country fixed half the races so unless you were in on the deal, why bother studying past performance charts?

By the seventh race, I was ahead by about a thousand and Dave was behind by a few hundred. I was betting the names of friends I knew and animals I liked and so on; he was playing a turf course Einstein.

At about that juncture, he turned to me and said: "You know, I was very happy to have you as my editorial page editor and … if I was still publisher, Tom Plate would still be the editorial page editor of the *Los Angeles Times*."

And then, at something like the eighth race, Dave hit a $2,000 long-shot bet.

By that time, I was down to a few hundred. He was ahead by more than a thousand.

Which is one reason why he was Dave Laventhol and I was just Tom Plate—he was always ahead.

> Jumping the midget doesn't always produce the best possible personal or professional consequences but if in your heart, mind and soul, you know it to be right, go ahead and do it anyway. Playing it 100 per cent safe is not any way to live a life … because you only get one life to live.

Conclusion

AFTER SO MANY PAGES, it might seem cowardly of me not to sum up my true feelings about journalism in an explicit way—it would be like, oh (a wild example plucked out of thin air!) a major newspaper not telling its readers of its preference in an important governor's race. Still, it is hard to summarize; the issue is complicated, professionally, intellectually and emotionally.

Perhaps one solid way of looking at the issue of a career in journalism is that two things can happen to you and maybe neither is good: One is that you go into the news media and end up a flop; the other is that you jump into journalism and are quite successful.

Even if it were the latter experience, when it comes at a young age, it can be especially tragic. I refer you back to the famous (but nameless) Manhattan architect who questioned why an apparently talented person would want to work for a magazine that even its founder, the great Clay Felker, once put down by quipping to his top aide: "But Milton, it's only a magazine!"

Let us assume for the sake of argument that Tom Plate has been, more or less, a successful American media man. That killed a bunch of decades, as you can tell from the last eight chapters. During that time I could have been saving babies from malnutrition as a public health professional, playing the clarinet in the New York Philharmonic (with plenty of practise, who knows?—I was good at it in high school) and creating musical beauty, curing cancer as a dedicated medical researcher (I was doing pre-med in college, at least until organic chemistry hit!) or helping an appropriate president of the United States or a skilled secretary of state articulate his or her vision as a top gun speechwriter (I interned in Washington once as a speechwriter).

But none of these or any other options were open to me as long as my mind was closed and set on journalism—and, worse yet, as long as the career was going reasonably well. Even when I screwed up, which was more than once, alas, I managed to land on my feet and get ahead. In some respects we become victims of our success, imprisoned by our achievements, not freed by failure. Be careful what you wish for, goes the saying, because you might just get what you want.

Though there are so many other wonderful things to do with your life, in the final analysis Alexis de Tocqueville was more right than wrong: we are probably somewhat better off with the American news media, for all its faults, than without it. But whether you want to be a willing participant and actually "commit to journalism" decade after decade is a tough personal and perhaps even spiritual question.

Here is what I call "The Ten Deadly Sins of Journalism Today:"

1. Money Madness: While playing the lead actor in "Citizen Kane," Orson Welles famously notes that making money is not difficult to do in life, if all you want to do with your life is to make money. For many media companies today, that is mainly what they want to do with the media's life, notwithstanding the many high-minded CEO speeches on Corporate Get-Together Day and so on. (Don't believe anything they say unrelated to the bottom line.) If the goal of a media company is no different from the goal of a soap conglomerate, why should a media company operate with the benefit of First Amendment protection? Think about it.

2. Professionalism: Unlike the legal and medical professions (which, to be sure, have their own share of serious problems), the American news media does not absolutely require core educational requirements for entry and no professionally administered testing, certification or mid-career re-education after that. This is a scandal. Consider my Andrea's respected but humble profession: social work. To be certified, she was required to pass entrance exams and, in the course of her career, undergo continual testing and professional re-education. Not with the news media, though. Its paucity of intellectual self-regard means that our increasingly complicated world is to be interpreted by those who are not only under extreme time pressure constraints (an endemic problem with which one has to be sympathetic) but who also may be intellectually ill-prepared for the substantive challenge. This is one reason the news media continually misses the onset or significance of major political, economic and social developments. Too many journalists just don't know any better.

3. Hypocrisy: News media executives and practitioners, in general, fail to apply the same norms of conduct to one another as they would to public officials and even corporate executives. There is no public financial disclosure required of business page columnists, for example (without such basic transparency, several such columnists have been caught touting stocks in which they had invested). The degree of intrusion into privacy to which the news media subjects public figures far exceeds that which they would deem allowable into their own, even though the editor of a major newspaper or magazine or high-level operative of a major TV station (not to mention network) has considerably more impact on society than many public officials. Yet all such shameless misconduct is justified under the skirt of the "First Amendment."

4. Partisanship: In the news-media profession in the United States, far too many journalists are out-and-out Democrats and far too many big media bosses are out-and-out Republicans. Partisanship is not a sin in and of itself, especially insofar as journalists can maintain a measure of fairness and non-partisanship in their journalism; but too few can, precisely because in their hearts they are reformers who seek to make things better, or a special kind of conservatives (that is, nineteenth-century liberals who want to keep things more or less as they are). Liberals in the US news media (that is, most reporters) hoping to spur change will promote negative journalism—a ten-part series on municipal corruption. But, in the end, the probability is that little will really change once the media caravan moves on to some other story, or that the resulting reforms will be designed to placate the media rather than relieve the problem.

5. Blurring lines: The above would be less problematic to the extent that journalists themselves could refrain from blurring the line between fact and opinion that they themselves claim had been erected to achieve precisely that goal. But increasingly that line has been blurred, compromised, even pulverized with new hair-splitting categories of journalism, especially the so-called page one news analyses

which I hate. They permit the reporter to disguise (barely) her or his opinion in the matrix of "analysis." But one man's or woman's analysis is another's opinion. (I once said to Higher Authority at a major US newspaper: "We don't need an editorial on that political issue for tomorrow's paper; the reader knows our opinion simply by reading the news analysis on our own front page this morning." This comment elicited extreme black skies/foul mood negative karma from Higher Authority.)

6. Pomposity: I don't think anyone loves an anchorman or anchorwoman as much as they appear to love themselves. They walk into a room of mere mortals and expect a standing ovation—for this is the age of the video image. Let a Nobel Prize winner in genetics walk into my UCLA classroom and—tragically—few will recognize the brilliant scientist, for she/he hasn't been on TV. But those who have been on TV are convinced that mere contact with the tube has lifted their IQs and trebled their self-worth. In fact, all it has done is to bloat their egos. On the whole, TV ruins true journalism because the story too readily becomes the reporter. This is the ultimate in nonsensical subjectivity. Some people are famous simply for being famous. Do we really need to care about Britney or why Dan Rather had to leave CBS?

7. The scoop: The scoop drives journalism the way germs drive epidemics—the end result is rarely any good. Scoops are artificial constructs of the news media that usually negatively correlate with events of social or political significance. A careful review of the last 1,000 significant scoops—as defined by the news media—would reveal how little of enduring value was unearthed. And yet the scoop is at the heart of the media phenomenon known widely as the "feeding frenzy"—the media vigil in front of the private home, the vicious attack on reputations, the perversion of human values, etc.

8. Privacy: There is less and less of it every day—who is a "public figure" and who is not? The courts understandably leave such definition-

making to the news media, just as they leave defining "what is news" to the news media. But because the news media is not an adequately self-regulated profession and sometimes behaves unprofessionally (that is, like a greedy brat), the net effect is to define virtually every citizen as a potential "public figure" and allow no part of anyone's life to be categorically off-limits to snooping. Technically, there is no privacy in America, except for the extremely skillful recluse. It is the news media in America (not the US government—too underfunded, too unmotivated) that has become Big Brother. Worry less about government spying than big media snooping.

9. Money: Where there is too much money sloshing around, there is corruption, whether in the form of felony venality or erosion of norms. Follow the media's money and at the end of the trail is crime and a criminal. And just as American media corporations are making too much money with their public trust, so are many journalists. Network stars make more money in a year or two than most Americans make in 20: How can these journalists stay in touch with the true needs of most people? At the *Los Angeles Times*, I was proud to rake in $250,000 on some given years but I also felt somehow that this was not quite right. Living in that compensatory bubble—with the leased car and the expense account—prompted me 15 years ago to begin teaching pro bono at a local school, the excellent Santa Monica College. This put me into weekly contact with real people struggling to make their way up a very rough-and-tough socio-economic ladder. I admired many of them far more than many of the media moguls I met whose high level of economic achievement so divorces them from the reality of American life.

10. Public trust: With exceptions, this has been betrayed. The American news media's behavior—towards excessive profit, privacy intrusion, lack of professional ethics and professional training and re-training, and conscious or unconscious bias—should morally require it to forfeit the Constitutional Protection of the First Amendment, and accept that it is, by and large, a profit-seeking commercial business

no different than any other. To make this admission would be the honorable thing to do. This will not happen because, on the whole, the US news media, despite its many honorable practitioners, is not as honorable as America's democracy needs it to be,

So, should you go into the news media business? I guess I would say only if you have nothing better to do with your life! I probably didn't. So, am I bitter? Not in the least. I had a fantastic time and felt very blessed. I am just not going to recommend it to anyone.

I guess what I am saying is this: if after reading this book, you still have the fever to be a journalist, then your disease is terminal and you might as well give up and do it. It's in your blood—you're a journalist and you'll just have to accept it.

As for myself, I'll always wonder how I would have done at Julliard.

I wonder why I didn't go there.

My Thanks

FOR STARTERS, I must thank some former and present students who helped me shape and edit and fact-check this book. They include Mimi Lu (first, foremost and always), Michelle Bologna, Sara Plummer, Diana K Lee, Satoko Yashuda and Anya Zabolotnaya.

While none of the editors or columnists I have met can truly rival the power of a president or a king or a prime minister, some of them are more than capable of competing in the charisma and personality department. The fascinating people drawn to journalism have kept my life colorful and my energy level high.

In no particular chronological order, let me quickly mention a dozen or so of them.

Sir David English was the legendary editor of *The Daily Mail*, for 20 years; and then editor-in-chief of Associated Newspapers. Almost every single minute I spent with David was like a scene from a terrific (madcap) movie. He would have more plots and intrigues cooking than in a crime thriller. Even after his untimely death a few years ago in London, his energy and personality never faded in my mind—and drive me to try to do better even today.

I certainly loved working at *Newsday* and *New York Newsday*, which featured towering figures like the sagacious David Laventhol, probably the finest boss anyone could possibly have, the high-voltage Don Forst, with whom I was to work twice more (he was the liveliest office mate in the world), Jim Klurfeld, the fairest of all supervisors, Robert Johnson, the most entrepreneurial and risk-taking of all publishers and Sylvan Fox, the magisterial, long-running editorial page editor who was one of the true gentlemen of the business.

At *Time* magazine, class acts to the max were Henry Grunwald and Ray Cave. Well, okay, they were not always that good for a laugh: we mid-ranking editors used to joke in private by dubbing Ray "Chuckles," or shake like a leaf when, on rare but ominous occasions, we were summoned to Henry's office, sometimes for a dressing-down. But they were brilliant editors who were good for their word, and inspired us lower editors to aim for the highest standards.

At the *Los Angeles Times*, the intellectually and sartorially elegant Shelby Coffey III was one of the most learned newspaper editors you would ever find (he was a voracious reader of every book you could imagine), and certainly in technical respects, one of the most accomplished. George Cotliar reminded me so much of Sylvan Fox—a true gentleman, thoughtful, caring (not so common traits in journalism). Committed journalists like Bob Berger, Janet Clayton, Jack Miles, Gayle Pollard, Robert Reinhold, Bill Stall and Tim Rutten provided intellectual stimulation aplenty.

At *New York*, there was Clay Felker, the legendary founding editor of *New York* magazine, where a dull moment was definitely a rarity. I wish all current young and would-be journalists could have worked there in the early days. He was a charming nightmare of a boss, with the intuition of a ready-to-pounce hawk—and quite fun to work with. The young staff (largely young—in the early days, he couldn't afford to hire more established and accomplished types!) kept the office charged with energy, ideas, zaniness and adventure.

At *The Los Angeles Herald Examiner*, James G Bellows, the last editor of the iconic *The New York Herald Tribune*, was as warm and inspirational a boss as one could hope to have and was—like David English and David Laventhol—an editor who encouraged me to view myself as a writer as well as an editor. Indeed, for a few years, Jim was almost a father to me—a role I had no right to ask of him and indeed one that no one should be asked to play.

At *Family Weekly*, published by CBS, let us not forget Patrick Linskey, the boss. He never got the respect he deserved, but he was the most underrated guy in the world. Sure, maybe he would have an extra drink or two from time to time)—saints are hard to find in this or any other business. But he had a genial sense of humor that could con even an accomplished con man, like me—and I miss him today.

I left many outstanding colleagues behind in New York when I made the big continental and conceptual leap to Los Angleles, to join the *Los Angeles Times* for six years as editorial pages editor, then to take up the challenge of a column and then to join the faculty at UCLA. I often miss seeing the warm and imaginative Arthur Cooper, the late, legendary editor of *GQ* magazine.

He was my predecessor as editor-in-chief of *Family Weekly* and was one of my boosters. I have a wonderful, long, taped session with him in which we exchanged thoughts (mostly his) on the art of editing, in case anyone would like to hear it.

Also at *Family Weekly*, the magnetic and surpassingly competent Kate White, until recently editor-in-chief of *Cosmopolitan*, who allegedly worked for me as number two, but who could have run this large-circulation magazine ALL by herself—and in fact, if CBS, Linskey and I hadn't been such sexists back then, perhaps she should have!

This book ends with my last desk job in journalism—with the *Los Angeles Times*. It was from the *Los Angeles Times* that the bridge to UCLA was managed. In 1994, Neil Malamuth and Jeff Cole—a pair of eminence grise at the great public university—came to the *Los Angeles Times* for lunch to ask for help. A last-minute emergency had created a teaching opening—one course, for three hours Wednesday afternoons. Was I interested? Not really. Flattered though I was, I never thought of myself as a professor, and when they told me the topic of the course, I almost died laughing. "Media ethics?" I laughed: "I'm a working journalist—what do I know of media ethics!!!"

To make the long story short, in the end they prevailed on my American-style desire to be a hero in a crisis. I came to UCLA one afternoon a week, and I loved it! The students, the campus, the colleagues—whether Professors Scott Waugh or Rory Hume or Archie Kleingartner or Paul Rosenthal or Tom Miller or Mike Intrilligator or Mark Kleiman or Bill Ouchi or, of course, Neil Malamuth—it was a slam-dunk affair of the heart as well as the mind.

Proceeding from part-time to full-time, I managed to launch my American column on Asia and America from my campus office. With the exception of Paul Krugman, who started his *New York Times* column while still on the faculty at Princeton, has any other campus in the US been home to an internationally syndicated column?

And so my next book will be either—Confessions of an American Columnist...or Confessions of a University Professor.

What is your preference?

Index

(Entries with page numbers in **bold** denote photos.)

ABC News, 188
Acheson, Dean, 42
"Adventures of Superman", 179
Advertising Age, 239
Age, The, 291
Akira Chiba, 51
alcoholism, 33, 82, 103, 110–111, 200–203, 244
"All the Presidents Men", 81
American Civil Liberties Union (ACLU), 54
American press ideology, 119
American Society of Newspaper Editors, The, 181, 329
Amherst College, 11–12, 51, 79–80, 89–91, 117
Amherst Student, 11, 79, 96
Amsterdam, Jane, 222
ANA Hotel (Tokyo), 51
Anderson, Walter, 240
"anti-Latino Proposition", 313
anti-Semitism, 211
Asia Pacific Media Network (APMN), 15, 40
Asian financial crisis, 69–70
Asimov, Stan, 263

Attention Deficit Disorder (ADD), 85, 134, 198, 212, 223
Auletta, Ken, 117
Australian, The, 137

Backbench, 178
Bacon, Ken, 52
BBC, 28
"Being First", 97
Bellows, James G (Jim), 114, 150–152, 156–161, 163–168, 182, 186, 189, 225, 241, 286, 324, 341
Bellevue Emergency, 201
Bergen, David, 52
Berger, Robert, 15, 286
Bernard, Walter, 91, 118
Bernstein Carl, 83, 85
Blair, Tony, 27–33, 38, 168, 175
"blood libel", 210
Bloom, Marshall, 96
Bloomingdale's, 118
Blue House, 47, 50
Blue Skies, No Candy, 125
blurring lines, 336
Boston Herald, The, 161
Bradlee, Benjamin, 80–85, 91, 92, 93, 223, 237, 325
Bradley, Bill, 60
Bradley, Tom, 176
Brady, James, 239, 269

Breakstone, Linda, 162
British press ideology, 119
Brodie, Ian, 28
Brown, Edmund ("Pat"), 317
Brown, Jerry, 317
Brown, Julie, 266
Brown, Kathleen, 317, 319
Bruton, John, **145**
Burby, Jack, 286
Bush Barbara, 235–236
Bush, George H, 166–167, 235–236

California Newspaper Publishers Association award, 306
caning, 53–54
Carter, Jimmy, 166, 297
Cave, Ray, 178, 215–217, 223–224, 340
CBS, 113, 181, 215–217, 221–226, 228, 243–244, 246, 299, 341
Chan, Anson, 64
Chan, Ronnie, 63–65
Chandler, Otis, 244, 274, 288, 305–308
Charles, Prince of Wales, **143**, 178
Charter Review Commission, New York City, 265
Chinoy, Mike, 66
China hysteria, 40
China Live, 66
China, People's Republic of, (PRC), 34–40, 57, 61
Chizuko Obuchi, 141
Christopher Commission on Police Reform, 262, 297–298
Christopher, Warren, 48, 51, 297–298
Church, Frank, 97
Churchill, Winston, 12, 20, 193

City News Service, 160
Clayton, Janet, 68, 160, 293, 332
Clinton, Bill, 20–25, 30, 36, 38–39, 41–49, 51, 69, 71–72, **145**, 167–168, 297
Clinton, Hillary, 263
CNN, 67, 81, 241, 269, 288
Coffey, Shelby, 91, 223, 274, 279, 288, 299, 326, 341
Cohen, Patricia, 268
Cole, Jeff, 342
Columbia University, 328, School of Journalism, 86–87, 133
"comments and corrections", 226
Conde Naste, 237
Connaught, The, 186
Conrad, Paul, 283–285, 294
Congressional Record, 97
Cooper, Arthur, 237, 341
copy-checking, 199–200
corporate interference, 279
corporate takeover, 238–239
Cosby, Bill, 218
Cosmopolitan, 118, 240
Cotliar, George, 341
Cowan, Dean Geoff, 87
Coward, Noel, 249
Cox, Christopher, 39–40
Cravath, Swaine & Moore, 265
Crime Pays!, 135
Crow, Elizabeth, 124

Daily Express, The, 163
Daily Mail, The, 31–32, 88, 98, 133, 150, 162–166, 168, 178–183, 186, 295, 340

Daily Telegrah, The, 33
Dale, Frank, 156, 187–189, 287
Dalmane (pain killer), 244
Daniels, Judy, 124
Danzig, Robert (Bob), 157
Das Kapital, 89
Davis, Patti, 232
Davos, Switzerland, 20–25, 63, 69
Day, Anthony, 215, 286, 314–315
de Tocqueville, Alexis, 114, 155, 335
deadlines, 83–84, 108, 164
"defeat" cigar, 192–195
DeLorean, John, 178
Democratic National Convention (New York City, 1980), 161
Des Moines Register, The, 156
Didion, Joan, 314–315
Dinkins, David, 256–262, 277
diversity training, 316
"Do the Right Thing", 256
Dobell, Byron, 117
Dolan, Mary Anne, 153, 162, 187–189, 305
Dorfman, Dan, 117
Dowd, Maureen, 26, 153, 206–209
Downer, Alexander, **146**
Du Brow, Rick, 162, 167
Dugan, Judy, 45, 68
Duke University, 114

editorial cartoons, 102, 255, 283–284
editorial pages, 102, 153, 156, 161, 187, 266, 273, 295, 300–302, 305, 307
endorsement process, newspaper, 257
English, Sir David, 30–32, 81, 88, 98, 133, 150–151, 162–168, 175, 177–182, 186, 245–246, 252, 267, 270, 323–324, 340–341
Erburu, Robert, 280
Esquire, 99–100, 104–106, 240
ethics, 26, 30–34, 127–128, 226, 295–296, 329, 342
ESPN, 107
ethnocentricity, 71

fact-checking, 211
Falk, Richard, 88
Family Weekly, 151, 223, 225, 228–230, 234, 236–237, 239–243, 246, 278, 299, 316, 341–342
Fay, Michael, 53
Federal Reserve, 207
Feinstein, Dianne, 312, 318, 321–323
Felker, Clay, 91, 106–107, 109–112, 114–121, 123–126, 129–136, 182, 240, 269, 323, 334, 341
Felker Magazine Program, 132
Financial Times, The, 174–175, 292
First Amendment journalism, 299, 305
Fleet Street, 26, 30, 33, 163, 168, 170–171, 175, 178–179, 183, 323
Fong Sze Yeung, 22–24
Ford, Gerald, 166–167
Forst, Don, 81, 125, 136, 151–152, 158–160, 225, 252–253, 311, 340
Four Seasons Hotel (Georgetown, Washington), 60, 245
Fox, Sylvan, 249, 250–251, 340
Friedman, Tom, 26
Friendly, Al, 80

gambling, 332–333

Gannett, 239–246
Gates, Daryl, 297–298
Gelb, Arthur, 208–209, 222
General Mills, 329
Gingrich, Newt, 60
"Gipper, The", 230, 232
   see also Reagan, Ronald
Giuliani, Rudolph, 259, 261–263
Glazer, Milton, 91, 117 118, 129
globalization, 21, 24
Goldmark, Peter Jr, 327
"Good Riddance" (electronic news flash, Times Square), 148–149
"Goodfellas", 122
Goodwin, Doris Kearns, 304
Gorbachev, Mikhail, 298
gossip column, 183–185
GQ, 222, 341
Graham, Donald, 96
Graham, Katherine, 238
Graham, Martha, **142**
Granger, David, 240
Greene, Gail, 117, 124
Greenfield, Meg, 153
Grover, Peter, 180–181
Gruner & Jahr, 124
Grunwald, Henry Anatole, 196–197, 217, 224, 238, 340
Guardian, The, 33, 119, 291
Guggenheims, the, 98, 244

Han Tao, 51
Harvard University
   Harvard College, 70, 80
   Harvard Crimson, 96–97, 265
   John F Kennedy School of

Government, 48, 80
Hayes, Harold, 99, 104–106
headline writing, 178
Hearst Corporation, 152, 155, 159
Hearst, Gina, 156–158
Hearst, Patty, 156–158
Hearst, William Randolph, 156
Hearst, William Randolph Jr., 157
Hefner, Hugh, 135, **143**
Henry III, William A, 209
Hicksville, 11–12
Hicksville Bugle, 11
Higher Authority, 15–16, 19, 58–59, 103, 113, 193, 212–213, 246, 275–278, 283–284, 291–293, 299–300, 302–304, 315, 317–323, 325–326, 337
Hitchcock, Alfred, 218
Hitchens, Christopher, 314, 316
Hiyakawa, S I, 309
hoax, 168–174
Hong Kong, 62–69
House of Commons, 27
Huffington, Ariana, 318
Huffington, Michael, 318, 323
Hume, Rory, 342
hypocrisy, 336

"Illegal Immigration Act", 313
in-depth profile writing, 176
"inside the deadline", 205
International Herald Tribune, 19
internship, 80
Intrilligator, Mike, 342
Iraq War, 75
Isaacs, Stephen D, 86

Isenberg, Steve, 291
Istana (Singapore), 54

Japan, 42–43, 51, 61, 71–77
job interviews, 92–93, 191
Johnson, Lyndon B, 83, 91, 99, 104–105, 109, 304
Johnson, Robert (Bob), 249, 250–251, 259–260, 276, 341
Johnson, Tom, 162, 269
journalism schools, 76, 118
Jerry Lewis, 170
jump the midget, 17–78, 81, 102, 136, 167, 207, 223, 232, 259, 333
Junichiro Koizumi, 38, 74

Kaufmann, Gerald, 26–27, 28–30
Kazuo Kodama, 51, 73–74, 76
Keil, Sally, 134
Keizo Obuchi, **141**
Kennebunkport River, 235–236
Kennedy, J F, 159
Kim Dae Jung, 59, **141**
Kim Young Sam, 47–48, 50
King, Rodney, 295, 297
Kirkpatrick, Jean, 206
Kissinger, Henry, 39, 59–60, 166
Kleiman, Mark, 342
Kleingartner, Archie, 342
Kluger, Richard, 88
Klurfeld, James (Jim), 251, 259, 265–266, 340
Koch, Ed, 25, 179, 254–261, 315
Koji Tsuruoka, 51, 73
Korda, Michael, 89
Korean Americans, 44

Korea Herald, The, 46
Korea Times, The, 46
Kraft, Joe, 326
Kramer, Michael, 117, 214
Kristof, Nick, 26
Krugman, Paul, 342
Kuok, Ean, **146**
Kuok, Robert, **146**

Labour Party, 175–176
Las Vegas, 333
Latham, Aaron, 12, 86, 99–100, 104–106, 109–111, 114, 116–117, 231
Latham, Earl, 97
Lane, Diane, 229
Lane, Eric, 265
Laventhol, David, 91–93, 98, 102, 104–105, 107, 110–111, **147**, 225–226, 241, 248–251, 253, 264, 267, 270–271, 274, 279, 285, 288, 291, 297, 299, 302–304, 308–311, 315, 325, 329–333, 340
Law of Unintended Consequences, 286
Le Monde, 103, 292
Lee Kuan Yew, 38, 52–61, **144**
Lebanon, 210
Levittown, 11–12
Lewinsky, Monica, 39
Lewis, Jerry, 170
Life, 117, 124
Linskey, Patrick, 228, 236–237, 239, 243–244, 341–342
Lloyd, John, 163
Los Angeles Board of Supervisors, 287
Los Angeles Police Department, 161, 262, 272, 297

Los Angeles Press Club, 288
Los Angeles Herald Examiner, The,
    150–159, 161–162, 183–184, 189,
    190, 215, 225, 261, 269, 285,
    287–288, 341
Los Angeles Times, 14, 19–20, 23,
    25–28, 30, 40, 45–46, 49, 53–54,
    57, 61, 67–68, 77, 83, 91, 95, 130,
    147, 152, 159–162, 186, 261–263,
    267–271, 272–274, 277–279,
    281–299, 301, 304–307, 311–313,
    316, 318, 320–333, 338, 340–342
    CALENDAR, 300
    CALIFORNIA, 300
    COLUMN LEFT / COLUMN RIGHT, 290, 294
    LETTERS TO THE EDITOR, 295
    OPINION, 323
    SPORTS, 300
    SUNDAY OPINION INTERVIEW, 294
    VOICES, 294–295
    WORLD REPORT, 289
Loeb Award, 154
Loos, Anita, 77
Love, Eulia, 160–161, 262
Luce, Henry, 196–197, 211
Lu, Annette, **140**
Lu, Mimi, 340

MacKenzie, Kelvin, 163
"The Mafia at War", 122–123
magazines, 113–117, 130
Magnuson, Ed, 198
Major, John, 27–28, 32, **147**
Malamuth, Neil, 342
Mandelson, Peter, 28, 32
Manhattan, 115

Manhattan, Inc, 221–222
Mayfair, London, 179
Mayflower Hotel, 83
McCurry, Mike, 51
McDaniel, Wanda, 162, 167
McLuhan, Marshall, 217
"Midnight Blue", 213
Miles, Jack, 341
Miller, Tom, 342
Ministry of Foreign Affairs, Japan, 51, 73
Mondale, Walter, 230–231, 234
money, 335, 338
Moore, Demi, 229
Moyers, Bill, 52, 91, 94–98, 102, 104
MS. Magazine, 125
Muller, Henry, 291
Murdoch, Rupert, 32, 136–137
Murphy, Franklin, 281
Murphy, Patrick V, 135

National Public Radio, 221
National Rifle Association, 305
Nelson, Bryce, 97
Nessel, Jack, 130
Neuharth, Al, 241–242
Newsday (New York), 14, 49, 33, 51,
    179, 248–271, 275–276, 315, 340
Newsday (Long Island), 94–96, 98–99,
    100–102, 104–105, 107, 110–112,
    136, 152, 163, 244, 248–249, 253,
    257, 264–269, 271, 325, 327, 340
    Sunday Newsday, 107
    CURRENTS, 251
    IDEAS, 107–110
Newsweek, 33, 80–81, 84, 90, 99, 190,
    197, 212

New York (magazine), 106, 109–111,
  114–125, 129, 131, 133–137, 151,
  214, 264, 269, 341
  interviewing for, 109–111
  daily routine, 128–130
New York Daily News, 107, 117, 248,
  252, 257–258
New York Fire Department, 136
New York Herald Tribune, The, 106, 114,
  150–152, 164–165, 341
New York Law School Law Review, 265
New York Post, 135, 137, 248
New York Times, 12, 25, 59, 71, 73,
  88–89, 107, 114, 118–119, 133, 189,
  196–197, 208, 221–222, 248, 252,
  257–258, 260, 265–266, 269, 271,
  273, 289, 292, 307, 315, 325, 328,
  342
New Yorker, The, 106, 117, 264, 314
Newfield, Jack, 121
Nixon Center, 59–60
Nixon, Richard M, 308
no-guts no-glory (tactic), 92
North Koreans, 41–42
"not for attribution", 68
"nothing but a flak", 51
"novelist's eye", 120

"off the record", 68
office layout, 214–215
Only Way to Go, The, 135
Orange County, 40, 273–274, 315, 319
Orange County Register, 273
Orchard Road (Singapore), 57
Ouchi, Bill, 342
Oval Office, the, 230–233

paparazzi, 172
Parade, 220, 229, 230, 237, 238, 240
Park Jin, 48, 50
Parkinson's disease, 308
Parks, Michael, 331
partisanship, 336
Passages, 125–127
Patten, Christopher, 68
Pentagon, 52
People, 218, 229
People's Action Party, 56
People's Liberation Army (PLA), 35, 68
Pigalle, 169, 171
Pileggi, Nicholas, 122
Playboy, 11, 135, 143
Plate, Andrea, 57, 77, 179, 186, 218,
  235–236, 245–246, 256–257, 259,
  270, 275, 308, 309
Plate, Ashley, 25, 51, 256–257,
  270, 324
Plummer, Sara, 340
"policy override", 211
political correctness, 293, 314
pomposity, 337
Prince Charles, **142**, 178
Princeton, 12–13, 86, 89–92, 100
  Woodrow Wilson School of Public
  and International Affairs, 12, 48, 86,
  90, 92, 323
Press secretaries, 50
Pretty Babies, 218
privacy, 337
professionalism, 335
Profiles in Courage, 126
Proposition 13 (anti-tax measure),
  285–288

Proposition 187 (also known as "Illegal Immigration Act"), 312–314, 317–318
Public Broadcasting Service (PBS), 98, 221
public trust, 338
"Puccini Theory of Life", 154
Pulitzer Prize, 27, 63, 96, 122, 232, 242, 244, 251, 253, 283, 309, 328–329
Push Pin Studios, 116, 129

Qian Qichen, 36
Quayle, Dan, 58
Quinn, John, 242

Raines, Howell, 289–291, 293
Raines, Theron, 89
RAND, 304
Ravitch, Richard, 259
Reader's Digest, 230
Reagan, Ronald, 142, 166–167, 180, 206, 230–232, 234
Red Pants, 120–121, 128
Reinhold, Robert, 341
Reeves, Richard (Dick), 52, 125
Republic of Korea, 41–50
Republican National Convention (Detroit, 1980), 161
Ribicoff, Sarai, 153–155, 158
Robarts, Jason, 81
Rockefeller Center, 199, 218–219
Rockefeller Foundation, 327
Rosenthal, Jack, 270
Rosenthal, Paul, 342
Rozenzweig, Dick, 135
Rubin, Robert, 69, 71

Rutten, Tim, 341

Saddam Hussein, 195, 284
Safire, William, 19–20, 59–60
"sales presentation", 283
Salinas, Carlos, **147**
Santa Monica College, 325, 338
Saturday Night Special, 306
Savvy, 124
"Scarface", 311
Schaap, Dick, 114
Schwarz, Frederick A O Jr. (Fritz), 265, 266
Scientific American, 89
scoop, 337
Seattle, 19, 21
Seattle Times, The, 290
Secret Police, 179
separation of Church and State, 132–133
"serenity walk", 253
Serling, Rod, 218
sexism, 205
Shangri–La Hotel (Singapore), 57
Sharon, Ariel, 210–211
Sharon versus *Time* (libel suit), 212
Shaw, David, 188
Shearer, Cody, 220
Shearer, Derek, 220
Shearer, Skip, 220
Sheehy, Gail, 114, 117, 120–121, 125–127, 134
Sigma, 234
Simes, Dimitri, 59
Simon & Schuster, 88–89, 135
Simon, Bill, 88
Singapore, 19, 52–62

slash-and-burn journalism, 39, 44
Smith, John, 29
Smith, Steve, 50, 190, 193–194, 208
Social Democratic Party, 176
"soft authoritarian", 56
Sorensen, Ted, 162
South Korea (Republic of Korea), 41–50
Sports Illustrated, 217
Stahl, Lesley, 181, 231
Stall, Bill, 341
Stanwyck, Barbara, 218
Staples Center, 330, 331
Steinem, Gloria, 125
Steven, Stewart, 182
Stewart, Connie, 156
Straits Times, The, 55
Summers, Lawrence O, 69–71
Sun, The, 32, 137, 163
"super editorial", 250

Talbott, Strobe, 213, 220
Tarkov, John, 240
Telegraph, The, 119, 174
television (TV), 213–214, 337
  "Ten Deadly Sins Of Journalism",
     334–339
    blurring lines, 336
    hypocrisy, 336
    money, 338
    money madness, 335
    partisanship, 336
    pomposity, 337
    privacy, 337
    professionalism, 335
    public trust, 338
    scoop, 337

Thatcher, Margaret, 164
Thomas, Frederick, 154
Tiffany's, 118
Tiffen, Pamela 114–116
Time, 11, 14, 50, 81, 98, 117, 150, 153,
    159, 178, 190–199, 201–213,
    215–218, 220–227, 230, 236–237,
    239
  BUSINESS, 197
  COMPUTERS, 216
  NATION, 192–193, 198–199, 203,
     205–213, 220, 223, 226, 340
  PUBLISHER'S LETTER, 215,
  WORLD, 199, 213
Time-Life Building, 199, 218, 225
Times Literary Supplement, The, 137
Times of London, The, 28, 137
Times-Mirror, 95, 223, 281, 331
Tobias, Andy, 117
Tollerson, Ernest, 268
Topping, Seymour, 328, 329
"trans-Atlantic journalism", 150, 189
Tsang, Donald 38
Tung Chee-hwa, 36, 62–67, **140**
Tunney, John, 309
Tuohy, Bill, 27–30, **147**
Turner, Ted, 241
twelve-hour shift approach, 193
21 (restaurant), 226

UCLA Media Center, 15
Ullman, Richard, 89
*Understanding Doomsday: A Guide to the
    Arms Race for Hawks, Doves, and
    People*, 89, 99
University of California, Berkeley, 97,

120, 133
   Graduate School of Journalism, 120
University of California, Los Angeles
   (UCLA), 13–15, 33, 34, 40, 70, 211,
   281, 296, 325–327, 330–331,
   341–342,
University of Southern California, 15,
   87, 218
   Annenberg School of Journalism, 87,
   218
"Urban Cowboy", 86
US News and World Report, 49, 190
US State Department, 13, 43–44, 90
USA Today, 242
USA Weekend, 223

Vanity Fair, 314
Vantage Point, The, 104
Variety, 218
Vesely, James, 290
Viagra, 75–76
Vietnam War, 52, 95–99, 104–105
Village Voice, The, 252, 264
Vogue, 118
Volcker, Paul, 221

Waldorf Astoria Hotel, 130
Wall Street Journal, The, 133, 155
Walsh, John, 102, 107
Wang Duohan, 36
Watanabe, Teresa, 155
Watergate, 83
Washington Post, The, 20, 79–85, 87, 90,
   94, 133, 153, 223, 237–238, 273,
   285, 314, 328
   FOR WOMEN, 94

STYLE, 94
Washington Star, The, 152, 189
Waugh, Scott, 342
Weaver, Sigourney, 229
Western journalistic culture, 175
Where the Boys Are, 12
White Boys New Republic Knee-Jerk
   Club, 277–278
White House, the, 44, 47, 49, 96,
   230–231
White, Kate, 240, 342
Whitman Window, 11
Willes, Mark, 330–332
Wilson, Pete, 312, 317–320, 322–323
Wolfe, Tom, 117, 128
Woodward, Bob, 20, 83, 85
working hours, 84–85, 192–193
World Economic Forum (WEF), 20–25,
   63, 69
World Trade Organization, 21, 36

Yeltsin, Boris, 298
Yeo, George, **144**
Yeo, Gwendoline, 52

Zalaznick, Sheldon, 114
"zipper, the", 267